TEXAS LIONS
1967-2017

A collection of Lions'
memories and stories of
sharing the vision of service

Compiled by
Everett J. "Ebb" Grindstaff

Acknowledgements

The significant acknowledgement of this book would need to be attributed to Past District Governor Carolyn Dorman, Chairman of the Long Range Committee, and by the Long Range Committee's Strategic Planning volunteers for the idea to publish a history book of the second 50 years of Lionism as we approach our Centennial Celebration in 2017. Carolyn is one of the most dedicated Lions that I have ever known. It is not only her tenacity, but her continuous request in such a manner that it was not known to you until you had spent days on the project.

LONG RANGE COMMITTEE/STRATEGIC PLANNING

District	District Representative	Term Expiration Date
T-1	PDG Jack King	June 30, 2017
T-2	PDG Joe Hargrove	June 30, 2018
T-3	PDG Frances Cherry	June 30, 2018
E-1	PDG Jerry Bentley	June 30, 2017
E-2	PDG Bob Mitchell	June 30, 2019
X-1	PDG Carolyn Dorman	June 30, 2018
X-2	PDG Leon VanAlstine	June 30, 2019
X-3	PCC Richard Robinson	June 30, 2018
A-1	PDG Lee Sigler	June 30, 2017
A-2	IPDG Roderick "Rod" Chisholm III	June 30, 2018
A-3	PDG Mark Todd	June 30, 2019
S-1	PDG Waldo Dalchau	June 30, 2018
S-2	PDG Charles Martin	June 30, 2017
S-3	PDG Charles Handrick	June 30, 2019
S-4	PCC Lewis Gardner	June 30, 2019
S-5	PDG Gordon Richardson	June 30, 2018

Carolyn was very persuasive in asking me to be a writer, collector and collaborator of this book. I would think, mainly, because I am the most mature (some would say oldest) Past Officer serving in the State of Texas, and now the oldest living Past President of Lions Club International. It was certainly a challenge to collect the information from the 16 Districts, International Officers and the Chairmen of Special Projects, along with the assistance and help of Carolyn, who served during this period of time. Past International Director, Mike Butler, who knew as much as me (or more) than I did because he got to watch from the outside, while I was working on the inside.

I am naturally indebted to Angelo State University for obtaining the discs for some of the pictures that have been accumulated and for some of my secretarial help, which consisted of Clydelle Selby, who worked with the "Judge" and me in the early 1970s (my father was also a Past District Governor of LCI in 1945-46), Ruby Carter, her daughter, Rhonda Carter Neal (who was the Executive Secretary and was with the Judge and my other partner, Ken Slimp and myself in Hawaii when I went out of office as President in 1983), Saam Geistmann, Monnie Davis, who has been with me for over 30 years, Rose Marie Englert, Theresa Patterson were the new kids on the block, Sydney Dankworth (who worked for me for two years prior to entering Angelo State University in the fall of 2014, and also the one who had the idea that culminated into the first Campus Club at Angelo State University), Abby Ocker, who worked for me as well as other high school students–McKenzie Arrott, who is only a Junior at Ballinger High School, but has done an excellent job in proofing and organizing and doing everything needed in the final stages, and was involved in Cross Examination debates (another one of the "Legal Eagles" as I call those that I have employed and trained for the past 35 years), Suzanne Campbell of the West Texas Collection of Angelo State University, special thanks to a new friend, designer of this book, and a Lion in Waco, Texas by the name of Kim Giles; and finally Bobby Broyles, my pastor of 14 years, and friend who was a counselor at the Camp many years ago. Of course, my greatest mentor in Lions International was Roy Schaetzel, the Executive Administrator and a true friend.

The list of District Coordinators that organized the Districts' history—whether shorter or longer—was done with pride and vision of service.

District Coordinators are:

T-1	Zoie White
T-2	Bernard (Bernie) Gradel, Jr.
T-3	Frances Cherry
E-1	Chuck Sims
E-2	Beverly Stebbins
X-1	Vinod Mathur
X-2	Barbara Lynn Nacol
X-3	John Noles
A-1	Charles Henicke
A-2	Sam Pantusa
A-3	Helen Muse
S-1	Waldo Dalchau
S-2	Art Drouin
S-3	Charles Handrick
S-4	Susan Wallis
S-5	Ronald Gay

Of course, none of this would have been possible without PDG E.C. "Judge" Grindstaff and Atha Grindstaff—my dad and mother. They inspired me from the beginning to serve and speak, and lighted the pathway to Lionism. Judge introduced me to Melvin Jones in Houston, Texas when he was District Governor and gave my nomination speech at the Convention in Atlanta, and my mother, a teacher (who said she taught 33 years and never got out of third grade) was always there to encourage and set an example; in fact they encouraged me to go to three International Lions Conventions with them—in San Francisco when Herb Petry was elected Third Vice President, and also to Philadelphia and Mexico City; then Jay and I, when I was President of Ballinger Noon Lions Club, went to Chicago in 1960. The Ballinger Lions Club, all of them, Aubrey Faubion, Weldon Brevard, Mark Travis, Fred Harwell, Jr. and Sr., Jerry Willingham, Darrell Rains, Sam McLarty, J. B. Arrott, Leo Williams, Gene Davis and many others paved the way to eventually reach our goals.

If it had not been for the patience of Jay and her furnishing ideas and offering her constructive criticism as she did when I was speaking, it would not have been possible to walk the talk. Jay has ridden the entire way with her support and suggestions since I became a Lion in 1954, the same year of our marriage. She is the most compassionate person I know and lives her beliefs by action and love for her fellow man. During this same time, she was involved in every community and church activity including the Woman's Club for over 50 years. Jeff and Michelle also gave their support and we missed out on some things together, but they felt that the sacrifice was worth the loss and effort.

Preface

Anything that is mentioned in this book as to imply that one individual is responsible for any acts that might be set forth herein, you should immediately realize that it is only because of each and every individual Lion that has served in the last 50 years has been a part of this history and a part of the projects that have been set forth herein.

Lions are some of the most humble people in the world, and all of them are leaders because they do not lead by power, they are all volunteers and believe in the love of their fellow man. They do not act by force, but by example, not by coercion, but by reasonable persuasion. Yes, these Lions and their work is only safe because they humble themselves to serve their fellow man and are willing to share their vision of service. Lions act because they care and are willing to share. HUMILITY is not thinking less of yourself, but thinking of yourself less, thinking more of others and focusing on serving others.

May you have enjoyable reading and good feelings as you read. Know that by joining hands in a sense of love and service, you are able to accomplish what no other organization has done.

We cannot keep up with the accomplishments of the young and old, especially the elders, such as the articles in the October 2015 edition of *Lions Magazine*:

Page 36 • <u>100</u>-year old Lion Eddie Munger—still involved and attending the Camp meetings.

Front page/Page 43 • Lion Ike Fitzgerald—88 years old and the one most responsible for the Recycling Center in Midland, Texas.

Both of these Lions are builders of our Lions world.

LIONS CLUBS INTERNATIONAL IS THE LARGEST AND GREATEST SERVICE ORGANIZATION IN OUR GLOBAL WORLD, AND WAS EXEMPLIFIED WHEN OUR ORGANIZATION WAS VOTED IN 2012 BY THE UNITED NATIONS AS THE NUMBER ONE NON-GOVERNMENTAL HUMANITARIAN ORGANIZATION IN THE WORLD.

Humility is not thinking less of yourself,
but thinking of yourself less, thinking more of others
and focusing on serving others.

A Short History of Texas Lionism

"Lions International" did not spring from the brow of some Zeus or Melvin Jones—fully-grown, armed and caparisoned. It had quite a gestation period and many of those events took place in Texas or involved Texas clubs. (Texas Lions 1917-67, Julien C. Hyer, page 6).

On Melvin Jones' invitation, Dr. W. P Woods, a surgeon in Evansville, Indiana and others came to Chicago on June 7, 1917 to the Hotel La Salle and met with Melvin's club called "The Business Circle" and others at a luncheon with Melvin Jones listed as Secretary. On July 31, 1917, Dr. Woods called for the "first convention of Lions Clubs, to be held in the city of Dallas, Texas on October 8, 1917."

The first Lions Convention was held in Dallas, Texas on October 8-10, 1917, with 40 men present from 23 different clubs. There were six other clubs, some known as Lions Clubs and by other names, that were not present, but agreed to go along with 50 men in attendance. Twelve of these clubs were from Texas, 10 actually in attendance and two not present, claiming thereby for their clubs the late privilege of being called "Founder Clubs."

It is agreed by all that after three days of meetings in the Adolphus Hotel, officers were elected, the name of our association was officially adopted, committees were appointed and generally a complete harmony was shown.

The 23 Clubs that were present in Dallas, Texas in 1917 are as follows:

Arkansas	Little Rock and Texarkana
Colorado	Denver and Colorado Springs
Missouri	St. Louis
Illinois	Chicago
Louisiana	Shreveport
Oklahoma	Oklahoma City, Tulsa, Ardmore, Chickasha, Muskogee
Texas	Port Arthur (4/23/17), Houston (4/2/17), Austin, (1/18/16), Waco (7/9/16), Fort Worth (9/26/16), Dallas (9/9/16), Paris, (2/8/17). Wichita Falls (7/16/16),

Texas, cont.	Beaumont (9/16/16) and Abilene (2/15/17)
Tennessee	Memphis

Clubs that were not present, but are counted today as Founder Clubs:

California	Oakland
Colorado	Pueblo
Oklahoma	El Reno and Okmulgee
Texas	San Antonio (1/17/19)* and Temple (6/21/17)
	*Inactive for a period

At this first Convention, Dr. W. P. Woods was elected our first President. Melvin Jones, who is now recognized as the "FATHER" of our Association, was elected Secretary-Treasurer. Dr. L. H. Lewis, President of the Dallas Club, declined the Presidency and was elected First Vice-President. St. Louis was selected as the site for the Second Convention in 1918.

Texas became known as District 2, having only one District Governor for the entire State, and having an official State Convention. Illinois was designated as District 1 due to the work of Melvin Jones as the names Founder of Lions International.

The first State Convention was held in Waco, Texas on June 19, 1919, and the 13th and last State Convention was held in Port Arthur, Texas on April 27-28, 1931. After this date, each district held its own District Convention. The delegates to the Convention voted to divide the State into five sub-districts, to be known as T–E–X–A–S. The year 1984 was the last year for the combination of District/State Convention. On May 17-19, 1985, the State Convention was held one week after the last District Convention.

Starting in 1917 with 12 clubs, Texas had grown to 242 clubs and 8,414 members by 1930. Due to the tremendous growth in Lionism in Southeast Texas, District 2-S divided into three districts in 1942; 2-S1, 2-S2 and 2-S3. At that time, there were 334 clubs and 12,091 members in Texas.

In 1947, the T District was divided, make sub-districts 2-T1 and 2-T2, this making 8 sub-districts in the State.

In 1958, the T District was divided again, and 2-T3 was added, making nine districts.

In 1959, the State had over 800 clubs and over 37,000 members and the State was divided into 15 districts, with 15 District Governors from over the

State which made up our state organization. The state was rearranged into districts 2-T1, 2-T2, 2-T3, 2-E1, 2-E2, 2-X1, 2-X2, 2-X3, 2-A1, 2-A2, 2-A3, 2-S1, 2-S2, 2-S3, 2-S4, and 2-S5.

In 1956, the Past District Governors of Texas Association was founded with George Jones of Corpus Christi as its first president. From District 2-S3, Robert Koennecke of Seguin served in 1971-72 as president and Freddie Wolters in 1981-82.

In July, 1949 during the International Convention in New York, the Directors of Lions International approved the project of the Texas Lions League for Crippled Children with permission to use the name of "Lions". By working together, more than 43,000 Lions of Texas have established:

- Summer Camp for Handicapped Children that provides two weeks of summer fun for the blind, deaf, mute and crippled youngsters of Texas at its Kerrville facility. (1953)
- The diabetic camp was established in 1970 when the South Texas Diabetic Camp was moved to Kerrville. Summer sessions exist for these special children under the direction of Dr. Stephen Ponder, University of Texas, San Antonio.
- After the Texas Center for the Blind was discontinued in 1984, the Outdoor Education Center was implemented to provide year-round service to handicapped children. (1984)

From 1953 through 1984, the Texas Lions Camp has served 25,323 handicapped campers (now over 70,000), 1,625 blind adults, 4,813 diabetic campers, and over 3,000 handicapped youngsters in the Outdoor Education Center program which is accredited by the Texas Education Agency as a private school. The Charter President of the League was Jack Wiech of Brownsville, Texas, while the first Executive Director was Frank Robertson of San Antonio, Texas. In 1975, J. L. McPherson succeeded Robertson as Executive Director, and our then current Executive Director, Glen Crawford succeeded McPherson in 1978.

Each of the 16 Districts are entitled to two elected directors on the Board of Directors from the Texas Lions Camp, with one director elected annually.

Table of Contents

History of Texas Lions

October 8, 1917 through Founder Clubs

For brief overviews of the first 50 years, there will be brief statements concerning those 50 years from 1917-1927.

October 8, 1917, at the Hotel Adolphus in Dallas, the International Association of Lion's Club held its first annual meeting. Forty delegates attended. Melvin Jones, the organization's founder, was also in attendance. This was to be the first "service" organization. Several Texas cities sent representatives: Abilene, Austin, Beaumont, Dallas, Fort Worth, Houston, Paris, Port Arthur, Waco and Wichita Falls. Those clubs were given the privilege of being called "Founder Clubs." At the meeting, a constitution and Bylaws, objects, code of ethics and an emblem of a lion's head holding a club marked "International" were adopted. Dr. W. P. Woods, from Indiana, was elected the First President and Melvin Jones was elected Secretary/Treasurer.

At the Second International Convention held in St. Louis, L. H. Lewis (1918-1919), from Dallas was elected as the first International President from Texas. Thus started Texas' long line of Presidents.

During the years 1927-1937, Lions growth was very large. With the encouragement of Melvin Jones, Texas was divided into five distinct districts—T-E-X-A-S—which continued until 1937. Texas also produced its second International President, Julien C. Hyer (1931-1932) from Ft. Worth. He was installed in Toronto, Canada. The Texas delegation went by train and carried the San Angelo Cowboy Band.

From 1937-1947, there was a growth of Lions. It was during this period that "T" was divided into two districts (2-T1 and 2-T2) and "S" was divided into 2-S1, 2-S2, and 2-S3.

Fourth decade—1947-1957

The fourth decade brought the establishment of the Texas Lions League for crippled Children in Kerrville. By July 1949, the corporation was chartered, the property was bought, and the International Board had given its approval. The camp opened its doors for the first kids in 1953. "…it may be said here that no other single act has so projected the spirit of Texas Lionism as much as this did…"

An interesting story about Texas Lions Camp (TLC): In support of the plan to fund TLC, Washington was approached (Veterans Administration) with a request to purchase their land in Kerrville (you will note we are neighbors with the VA hospital, because what is now TLC and the Kerrville Little League and KISD were all one parcel owned by the VA). The Government responded with a "challenge grant" that mandated that if the Lions could raise $100,000 in six months to demonstrate their intent and resolve, the land would be sold to TLC for that sum. The Lions were able to raise $80,000 while the deadline loomed. As the time for a final status report matured, then Lion Governor Sealie McCreless stepped forward to present a $20,000 check to fund the balance and tip the shortfall into TLC's favor. The only problem was, he didn't have $20,000 at the time, but had the courage to make the pledge nevertheless. With the final pledge in hand, the VA was informed that $100,000 in pledges had been achieved, and the Lions were granted the deed for $100,000. By the time the cash was to be transferred to the Government to close on the land, other donors and fundraisers had been added to the $80,000 figure, and the $20,000 pledge by McCreless was forgiven. His check was never cashed.

As a reminder of one person's determination and courage, TLC still has (and celebrates) Governor McCreless' act with that original check. A copy of the uncashed check that bridged the "eleventh-hour" hangs in the TLC museum—while the original is safely tucked away in TLC's safe-deposit box at Broadway National Bank.

The courage that it took McCreless to be the catalyst to tip the scales in TLC's favor is both celebrated and repeated on many levels even today, as individuals step forward and say, "I'll be the one to guarantee TLC's forward movement and continued success. It is a lesson in fortitude, creativity, blind-faith and a testament to the power of self-less leadership."

Also, Lion Herbert C. Petry, Jr. was elected President and served during the Lion year 1950-1951.

1957-1967

During this decade, David A. Evans (1968-69) from Texas City, served as International President. During this decade, the districts were divided into 15 districts. And so, the birth of District 2-X2 as we know it today occurred.

The District Governors that officially served are:
Paul Boseman, 1975-76
Chester Penick, 1976-77
George Futch, Jr., 1976-77
C. F. Kuykendall, 1977-78
Donald Hamilton, 1978-79
Dr. Roger Cheatham, 1979-80
Frank Keas, 1980-81
Robert J. "Jim" Williams, 1980-81
Larkin Gooch, 1981-82
C. J. "Smokey" Stevens, 1982-83
Johnny D. Mooney, 1983-84
Garvis Gilbert, 1984-85
Harry K. Poulan, Jr., 1985-86
Herbert Daniels, Jr., M.D. 1986-87
Harold Spivey, 1987-88
Ray Ashlock, 1987-88
Jack M. Heilman, 1989-90
Ernie Barbee, 1990-91
"Happy" Jack Wakin, 1990-91
Harvey Clements, 1991-92
Carol French, 1992-93
Dale Halyard, 1993-94
Brian Whitenack, 1994-95
Bill Roop, 1995-96
Joan Houser, 1996-97
Glenn Jennings, 1997-98
Gid Terry, 1998-99
Patrick Smith, 1998-99
Everett Van Hawes, 1999-2000

H. L. Ashcroft, 2000-01
William A. "Bill" Hurst, 2001-02
Gerald Townscnd, 2002-03
Harold Raines, 2003-04
Don Francis, 2004-05
Leon VanAlstine, 2005-06
Zac Gray, 2005-06
Rebecca "Becky" Whitenack, 2006-07
Jim Merritt, 2007-08
John Samples, 2008-09
Richard "Sandy" Sandberg, 2009-10
Barbara "Lynn" Nacol, 2010-11
Alonzo C. (A. C.) Ellis, Jr., 2011-12
Traci Francis, 2012-13
Nancy VanAlstine, 2013-14
Jasper (Jimmy) Strickland, 2014-15

The writer is not involved in any legal decision or otherwise as to the first Club in Texas or Lions International. Most of the material was taken from the early pages of Judge Hyers' book.

FOUNDER CLUBS

From the *Texas Lions 1927-67* by Julien C. Hyer

Club	Charter Date	District
Austin	1-18-1916	S3
Dallas	9-09-1916	X1
Waco	9-19-1916	X3
Fort Worth	9-26-1916	E2
Abilene	3-23-1917	E1
Houston	4-02-1917	S2
Port Arthur	4-23-1917	S1
San Antonio	1-17-1919	A2
Paris	6-04-1921	X2
Beaumont	10-14-1921	S1
Wichita Falls	10-22-1921	E1
Temple	3-26-1924	X3

Lionism comes to Texas!

It began in 2-S-3 with the formation of the Austin Founders Club on January 18, 1916 prior to the first Lions Convention held in Dallas on October 8, 1917.

"The International Association of Lions Clubs". Illinois was designated District 1 in honor of Founder Melvin Jones (his home state). Texas was designated District 2 and continued to operate that way until 1930 when the "S" from TEXAS was added. At that time District S2 was the third largest of 5 districts representing 53 counties and 48,888 square miles.

Texas, District S2, boasted of four Founder Clubs—Austin, Houston, Beaumont and Port Arthur—each of which had representatives at the memorable Dallas Convention in 1917.

In the first few years, the State Convention was held in cities in those areas: Houston (second and eighth) and Beaumont (fourth and seventh). Then, in 1943 as a war-time economy measure, the work was divided into districts 2-S1, 2-S2 and 2-S3 and continued that way until the 1959 "grand rearrangement" of the entire state when District 2-S4 was added. That division continued until 1989 when District 2-S3, with approximately 125 clubs, was divided into two districts, basically east and west, and District 2-S5 was created. The eastern portion became 2-S5 and the western portion remained 2-S3.

Chartered on August 261923, the oldest club in District 2-S5 is the Bryan Lions Club, commonly referred to as Bryan Noon Lions. Lions Clubs International Founder and Secretary General, Melvin Jones, attended their 25th Anniversary in 1949. Julian C. Hyer, International President 1931, spoke at their 50th Anniversary in 1973.

District 2-S5 has benefitted greatly from the service and contributions of 6 living PDGs and others who have passed away who served as District Governors in S-3 before our district became 2-S5. Those PDGs have remained active throughout the years and served the district in many capacities, including cabinet members, committee and convention chairmen, zone chairmen, members of the boards of the Texas Lions Camp and Lone Star Lions Eye Bank and as trusted advisors.

Those still with us include PDG Charlie Briggs, PDG David Kahlich, PDG PID Joe Al Picone, PDG Mark Anderson, PDG Don Mayer and PDG Gordon Richardson. Several of these distinguished PDGs have been inducted into the Texas Lions Hall of Fame.

Austin Founder Lions Club
Highlights of 1979-1980

Officers:
President, J. P. Kirksey (63rd President to serve)
1st Vice President, Charles Mathews
2nd Vice President, Tommy Cowan
3rd Vice President, Arvin Harrell
Secretary/Treasurer, Doug Shannon
Lion Tamer, Jack Heacock
Assistant Lion Tamer, David Kerbow
Tail Twister, Jim Garrison
Assistant Tail Twister, Bill Anderson
Immediate Past President, Moton Crockett
Directors, Tom Lokey, Don Schroeder, Charles Smith, Larry Meriage, Jon Wisser

International President, Lloyd Morgan from New Zealand
International Theme – A World Together
International Convention – Chicago, IL

Membership
7/1/1979 = 166;   6/30/1980 = 169
Added 19 new members Net Gain = 3
Average Weekly attendance = 46% (76 Lions)
President J. P. Kirksey qualified for and received LCI 100% President's Award

Meetings in Ballroom of Stephen F. Austin Hotel, 7th and Congress Avenue
Meal Cost $2.50
Dues $132/year
Committee established to administer Hornberger Scholarship Fund
Office located in room 412 of Stephen F. Austin Hotel

Executive Secretary Katherine Holmes

Notable projects:

April 1979 – Sponsored blind student at TSB, Leno Pena, to ski trip in Vail, Colorado. Partnered with Continental Airlines and Vail Associates.

July 1979 – Hosted 40 international youth and their sponsors from the Julien C. Hyer Youth Camp

October 1979 – World Services Day project: donated and planted three ash trees on campus of Girlstown, USA. Also, Lion Dennis Cowan built and installed two picnic tables.

Feb 1980 – Board established a memorial contribution program to add to the Hornberger Fund. Contributions could be in memory of deceased Lions or other worthy individuals.

Feb 1980 – Club sponsored John Tamez, graduate of Texas School for the Blind to National Blind Olympics in McComb, Illinois. Distance Runner and Go-Ball contestant.

March 1980 – Paper Drive (Magazines and Newspapers recycled for cash)

April 1980 – Provided tricycle to John Paul Miller, an indigent child with cerebral palsy and visually impaired. Very rewarding when several of us delivered the tricycle to the Miller family.

June 1980 – Funded expenses for eye examination and corrective lenses for 5-year-old Lorie Ann Thorp.

Notable Weekly Programs:

08/02/1979 – Dick Lillie, Planning Director, City of Austin

08/16/1979 – Dr. Peter Flawn, President-Elect, UT Austin

08/28/1979 – Humble Oil/Exxon Southwest Conference Football Highlights with Kern Tips. Program brought by Pup Kindle who was presented a plaque commemorating 30 years for bringing program.

09/20/1979 – Head Football Coach Fred Akers, UT Austin

09/27/1979 – Bob Bullock, Comptroller of Public Accounts

11/01/1979 – Judge Jack Pope, Associate Justice, Supreme Court of Texas

11/15/1979 – J. Neils Thompson Appreciation Day for his service to UT and Austin, Speakers Bill Little, Darrell K. Royal and Frank Erwin assisted by Roy Vaughn, Executive Director of UT Ex-Students Association.

12/06/1979 – Charles Herring, General Manager of LCRA

01/24/1980 – Dr. Bailey Marshall, Director General, University Interscholastic League

02/07/1980 – Annual Sportsmanship Award

03/06/1980 – Dr. Donna Lopiano, Director of Women's Athletics, UT Austin

03/13/1980 – Bob Armstrong, Texas Land Commissioner

03/27/1980 – Mark White, Attorney General

04/03/1980 – Reagan Brown, Texas Commissioner of Agriculture

05/01/1980 – Longhorn Dixieland Band, director Dr. Tom Lee and Jerry Junkin

05/08/1980 – Warren G. Harding, Treasurer, State of Texas

05/15/1980 – George W. Strake, Jr., Texas Secretary of State

05/22/1980 – Police Chief Frank Dyson Appreciation Day for his service to the City of Austin. Speakers PDG Judge Zollie Steakley and Mayor Carol Keeton McLellan.

June 1980 – Outstanding program from Texas Lions Camp

Other Pertinent Information

Paid Staff/Executive Secretary

Exa Robb – 1947 to 1976

Katherine Holmes - 1976 to unknown

Ginny Godfrey - unknown to 2004

Past District Governors in the club

1925-1926	E. P. "Eddie" Cravens
1932-1933	Bob J. Lyles
1933-unknown	Dr. John Barclay (DG in North Carolina)
1963-1964	Dr. Tom Caldwell (DG from South Austin Lions)
1969-1970	Neil Gilligan (DG in District 2-A3, Laredo, TX)
1969-1970	Jim Kaster (DG in District 2-T3, El Paso, TX)
1940-1941	C. Mel Miller
1944-1945	Willie I. Kocurek (appointed)
1947-1948	Harry Kelly
1952-1953	Judge Zollie Steakley
1959-1960	J.J. "Jake" Pickle
1962-1963	R. J. "Red" Lewallen
1972-1973	Bill Raschke

Past District Governors in the club, continued

1991-1992   James T. "Tom" Lokey

2012-2013   J. P. Kirksey

Texas Lions Hall of Fame Members

1992   PDG Willie I. Kocurek

2007   Lion J. P. Kirksey

District 2-S3 Harry Reasonover Award Recipients

1973   PDG Willie I. Kocurek

1975   PDG Bill Raschke

1992   Lion J. P. Kirksey

2001   PDG James T. "Tom" Lokey

Notable Gifts to City of Austin

1925-1930s – Lions Municipal Golf Course. Club promoted bond sale and built two 9-hole segments of course and Club House on land leased from University of Texas on Lake Austin Boulevard near Lake Austin (at the time and for many years afterward, the land was considered undesirable for any other use).

1938 -1940 – Planted Pecan trees along Barton Springs Road
Note: Confirmed from Lambert's book

1947 – Organized effort and funded construction of scoreboard at House Park erected as permanent memorial to Austin citizens who were killed in World War II. *Note:* Lambert's book

1966-1967 – 50th Anniversary: (we think) Five water fountains installed in Town Lake west of 1st Street (Drake) Bridge near bank of Auditorium Shores

1976 – USA Bicentennial. Donated funds to beautify Auction Oaks Section of Republic Square, which was named by Lion Harris Brush, a member of the City Parks Commission.

1981 – 65th Anniversary

1982 – Planted oak tree on berm in Republic Square (has since been removed)

1991 – 75th Anniversary Purchased and installed Lion Drinking Fountain in Zilker Park, along with playscape improvements.

Other notable events beginning in the 1970s:

Dec 1972 – Club received contribution from Estate of Margaret C. Hornberger for purpose of establishing a scholarship for deserving students. It is believed that Ms. Hornberger was a former school teacher in AISD.

1974 – First annual Lions Sale for Sight organized by Willie Kocurek to provide funds for purchase of Lions Drinking Fountain at Texas School for the Blind (installed in 1975). Event grew and became well-known in the community and continued quite successfully as the primary fundraiser for many years under the leadership of several Lions Club members. Held in various venues all over Austin including: former Big Bear Food store on S. Congress and Barton Springs Road, Shipe Hall on W. 38th Street (former home of North Austin Lions Club), vacated auto repair shop on W. 5th Street, empty drive-in restaurant on Riverside Drive, vacated service station at corner of South Congress and Barton Springs Road, Christie's Restaurant building on Town Lake, Whitley Printing Building on Brazos. Sale continued until Rose Day began.

1974 – PDGs Willie Kocurek and Bill Raschke were actively involved in formation of the District 2-S3 Lions Eye Bank (now the multi-District Lone Star Lions Eye Bank) that was originally housed at Seton Hospital.

June 22, 1975 – President Max Noe and Lions Moton Crockett, J. P. Kirksey, Tom Lokey attended first-ever reunion of Founder Clubs during LCI Convention in Dallas, Texas. Meeting was held in Ballroom of Adolphus Hotel (same room as founding convention in 1917) and hosted by Dallas Founder Lions Club.

June 9, 1979 – Donated funds to furnish room at Texas Lions Camp in memory of Lion Bill Simpson (effort spearheaded by President Moton Crockett during his year)

May 1980 – Past President and PDG Willie Kocurek graduated from the University of Texas Law School as the oldest graduate ever at age 70. He and Maureen appeared on national TV on *Good Morning America* proudly wearing his Lions lapel pin.

Jan. 14, 1995 – "Welcome Home Jake Pickle" day/party at Camp Mabry. Event hosted by Austin Founder Lions Club with several other organizations participating. Attended by approximately 2,500 well-wishers and emceed by local radio personality, Bob Cole. Planning Committee chaired by J. P. Kirksey.

Nov 2, 1995 – "Roastie–Toastie" for Willie I. and Maureen Kocurek held at Wyndham Austin Hotel at I35 and Ben White Blvd. Planning Committee chaired by J. P. Kirksey. Net proceeds from event distributed between Adult Services Council, Austin Groups for the Elderly, Boys and Girls Club, South Austin Civic Club, Sprout Scouts, and Austin Founder Lions Club Activity Fund.

Over the years, numerous of our members have attended the annual Lions Clubs International Convention beginning with the first Convention in Dallas in 1917. Officers and Delegates have traveled to Atlanta, Boston, Chicago, Dallas, Denver, Honolulu, Miami, Mexico City, Montreal, New Orleans, Phoenix, Seattle, San Diego, San Francisco, St. Louis, Australia, South Korea, Toronto, Germany, and other locations around the US and the world.

Beginning in 1975, many of the domestic excursions were on Crockett Airlines; i.e., Lion Past President Moton H. Crockett, Jr. and his sleek plane.

Lion Past President and Past District Governor J. P. Kirksey has represented the Club at 25 International Conventions beginning in 1976 – 24 of them as a voting Delegate. J. P. was also chair of either the District 2-S3 Convention or Mid-Winter Conference for many District Governors since 1978. In addition, our Club facilitated very successful State Lions Conventions in Austin in 1997 and 2013.

In 2018, our Club will be honored to have the first-ever member to be installed as President of the Past District Governors Association of Texas.

History of Dallas Founder Lions Club

As I remember and experienced,

and as given to me by then-President Ron Pearce

by PCC John Eads, MD2-Texas and PDG District 2-X1

The story I am about to tell is based on what I remember and experienced in my dealings with the Dallas Founder Lions Club over the years. (My apologies to all Lions, if I do not state it exactly right, but my heart is in the words I write). I am privileged to be one of only two honorary members of the Dallas Founder Lions Club. The other honorary member was PDG Rex Coppedge, who has since passed on. My association with Dallas Founder Lions Club really began early in my Lion's career through my meeting and becoming associated with PDG Surry Shaffer, Jr., who was a member of the club, around 1973. This was the year I was the President of the DeSoto Lions Club and had been a Lion for only seven years. Over the years, I had attended many of their Lions Club meetings, spoke to the Club as their speaker on numerous occasions on different topics and was honored to be the Master of Ceremonies at their 90th Anniversary Celebration at the Adolphus Hotel on September 21, 2006.

This was a dynamic and active Lions Club in my years of close association with them. There were a number of elected judges, lawyers, mayors and businessmen as members in the Club. They were active in District 2-X1. They met at most of the meetings I attended at Union Station near the downtown court houses. It was not unusual for them to have 35 to 40 of their members or more present at their meetings. The lunches served were really outstanding. One of their major fundraisers/service projects was providing clothing to underprivileged children. The Lions would set a date and take them shopping in downtown Dallas at the various department stores and pay for their clothing. Through the efforts of PDG Surry Shaffer, Jr. working with Judge Julien C. Hyer, they were very much involved in Youth Exchange and the Julien C. Hyer Lions Youth Camp was named after PIP Judge Julien C. Hyer.

The Club was chartered September 9, 1916, a full month prior to the First International Convention at the Adolphus Hotel in Dallas, Texas on October 8-10, 1917. The first International President Dr. W. P. Woods, of Evansville, Indiana was the Keynote Speaker. I remember a lot of "bragging conversations" at various times by the members about being the first Founder Lions Club of Lions Club International, since it hosted the first Lions Clubs International Convention in 1917 at the Adolphus Hotel. There was a rivalry to some degree with the Austin and San Antonio Founder Clubs. I believe Austin Founder Club may have been chartered before the Dallas Founder Club.

President Ron (now deceased), a long-time member, two time President and a British fighter pilot in World War II, wrote the following history that he presented in 2006 at the 90th Celebration:

"The Dallas Founder Lions Club (original known as the Dallas Lions Club) was organized March 31, 1916 and Chartered September 9, 1916. The Club hosted the First International Lions Convention in 1917. Prominently covered by the Dallas Morning News with headline, October 8 'Lions International Meeting Opens Today' and subsequently chronicled in great detail by Judge Hyer in his book "Texas Lions 1917-1967." We have gone on from this point, uninterrupted for 90 wonderful years in Lionism.

We proudly claim a number of firsts, Past International Presidents L. H. Lewis (our Club President in 1916), Judge Julien C. Hyer, George R. Jordan, all members of our Club. Three Past International Presidents in one Club is unmatched. Through the years, we have hosted many dignitaries, 5 International Presidents, many International Board members and Helen Keller, best remembered for her presentation at the International Convention in 1925 to adopt the Sight Conservation program.

As to club sponsorship, Oak Cliff, Park Cities come to mind, followed by Inwood, Dallas Central, Carrollton, East Dallas, and Dallas South. We also established Lionism in Egypt with sponsorship of the Lions Club of Cairo.

A Youth Exchange Program was pioneered in 1963 with High School Students being sent to stay with Lions families in overseas countries. Judge Hyer took this highly successful program to the International Board who adopted the idea. In recognition of the Judges services, we established the

Julien C. Hyer Youth Camp (near Dallas) and it flourishes to this day.

The popular Gavel Travel idea came from our Club and has extended to many other countries. As to our membership, it has read like "Who's Who" in our city, most major banks and businesses were represented including three mayors and an ambassador. We are proud to have served our fellow man for 90 years, and are dedicated to continued service in the spirit of "We Serve" in the future. We have a long history and proud heritage and take pride in being a club with members in the greatest service organization in the world—The International Association of Lions Clubs." (I remember how proud Ron and the members of Dallas Founder Lions Club, including PDG Surry Shaffer, Jr. were that evening of their accomplishments and history).

The County of Dallas and the Mayor of the City of Dallas proclaimed September 21, 2006 as Dallas Founder Lions Club Day on the 21st day of September 2006 and they presented the proclamations to Lion President Pearce at the 90th Celebration. The guest speaker for the celebration was our own Texas President of Lions Club International Lion Jimmy Ross. The Club history and the history of the First Convention were at one end of the room. Included in that presentation was the guest book signed by those in attendance at the First International Convention. There was a commemorative plaque signifying the First International Convention that hung in the Adolphus Hotel lobby for many years. There was a copy of the program for the Convention, along with pictures of the First Convention attendees. The exhibit also included the Club Charter, some place cards for the attendees with their names, a menu, newspaper articles and many other pieces of the history of the Club and the First International Convention.

MD-2 Texas Lions will have a Centennial Celebration in Dallas to celebrate 100 years of service to others by Lions Club International. We will also quietly celebrate the 100 years of service of the Dallas Founder Lions Club and other Founder Clubs across the State. "Where There's A Need THERE'S A LION Since 1917" is the theme of Lions Clubs International Centennial Celebration.

I am proud to be a Lion. Thank you, Melvin Jones!

Brief History of the Waco Founder Lions Club

The Waco club itself was organized at an initial meeting on July 19, 1916. This inaugural event was actually a banquet which was held in the Gold Room of the historic downtown Raleigh Hotel and which was presided over by the first President, Mr. W.V. Crawford. There were forty-five charter members present that evening. The event was described as follows: "Another voice has been added to the chorus of organizations whose tunes are pitched high on the scale of Waco progress - It's a roar!" The club was organized locally for the specific purpose of bringing individuals of ability, from all lines of business and from every profession, together for the interests of Waco.

Since its beginning, the Waco Founder Lions Club has continued to be engaged in numerous charitable efforts for the local community, the State of Texas, the nation, and the world. Club members have enthusiastically supported a variety of projects, including the Texas Lions Camp, programs to assist the visually and hearing impaired, drug education activities, and various scholarships for local youth. Finally, the Waco Founder Lions Club has sponsored and helped organize many new Lions clubs in the surrounding area. Included here are those in Bellman, Gatesville, Mart, McGregor, Valley Mills, East Waco, and, most recently, Crawford.

Early Notes of Interest as Taken from the *Waco Morning News*

Dr. Alton B. Lee, Past District Governor of Texas' District 2-E, came to Waco in September, 1955 to serve as Registrar and then Dean of Admissions and Public Records for Baylor University. He joined the Waco Founder Lions Club that same month on transfer from the Abilene Lions Club in Abilene, Texas. In Abilene, he was with Hardin-Simmons University, which conferred on him an honorary doctorate in recognition of his valued contributions to education.

Dr. Alton B. Lee first saw the light of Lionism when he was teaching in

Decatur, Texas—first in public schools and then at Decatur Baptist College. He served in many capacities in the Decatur Lions Club and held various offices, including President. For many years, he was club bulletin editor.

In 1941, the Lions of District 2-E, Texas selected this remarkable Lion as their District Governor. He certainly lived up to their expectations and gave the District a memorable year in 1941-1942.

In 1947, Lee transferred to the Abilene Lions Club, when he took on duties at Hardin-Simmons University. He served on the Abilene Board of Directors, filled many committee posts, and was a valued member. When Joe Williamson, veteran secretary for over 30 years of the Abilene Lions sent a transfer form to Waco Lions on Dr. Lee, he added his comment, *"Was one of the best Program Chairmen this club has ever had. Get him in and put him to work."* (Dr. Alton Lee was a cousin of Past International President Grindstaff's mother, and had known PIP Grindstaff all of his life).

Dr. Lee retired from his position of Dean of Admissions at Baylor University in June, 1976. One of his comments upon retirement was to the effect that now he would have more free time to give to his Lions Club. How blessed can we be?

Laura S. Farmer, Executive Secretary
1951-1979

In many ways, perhaps she was the best "Lion" of us all. She had helped as an "extra" to put over the big Lions Club Minstrel the year before and had proved her ability and worth. Early in 1951, this led the discerning officers of Waco Founder Lions Club putting her to work full-time as executive secretary. She was on-hand in time to become a casualty of the tornado that hit Waco in May, 1953, and was injured by flying glass as she raced about the downtown office of Waco Lions, then located in the Roosevelt Hotel.

Her unusual abilities in managing the day-to-day affairs of Waco Lions asserted themselves, as well as her keen interest in Lions affairs both far and wide. Not only did local Lions come to depend upon her, but also Lions from over the district and even in International headquarters. When an answer about Lions matters was needed, Lions knew where to get it and sought Laura's assistance from time to time. She attended the district conventions and the International conventions, and soon became known to one and all as the very knowledgeable "Laura from Waco Lions."

On February 11, 1976, Waco Founder Lions staged a special appreciation banquet for Laura, commemorating her 25 years of service, which was well attended—not only by members of her own club, but also many members of other clubs in the district.

At her own request, Laura was relieved of her duties as executive secretary after 28 years of devoted service to Lions and Lionism, her retirement becoming effective August 9, 1979.

Lions, we are debtors. May our gratitude to Laura live on and on.
—Alton B. Lee

Also in a tribute to all PDGs, Bill Miller will be remembered by those who knew him, as he organized 10 clubs in 1982-1983 as we reached the coveted 45,000 member mark. Bill passed away in late 2016, and had also been President of the World Jaycees in addition to his Lion's career.

Waco Founder Lions Club Past-Presidents

Bill Miller	1980-81	Also a PDG/Deceased
Tom Bentley	1981-82	Deceased
Carl Shamburger	1982-83	
Paul Marable	1983-84	
Jack Nelson	1984-85	
Ronald Nelson	1985-86	
Mark Boyd	1986-87	
Towne V. Adams	1987-88	
Donald Gunn	1988-89	
David L. Keathley	1989-89	Died in office
Royce Brownfied	1989-90	
Charles Doherty	1990-91	
Ronald Holze	1991-92	
David T. Corbitt	1992-93	
John Low	1993-94	

Waco Founder Lions Club Past-Presidents, continued

Meg Garland	1994-95
Jay McCullough	1995-96
Gary McWilliams	1996-97
Lin Mills	1997-98
Samuel Shreffler	1998-99
William S. Martin (Bill)	1999-00
Timothy Nemel	2000-01
Robert (Bob) Kinney	2001-02
Curtis Holland	2002-03
C.C. Sinkel, Jr.	2003-04
Keith R. (Hap) Nielsen	2004-05
J. Brady Bass	2005-06
William A. (Bill) Gohring	2006-07
Harry A. (Buddy) Powell	2007-08
Carolyn Hafercamp	2008-09
Lori Roller	2009-10
Terry M. Sutcliffe	2010-11
Tim Riley	2011-12
Karen Conine	2012-13
Gene Gooch	2013-14
Louise Powell	2014-15
Buck Rogers	2015-16
Richard Kruger	2016-Present

Fort Worth Founder Lions Club

Lions Clubs International was loosely organized in August 1911-17 under a number of names. Starting about 1911 with "The Royal Order of Lions" in Indiana by Dr. W.P. Woods, who owned the title "Royal Order of Lions". Melvin Jones had the "Business Circle" in Chicago. E.N. Kaercher had the "Vortex' in St. Louis. Gust Gessing of St. Paul had the "Business and Professional Men's Association".

Melvin Jones, Dr. Woods and all the other club representatives met in Chicago on June 7, 1917. Dr. Woods called for a meeting to be held in Dallas, Texas. This was called the first convention of this organization, it was held on October 8-9, 1917 at the Adolphus Hotel.

There was about 44 men from 23 different clubs, also six other clubs involved under the different collection of names. At this meeting, Dr. Wood relinquished his title to Royal Order of Lions. The delegates at the business meetings then adopted the name "International Association of Lions". This name was picked over National or General.

Delegates then voted to adopt a constitution and by-laws. There were many committees set to work. They adopted to accept businesswomen. Clubs were called "Dens". Delegates at the convention named Chicago the "Birth Place of Lions".

Of the 29 Founder Clubs at the Convention, 12 were from Texas.

San Antonio	1915	Paris	2-08-17
Austin	1-18-16	Abilene	2-15-17
Dallas	9-09-16	Temple	6-21-17
Waco	7-09-16	Houston	4-02-17
Beaumont	9-16-16	Wichita Falls	7-16-17
Fort Worth	9-26-16	Port Arthur	4-23-17

Mr. L.H. Lewis of Dallas was nominated President. He declined, because he felt that Dr. Woods of Indiana should be the first President. Delegates then voted Dr. Woods as the Association's first President.

Mr. Lewis was elected as First Vice President. Melvin Jones was elected Secretary and Treasurer.

At the convention, Texas was assigned District 4, but this was changed at the 1921 International Convention. District 1 was assigned to Illinois in honor of Melvin Jones, and District 2 was assigned to Texas because they had the most clubs at the first convention.

A Brief History of Abilene Founder Lions Club

According to early records and newspaper clippings, Dr. Cyrus N. Ray—a local osteopathic physician—decided in 1916 that Abilene needed a businessmen's luncheon club. At that time the town was 34 years old, with a population of about 10,000. Dr. Ray convinced 16 men to agree to help organize such a club, and Rotary International was contacted to form a Rotary Club. Rotary International advised that Abilene was too small for a Rotary Club and recommended that the group wait until the population increased to at least 20,000.

A short time later, E. A. Hicks—an organizer for the International Association of Lions Clubs of Evansville, Indiana—called on Dr. Ray and presented him a letter from his brother, Dr. T. L. Ray of Fort Worth. Dr. T. L. Ray had recently been installed as charter president of the new Fort Worth Lions Club and was recommending that Dr. Cyrus Ray work with Hicks to organize a Lions Club in Abilene.

A meeting of interested businessmen was called by Dr. Ray and the first organizational meeting of the Abilene Lions Club was held on Thursday, February 15, 1917 in the Red Room of the Grace Hotel, at which time, 15 men signed up as charter members. Twenty were required in order to apply for a charter, and by the following Saturday, 11 more had been recruited. The group sent in a charter application to Dr. W. P. Woods, president of the International Association of Lions Clubs.

The *Abilene Reporter* reported that the first weekly luncheon of the Abilene Lions Club was conducted Thursday, March 8, 1917 in the dining room of the Grace Hotel. The club has continued to meet regularly on Thursday at noon ever since. The official charter for the club was issued March 23, 1917.

The Abilene Lions Club was among 27 Lions Clubs (13 in Texas) which were represented by Dr. Woods when he met at the Business Circle luncheon with Melvin Jones and members of Optimist Clubs, Vortex Clubs, and Business and Professional Men's Association at Hotel LaSalle in

Chicago on Thursday, June 7, 1917, where the group agreed to accept charters in Dr. Woods' International Association of Lions Clubs, Chartered in Indiana.

F. A. Matthes, charter president of the Abilene Lions Club, represented the club at the first annual convention of the International Association of Lions Clubs on October 8-10 at the Adolphus Hotel in Dallas, Texas. He was appointed to the credentials committee for the convention by Dr. Woods, who chaired the convention session.

The club was officially named Abilene Lions Club, but unofficially adopted the name Abilene Downtown Lions Club when it sponsored the organization of a second club in 1953. The name was officially changed to Abilene Founder Lions Club in 1984, when the word 'Founder' was added in recognition of the fact that the club was in existence before the international organization was formed, and is recognized by the International Association of Lions Clubs as a Founder Club of the association.

The club had only four regular meeting places in its 86-year history: Grace Hotel, Wooten Hotel, Hilton Hotel (later renamed Windsor), and since January, 1982, the Briarstone Manor. The Grace Hotel, after sitting vacant for several years, was renovated and restored as a historical site and converted into Grace Museum in 1992. The club held its 80th anniversary celebration in the ballroom of the Grace in 1997. The club moved its meeting place to the new Hilton Hotel in the heart of downtown when it opened in 1927. The hotel was renamed Windsor Hotel in 1945, but the club continued to meet there until the hotel was closed in 1982 and the club moved to its current location at the Briarstone Manor. The Windsor also was renovated and restored in 2001, and the club held its 85th anniversary celebration in 2002 in the refurbished Windsor Ballroom where the club had held its weekly luncheon meetings for 55 years.

Among the club's earliest service projects were assisting the city in paving the streets of the young city and sponsoring the development of a city park. During World War II, Abilene Lions were active in bringing Camp Barkeley to Abilene. The club promoted a highway shelter for GIs commuting between the camp and downtown, sponsored recreation programs at the camp, assisted with blood drives, and helped the Red Cross. At one of its luncheon meetings, the club conducted a War Bond drive and $1,000,000 worth of bonds were purchased.

Through the years, the club's major efforts have been toward providing eye exams and glasses for school children, supporting the Texas Lions Camp for children with physical disabilities and diabetes, and participating in the District 2-E1 Lions Tissue and Eye Bank. The club has helped support many local charitable groups such as Meals on Wheels, Ben Richey Boys Ranch, Food Bank of Abilene, Big Brothers/Big Sisters, and others. In earlier years, the club maintained a student loan fund, providing interest-free loans to needy students of the three colleges in town. Since 1974, the club has awarded over $63,000 in scholarships to graduating seniors from the local high school. The club contributes to various district, state, and international Lions-related enterprises, and conducts an annual White Cane Day drive to promote sight conservation.

Fundraising projects have included collecting waste paper and tin cans during World War II; selling mops, brooms, light bulbs, trash bags; minstrel shows, musical concerts, fashion shows, garage sales, concessions at athletic events, and charity football games. Our two current major projects are an annual fish fry and an "old-fashioned supper"—serving sausage and beans, coleslaw and cornbread.

Shortly after women were admitted to the Lions Club, the club held a "Cub Shower" during one of our luncheon meeting for two young married women in the club who gave birth to a baby boy and girl within a two-week period. The club currently has 14 women on its membership roster. Two women have served as president of the club. Several others have served on the board, including our incoming third vice president.

Our membership has ranged from the original 27 to as high as 265 in the early 1960s. The club has dropped in membership over the past few years to 26 members in 2015. There have been several deaths the last few years. At the present time, the club has 26 members—21 men and 5 women.

Beginning August 6, 2015, the Abilene Founders Lions Club will be having their noon meetings at Al's Mesquite Grill on Buffalo Gap Road.

The club's main project the last few years is the American Flag Project.

The Abilene Founders Club has had 92 presidents and 14 secretaries since the club was organized on March 8, 1917.

We hope to see our membership increase this year.

—*Mary Beth Sharp, Secretary*

History of the Houston Founder Lions Club

The Houston Founder Lions Club was organized on April 2, 1917 by Mr. Marlowe Fisher under the name "Houston Central Lions Club", and later was changed in 1995 to the "Houston Downtown Lions Club". The first president of the club was Mr. J.J. Boyle. Texas was the birthplace for Lions International, and the Houston Central Lions Club was there to witness its birth. Delegates from Houston attended the first Convention of Lions International in October of 1917 in Dallas, Texas and, earned the club the distinguished title of "Founder Club." The club charter was signed by Dr. Melvin Jones, the founder of Lionism.

Since that first convention in Dallas, Lions International has grown to 45,000 clubs in over 200 countries with 1.35 million members, making it the largest service organization in the world. In 1940, the Houston Central Lions Club was the largest Lions Organization in the United States and one of the largest in the world. The Houston Central Lions Club has help spread the vision of Lionism in the Gulf Coast area by sponsoring and helping to organize approximately 70 Lions organizations, including 30 in Houston itself.

The Houston Founder Lions Club has had many influential members. Notable was G.M. Cunningham, a contemporary of Dr. Jones, and an organizer of many clubs in the Southern United States. The club has provided many District Governors and office holders in the State, National, and International levels. After World War II, the club welcomed a large number of distinguished veterans, several of them are still very active in the club today.

"We Serve" is the motto of Lions International, and the Houston Founder Lions have most certainly served the city of Houston. In 1939, the Houston Central Lions Club started the Lighthouse for the Blind, which serves the blind community of Houston and the surrounding area. In 1949, the club was instrumental in organizing the Crippled Children's Camp of Texas, which later became the Texas Lions Camp in Kerrville. In 1953, the Houston Central Lions Club, along with other Lions Clubs in the

Gulf Coast area, established the Lions Eye Bank at the Baylor College of Medicine. The Lions have always been active with helping in the community with mainly sight-related projects and support for other community projects. Interestingly, the Houston Central Lions were instrumental in organizing Little League baseball in the early 1950s.

Almost from its founding in 1917, the Houston Central Lions Club met at the Rice Hotel, one of the most historic hotels in the city of Houston, located at the site of the first capitol of the state of Texas. The Rice was "home" for the club, until it was vacated some 35 years ago. In 1995, the Houston Central Lions Club changed its name to Houston Downtown Lions Club, and recently in 2012, changed its name to Houston Founder Lions Club, which recognizes the club as the original, founding Lions Club in Houston and Lions District 2-S2 in Texas. The club now meets at the Tellepsen Downtown YMCA at 808 Pease Street on the 2nd and 4th Tuesdays at 12:00 p.m.

All of the donations and money received from fundraising efforts is given back to children in need and deserving families. We appreciate any and all support given to this historical organization.

History of the Port Arthur Founder Lions Club

Organized 4/23/1917 • Chartered 10/15/1917 • 12 Charter Members

In the beginning, the club president only served six months. The first was Lion A.W. Dycus in 1917. The first President in 1918 was Lion F. E. Gifford, and the second, Lion R. Lyles.

Port Arthur Founders who were Hall of Fame members were: PDG Wilbur Abbey; PDG Robert "Bob"Price; and PDG Wilbert Boulet. Lions District 2S1 Past District Governors were Lions: Nate Brown (35-36); James W. Long (41-42); Mack J. Thomas (43-44); Wilbur Abby (54-55); Marshall Elliott (59-60); Robert E. "Bob" Price (67-68); Wilbert C. Boulet (85-86) and Captain James K. Manry (87-88). The club has had 20 Melvin Jones Fellows; currently there are six members. In the past there were 16 Jack Wiech Fellows.

In 1898, planners of the layout of Port Arthur set aside land for Lake-shore Park along the Sabine Lake shoreline. In 1920, a portion of the park was named for Lions Park in honor of the Lions club members who made numerous improvements including, playground equipment, water fountains, landscaping, picnic tables, and in 1954, a two-story southern colonial style bandstand (gazebo) which became a focal point of community social, political and recreational activities. In September 1989, the park was donated to Lamar University. The Port Arthur Founders has supported all the Lions Charities, in particular, the Texas Lions Camp and the Lions Eye Bank of Texas. Present member Lion Howard Collins (100 years young) is a Charter Century Club Member of the Camp, and is still a member. Currently, there are seven Century Club Port Arthur Founder Lions. This club has always rung the bell for the Salvation Army, and continually supports it with funds, food for the needy and Christmas presents for families each year. Every year, the club has at least one White Cane Sale to raise money for the Lions Eye Bank of Texas. Also supporting the LEBT, the club sponsors a golf team in the annual District 2S1 Golf Tournament for the LEBT.

The club provides eye exams and glasses for school children and adults who cannot afford them.

During the 1930s, the Port Arthur Founders chose (and sponsored) a Junior Lion who was an outstanding high school boy. The club always sponsored a princess in the Port Arthur Cavoilcade. The club provides five to six $500 scholarships for students to attend Lamar College-Port Arthur each year. In order to raise money for these projects, through the years the Founders have had dance recitals, sold light bulbs, had fried chicken dinners, fish fries, and garage sales. Later fundraisers have been gospel singing concerts, pie sales and recipe books.

.

San Antonio Founder Lions Club

Our story began in 1915 when San Antonio was the largest city in Texas, boasting a population of almost 120,000. Our club was organized by Mr. E.A. Hicks. Our Charter Banquet was held at the Gunter Hotel on October 8, 1915, with 53 members in attendance. Our Charter bore the name "San Antonio Den of the Royal Order of Lions." The Den's objective was various forms of civic improvement such as paving the street in front of the Alamo, encouraging the construction of sidewalks downtown, etc.

Mr. Hicks had, one month before, organized a Royal Order in El Paso, but itsubsequently folded.

Early on, the relationship between the San Antonio Den and the Indiana Headquarters was disrupted upon receipt of the Charter documents for the Royal Order of Lions, whereupon it was discovered that the Royal Order was in truth a secretive "fraternal" organization, considered unsavory…thus by 1916, many left the organization.

In came Dr. William Perry Woods, a prominent medical surgeon in Evansville, Indiana. In consultation with Mr. Hicks, Dr. Woods proposed that those clubs who resented the "fraternal" aspects would form a new organization. Thus, on October 24, 1916, the International Association of Lions Clubs was incorporated in Evansville, Indiana.

In the summer of 1917, Dr. Woods sent out invitations to 33 southern clubs to join him in October of 1917 in Dallas, at the Adolphus Hotel. The San Antonio Club received its invitation, but because of the World War I effort, it was unable to send a representative. It nevertheless elected to support the outcome of the meeting.

Dr. Woods, the Founding Father of Lionism, was subsequently elected to be the first President of the International Association at the Dallas Convention, and the San Antonio club became a part of the newly incorporated association. Of all the clubs invited to the Dallas Convention, the San Antonio Club had (and still has) the earliest date of organization as a Lions Club.

The San Antonio Founder Club's 100th Anniversary Gala was held on Friday, October 9, 2015 at the Gunter Hotel with Past District Governor and President of the Texas Lions Camp, Sam Lindsey as its guest speaker. A Special Addition newsletter was prepared showing the 100th Anniversary Gala of San Antonio. The program honored Past District Governor Rod Chisholm and Past President George Harvey for their continuing service to the Founder Club. Special proclamation in honor of the 100th Anniversary was witnessed at the City Hall by the signing of the proclamation with several Lions in attendance.

One of the official items in the program that lends credence to their birthday is the official congratulations to the members of the Lions Club for the formation of the City of San Antonio Club on October 8, 2015, signed by Ivy R. Taylor, Mayor. Of course this brought up several stories; some of the older Lions and their acquaintances, which would include Past District Governor A. C. Schwethelm who served in 1961-62 and his wife, Marilyn, President of the Comfort Lions Club, Past International Director Mike Butler and his Lion bride, Sheryl, Past District Governor Jim Weed and his wife Marilyn, and the list could go on and on. It brought back memories to me of one visit to the Club in 1982–83, when Past District Governor Mike P. Butler installed Lion John E. Stacey as President of the Club. On that occasion, Ebb Grindstaff had the opportunity to address the Club as President of Lions Clubs International, and for the occasion, they gave $12,000 to the State Lions Camp in his honor, which was a very, very special occasion in his life.

Paris Founder Lions Club

The Paris Founders Lions Club dates back to May 12, 1921. Lion Jim W. DeWeese was an unofficial delegate at the first National Lions Convention in Dallas in October 1917—thus the pioneer title of "Paris Noon Lions Club". The first charter was presented in Paris on January 10, 1922 by District Governor L. H. Lewis, who later became President of Lions International.

The club soon became active in community projects. Funds were raised for the Girl Scouts to build Bluebonnet Lodge. Later, a cabin was built at Camp Gambill. The Lions secured the land for Bywaters Park with administration by the Paris Parks Council.

At the Lions Club International Convention in 1925, Helen Keller called on the Lions to take up the cause of the visually handicapped when we were told, "You can become Knights of the Blind in a crusade against darkness". Lion Morrison George wrote a letter to Helen Keller in 1933 and later gave a report to the International Convention in Hawaii. Helen Keller included her autograph in her reply, which is still in the George family collection—too difficult to duplicate, but shows it was sent from England.

From an International aspect in 1927, membership stood at 50,000 with 1,183 active clubs. Panama, in 1935, became the first Central American nation to have a Lions Club. The following year, the first South American Club was organized in Colombia. Lionism reached Europe in 1948 when clubs were charted in Sweden, Switzerland and France.

Sight conversation has been a major project for all Lions clubs. For many years, the Paris Lions Club sold light bulbs door-to-door throughout the entire city. These funds were used to furnish eyeglasses to school children of Lamar County when referred by the schools. Eyeglasses are still furnished to school children who need glasses and cannot afford them. The Westinghouse light bulb packages were labeled "Buy Light, Save Sight".

There was a very interesting article by William H. George, D.D.S. that was sent to Lynn and recites that his grandfather, Jack Hathaway, was a

Charter Member of the Paris Founder Lions Club, and was President in 1929-30, and that George's father was President in 1982-83, and was the one who actually received the letter from Helen Keller, whose copy we did see and to also discover the Original Charter hangs in the office of Dr. George at 604 Lamar Avenue, Paris, Texas 75460.

There is active support of the Texas Lions Camp at Kerrville for disabled and diabetic children. Our club has had a 100% member participation in this project since 1976. Paris Lions also have 100% member participation in Lions World Services for the Blind, Lions Club International Foundation, Texas Lions Foundation, East Texas Eye Bank, Texas Lions Eyeglass Recycling Center and Leader Dog program.

Other community service projects included support and donations for Lamar County Big Brothers Big Sisters, Habitat for Humanity, Boy Scouts and Girl Scouts, CASA, Paris Junior College scholarships, Salvation Army, Project Graduation and African-American Student Union at Paris Junior College.

Current fundraising projects include the selling of hamburgers and refreshments at the Red River Valley Fair. We also hold the Annual Charles Woodfin Golf Tournament and an Annual Fish Fry.

The Paris Founders Lions Club continues to represent the ideals of Lionism in Paris, Texas. This brief history bears out our motto, "We Serve".

Beaumont Founder Lions Club

The Beaumont Founders Lions Club was organized in 1916, and is one of the 12 clubs from Texas that formed Lions Clubs International in 1917.

They met in the "Rose Room" ballroom on top of the Hotel Beaumont which was located in the downtown area, and was called by many people the "Downtown Lions" for that reason. After many years, they moved to Moncla's Restaurant not too far from downtown, and met there for many years until the restaurant closed. They met in various restaurants over the years, and have been meeting in the Cattle Company restaurant now for several years.

A few of the many notables who have been active in the club are Rose Maceo, founder of the Texas Coffee Company, makers of Seaport Coffee and other products; Past International Director, Federal Judge Joe Fisher; Charlie Schmucker, who delivered the news, weather and market report for many years; David Hearn, who led the singing for what would be a lifetime for many, as he was active in the club for over 65 years and lived to be 102 years young; Past International Director Marshall Cooper, and many others.

The club had many different fundraisers over the years. We went door-to-door selling brooms at one time, and light bulbs at another time for the Lighthouse for the Blind which was located in Houston.

Charlie Schmucker had a SECRET recipe for fried chicken that we cooked and sold in store parking lots from time-to-time. Unfortunately, Charlie took his secret recipe to the grave with him, so that was the end of chicken sales. At one time, we were having an annual garage sale and auction of new donated items. For the last 23 years, we have been producing the "Willie Ray Smith Football Awards Banquet." Willie Ray Smith was a legendary football coach of one of the formerly all-black high schools. Two of his sons, Bubba and Tody, went on to play professional football, as did many of his other players. The event was created to honor the memory of coach Smith and the best of the area high school players.

There is an award for the best offensive player, and one for the best defensive player. Many of the winners have gone on to play at college level, and quite a few have gone on to the professional level. For instance, Earl Thomas and Christine Michael were Seattle Seahawks players in the last two Superbowl games.

We have supported many charitable activities. We are a big supporter of the Texas Lions Camp at Kerrville. We have collected used eyeglasses for many years. We have purchased eye exams and glasses for indigent adults and schoolchildren. There have been many instances of filling needs of specific individuals with special needs, such as a specially-built bicycle for a child who had no use of his legs. And of course we participate in the District's new capability to clean, read prescriptions and dispense used eyeglasses locally.

We believe we can say proudly that "WE SERVE".

Wichita Falls Founder Lions Club

District 2E-1
A Short History for the Centennial Year
of Lions Club International 2-7-2017
Submitted by Lion Joe Cullen, Secretary

An excerpt from *A Few Moments of History* by Lion M.J. Weaver , District Historian in 1978 tells us the following:

Lions International was started under the leadership of Melvin Jones, a businessman from the Chicago Area. He called together business leaders from the mid part of the nation to a meeting in Dallas in October 1917. Those attending represented independent civic clubs. Wichita Falls Downtown Lions Club sent B.F. Johnson to this meeting, known as the first "convention."

The Wichita Falls Downtown Lions Club was organized in July 1917 by G. M. Cunningham. The Lions in the "Falls" have always dealt themselves a hand in what is going on in Lionism.

In 1926, the Wichita Falls Lions had a famous Lions quartet made up of Joel McGregor, Francis Hansen, H.W. Gray and Erwin Bohmfalk, and they were great. They sang all through the District at Ladies Nights, and at Lion Conventions. One year they sang at the State Convention in McAllen. Their best number was "Sweet Adeline."

From a History written by Dr. Whitney A. Snow an MSU professor, entitled *The Wichita Falls Municipal Zoo* states that on November 21, 1927, in the "Wichita Daily Times" was the announcement that the local Chapter of Lions sought the creation of a zoo in Wichita Falls. Club President Dr. R.H. Graham decided—with the support of the chapter—to talk with city officials. He, along with Tom Sorey, H.J. Bruce and W.P. Bolding spoke with the City Council. During the meeting Sorey who was an architect proposed an outline with an aviary, surrounded by 32 cages. The location is to be in proximity to the Wichita River, in an area know as Scotland Park. The expense was to be handled by public donation, and received the blessing of Park Superintendent Charles Bennenberg and Mayor R.E. Shepherd. Immediately, the Lions Club started receiving animals. In March of 1928, the city received the following: four armadillos, two guinea pigs, two pigeons, two lynx, one horned owl, and one bobcat. These animals—as well as 32 pigeons, one wild hog and two deer—were the initial animals at the zoo. By April 9, 1928, 15,000-20,000 people visited the zoo in one day.

On July 2, 1928, the pride of the zoo, an elephant named "Miss Sugar" was added to the zoo, along with a zebra. Financially and legally, the zoo limped along until, due to lack of funds, Miss Sugar and the other animals were sold. The Lions Club Zoo closed on September 28, 1934.

In 2017, the Wichita Falls Founder Lions Club will purchase a historical sign, which will be erected in the Scotland Park area to sustain this piece of history, uniting Wichita Falls and the local Lions Club.

The history of District involvement continues with Lion Dr. Graham elected District Governor in 1930. Doc was also Chairman of the Texas District Council, yet dreaded public speaking; however, he was able lead the District through serious problems.

It was 10 years before Lion Frank Criplever was elected District Governor, as he took office in 1940. Everybody in the District loved and admired him as a Lion, He was a diligent and industrious official.

It was 20 years before another District Governor came from a Wichita Falls Club. By then our club was known as the Wichita Falls Founder Lions Club. One of our favorite sons, D.L.(Podner) Ligon in 1960 became our District Governor. Podner was born in Denton County and in 1937 came to Wichita Falls, and became Hardin Junior College's (Now Midwestern State University) Director of Physical Education. His service to the University continued for 53 years, and during that time he coached basketball, baseball, track and tennis while maintaining teaching and administrative duties. In 1975, the MSU Coliseum was renamed the "D.L. Ligon Coliseum " During this time he also gave 100% effort to his service with the Wichita

Falls Founder Lions Club. He was president in 1957. Followed by Zone Chairman, and District Governor in 1960. He served our club and district well throughout the years, and garnered the reputation as one of the most devoted, enthusiastic Lions in our Club's history .

The Founder Lions Club has continued to serve MSU as a guide to the Midwestern State University's Lions Club. Many of the MSU Students have received Founder Lions Club scholarships. The spirit of D.L. Ligon lives on in the form of a sign on the MSU Campus near the Coliseum—purchased and dedicated by the Wichita Falls Founder Lions to Lion D.L. Ligon in 1983.

In 1963, Lion Charles E. Davis became the District Governor from Wichita Falls Founder Lions Club. He was a strong educator of other District Governors, and he did a good job.

To continue our strong Support of Texas Lions Camp, Lion Walter Colman was a Director of the Kerrville Crippled Children's Camp.

Strong support for District activities continues today as Lion Rodney Foyce, Past President, Past Zone Leader and Past District Vice Governor now serves for the year 2016-17 as District Governor.

The premier event of the Wichita Falls Founder Lions Club is our annual Texas/ Oklahoma Fair. The year 2016 marks the 22nd year that the Club has reestablished the Fair which began in 1922. After 5 years, it failed, it then moved to Iowa Park, Texas as the Wichita County Free Fair. It expanded to a two-state festival and again became Texas/Oklahoma Fair in 1947. Only in 1942 was the fair canceled. The horror of September 11, 2001—the opening day of the fair—did not crush the "spirit" of exhibitors or visitors as the events were dedicated to the memory of those murdered in the attack on America! Attendance in 2002 bounced back and went over 117,000.

In Wichita Falls, the active members of the Wichita Falls Founder Lions Club, volunteers, and the adopted squadron, the 366th from Wichita Falls Sheppard Air Base, continue to produce this annual event in Wichita Falls. Since 1995, the Fair has taken place on the third week in September at the MPEC and the Bridwell Ag Center. It is an event that hosts the Evans Carnival, exhibit booths, livestock shows, indoor and outdoor entertainment, creative arts and home skills. The Fair Board is always working creatively to produce a more entertaining fair for thousands of people, and providing $40,000–$50,000 in support to local non-profit organizations, and annual scholarships.

The Wichita Falls Founder Lions Club is active with 46 members, meeting weekly at Luby's Cafeteria to provide Lion updates, and an informative local program. We continue to serve with our committees and attendance at District events. The future is bright, as we are always looking for new ways to Serve and Increase awareness of Lionism in Wichita Falls.

History of the Temple Founder Lions Club

In 1916, George M. Cunningham, along with H. K. Orgain and W. J. Basset, represented the Young Men's Business League of Temple, Texas at a Dallas meeting to form an organization of civic clubs. This gathering spawned founding sessions for Lions Clubs.

The organizational effort begun in 1916 came to fruition November 1, 1917, with establishment of Temple Lions Club. Research shows Temple Founder Lions Club as the 8th oldest Lions Club in the State of Texas.

In addition to Cunningham, Orgain and Basset, charter members included Dr. J. M. Woodson, B. A. Hodges, J. C. Mitchell, John A. Cole, Dr. O. F. Gober, H. P. Robertson, Jr., W. E. Willis, W. F. Lucas, Andrew McBeath, H. L. Daily, W. O. Cox, W. W. Clement, Dr. J. M. Murphy, W. H. Knickerbocker and P. L. Downs—the club's first President.

Temple Lions began weekly meetings at the Martin Hotel. After a few relocations over the years, today the Temple Founder Lions Club meets at noon each Wednesday at the Lion's Den in the Gober Party House. Gober House is a city meeting facility in the center of town named in honor of founding Lion Dr. O. F. Gober.

Temple Lions Club was established with 18 charter members in its inaugural year. Almost a century later, Temple Founder Lions Club is 117 members strong.

The Early Years

Early club minutes document members as interested in community cleanliness and appearance, patriotism and high ideals for the membership.

The first club projects supported the sale of "Liberty Bonds" and assisted with record-keeping on the draft of men into military service. Temple Lions also staged a "Victory Sing" for community morale in the early days of World War I.

The Club's "City Beautiful" project was launched in February 1918. During the first campaign, townspeople were inspired to haul off 319 truckloads of trash from Temple's downtown area.

Minstrel shows became an early mainstay fundraiser beginning in 1936. The tradition continues today in a variety show format held in the spring of each year. The show's foolishness takes gentle pokes at local individuals, organizations and the news media, which continues as an important part of today's show, in addition to incorporating a limited amount of legitimate talent. Now known as the "Lions Follies," the 2015 performance marked 76 consecutive years of Temple Founder Lions Club hosting this event.

In 1941, then Lions President D. Q. (Jack) Baskin reported the Lions had contributed to almost 300 cases of children's medical needs in the previous seven years under committee chairman Tom S. Wright's supervision. Civic projects, such as funding numerous baseball fields, fill the archives of Lions activities.

Community Impact

Of all the thousands of dollars Temple Founder Lions have directed to our community, several projects stand out as highly-visible Lions efforts in our service area.

Leading up to the 1965 groundbreaking for Temple's Crippled Children's Rehabilitation Center, club members sold small bricks to raise funds in a "Bricks for Braces" campaign. Since its mid-60's beginning, the Rehab Center has served countless thousands of children who face physical challenges on a daily basis. The facility has been enlarged by other Lion-supported efforts throughout the years. Today, the facility is known as the Central Texas Children's Center.

The largest single club project involvement prior to 2000 is the creation and continued development of Temple Lions Park. A joint project of the City of Temple and the Temple Founder Lions Club, the Club initially borrowed $160,000 from banks in our community to build the Temple Lions Pool in Lions Park. Temple received a Parks and Wildlife Department grant to assist with the pool's funding.

Through the years, the Lions Club, the city and other organizations have continued to support the development of Lions Park. Today's park includes the 4-field A. J. Mercer Softball Complex, Lions pavilion, Rotary pavilion, South Rotary playground for disabled children, soccer fields, hiking trail, dog park and fishing pond. An outdoor amphitheater was added in 2013 with funds from Temple Lions Club Parks and Charities and the Temple Parks Foundation. This "Lion Sam Farrow Amphitheater" honors a long-time life member of the Temple Founder Lions Club who singularly sponsored more than 70 members into our club. Lion Farrow passed away in 2015. The hiking trail was recently named for long-time club Secretary and former District Governor, the late Lion Charles Stout.

In the early 1990s, Temple Founder Lions Club was among the first clubs to bring the "Lions Quest" program into Temple schools. Club donations to Temple schools for Quest programs and training have totaled around $40,000.

Service Outreach

Temple Founder Lions Club is proud of its record of humanitarian involvement and support of needy and disabled individuals. For 100 years, individual Lions clubs—including our own—and districts in the U.S., Canada and several other countries have collected used eyeglasses for distribution to the needy in developing nations. The general public is encouraged to donate their used eyeglasses and sunglasses to their local Lions club, or to send them to the Texas Lions Eyeglass Recycling Center, located at 200 Plaza Street, Midland, TX 79701.

Each year, our club spends about $3,000 to fund eye exams and eyeglasses for needy children in our community who are referred by school nurses. We currently provide a limited number of glasses and eye exams for needy adults. Temple Founder Lions Club recently purchased a portable, hand-held Spot Vision screening device, and a number of our Lions are now certified to use the unit to screen for vision abnormalities. This device is one of three made available on loan to clubs within District 2X-3.

The Central Texas Lions Eye Bank is another project supported by the Temple Lions Club. The Eye Bank started as the District 2-X3 Eye Bank in association with regional hospital Scott and White. In recent years, the Central Texas Lions Eye Bank supplied more than 1,000 corneal transplants annually at Central Texas hospitals.

Texas Lions Camp in Kerrville, Texas is the cornerstone project of the Club. Texas Lions Camp has been providing camping experiences for children with special medical conditions since 1949. Expenses associated with these experiences are paid in full by the Lions Camp Organization so children may attend completely free-of-charge. In many instances, transportation to and from Camp is provided as well.

Annually, Temple Founder Lions Club is a 100% (or more) contributor to several Lions humanitarian projects: Lions Clubs International Foundation, Texas Lions Foundation, Leader Dog for the Blind, Texas Lions Camp, World Services for the Blind, the Lone Star Lions Eye Bank, and Lions Efforts Against Drugs (L.E.A.D.), as well as numerous local charities. Temple Founder Lions Club is proud of our record of service to the Temple area and beyond for the past 98 years! To learn more about the club, fully explore our website at templelionsclub.org or visit our Facebook page at facebook.com/TempleFounderLionsClub. The Lions Clubs International website is www.lionsclubs.org.

Humanitarian Service

A leader does not lead by power, buy by love of fellow man. Not by force, but by example. Not by coercion, but by reasonable persuasion. Leaders have power, but power is only safe in the hands of those who humble themselves to serve.

Anyone can be humble. At the outset of this resume for the HISTORY OF LIONISM FOR THE LAST 50 YEARS, or basically from 1967 to 2017, some of the things that I will say may seem to be prejudicial.

HOWEVER, it is my sincere desire to give credit to all those who have served in any capacity as a Texas Lion, because they have done so only because of the fact that they care and are willing to share. HUMILITY is not thinking selfishly of yourself, but thinking of yourself less, thinking more of others, and then be focused on serving others.

This does not mean that we always act in complete agreement with everyone in order to reach a desired purpose or goal, but it does mean that we are thinking of other people who are willing to share a way of life.

If expressing ourselves, Benjamin Franklin said, "If advancing something that might be disputed, we should not use the words 'undoubtedly' or 'arrogance,' but rather 'I conceive this to be the matter in which we should act' or 'I apprehend that this is the way that this should go.' "

We can join together and even do things unintentionally on our own part, while exalting ourselves in pride of what we've accomplished, but it's because we believe in sharing. It gives us a deep understanding of the feeling of the result therof. Why? It is because we think globally and act locally, which has been the underlying cause of the great growth of service in humanitarian efforts.

Redistricting of Texas

Early in Lionism, the entire state of Texas was given the designation of District 2. The first District Governors did not have too many clubs to visit during their tenure of office, but the mileage they drove was a tremendous problem. In those days, Lions clubs were located (for the most part) in populated areas such as El Paso, San Angelo, Abilene, San Antonio and Dallas.

As the years passed, five new districts were formed and they were known as T-E-X-A-S. This took care of the situation for a time, but it wasn't long until the heavily-populated area of East Texas began to present a very formidable problem to a District Governor.

After a bitterly-contested convention, and many predictions that it would never work, District 2-S was divided into three—known by the names of 2S1, 2S2 and 2S3. A short time later, the district of 2T, which extended from the Oklahoma border in the panhandle area to El Paso and Presidio on the Mexico border, divided into 2T1 and 2T2. This left my own District 2-A the largest in land miles, and the largest in the number of clubs of any district in the world. It quickly became apparent, however, that the heavily populated area of 2-X would soon pass even District 2-A in number of clubs, which it did shortly after Dr. A. Lewis Kline's administration as Governor.

The situation of 2-X having some 198 clubs and 2-A having some 150 clubs began to create considerable discussion in various areas. Several good Lions of both Districts attempted in one way or another to get some type of satisfactory division worked out, but without any tangible results. It became apparent that the only feasible way to eliminate the inequalities of districts in Texas was a complete redistricting of the state without any regard for present district boundaries. After 2-T2 voted in 1957 to divide themselves again, leaving only 36 clubs per district, the subject of redistricting the entire state was again brought under discussion.

At the San Francisco convention in 1957, Lions International made it very clear that they did not approve of large districts by decreeing that each Governor—in order to qualify for the 100 percent award—had to visit each and every club in his District, and that they preferred that such visits be made during clubs' regular meeting times. This situation was alleviated somewhat through the work of our own Past International President, H. C. Petry at a board meeting in Hot Springs, Arkansas.

During the Board of Governors meeting in Midland, Texas, International Director Joe Childers reported that International was very interested in seeing Texas do something about her tremendous districts. He also indicated that if Texas didn't do something on her own, that sooner or later International would have to do something, but preferred that we work it out on our own. Several past Governors were consulted at once—one being Roy Minear, President of the International Counselors Association—and after much preliminary groundwork, it was decided by the Board of Governors to set the wheels in motion and prepare a resolution in the form of a constitutional amendment to be presented to the Lions of Texas at each of their District conventions, calling for the redistricting of Texas from nine to 15 Districts.

A map of Texas was prepared, showing county lines, potential convention cities, Lions clubs and membership of each. District lines were worked out from this map at a later meeting in Austin. The map was completed and the resolution was prepared for the approval or disapproval by the Lions of Texas. You know the story. The amendment carried by an overwhelming majority. The Board of Governors for the year 1957-1958 gave the Lions of Texas an opportunity to vote on the redistricting issue, and the Board of Governors of 1958-1959 did an outstanding job of organizing and preparing the Lions of Texas for the great step that took place with the beginning of the fiscal year, July 1, 1959.

"Many would miss many of their old friends, but would make many new ones, and Lionism in Texas would embark on a period of new phenomenal growth. Would this be the last time Texas will find it necessary to institute a redistricting program? I say an emphatic NO! Lionism will always continue to grow and develop—making it necessary for more changes in the future because of man's willingness and desire to always be of service to his fellow man. We will always be able to say, again and again, 'IT'S GREAT TO BE A LION.' " —Neil Mathena

Pre-1967

Pre-1967 was historical by the groundwork laid by the great leaders of Texas for international growth in the next 50 years. In an emerging global world, this leadership and inspiration was instilled by the many Texans, but none surpassed those of Roy Keaton, Director General of Lions Clubs International, and Herb C. Petry, Jr., Past President of Lions Clubs International, who was also very active in all the politics in South Texas and served on the State Highway Commission for many years. In fact, Lion Petry served longer than any person on the State Highway Commission and many other different boards and titles too numerous to mention, other than the Lions State offices, along with the esteem he held in the legal profession in South Texas. These two were driving forces behind the global expansion of Lionism.

Lack of communication has caused our society great problems in all phases. Roy Keaton had the greatest gifts of speech and writings of any person I have ever known or heard spoken. Yet Roy Keaton spoke and wrote a simple message of inspiration and enthusiasm. My association with Roy was as a friend and mentor.

The highlights of my life began in my high school years when my father was District Governor of District 2-A in Texas, and had the high honor of going to Houston to shake the hand of Melvin Jones. Later, I became District Governor, and my dad and I were the first father-son District Governors. At that time, a District, State and monthly newsletters came out from Lions International; and on the front page was always an article written by Roy Keaton, Director General. I began to read those articles in high school in high regard, and put them in a file entitled "Roy Rides Again," because they were so practical and important in our every day attitudes and life. I always felt that I would be involved in some type of service profession in life.

When preparing my inaugural speech for Atlanta, Georgia in 1982, we were in Florida for a couple of days of RandR and sunshine...and work. I re-read those articles in the file from the 1940s written by Roy Keaton. Many of the ideas in my speech then and thereafter say, *"Amen and sit down"*—

were generated from Roy Keaton and his monthly newsletter. Other ideas and thoughts came from my mentors: my dad, Herb Petry, and executive administrator, Roy Schaetzel.

Here are just some of the titles of the articles by Roy Keaton which divulged the practicality of Lions using this information for the growth of Lionism:

Being with Others	*TNT—Today not Tomorrow*
Control Your Attitudes	*He Can Who Thinks He Can*
Three little words "And then some"	*Knock the "T" Out of Can't*
The Best Gift is Yourself	*You Are Important*
The Colors in the Sunset	*Enthusiasm: a Leader's Asset*
The Face in the Mirror	*Words Work Wonders*

This was part of his philosophy in accepting the position in 1934 as special representative for Lions International. He established and reorganized Lions Clubs across the United States, Mexico and Canada. In 1945, he was named Assistant Secretary General of Lions International and heir apparent to succeed Melvin Jones, Chief Administrative Officer and head of Lions International. However, when Melvin Jones retired in 1948, Roy Keaton was named Director General of Lions International and became the head of the world's largest service organization. During the first 10 years of his tenure as Director General, the countries with Lions Clubs founded around the world increased from 28 to 102, and the number of clubs more than doubled from 8,000 to 16,000. Under his leadership, total membership grew from 380,000 to more than 600,000. Today, there are more than 1,500,000 members of Lions in over 200 countries and geographical locations around the world.

It is undisputed that the unprecedented growth of Lions International is largely because of the dynamic leadership and tireless efforts of Roy Keaton and Past International President Herb Petry. One writer said, *"He ignited the fire and provided the zeal, the zest, the enthusiasm, talent and dedication which made it all happen."* When he retired in 1960, his title of Director General was also retired by the Board of Directors in tribute and respect to his incredible accomplishments. His contributions made the world a better place for millions of people. More than one million men's and women's lives were enriched by his unselfishness and compassion.

His motto was "To serve." Roy also wrote, *"Through the service we contribute something useful, helpful, and beneficial to society. We perform acts of kindness to others, contribute needed service, give encouragement, solace and comfort. Making the world a better place, LIVING IN THE PRESENT, TRUSTEES OF THE PAST AND GUARDIANS OF THE FUTURE: WE SERVE!"* That was his life.

HE WAS AN AMAZING MAN, LOVED BY ALL WHO KNEW HIM, POSSESSED A BOUNDLESS ENERGY, RARE INTELLIGENCE AND REMARKABLE TALENT. A GIFTED WRITER, MASTER OF ORATORY, QUICKNESS OF MIND, SPARKLING HUMOR, BUT ALWAYS WITH AN ESSENTIAL PURPOSE AND AN INFALLIBLE DESIRE TO BE OF SERVICE.

There were hard times and things weren't selling well, but Roy sold Lionism in such great volume that they changed the face of all of Texas— bringing it to a new life and vigor, and new hope to people in the scores of depression, recession-hit communities. He organized some 200 Lions clubs in the state of Texas alone.

By the way, I forgot to mention that ol' Roy Keaton and Past International President Herb Petry were the men who organized the first Lions club on the European continent in Stockholm, Sweden. They also organized the first Lions club in Geneva, Switzerland, and in Paris, France. Lionism moved forward on the European continent because of the vision of Roy Keaton and Herb Petry.

One of my greatest hours in Lionism was to attend the special tribute by the Weatherford Noon Lions Club, where a memorial plaque honoring R. Roy Keaton was erected, and I had the honor of sharing some of the facts and figures of Roy spreading Lionism throughout North America and beyond. I was very fortunate because there is no one that could have been a better friend and mentor. Thank you, Roy Keaton.

Dave Evans

It is certainly worthy of mention that David A. Evans was elected President of our association at the beginning of the second 50 years of Lionism in Texas, 1968-69. His story is best told by David A. Evans in his own history in letters to the Texans.

My Texas Lions History by David A. Evans

It started on April 16, 1947 at 9:12 a.m., with a roar that could be heard for 100 miles and that shattered windows as far away as Houston. A sudden explosion of the freight ship "Grand Camp," laden with ammonium nitrate to be used for fertilizer, exploded and killed 502 people in the harbor in my hometown of Texas City.

At that time, I was a member of a volunteer rescue squad. Out of the 23 members of this squad, I and one other person were then the only ones left alive. The volunteer fire department suffered the same fate, all being killed with the exception of the Fire Chief, who was out of town.

All this may seem to you to be far removed from Lionism, but was actually my start as a Lion, even though I was not to become a member for another four years. I saw the way that the Lions Club in Texas City went into action, even though the five top officers of the Club had been killed in the explosion, I saw how the Lions from all over the world started to send money and supplies to the local club for use in this disaster. I saw how men who had their own businesses to run, their own families to look after, worked night and day for those people whom they did not even know.

I wondered to myself, what kind of man is this that would do all these things without expecting anything in return? What kind of people do we have in this world, who would send money to a little community that they had never heard of before to help those in need?

I decided that I must find out what made these people tick, and if possible, to become one of them. I soon learned that the only way to get into a Lions club was to be invited, and this invitation did not come until January 1951. So needless to say, when the invitation did come, I was ready!

There are many people who become members of a Lions club and never become Lions. Fortunately, soon after my business as a builder, I was given the assignment to work on a project of erecting a monument to those Lions who were killed during the explosion four years earlier. I was so enthusiastic about the project, I did it singlehandedly, even though I was not the chairman, and there were eight other members on the committee. Three days later, I reported to the club that the project had been finished, they could hardly believe it was true. So, I did become a Lion shortly after becoming a member, and I feel that I have been a Lion ever since.

I continued to be happy to serve on committees, to work for the community, to work our fundraising project, as a member of the Minstrel Show, to expect nothing in return, until one year I found myself nominated for a Director of the club. I won the election and served for two years as a Director, and all went well until the following year when I was elected "Tail-Twister."

My enthusiasm for the position soon caused me problems. I was thrown out of the club on several occasions, and soon found that there were two members of the club who did not believe in fines. In my persistence to fine these members, I found myself involved in a hot argument that caused me to offer my resignation from the club. Because of good friends who came to me and insisted that the organization was bigger than these two men who did not like to go along with the rules, I was persuaded to stay in the club. The following year, I was elected Third Vice-President. Anticipating that it would take me at least three years to become President of the club, I was really surprised when I was nominated for President the following year in a field of three candidates. I won the election. I became the first member of my Club to jump from Third Vice-President to President.

As President, I tried a new experience in appointing members of the club who had been members for many years—but had never shown any inclination to work—as chairmen of certain committees. To the surprise of all those in the club, these people who had not worked in the past suddenly came alive and made some of the finest Lions in our entire club. Most of these members are still in the club today.

I went from President to Zone Chairman to Deputy District Governor, and when the State was divided into 15 districts, and the area where I lived was made into the new District 2 S-4, I became a candidate for District Governor. Having no opposition to the post, I won very handily.

After serving as District Governor, the following year I decided to become a candidate for International Director. To add many other things that confronted me at the time, we had a visit from an old sister called "Carla." This hurricane brought 13 feet of water across the seawall in Texas City, and deposited two feet of water, mud, soot, chemicals and raw sewage into our home. Not to be outdone by any wet lade, we immediately set about cleaning up and rebuilding, while at the same time, campaigning for the nomination within the State.

Having an opponent who was very well known, I found that getting the nomination was not an easy task, but at the last convention held in Amarillo, it was finally confirmed that I had received the nomination. We went on to Nice, France to campaign on the international level. We were fortunate in having only nine candidates for eight positions, and I won the office of International Director.

The following January, after being elected as Director, the Dallas-Fort Worth Lions held a banquet in our honor. At this banquet, it was decided that we would again try to get the International Convention to Dallas. In the next three months, we carefully laid our plans, contacted our known friends on the Board, gathered our ammunition, and in April, we headed to the Board meeting in Tokyo.

All the Board members assembled in Vancouver, British Columbia. At this point, we presented every Director and Past President with a Texas Stetson. When we got off the plane in Tokyo, it looked like a meeting of the Southwestern Cattlemen's Association. From the time we left Vancouver, we had the situation well in-hand. The night before we were to vote on the convention site, the Board attended a cocktail party hosted by the Atlantic City convention Bureau. Even their convention manager conceded we would win. When the vote was taken the next morning, the vote was so overwhelming for Dallas that they would not announce the three votes that we did not receive.

I served two years as International Director, and then announced my candidacy for Third Vice-President. This was probably one of the most enjoyable experiences of my entire Lionistic career, running for this office at the Los Angeles Convention. To sum up the Los Angeles Convention, I refer to the letter I wrote immediately after my return from Los Angeles:

Texas City, Texas
August 1, 1965

My dear Texas Lions,

THEY SAID IT COULDN'T BE DONE, but you and all the other Lions of Texas joined ranks and won the greatest victory ever for the Texas Lions. I felt as they must have felt on that day of April 21 many years back when they unfurled the Lone Star Flag at San Jacinto.

This was not a grudge fight, and we were not trying to vindicate anything. We won with dignity maintaining our self-respect and the respect of others along the way. We won because we had an excellent campaign manager in R. A. "Lip" Lipscomb. He is one of the greatest men I have ever known and his devotion to Lionism is unquestionable. His wife, Irene…there are not enough adjectives to describe Betty's and my feeling toward her. In Spanish, I would call her, "Mi princesa Simpatico." She and Lip are our dearest friends and have won the respect of all Lions they have met, from the Past Presidents of Lion International to the newest Lion.

Then there was our advisor, Past International President, Judge Julien C. Hyer. He talked to me like a father, directed me like a coach, counseled me like a judge and advised me and our organization to a victory. What more could you ask of any man? He was our inside man and did a terrific job for Texas.

And Herb Petry, in his subtle way acting mostly behind the scenes during the early stages of the campaign did an outstanding job of molding and solidifying our State into one united front, always being there when we needed him.

International Counselor, Don Buckalew of Conroe, and my neighbor Lon Charles Barre, flew out with us and it befell their lot to be the peons and do all the work until reinforcements arrived. They accepted the responsibility without looking back and attacked the multitude of problems with usual Texas Lionistic vigor.

One lone reinforcement appeared on the scene Saturday. This was In-

ternational Counsellor Charles Carruth of Andrews. Most of you remember him as our Chairman of the Council for 1963-64. Charlie flew his own plane to California and spent half a day trying to locate Los Angeles through the smog. No sooner had he landed, he and Don set up an assembly line putting our banners together. International Counsellor Charlie "Clem" Daniels of Norton, Virginia (no relation to Jack) joined our "peace corps" project and set out to hang the banners in the different hotels. He headed for the airport area and Hollywood while Charles Barre and his two sons John and Herbie invaded the Biltmore (which housed all Governors and Governors-elect). It didn't take us long to find out that Los Angeles had some sort of ordinance against such banners unless they are flame proofed. Even though our banners were of a weight heavy enough to be exempt we couldn't convince the hotel managers.

Not to be outdone by this unfriendly approach taken by the hotels District Governor, Bill Stein took the venetian blind cord, tied it to one of the banners and let it down the outside of his hotel room. The hotels eventually relented and by Wednesday morning we had the city covered like a heavy snow.

Don Buckalew (a Chevrolet dealer) was elected to be the chauffeur and we immediately dispatched him to North Hollywood to pick up a new Pontiac station wagon that had been made available to us through the generosity of the Pontiac division of General Motors. On his return to the hotel, Don installed a Texas flag on each front fender and from that moment on we owned the city.

On Sunday, Abe Houston, our Convention Chairman arrived at the International Hotel and started setting up his control center. NASA could learn some things from Abe on his operation of this center. It was highly organized with contacts into each hotel and motel where Texas were staying.

International Counselor John Painter and ZotZottarelli were also on the scene early, getting their committees into shape. They traveled halfway across California to find a tank of helium to fill the balloons. They missed most of the Wednesday morning convention session getting ready for the parade on Wednesday night. Man, what a parade...Zot and his committee were really clicking. The California TV stations televised the first two hours of the parade and most of that two hours was taken by Texas. The narrator of the TV show would say after each Texas band passed, "Well, this concludes the

Texas Part," after about the sixth band had passed he was heard to say, "My gosh, they brought the whole State with them."

These wonderful people stood there for over an hour before the magic moment came. When it did, there is only one way to adequately describe it and this is to use Arby Verbage, "All hell broke loose." I have never seen a demonstration like this before. We were allowed only 15 minutes, and it took longer than that just to get our Texans through. Betty and I were on the stage, and from our vantage point it was an impressive sight. I'm not ashamed to admit that more than once I had to brush away the tears. I was never before so proud of my Texans and never more proud to be a Texan. Our daughter Tanya insisted on marching in the demonstration and did fine for the first few minutes, but after that pent-up emotion came through. Visualize a little girl of 13 marching placard in one hand and wiping tears that were flowing copiously, with the other. Our neighbor girl Shirley Zenthoefer had gone with the band to California and had lost a toenail in a little accident but was marching in the demonstration, quite a feat I would say. No stone was left unturned, everything was perfect. International Counsellor Don Buckalew came upon the stage and presented to Betty, Texas yellow roses. Lip and Dick were standing with us. Julien and Herb escorted us to the center of the stage. John Painter and his committee had the demonstration organized so well that no once was the procession stopped.

Thursday afternoon we spent visiting caucuses, pigeon-holing delegates, entertaining the leaders, and once or twice sitting down and pulling our shoes off. Thursday night was "Florida Night" and the Sports Arena. They presented a fine show (so I'm told, I slept through most of it) and our new President and his wife were radiating enthusiasm. One of the funny things of the night was when one of the helium-filled balloons, shaped like a clown's head (that was released during the morning demonstration) floated down from the ceiling and drifted to within 18 inches of the microphone during the performance of the Four Saints. It appeared as if the balloon had joined in the singing. Of course these balloons had printed on them "EVANS FOR THIRD" and we were accused of having them radio controlled.

Saturday was a big day for Texas. Everyone was out early to vote and most all the Texas delegates voted, not all, but a good percentage. Former Vice-President Richard Nixon spoke on the Vietnam problem and was well received.

Then came the big moment for us, the announcement of the new Third Vice-President. And once again, John Painter's crew took over the Sports Arena and an even better and larger demonstration, than before, took place.

When the tooting of horns, the beating of drums, the clash of symbols, the shouts of joy and the shuffle of feet had finally died down, the past president of the Rio Piedras Lions Club of Puerto Rico presented to Kermit Agee the New President of the Texas City Loins Club the banner of the Third Vice-President. It was a wonderful, thrilling moment for all of us and all of Texas. It was made possible by the united efforts of all Texas Lions. I am proud of you and I commend each and every one of you.

We captured many prizes in the parade. The Texas City Band won second place which is more than the top honor considering our State had a candidate.

The White Oak Band was terrific and came up with the fourth prize. The Texas AandI Band won first place in the adult division. Jacksboro and Carthage both took honors in baton twirling.

The entire group form the International family stood as the strains of "The Eyes of Texas" reverberated up and down Hollywood Boulevard, an act never before witnessed by any Lion.

Thursday morning broke through the smog-laden valley even before Wednesday night had ended. Being the morning for the Texas Breakfast, which was being held 18 miles away at the International Hotel, we had to leave the Statler early and fight the peak traffic hour to be on-hand for the greatest breakfast ever held. There were over 430 District Governors and their wives there. We had a good representation of the International family there, we had "millions" of Texans there. We had a total of 1,053 people at this breakfast, and all-time record for the size of any State breakfast. The Midland Lions Club Bank was on hand to help awaken those still asleep with their wonderful renditions. They were followed by the Lamesa "Slumtown Symfunny," composed of Lions and business leaders of Lamesa. What a great impression these two groups made, not only at the Texas breakfast, but at every function where they appeared.

International Counsellor Bert Belcher of Seagraves was in charge of this entertainment and he was covering more places, at more time, with less groups than seems possible. Bert is the kind of Lion that can do the impossible.

While we were on the subject of breakfasts, I must mention the terrific job done by Past International Director Dick Self of Dallas. Dick was, among other things, also in charge of the speakers' bureau for all breakfasts. He had this organized down to the last detail and left nothing to be desired. He met with each speaker, coached him in the things to do, provided him with all the ammunition he needed, and sent him in his way…but… it didn't stop there. Dick was up each morning long before breakfast time checking to see that the assigned speaker was up and ready to go. After giving each of them a pep talk, he would then turn his efforts toward other duties for the day. He watched these breakfasts so closely that when "yours truly" did not show up at the Kansas breakfast as scheduled he was there in my place without any advance warning. What a great, dedicated and devoted Lion this man is and that also apples to his wife, Louise.

Following the Texas breakfast we all (some 3,500 Texans) converged on the Los Angeles Memorial Sports Arena to await the nominations. As usual the program was running late and our group was getting restless. Can you imagine some 3,500 Texas men, women, and children, nine large bands and States like Pennsylvania and Oklahoma wanting to join us, all bunched up behind a rope waiting to let off their steam? One shot and they would have stampeded through the walls of the arena.

The District Governors of 1962-63 took the initial step and laid the ground work. The Governors of 1963-64 picked it up and got it off the ground and the Governors of 1964-65 carried it to victory. We owe a lot of these men and especially to the 1964-65 Governors who carried a double load. Mt hat is off to them all.

To the International Counsellors Association who lent their support and contributed greatly to our success, to the Governors with whom I served in 1959-60 who worked so hard, to the District Chairmen of each District, to the Promote Texas Chairmen and especially to International Counsellors Charles Davis who handled this fund in such a fine manner. To the campaign Committees in Los Angeles under the great leadership of International Counsellor Abe Houston to men like Buckalew, Carruth, Barre, Palmer, Painter, Zottarrelli, Redmon, Puig, Schwartz, Kelly, Cornett, J.T. Jones, Nelson, Carrington, Dyer, Belcher, Houston, to the Governor-elect who performed like troupers, to many, many others that

I would like to mention by name if space permitted but my thanks to *you as much as to everyone else. To Dick and Louise Self, to Lip and Irene, two great past Directors who served so willingly, so tirelessly and so efficiently; to Julien Hyer, my advisor, my confidant, my dear friend and to his sweet wife, Agnes; to Herb Petry who was near when I needed him, who lifted me up when I was down and to beautiful Jo; to all Texas Lions, their ladies, their children; to the Paris, Andrews, Jacksboro, Carthage, White Oak, Harper, Texas AandI, and the Texas City Banks, to the Midland Lions Band, the Slumtown Eymfunny and the Castleberry Choir.*

To all my friends both mentioned and unmentioned herein from Berry and me we say thank and God bless you. May you carry Texas Lionism to greater heights than ever before.

Sincerely,
David A. Evans, Third Vice-President

At the convention in Los Angeles, one of the bands that went to the convention was from Harper, Texas—now the home of Trish Wilson, Development Director of Camp Operations at the Texas Lions Camp. It was during this time as you will note in the letters that Don Buckalew and some other District Governors were referred to as International Counsellors, which was the case in 1963, but in 1964 at the time I became Governor, they changed the name to 'District Governor' and I and others for that one year, could be known as International Counsellors and District Governors, which did not make that much difference since we were all proud to be in that position whatever we were called.

It is worthy of note that one of the International Counsellors (or District Governors) Don Buckalew from Conroe and one of the stalwart campaigners during the Evans years later became Past International Director in 1974. In addition, he had to be one of the youngest District Governors in the association upon his election at the age of 29.

Interlude–Patrick Henry

If we go back into history, some of the most remarkable words said by an individual were Patrick Henry's, *"Give me liberty or give me death."*

Which reminds me of the sixth grade history buff who always finished every theme with that famous quotation, *"Give me liberty or give me death."* The teacher became so put out with the same quotation on every theme that she decided to give an assignment whereby he would not be able to use it, so the title of the next theme was supposed to be "Horse Colic." The papers were all turned in and she immediately thumbed through the papers to little Patrick Henry. And he wrote: *"Horse Colic. Horse Colic is something that is found in horses. It is found in the stomach of horses, and it is caused by gas pains hollering, "Give me liberty or give me death.' "*

The words immediately before that famous challenge by the American patriot were perhaps equally courageous. He said, *"But as for me"*...which has to be among the greatest examples of an individual accepting his responsibility.

16 Districts

T-1, T-2, T-3
History of District 2-T1 Lions

District 2-T1 was established in 1947 when District "T" was divided into T1 and T2. District 2-T1 had 27,513 square miles—with the oldest club being Amarillo Downtown, Dalhart was second oldest and Clarendon the third. In 1959, the Multiple District was re-districted, statewide, and "T" got still another sub-district, known as T-3. This status remains until now. That reduced 2-T1 to the upper 26 Counties of the Texas Panhandle covering 25,823.9 square miles. By 1967, there were sixty-six Clubs and 2,675 members in District 2-T1.

Amarillo Lions set in motion the momentum that put over the High Plains Eye Bank, Inc. Starting out in 1958, under such leadership as Lions Omar Hermsmeyer, Jim Wheeler, Joe Tooley, and Ed Skypala, they made a District project out of it 1962. The project continued until 1998 when it was dissolved and the Lions Eye Bank of District 2-T1 (a support group and not an Eye Bank) was formed.

In 1969, PID Ed Flood organized a District project that was known at that time as The Girlstown Coat and Shoe Shopping Spree where every girl from Girlstown could purchase a coat and a pair of shoes. Held in November each year prior to Thanksgiving, this continues to be a District project although Boys Ranch has taken over Girlstown.

In October 1995, under direction of Lion Charles Kuntz the Panhandle of Texas Lions Foundation was formed to collect and disburse District funds.

Good times were to be had at District Conventions, such as in 2002 when John Nash was running for District Governor, the song "Big Bad John" was revised and preformed as his nominating speech. Then Ray White was running for Council Chairman in 2007 and the Whistling Bellies were called in. District 2-T1 has had it all from grass skirts and coconut halves to ugliest shirt contest. District 2-T1 is one of the few Districts in Texas that still has a "Queen's Contest" with Sweethearts from different Clubs competing.

In 2002, District Governor Jim Wilson established a District 2-T1 Lion Legacy Award to recognize an outstanding Lion within the District, a tradition which continues today. The first recipient was PDG Raymond White from Hereford.

There have been two outstanding Lions from District 2-T1 to serve as President of The Texas Lions Camp, those being PDG Raymond White from Hereford, and PDG Jack King from Amarillo Downtown.

Of course District 2-T1 was put on the map in 2007 when one of its own, Lion Jimmy Ross from Quitaque was elected President of Lions Clubs International.

Following are the Texas Lions Hall of Fame recipients from District 2-T1:
PID E.B. "Tex" Mayer (1972)
PDG D. D. (Don) Zimmerman (1973)
PDG W. L. "Preach" Edelman (1975)
PID Edwin "Ed" Flood (1979)
Lion Ed Skypala (1981)
PDG Larry Fuller (1984)
PDG Raymond White (1987)
PDG Jimmy Pigman (1990)
PIP Jimmy Ross (1993)
PDG James Wheeler (1996)
PDG Rick Garrett (1999)
PDG Dr. Kenneth Waugh (2002)
PDG Earl Long (2005)
Lion Jim Wilson (2008)
Lion Wayne Smith (2011)
PDG Jack King (2013)

Centennial Events in District 2-T2

1959 • District 2-T2 was formed from the subdivision of District T. Multiple District 2.

First District Governor • PDG Glen Jones and First Lady Winona from Anton, Texas, 1959-60.

Girlstown, USA in Whiteface - 1949 to present

Home for girls, now affiliated with Cal Farley's Boys Ranch program since 1987.

Amelia Anthony founded Girlstown, U.S.A. in 1949 when she opened a temporary shelter for girls at Buffalo Gap, Texas. In July of that same year, Thomas B. Duggan, a rancher in Lubbock, Texas, donated 1,425 acres of land a few miles south of Whiteface, Texas. Shortly thereafter, Ms. Anthony and her nine girls took up residence.

The Lions of District 2-T2 have assisted through service and in the support of Girlstown, USA since the District's founding.

Texas Boys Ranch at Lubbock - 1972 to present

Texas Boys Ranch was first considered by concerned citizens of Lubbock. They wanted to make a difference in the lives of homeless, neglected and dependent boys of the South Plains area.

The Ranch has served over 1,000 young boys and girls since inception. Girls have been a part of the program since 2010.

Past Council Chairman and Board of Director Appointee Lion Art Cook and his wife, Jody, were very instrumental in the founding of the Ranch. The Lubbock Lions Club and the Lions of District 2-T2 built the second and third cottages.

Great Plains Lions Eye Bank - 1974 to present

Founded by the Lions of District 2-T2, the GPLEB encompasses 22 counties surrounding and including Lubbock County. The Lions are dedicated to their eye bank which has served the good people of West Texas and the South Plains for almost 30 years. The project is locally-owned and operated by hometown people taking care of hometown people, not a satellite office in West Texas operating under the corporate scheme of a major metropolitan city.

Since the eye bank's inception in 1974, we have provided more than 1,500 corneas, and countless other eye tissues, to recipients for "sight-restoring" transplant surgeries.

District 2-T2 Hearing Bank - 1997

The bank was formed to service disadvantaged adults and some special needs children with hearing disabilities. Over 100 clients have benefited from hearing aids since the Hearing Bank began.

Texas Lions Camp - 1953 to present

The Lubbock Lions Club has built the first health lodge and two swimming pools at the Camp. District 2-T2 has assisted with the transportation of children with disabilities to the Camp since its inception, with a full bus of 38 children being sent annually for the past 10 years.

District 2-T2 Eyeglass Recycling and Children's Eyeglass Program · 2010 to present

Fitted over 1,000 disadvantaged children with eyeglasses to-date.

Texas Lions District 2-T3

Lions District 2-T3 was formed in 1958. Several other subdivisions have occurred since 1958, but Lions District 2-T3 remains the district that governs Lionism in Far West Texas. One of the oldest clubs in Texas is the El Paso Downtown Lions Club, chartered in 1923. El Paso Downtown Lions Club began sponsoring other clubs and District 2-T3 grew.

Lions District 2-T3 includes 36 clubs, organized in eight zones in cities large and small from El Paso, Fabens, Horizon City, Andrews, Odessa, Crane, Ft. Stockton, Iraan, McCamey, Alpine, Ft. Davis, Sanderson, Van Horn, Kermit, Monahans, Pecos and Wink.

The many activities of clubs in District 2-T3 over the years have included support to the Texas Lions Camp, hearing and speech programs, vision health and screening programs, food drives, war efforts, various crisis centers, the Boys and Girl Scouts of America, various rescue missions, the Salvation Army; local schools, local athletic teams, children with special needs, Habitat for Humanity, various rehabilitation centers, and Meals on Wheels programs, to list a few.

Fundraising activities across District 2-T3 have included: staging minstrel shows, rodeos, circuses, chili cook-offs, spaghetti dinners, operating concession stands at local schools and universities, selling roses and fruit baskets for special occasions, sponsoring casino nights, Bingo, and even sponsoring gun shows and golf tournaments.

While supporting local activities, clubs across District 2-T3 have achieved unique milestones such as: establishment of a Children's Camp in El Paso for children that did not qualify to attend the Texas Lions Camp, establishment of a Deaf Center and a Miss Deaf El Paso Pageant to serve the deaf and hard of hearing community, participating and anchoring the Sun Bowl Association Thanksgiving Day Parade, establishment and participating in the Fourth of July People's Parade, establishment of "El Leon" the "Conquistador" awards for outstanding Lions and citizens in El Paso, conducting a district-level pageant to crown a district queen, establishment of the first University Club in West Texas, establishment of the all-women Professional Women's Lions Club and the Special Needs Lions Club in El Paso.

Of course, some of the outstanding Lions of T-3 have included Roy J. Davenport, Roy C. Chambliss, William and Susan Driscoll, and Donald R. Peppard. One of the oldest Lions in T-3 was Roy J. Davenport, truly a character in his own right. Roy C. Chambliss was a principal at Yselta High School, then later moved to Clovis, New Mexico, where he was a District Governor. William and Susan Driscoll were also truly extraordinary. Bill had quite a career as a secret service agent, before coming to El Paso and meeting Susan. They were married and became two of the outstanding Lions of that District of Texas. Donald and Irene Peppard have been some great leaders and Donald served through the chairs of the Past District Governors Association.

Through 56 Past District Governors; including the two Past District Governors that were very active, Joe Parish, who served from 1978-1979, and Garland Tiner, who served 2009-2010. Also along with countless past and present District Officers, Zone Chairmen, Club Presidents, Club Officers and individual Lions, District 2-T3 has proudly and with a special Texas flair, upheld through its activities, the basic core values of the Lions Club International Association. Lions District 2-T3 is, and will always strive to be the personification of our guiding principle. In Lions District 2-T3, we serve and, we serve–Texas style.

E-1, E-2

History of District 2-E1

District 2-E1 was created in 1959 when District 2-E was divided into 2-E1 and 2-E2. This occurred when the state was redistricted into 15 sub-districts. There are two Founder Clubs—Abilene Founder and Wichita Falls Founder—created in 1917. The District is comprised of clubs located in 23 counties.

Lion M. E. Carothers of Anson Noon was District Governor for 1968-69, and nine new clubs were organized during his tenure (the most new clubs in one year). One of these new clubs had the honor of being the 1,000th Lions club in Texas—the Graham Evening club, sponsored by Graham Noon. International President Dave Evans of Texas City was the speaker for their charter night banquet.

One of the youngest District Governors in history was elected at the 1969 convention in Graham, as Jerry K. Vandiver of Wichita Falls Southwest took over the reins. Governor Vandiver stressed youth work and saw the District's first Leo Club organized at Graham. He also presented charters to three new Lions clubs.

Delegates to the district convention in 1973, with Loren Maples of Graham Noon Club as Governor, voted to proceed with the organization of a District 2-E1 Lions Eye Bank. The organizational meeting for the District 2-E1 Lions Eye Bank, Inc. was held during the Mid-Winter Conference in Vernon on January 12, 1974 during District Governor Tom Lindsey's term. Articles of Incorporation were prepared by attorney Bryan Bradbury, a member of the Abilene Founders Lions Club, and signed by James D. Taylor of Vernon, Charles Davis of Wichita Falls and James H. Wheeler, Jr. of Abilene. The Eye Bank began operation on August 10, 1974, in Stamford, Texas. Under the guidance, direction and hard work of many Lions—but particularly PDG Charlie Davis, PDG Irvin Hiler, and PDG James Wheeler—the Eye Bank has evolved into a very successful operation. The District Eye Bank joined with Districts 2-E2, 2-X1, and 2-X2 in 1994 to work with Transplant Services in Dallas. Because of our close affiliation with Transplant Services Center at U.T. Southwestern Medical Center, we changed our name to District 2-E1 Lions Tissue and Eye Bank, Inc. in November 1996.

Many members have given years of service to the Texas Lions Camp as directors, committeemen, and workers. PDG James P. McCracken of Cisco served two terms as president of the board of directors. PDG James Wheeler of Abilene, PDG John Kendrick of Mineral Wells, and PDG Hal Griffin of Abilene have also served as President of the camp. PDG James H. Wheeler Jr. was named chair of the Camp Improvements Committee by Camp President E.H. Munger in 1967. He has served in that position until today in 2015, except for his time on the Camp's Executive Committee from 1975 - 1981. PDG Wheeler received the prestigious Ambassador of Good Will award in 2004 from Lions Clubs International President Dr. Tae-Sup Lee for his service on our District Tissue and Eye Bank as well as the Texas Lions Camp.

PDG John W. Longley of Stamford, in the position of Extension Chairman for many District Governors, was very effective in his work in organizing new clubs. He was recognized by Lions International for 20 new clubs and received the award for excellence in this area from Lions International. He was presented the Ambassador of Goodwill Award, Lionism's highest award, by International President Joe McLoughlin in Kerrville on August 5, 1977.

The District has actively supported Leo Clubs since the first one was organized in 1969. There are currently 4 Leo Clubs in the district.

E-1

Sue Smith, wife of our faithful Past District Governor, passed away on July 11, 2015, but C. Lee kept up his duties the eight years she had been ill and continued on the next week. There is not another like him.

Two of the most active members of this District during the later years have been Hal and Sandy Griffith. Sandy Griffith was first on the scene, she was State Chairman of the Leader Dog for over 12 years. Sandy gave great programs about Leader Dog and helped raise many puppies (pups) for assistance to blind individuals. Because of her involvement, Hal then became more involved in many activities and received seven Presidential Awards—finally reaching the pinnacle of being the area's GMT. For the year 2015-16, Hal is a new club consultant for the entire area. Our hats off to two great individuals and Lions.

Who could forget Gary Sult, who chased after my hat during a golf tournament in E-1, and his contributions to the Camp and all aspects of Lionism; Scott Evans and a contributing Lion for many years and Art Dearing (I call him my spy) who have been involved so much in District affairs.

District 2-E2
First and Only

Who would have thought that anyone would have a Charter Night at Billy Bob's arena in Ft. Worth, Texas? But Gib Lewis, then Speaker of the House, and Ebb rode out on horses (real Cowboys dressed in suits and hats that did not properly fit) and both jumped off their horses and conducted the Charter Night for a Lions Club!

WHO KILLED J.R.?

On my first flight to England on Braniff Airways, we rode first-class. Before the flight began, I was talking to a lady in the front seat (we were in second row seats), and she was a very lovely lady and a very good conversationalist. All at once, Jay (my wife) punched me. I turned around and there was J. R. (Larry Hagman) coming up the aisle in a robe and boots! He sat down in the first row seat next to the lady I had been visiting with... his wife, Maj! The conversation quickly turned to boots between J. R. and I, and he asked where I had my boots made. I told him at Leddy's, and he told me he had most of his made at Casey's in San Antonio, but he had had a pair or two from Leddy's in Ft. Worth. The reason we began our conversation was because of the introductions. He was familiar with the Grindstaff name because my uncle was a lawyer in Weatherford, and J. R.'s dad was a lawyer who was married at one time to Mary Martin, also from Weatherford. Larry visited on occasion, and knew my family name because of the legal ties.

J. R. was also a jogger, and we had plans to both meet and jog in Hyde Park in London. Our plans did not work out, even though Larry did jog in London in Hyde Park, as his picture was in the paper.

In 1917, Texas was designated District 4, with 12 Clubs and 360 members.
In 1922, Texas was designated District 2, with 22 clubs and 1,444 members.
In 1930, Texas was divided into 5 Sub-Districts—called T-E-X-A-S—with 242 clubs and 8,418 members
In 1959, District 2-E was divided into 2-E 1 and 2-E 2

District 2-E 2 International Lions Officers

Julien C. Hyer, Fort Worth	1 year International Director	1922
(never served as a Governor)	Third Vice President	1928-29
	President	1931-32
PID Beverly Stebbins	Arlington	2008-10

Texas Lions Hall of Fame

PDG Charlie Williams	Fort Worth	1973
PDG Vern Carrington	Denton	1979
PDG Albert W. Brown	Denison	1983
PDG Bill Hudson	Denton	1986
PDG Harry Rankin	Fort Worth	1989
PDG J.T. Hinkle	River Oaks	1992
PDG Edward Stebbins	Arlington	1995
PDG Jack Harris	Fort Worth	1998
PDG Jack Adkison	River Oaks	2004
PDG Bill R. Graham	Gainesville	2007
PDG Al Jara	Fort Worth	2010
PDG Beverly Stebbins	Arlington	2011
PDG Rick Stoorza	Aledo	2013
PDG Otis Pharr	District 2 X1/Pantego	2001

District 2-E2 District Governors
The Second 50 Years

1967-68	**PDG Raymond Meissner**	Fort Worth
1968-69	**PDG Loyd Chapman**	Fort Worth
1969-70	**PDG A.H. "Brink" Brinkman**	Denton
	Melvin Jones Fellow	
1970-71	**PDG Dr. Louis A. Griffith**	
1971-72	**PDG J.T. Hinkle**	River Oaks

Melvin Jones Fellow, Texas Lions Hall of Fame 1992, four extension awards, helped organize 2-E2 Organ/eye Bank 1971-72. Exec. Director and President. President of MD2 Eye Banks Association of Texas 1st. Lt. Gov. in 2-E2.

PDG J.T. Hinkle, continued
Served on MD-2 Committee to form the Texas Lions Hall of
Fame. Inducted the first Hall of Fame member, PIP Julien C.
Hyer. Chairman of Lions International Parade in Mexico City
in 1972. Life Member of Lions Clubs International.

1972-73	**PDG Albert W. Brown**	Denison

Progressive Melvin Jones Fellow, 2, Ruby white Gold,
Lead Donor LCIF Campaign Sight First 1991. Texas Lions
Hall of Fame 1983. Past President, PDG's Association of Texas
1999-2000. Past President Texas Lions Camp. MD2 LCIF
Campaign Sight First Chair. Host Committee Advisor, USA/
Canada, Fort Worth 2002 Albert and Violia Brown Humani-
tarian Award named for him.

1973-74	**PDG John L. Bigler**	Forest Hill

Melvin Jones Fellow

1974-75	**PDG John Seelig**	Fort Worth

Melvin Jones Fellow

1975-76	**PDG W.S. "Dub" Horn**	Fort Worth

Melvin Jones Fellow

1976-77	**PDG Bill Hudson**	Denton

Texas Lions Hall of Fame, 1986. Past President, PDG's
Association of Texas, 1982-83.

1977-78	**PDG Charles Wilson**	Fort Worth

Melvin Jones Fellow. Organizer of Lions Clubs.

1978-79	**PDG Clifton Ramsey**	Denison

Melvin Jones Fellow

1979-80	**PDG Jack Harris**	Fort Worth

Progressive Melvin Jones Fellow, 4 Diamond White Gold.
Texas Lions Hall of Fame, 1998. MD-2 Texas Lions Foundation
Chair. MD-2 Council Chair. MD-2, State Chair, USA/Canada.
Host Committee Chairman USA/Canada Fort Worth, 2002.
USA/Canada site selection committee.

1980-81	**PDG Frank Keas**	Denton
1981-82	**PDG Bill Butcher**	Fort Worth
1982-83	**PDG 'Buck' Barajas**	Fort Worth

1983-84	**PDG E.L. Atkins**	Arlington
1984-85	**PDG Joe Goetz**	Fort Worth
1985-86	**PDG "Pockets" Hartwick**	Fort Worth
1986-87	**PDG Pat Waddle**	Denton

Progressive Melvin Jones Fellow

1987-88	**PDG Jan Carrington**	Denton

Progressive Melvin Jones Fellow

1988-89	**PDG Al Jara**	Fort Worth

Melvin Jones Fellow, Texas Lions Hall of Fame, 2010. Host Committee, Printing, USA/Canada, Fort Worth, 2002

1989-90	**PDG Ron Layland**	Cleburne

Progressive Melvin Jones Fellow, 6 Diamond Yellow Gold .MD-2, Membership Chair, 1993-95. MD-2 Leader Dog Chair, 1996-99 MD-2, Retention Chair, 2001-2005 .MD-2 Eyeglass Recycling program Chair. LCI Membership key for 300+ members. LCI Extension Awards, 25 Lions International President Certificates of Appreciation, 8. Over 15 years as #1 in Membership, Texas Lions PDG's Association.

1990-91	**PDG Bob Brady**	Fort Worth

Melvin Jones Fellow, MD-2 Long Range Planning Commission.

1991-92	**PDG Edward Stebbins**	Arlington

Progressive Melvin Jones Fellow, 9 Diamond Yellow Gold. 8 New Lions Clubs, LCI Extension Awards and LCI Membership Key Award. Director Lions World Service for the Blind. Texas Lions Hall of Fame, 1995. Past President PDG's Association of Texas, 1999-2000. Past President Texas Lions Camp. LCI Elections Committee, multiple times. LCIF District Coordinator 1992-93

1992-93	**PDG Jack Adkison**	River Oaks

Progressive Melvin Jones Fellow. MD-2 Council Secretary. USA/Canada Discussion Leader. USA/Canada Host Committee, Protocol / VIPs, Fort Worth, Texas, 2002. Texas Lions Hall of Fame, 2004. 4, LCI Extension Awards. Life Member Lions Clubs International. 10, International Presidents Certificate of

PDG Jack Adkison, continued
Appreciation. LCI Guiding Lion Medal. Past President, PDG's
Association of Texas 2014-15.LCIF District Coordinator, 1993-95.
District LCIF Coordinator, 2011-17. LCI Membership, Senior
Master Key, 25 members.

1993-94 **PDG Charles Brinkley** Fort Worth
Melvin Jones Fellow. LCI Membership Key Award for Members.
LCIF District Coordinator, 1994-95.

1994-95 **PDG Billy Graham** Gainesville
Progressive Melvin Jones Fellow. Texas Lions Hall of Fame, 2007.
USA/Canada Host Committee, Transportation, Fort Worth,
Texas 2002 MD-2 Director Lions World Services for the Blind.
Multiple Times.

1995-96 **PDG Fred Tramel** Fort Worth
Melvin Jones Fellow, LCIF District Coordinator, 96-97.

1996-97 **PDG Truman Wester** Denison
Progressive Melvin Jones Fellow, 4 Diamond yellow Gold.
LCIF District Coordinator, 1997-98.

1997-98 **PDG David Gramm** The Colony
Melvin Jones Fellow, Texas Lions Foundation Trustee, USA/
Canada Host Committee Facilities, Fort Worth, 2002.

1998-99 **PDG Richard Stoorza** Aledo
Melvin Jones Fellow, MD-2 Council Chair, Texas Lions Hall
of Fame, 2013. MD-2 USA / Canada Chair. USA/Canada Host
Committee, Vice Chair, Fort Worth, 2002. Past President,
Texas Lions Camp.

1999-2000 **PDG Beverly Stebbins** Arlington
Progressive Melvin Jones Fellow, 9 Diamond Yellow Gold.
USA/Canada Host Committee, Vice Chair, Fort Worth, 2002.
USA / Canada Discussion Leader. International Director,
2008-10, Texas Lions Hall of Fame, 2011. MD-2, International
Relations / Liaison, 2010-13. MD-2 GLT. Lions International
Ambassador of Goodwill.

2000-01 **PDG Jim Coleman** Lewisville
Melvin Jones Fellow, Texas Lions Foundation Trustee. MD-2

PDG Jim Coleman, continued
World Services for the Blind Chair. USA /Canada, Host
Committee, Airport Services, Fort Worth, 2002.

01-02 **PDG Ted Whitley** Burleson
Melvin Jones Fellow, MD-2 Outstanding Youth. Multiple
years USA / Canada Host Committee, Secretary/Treasurer,
Fort Worth, 2002 Year ending + membership.

02-03 **PDG Bill McCarty** Denton
MD-2 Woman's Membership and Development Chair.

03-04 **PDG Barry Beeson** McKinney
Melvin Jones Fellow

04-05 **PDG Robert "Bob" Mitchell** The Colony
Progressive Melvin Jones Fellow. MD-2 Vice Council Chair.

05-06 **PDG H.M. "Skip" Nuss** Mansfield
Melvin Jones Fellow, MD-2 Lions Quest Chair, Multiple
Terms. LCIF District Coordinator, 2009-10

06-07 **PDG Carolyn Gramm** The Colony
Melvin Jones Fellow, USA /Canada, Host Committee,
Manpower, Fort Worth, 2002 .International Presidents
Certificate of Appreciation.

07-08 **PDG Craig Spencer** Bedford
Melvin Jones Fellow

08-09 **PDG Dr. Don Yandell** Cleburne
Melvin Jones Fellow

09-10 **PDG Margie Nuss** Mansfield
Melvin Jones Fellow, MD-2 Lions Quest. Year ending
Membership, 1-Club, +1. LCI Extension award, 1.

10-11 **PDG Jeanne Adkison** River Oaks
Progressive Melvin Jones Fellow, MD-2 Vice Council
Chair. Texas Lions Camp Executive Board, 2007-08. 7, Inter-
national President's Certificate of Appreciation. USA / Canada
Discussion Leader. 4, LCI Extension Awards. Year ending
Membership, 4-Clubs, + 29.

11-12 **PDG Tom Westerman** Colleyville
Melvin Jones Fellow. 4, LCI Extension Awards. Year ending
Membership, 3, Clubs + 14.

| 12-13 | **PDG John Paul Burnett** | Colleyville |

Melvin Jones Fellow, MD-2 Leader Dog Chair. Multiple years. Texas Lions Camp Executive Board, 2013-14. 1 LCI, Extension Award. Year ending Membership, 1, Club, +26.

| 13-14 | **PDG Suzi Schneider** | Denton Triangle |

Melvin Jones Fellow, MD-2 GLT. Albert and Viola Brown Humanitarian Award, 2009-10. 4, LCI Extension Awards. Year ending Membership 4, Clubs +37.

| 14-15 | **PDG Suzanne Henderson** | Fort Worth |

Melvin Jones Fellow

Important events for District 2-E2

The Mother Club–Fort Worth Founder

The Fort Worth Lions Club was originally chartered on September 26, 1916. An organizer by the name of Elbert A. Hicks, working for Dr. W.P. Woods and his "International Association of Lions Club", came through Texas organizing "Dens". This title was presumptuous, because at that time they were neither "International" nor a true "Association". The first President of the Fort Worth Club was Dr. T.L. Ray.

At the organizational meeting with Melvin Jones and representatives of other Business Men's Clubs in Chicago, Illinois on July 7th.1917 the Fort Worth Lions Club was represented by W.W. Wren and A.E. Corebett .It was at this meeting that they agreed to have the first Convention in Dallas, Texas, on October 8,1917.

At the first Convention in Dallas, Texas the representatives were W.W. Wren and W.A. Grimes as Delegates and A.E. Corebett as an alternate. At this Convention the current Fort Worth, Lions Club President Harry G. Brickhouse's name was placed in nomination to be a 1 Year International Director. President Brickhouse was one of five Lions nominated and he was not elected.

There was 73 signers of the Charter for the Fort Worth Lions Club, Dated October 8, 1917. The Fort Worth Lions Club had a young lawyer out of South Carolina by the name of Julien C. Hyer that Lion P.H. Edwards

invited to visit the club in December of 1919. For some reason, he did not
join until June of 1920.

Julien C. Hyer was elected Club President in January 1922. At the International Lions Convention in Hot Springs, Arkansas, he was elected to
a 1 year term as International Director. At the International Convention in
Des Moines in 1928, he was elected to International 3rd. Vice President
and proceeded up the chairs, until at the Convention in Toronto, Canada
in 1931 he was elected as International President of Lions Club International.

Julien remains the only Lion from the Fort Worth Lions Club to hold
an International office. There have been 9 District Governors from the
club. Dr. William J. Danforth in 1933-34, Tom Gillis 1937-38, Charles F.
Williams 1942-43, W.R. McDonald, 1955-56, Judge Marvin B. Simpson
1958-59, John Seelig 1974-75, Joe Goetz 1984-85 and Suzanne Henderson
2015-16. International President Julien C. Hyer never served as a District
Governor.

1983 War on Drugs

International President Everett J. 'Ebb" Grindstaff kicked off his signa-
ture event for his year as President in District 2-E2 at the River Oaks Lions
Club's annual International Night Dinner. The International "Drug Aware-
ness" and "Texas War on Drugs" event was held at the Shady Oaks Country
Club in Fort Worth, Texas. President Grindstaff presided over the meeting
that was attended by Dr. Turner of Washington D.C. as a representative of
U.S. President Ronald Reagan, to start the National War on Drugs campaign.
The Speaker was H. Ross Perot of Dallas, Texas.

District 2-E2 has hosted a number of State Conventions and Council of
Governors meetings. Hosted the USA / Canada Forum in Fort Worth, 2002.

Past Director General Lions Clubs International

R. Roy Keaton, a Weatherford, Texas native became Special Representative for Lions Club International in 1934, establishing Lions clubs across
the United States, Mexico and Canada. Roy was named Assistant Secretary
General in 1945 and heir apparent to succeed Melvin Jones, the founder of
Lionism. In 1948, Roy Keaton was named Director General becoming head
of the world's largest service organization. Under his leadership, Lions

clubs membership increased from 380,000 members to more than 600,000 Lions, and the scope of Lionism spread from 28 to 102 countries.

As of January 2015, there are 1,381,034 members in 46,394 clubs, and 755 districts in 210 countries and geographic areas. The unprecedented growth of Lions clubs was largely because of the dynamic leadership, vision and efforts of Robert Roy Keaton.

Roy is buried in Oakwood Cemetery in Weatherford, Texas at Rusk and Front Street near the Weatherford Evening Lions Club where he attended regular meetings until his passing. There is a Lions Club International Marker at his gravesite.

Lions Clubs International Foundation

District 2-E2 had a Lead Donor for "Campaign Sight First: PDG Albert W. Brown, Denison Lions Club.

District 2-E2 has 2 clubs with 100% Melvin Jones Fellow members, only 2 in Texas and 2 of 355 in the world: Pantego Lions Club and Arlington Greater Lions Club.

International Officers

International President, Julien C. Hyer, Fort Worth Founder Lions Club, Fort Worth, Texas. Elected to the office of President, at the International convention, Toronto, Canada. 1931. Served 1931-32.

International Director, Beverly L. Stebbins, Arlington Lions Club, Arlington, Texas. Elected to the office of International Director at the Convention in Bangkok, Thailand. Served 2008-10.

Fellow

Melvin Jones conceived the idea that Lions, in addition to meeting, eating, trading with each other and calling each person by their first name, should do service to others—that Lions should be a service club.

This tradition has served as our mission in District 2-E2. "WE SERVE" carries on in all our entities we support.

Texas Lions Camp

At the 1949 Lions International Convention in New York, the International Board approved the Charter of the Texas Lions League for Crippled Children. Since the Camp's opening in 1953, over 60,000 children have attended. District 2-E2 is entitled to two Elected Directors, one Director elected each year. In addition, the Governor and the IPDG serve as Directors. The Past Presidents of District 2-E2 also serve as Directors for life. The Charter President was PDG Jack Wiech.

The Presidents of the Camp from District 2-E2:

PDG Albert W. Brown

PDG Edward Stebbins

PCC Richard Stoorza

Julien C. Hyer Lions Youth Camp

Established in 1973 to foster and create a spirit of understanding among the peoples of the world. Named in honor of Lions Past President Julien C. Hyer of District 2-E2. PCC Jack Harris was one the founders and served until his passing. The president's position is rotated between District 2-E2 and our co-founder, District 2-X1. The board is also split between the two districts. The 1st Vice District Governor automatically serves on the board.

Lions Clubs International Foundation

LCIF was established in 1968, with the Melvin Jones Fellowship added in 1973. An international foundation that administers grants and supports disaster victims, those with disabilities, youth programs, preserves sight, and meets humanitarian needs. Over $30 million in grants are disbursed each year.

LCIF took off with Lions when the Association started Campaign SightFirst in 1990. PDG Albert W. Brown of District 2-E2 was one of the lead donors. This was followed next with Campaign SightFirst 2. Both of these campaigns were very successful in obtaining funds to enlarge our grants and Disaster relief services.

As of April 2015, District 2-E2 has over 655 Melvin Jones Fellows and a total of 49 Progressives, with a mix of Diamonds and Rubies.

The Texas Lions Foundation was established in 1984 by the Texas Council of Governors and ratified by the delegates at the State Convention. The Foundation has given humanitarian service grants and disaster relief services to victims of natural disasters that cause mortality, injury and property damage within the State of Texas—and have been of major assistance to worthy projects in Texas. Trustees have been PCC Jack Harris, PDG David Gramm and PDG Jim Coleman.

World Services for the Blind is a rehab facility for blind or visually-impaired adults offering a unique combination of independent living and career training to help students reenter life independently and be able to attend to their activities of daily living. Established in Little Rock, Arkansas in 1947. District 2-E2 in 1992. Trustees have been PDG Edward Stebbins, PDG Billy Graham and PDG Jim Coleman.

The District 2-E2 Drug Awareness Council exists to further educate youth on the pitfalls and dangers of various drugs—both illicit and legal. Council has many programs for individual clubs and Lions to support the awareness of drugs in our communities. DAC has a president and board members with terms, elected at the district convention.

The District 2-E2 Lions Eye and Organ Bank was established in 1972 as a dream of PDG J.T. Hinkle. He not only founded, but was instrumental in locating the office at John Peter Smith Hospital with a grant.

The LEOB promotes the conservation, restoration and transplanting of human organs and eyes. With the prevention, treatment and research of blindness and diabetes. There is an Adult Eye Clinic, Transplant Service Center the Garden of Life, Thanksgiving of Life, the Mobile Vision Unit and the Eyeglass Recycling Center. The LEOB has a president and board members with terms, elected at the District convention.

The Leader Dog Program empowers people who are blind, visually-impaired or deaf-blind with skills for a lifetime of independent living. Matches the person with a leader dog that has been trained to make the person as independent as possible. This program helps a person re-enter society and contribute to their community.

Texas Lions Eyeglass Recycling Center volunteers collect used eyeglasses and deliver them to the District 2-E2 recycling center. They are cleaned, sorted, lenses strength checked, catalogued, and then distributed to missions in foreign countries and people in need.

Sports Extravaganza is a relatively new entity for District 2-E2, shared with District 2-X1. Its purpose is to empower sight-impaired children to compete in competition for awards and to build confidence in themselves.

.

District 2-X
1931-1959

1931-1932   Julien C. Hyer
               Ft. Worth Founder and Dallas Founder Lions Club
               International President; Honoree Texas Lions Hall of
               Fame 1972

1942-1943   Jesse Guy Smith
               Commerce Lions Club
               Honoree Texas Lions Hall of Fame 1974

1946-1947   A. M. "Buck" Morgan
               Grand Prairie Lions Club
               Honoree, Texas Lions Hall of Fame 1980

1950-1951   James H. Harbin
               Waxahachie Lions Club
               Constitution and By-laws Chair of District 2-X1 for many
               years; candidates could not think of running for District
               office without an interview from him.
               Honoree, Texas Lions Hall of Fame 1983

1951-1952   R. A. "Dick" Self
               Dallas Oak Cliff Lions Club
               International Director 1954-1956
               Honoree, Texas Lions Hall of Fame 1972

1956-1957   George E. Bushong
               Dallas Park Cities
               Made badge boxes and gave them to newly-formed clubs;
               very active in Guiding Lions programs
               Honoree, Texas Lions Hall of Fame 1992

1959-Present District 2-X1

1959-1960	Weldon Guillickson Dallas Westcliff Lions Club
1960-1961	Marion B. Snider Dallas Park Cities Lions Club International piano entertainer LCI Conventions for 10+ years; recipient Ambassador of Good Will; Honoree, Texas Lions Hall of Fame 1995
1961-1962	Ross T. Bowling Dallas Trinity Industrial Lions Club
1962-1963	M. M. "Pop" Myers
1963-1964	Cecil Cooper Garland Host Lions Club
1964-1965	Hugh Childress Instrumental in forming the District 2-X1 Lions Sight and Tissue Foundation
1965-1966	Frank Conrad Dallas Park Cities Lions Club
1966-1967	Chick Knight (Ovella) Duncanville Lions Club
1967-1968	W. "Dub" T. Nelson (Daisy Fern) Dallas Exchange Park Lions Club Served as District T Governor in 1955-1956, then again in 1967-1968 for District 2-X1. Served as President of the MD-2 Past District Governors Association in 1964-1965 Honoree, Texas Lions Hall of Fame 1989

1968-1969   J. A White (Ovella)
Mesquite Lions Club
Mr. Extension for Lions Clubs in North Texas area;
served as MD-2 State Extension Chairman

1969-1970   Olin H. Hill
Quilian Lions Club

1970-1971   James E. Borman (Ima Gene)
Dallas Wynnewood Lions Club

1971-1972   W. G. Franklin (Deanna)
Served as MD-2 Council Chairman, the first from District
2-X1. Later, he moved to Kentucky and served as District
Governor and Council Chairman for Kentucky.

1972-1973   C. W. Woodson (Angie)

1973-1974   A. Lewis (Pat)
Richardson Host Lions Club
Always wore red socks for all events.

1974-1975   Sylvan Moritz (Mickey)
Dallas Oak Cliff Lions Club
Lion Sylvan never served as a President of a Lions club.
However, soon afterwards, Lions Clubs International
changed the criteria of becoming a District Governor.
Lion Sylvan was instrumental in the formation of the
Lions Foundation for Shadow Children of District 2-X1.
An active member of his club, serving every week
to distribute food for Meals-On-Wheels program,
Red Ribbon Lion, Honoree, Texas Lions Hall of Fame 1998

1975-1976   F. X. "Pancho" Luna (Ale)
Dallas Central Lions Club
Lion Pancho was instrumental in getting the Mexican
Constitution changed to allow cornea transplants in Mexico.

He "smuggled" corneas for the blind to Monterrey, Mexico for many years; ran for Texas candidate for International Director; Honoree Texas Lions Hall of Fame 2001

1976-1977   Surry Shaffer, Jr. (Dori)
Dallas Founder Lions Club
Lion Surry was the founder and organizer of the Julien C. Hyer Lions Youth Camp founded in 1973, and hosted first youths in 1974; instrumental in making Lion Clubs International Youth Exchange Program a success; personally knew many influential Lions all over the world; hosted many in his home and had block parties where neighbors would participate in hosting the Lions; instrumental in establishing Gavel Travel in the District where Lions club representatives would visit clubs and take their gavel, causing them in-turn to come to their Lions club to get it back.

1977-1978   Odis Pharr
Dallas Park Cities Lions Club
"Stand Up, Odis," a Lion of small stature, but a big heart. Would always get emotional at meetings.

1978-1979   F. Hall Brown (Helen)
Dallas Wynnewood Lions Club
Lion Hall was a great extension chair. He never would take "No" for an answer. He served as MD-2 State Extension for several years; Co-founder District 2-X1 Diabetic Day Camp. He was one of the original Directors/Officers of the Lions Sight and Tissue Foundation; Honoree, Texas Lions Hall of Fame 1986

1979-1980   Robert Binder (Betty)
Commerce Lions Club

1980-1981   Bill Melton
             Dallas Oak Cliff Lions Club
             Recipient Ambassador of Good Will
             Honoree, Texas Lions Hall of Fame 2007

1981-1982   Howard Synder (Dorthea)
             Dallas Preston North Lions Club
             Lion Howard was instrumental in assisting the Lions
             Sight and Tissue Foundation of District 2-X1. He was very
             involved in sight conservation and world wide Eye Bank
             organizations. Honoree, Texas Lions Hall of Fame 2004

1982-1983   Charles Norwood (Daisy)
             Richardson Host Lions Club
             In 1983, Lion DG Charlie began a District 2-X1 program
             of District Lion of the Year which has continued since his
             term as Governor.
             Honoree, Texas Lions Hall of Fame 2013

1983-1984   Eugene Cooper (Regina)
             Dallas Inwood Lions Club

1984-1985   Don Anderson (Elizabeth)
             Grand Prairie Host Lions Club

1985-1986   John Eads (Joanna)
             DeSoto Lions Club
             Lion DG John began an annual program of "Grass Root
             Lion" to honor Lions in clubs who had been in Lions less
             than a five years. Lion DG John began an annual program
             called "Dr. R. 'Dick' A. Self Outstanding Club Award."
             It is presented by the District Governor to the Lions Club
             deemed to be the most outstanding Club in the District.
             It was named in honor of Lion R. A. Self, who served as
             District -X Governor in 1951-1952, and Lions Club
             International Director in 1954-1956. State and Interna-
             tional Campaign Chairman for PID Ray Hughston and
             PID Connie De La Garza.

1985-1986 John Eads, continued
Served MD-2 as Finance Chair for seven years. Served as
MD-2 Council Chairman in 1986-1987. Served as President
of the MD-2 Past District Governors Association in 1993-
1994. Will serve as President of the Texas Lions Camp in
2018-2019. Recipient, Ambassador of Good Will Award,
two Presidential Awards.
Honoree, Texas Lions Hall of Fame 2010

1986-1987 Martin Reese (Jimmie)
Dallas Town North Lions Club

1987-1988 Rex Coppedge (Vivian)
Plano Early Lions Club

1988-1989 Wes Jespersen (Ann)
Duncanville Lions Club

1989-1990 Joseph "Joe" L. Montag (Lucille)
Carrollton Evening Lions Club
Served as MD-2 State Constitution Chair in 1987-1988
before becoming District Governor. Served as MD-2 State
Leadership Chair in 1995-1998. Served as MD-2 State
Finance Chair for eight years. Served as MD-2 Council
Chair in 2002-2003. Serves on the Melvin Jones Lion
International Memorial Foundation, Ft. Thomas, Arizona
since 2011, when appointed by the Lions of Arizona.

1990-1991 William Weston, Jr.
Dallas Founder Lions Club

1991-1992 Norwood Brenneke (Carol)
Plano Host Lions Club
Served as MD-2 State Finance Chair for 5 years. Served as
President of the Texas Lions Camp in 2000-2001.

1992-1993 Robert Morris
Dallas Skyline Lions Club

1993-1994 Don Johnson
Dallas South Lions Club
Known as "the Energizer" when serving as District
Governor, still called the Energizer today.

1994-1995 Barbara Babcock
Dallas SMU Lions Club
The first woman District Governor to serve in MD-2.

1995-1996 A. K. Mago (Monica)
Dallas Indian Lions Club

1996-1997 Robert "Bob" Lange
Dallas Town North Lions Club

1997-1998 Dale Massey (Judy)
Carrollton Evening Lions Club

1998-1999 Randall Morris
Dallas Skyline Lions Club

1999-2000 Jim Bob Wilson (Sue Ann)
Ennis Host Lions Club

2000-2001 Julia Johnson
Dallas Town North Lions Club
Served as President of the MD-2 Past District Governors
Association in 2008-2009.

2001-2002 Skip Johnson (Patricia)
Grand Prairie Host Lions Club

2002-2003 Frank Pickens, II (Rena)
Carrollton Evening Lions Club

2003-2004 Wayne Meachum
Dallas Oak Cliff Lions Club

2004-2005 Pat Jones
Greenville Lions Club

2005-2006	Kathy Fletcher Dallas Metro Lions Club
2006-2007	Carolyn Dorman (Carlton) Plano New Millennium Lions Club (Now Plano Evening) 2013 District Global Leadership Team Coordinator, was instrumental in implementation of 2-X1 University.
2007-2008	Wallace Roberts (Joy) Ennis Host Lions Club
2008-2009	Alice Conway Dallas Filipino Lions Club
2009-2010	Mark Dean (Sylvia) Grant Prairie Host Lions Club
2010-2011	Dan Busdiecker (Linda) Irving Noon Day Lions Club
2011-2012	John Landrum (Hilary) Waxahachie Lions Club Will serve as MD-2 Council Chair in 2018-2019. Planning for 2-X1 University was started.
2012-2013	Ken Gleason Plano Early Lions Club Served as President of the Texas Lions Camp in 2008-2009. 2-X1 University was held for the first time, and was implemented by GLT-D PDG Carolyn Dorman. Served again as 2-X1 District Governor in 2014-2015.
2013-2014	Darla Wisdom (Danny) Dallas Oak Cliff Lions Club
2014-2015	Ken Gleason Plano Early Lions Club Served as President of the Texas Lions Camp in 2008-2009. Served earlier as 2-X1 District Governor in 2012-2013.

History prepared/edited by PCC Joseph Montag, PCC John Eads and DG/PDG Ken Gleason

Lions 2-X1 University

Teamwork gives you the best opportunity to turn your visions into reality

When Lions Clubs International formed the Global Leadership Team in 2011-2012, District 2-X1 Lions decided that we should develop a training program that would take all of the Lions in our District to a higher level of knowledge. GLT-D PDG Carolyn Dorman formed the GLT Team with 14 members. Each member was given a specific job to develop curriculum for each of the classes that would be taught to 2-X1 Lions that were going to become club officers. The planning for 2-X1 University was started during the year that PDG John Landrum was Governor. The first year that 2-X1 University was held was 2012-2013 when PDG Ken Gleason was governor. It is held each year at Collin College in Plano, Texas.

Courses offered train the Club President, Vice Presidents, Club Secretary, Membership Chair and Tail Twister. Financial curriculum, including club Treasurer and all District charities financials was developed by Lion Bill Smothermon, a Lion and partner in a CPA firm.

Communication was developed by Lion Bob Sander that included LCI online training, social media that informed clubs about events, District meetings, conventions, websites, all leadership training for district, MD-2 and Lions Clubs International opportunities. The first year 2-X1 University was held, 135 Lions attended. District 2-X1 had never had that many Lions attend an officer training.

From that beginning, new courses have been added each year. The new courses include Membership, Mentoring, Event Planning, Goal Setting, Conflict and resolution, 2-X1 Charities, and Why Leadership is Important. The Guiding Lion training has been developed including LCI information and has included Customer Service, Mentoring, Lions Orientation, and Constitution and By-Laws. Zone Chair Training is held in a special class with curriculum using LCI material that will help the Zone Chairs to do their jobs better.

We added Club Membership Chairperson Training and 57 Lions attended the first year it was offered.

Lions 2-X1 University offers a good speaker for the opening session, lunch and the graduation. PID Mike Butler, PID Dennis Cobbler, PID Joe Al Picone, PID Beverly Stebbins, PDG Aubrey Cherry, and Lion Jeff Senour have all been featured speakers.

The first year, PID Mike Butler opened the Red Carpet event on Friday evening prior to classes on Saturday with Texas History. Lions of 2-X1 and other Lions from all over the State of Texas enjoyed an evening of knowledge, laughter, good food and fellowship by all who attended.

The first GLT Team consisted of PDG Carolyn Dorman, Lions A P Haridas, Bill Smothermon, Bob Sander, John Joy, Bonita Shrestha, Tommie Worthy, Billy Ketner, Cabinet Secretary Kathleen Tyre, and PDG Frank Pickens. Governors were DG John Landrum, Ken Gleason, and Darla Wisdom.

The fourth year of Lions 2-X1 University was held June 13, 2015 at Collin College.

Interlude
Real Talent: Marion and Gordon

Even though they were not officially a Director or a President of Lions Clubs International, they were the heart and soul to help Lions Clubs International with the timing and arrangements for many conventions.

These two Lions—Marion Snider and Gordon Rea—were vital at the Conventions, with Marion as the official pianist (boy, could he beat on that piano, beginning his career with the Gaither Brothers in the early days) and Gordon, the official singer for the Conventions during the time of Past President Dave Evans, continuing on in the 1970s and up to my year of 1982-1983.

They started with us in Mexico City in 1972-1979 when I was elected Third Vice President of Lions International, and then on through 1983 when I was going through the Chairs.

We had the honor of having both of them perform in 1983 in Ballinger, Texas at our daughter, Michelle's wedding.

These two Lions were known throughout the world for their talent.

History of District 2-X2

For brief overviews of the first fifty (50) years, there will be brief statements concerning those fifty (50) years, 1917-27.

October 8, 1917, at the Hotel Adolphus in Dallas, the International Association of Lion's Club held its first annual meeting. Forty delegates attended. Melvin Jones, the organization's founder, was also in attendance. This was to be the first "service" organization. Several Texas cities sent representatives: Abilene, Austin, Beaumont, Dallas, Fort Worth, Houston, Paris, Port Arthur, Waco, and Wichita Fall. Those clubs were given the privilege of being called "Founder Clubs" At the meeting, a constitution and by-laws, objects, code of ethics and an emblem of a lion's head, holding a club, marked "International" were adopted. Dr. W. P. Woods, from Indiana, was elected the First President and Melvin Jones was elected Secretary/Treasurer.

At the Second International Convention held in St. Louis, L. H. Lewis (1918-1919), from Dallas was elected as the first International President from Texas. Thus started Texas' long line of Presidents.

During the years 1927-1937, Lions growth was very large; with the encouragement of Melvin Jones, Texas was divided into five distinct districts, T,E,X,A,S, which continued until 1937. Texas also produced its second International President, Julien C. Hyer (1931-1932), from Ft. Worth. He was installed in Toronto. The Texas delegation went by train and carried the San Angelo Cowboy Band.

From 1937 to 1947, there was a growth of Lions. It was during this period that "T" was divided into two districts, 2-T1 and 2-T2, and "S" was divided into 2-S1, 2-S2, and 2-S3.

Fourth decade: 1947-1957

The fourth decade brought the establishment of the Texas Lions League for crippled Children in Kerrville. By July 1949, the corporation was chartered, the property was bought, and the International Board had given its approval. The camp opened its doors for the first kids in 1953. "…it may be said here that no other single act has so projected the spirit of Texas Lionism as much as this did…"

An interesting story about TLC:

In support of the plan to found TLC, Washington was approached (Veterans Admin) with a request to purchase their land in Kerrville (you will note we are neighbors with the V.A. Hospital because what is now TLC and the Kerrville Little League and KISD were all one parcel owned by the V.A.). The Government responded with a "challenge grant" that mandated that if the Lions could raise $100,000 in six months to demonstrate their intent and resolve, the land would be sold to TLC for that sum. Lions were able to raise $80,000, while the deadline loomed. As the time for a final status report matured, then-Lion Governor Sealie McCreless stepped forward to present a $20,000 check to fund the balance and tip the short-fall into TLC's favor. The only problem was, he didn't have $20,000 at the time, but had the courage to make the pledge nevertheless. With the final pledge in hand, the V.A. was informed that $100,000 in pledges had been achieved, and the Lions were granted the deed for $100,000. By the time the $100,000 in cash was to be transferred to the Government to close on the land, other donors and fundraisers had been added to the $80,000 figure and the $20,000 pledge by McCreless was forgiven. His check was never cashed.

As a reminder of one person's determination and courage, TLC still has (and celebrates the Governor's act with) that original check. A copy of the uncashed check that bridged the "eleventh-hour" hangs in the TLC museum, while the original is safely tucked away in TLC's safe-deposit box at Broadway National Bank.

The courage that it took McCreless to be the catalyst to tip the scales in TLC's favor is both celebrated and repeated on many levels even today, as individuals step forward and say, "I'll be the one to guarantee TLC's forward movement and continued success. It is a lesson in fortitude, creativity, blind-faith and a testament to the power of selfless leadership."

Also, Lion Herbert C. Petry, Jr. was elected President and served during the Lion year 1950-1951.

1957-1967

During that decade, David A. Evans, 1968-69, from Texas City served as International President. During this decade, the districts were divided into 15 districts. And so the birth of District 2-X2 as we know it today occurred.

The District Governors that served officially are the following:

Paul Boseman, 1975-76

Chester Penick, 1976-77

George Futch, Jr., 1976-77

C. F. Kuykendall, 1977-78

Donald Hamilton, 1978-79

Dr. Roger Cheatham, 1979-80

Frank Keas, 1980-81

Robert J. "Jim" Williams, 1980-81

Larkin Gooch, 1981-82

C. J. "Smokey" Stevens, 1982-83

Johnny D. Mooney, 1983-84

Garvis Gilbert, 1984-85

Harry K. Poulan, Jr., 1985-86

Herbert Daniels, Jr., M.D. 1986-87

Harold Spivey, 1987-88

Ray Ashlock, 1987-88

Jack M. Heilman, 1989-90

Ernie Barbee, 1990-91

"Happy" Jack Wakin, 1990-91

Harvey Clements, 1991-92

Carol French, 1992-93

Dale Halyard, 1993-94

Brian Whitenack, 1994-95

Bill Roop, 1995-96

Joan Houser, 1996-97

Glenn Jennings, 1997-98

Gid Terry, 1998-99

Patrick Smith, 1998-99

Everett Van Hawes, 1999-2000

H. L. Ashcroft, 2000-01

William A. "Bill" Hurst, 2001-02

Gerald Townsend, 2002-03

Harold Raines, 2003-04

Don Francis, 2004-05

Leon VanAlstine, 2005-06
Zac Gray, 2005-06
Rebecca "Becky" Whitenack, 2006-07
Jim Merritt, 2007-08
John Samples, 2008-09
Richard "Sandy" Sandberg, 2009-10
Barbara "Lynn" Nacol, 2010-11
Alonzo C. (A. C.) Ellis, Jr., 2011-12
Traci Francis, 2012-13
Nancy Van Alstine, 2013-14
Jasper (Jimmy) Strickland, 2014-15

X-3

by PIP Ebb Grindstaff

My first real introduction to State Secretaries or Lions paid representatives was Tom Kirkham. An excellent book was published by Lion Glenn A. Craig, 3107 Live Oak Ave., Waco, Texas 76708 in 1974 and was printed in Waco, Texas by the Library Binding Company of Waco. The book was compiled and edited by Lion Glenn A. Craig, concerning *My First Million Miles for Lionism* by Lion Tom P. Kirkham, Jr.

Tom P. Kirkham, Jr. was the hardest-working individual that I have ever known in Lionism as he drove, and drove, and drove, night after night to get to another place to speak to another Lions club, to begin to organize another Lions club, or whatever his duty was at that particular time.

Tom's book is a collection of memories of over 30 years of service to Lionism. Lion Tom served in every elected position through Deputy District Governor, and was appointed to finish an unexpired term as District Governor.

As a professional, he served as State Secretary of Florida, Texas and Alabama. He organized and reorganized over 600 Lions Clubs in 45 states. He gave over 9,600 inspirational talks on Lionism. Included in his book are some of the best.

Tom held many positions in the states, which included fourteen (14) years of Lionism in other parts of this old nation of ours; a short time in Colorado, then to Florida for three years as their first State Secretary; Texas came next, in the same position, staying there for almost eight years, and finally to Alabama, where he opened up their state office, and served as their secretary until retirement.

FACTS ABOUT LION TOM KIRKHAM

- Joined the Lions Club of Sun Ray, Texas June 15, 1943
- 100% Attendance for 30 years
- Elected to every position through Deputy District Governor
- Served as District Governor to finish unexpired term of a friend and missed time necessary to be official Past District Governor by only a few days

- Lionism became his profession in 1951.
- Worked in 45 states.
- Opened first Florida State office in 1956.
- Served as State Secretary of Texas for nine years.
- Opened Alabama State Office in 1966.
- 100% President (twice)
- 100% Secretary (twice)
- Merit Award (twice)
- Citizenship Award (five times)
- International Service Award (four times)
- International Presidents Award (six times)
- District Governor's Appreciation Award (46 times)
- Two Special International Presidents Awards, of which there were only a total of seven in the world. No one else had more than one.
- Gave over 9,600 inspirational talks on Lionism.
- Organized and reorganized over 600 Lions Clubs.
- Life Member of Northwest Waco Lions Club.
- Life Member of Texas Lions Camp for Crippled Children.
- Quarter Century Lions Medal.
- Author of two books on Lionism.
- Author of handbook for Tail Twisters.
- City Councilman of Lorena, Texas at the time of his death.

Throughout this story as told by Tom, from his experience, not only in the book, but by personal knowledge are ones that I used and inspired me through my early years as District Governor and while running for International Director in Mexico City in 1972. One idea that I never forgot for a very long period of time was his "Lions Membership Garden":

First, plant four rows of peas:
Presence, Promptness, Preparation and Perserverance;
Next to these plant three rows of squash:
Squash gossip, Squash indifference, Squash criticism;
Then, plant five rows of lettuce:
Let us be loyal and unselfish,
Let us be faithful to duty,

Let us be true to our obligations,
Let us love one another,
Let us live up to our motto "We Serve";
No Garden is complete without turnips:
Turn up for the meetings,
Turn up with a smile,
Turn up with new ideas,
Turn up with determination to make everything count for something good
and worthwhile.

Of course, Tom was known for his working on clocks during his time to travel, and fixing old clocks certainly kept him busy during his retirement after his previous 23 years of traveling for Lions International. "Traveling" is the word he used to describe driving 1.5 million miles in 45 states organizing Lions Clubs. As he said, "That's just the driving now, that isn't the flying, the buses, the trains nor the hitchhiking." He drove this 1.5 million miles in every state but Maine, New Hampshire, Vermont, Hawaii and Alaska, with a clock repair kit in the trunk of his car. Why not? "I've worked on clocks for 52 years, ever since I was 11 years old," he added.

Yes, Tom loved old clocks, and everybody loved Tom for what he meant to us as Governors, and especially during the late 1960s and early 1970s as so-called leaders of Lionism in Texas during that period of time, which credit was really due to our Pension Representatives or State Secretaries, or paid leaders of Lionism in Texas whose love for the game was always the most important. Not all of the State Secretaries are recalled by the undersigned, but I remember Marlowe Fisher from Austin, Texas and Ed Skypala from Hereford, Texas from the days that my dad was District Governor in the '40s. Ed was the organizer of the first Forum that we had in Austin, Texas, and was another one of those that would go anywhere in the state at the drop of a hat to speak on Lionism, to organize new Lions Clubs or whatever was needed; thereafter, Pat Nations served as Secretary or Executive Secretary, but was really an office State Secretary and did not go out in the field as the guys before her. She served very faithfully for several years until our present pride and joy, Sandy Merritt, the Executive Secretary for the Council of Governors while we had the offices on the highway and was also involved in the purchase of the property between the highway, the YO and the Camp. Sandy is a real joy to be around andis very efficient. That can be testified to anyone that knew her.

There were many outstanding Governors from X-3, including but not limited to PDG Abe Houston, PDG Ike Carroll, PDG Ben Baker, and PDG Herb Barsh, who was also President of the Camp.

Bill Miller from X3 was President of the World Jaycees prior to becoming a Lion, and while District Governor of the Lions in '82-83, he organized 10 Lions Clubs—the most of any other Governor in the United States. Bill was very generous and loved to entertain, even though he was the most avid Longhorn fan I have ever seen. He had an orange convertible with horns on the front of it that he took to all the meetings, and there was a certain way that he always addressed his wife, Martha Sue. It cannot be put in writing, but it's something still – it's "Matha Soo". It's just the way he said it.

The Lions in Killeen moved to the forefront of leadership in 2-X3 along with others previously mentioned with Mutt and Jeff (PDG Gladys and PDG Johnnie Tramp), PDG Bob Crabtree (District Governor for 2-X3 in 2012-13 and the GMT for 2-X1 in 2014-15), and his wife Becky (the President of the Kosse Lions Club, the Cabinet Secretary of 2-X3 in 2015-16 and the owner of 5" heels that move smoothly across the dance floor); Jodye Lindsey, the Charter President of the Kosse Lions Club (by the way, if you have not been to Kosse, you do not know what you have missed, and neither do I, but Sam Lindsey can tell you all about it).

INTERLUDE

In addition to our great projects, there is always a moment when you are humbled in several ways—some by the lack of definition of new words, such as "lexophile" as presented at one of the meetings in Kerrville by Past District Governor, Waldo Dalchau. He has been in more than one district, but at one time was a coach and has done a great job in each district in which he has served.

The occasion arose because he came to me in Kerrville and asked for a definition of a will. I immediately started on a program of explaining that it depended upon the type of will, the individuals involved, and the family. Wherein he asked for a two-word definition of a will and I told him that was impossible, until he told me that lexophile was a word used to describe those who have a use for words, and in this particular case a will was defined as a "dead giveaway". How could you argue such a point? But it did lead on to some other lexophiles which might be of interest, and might come at a time when you need a pep in your step or in your talk, some of which are described below:

1. You can tune a piano, but you can't tuna fish.

2. To write with a broken pencil is pointless.

3. A thief who stole a calendar got twelve months.

4. A boiled egg is hard to beat.

5. When you've seen one shopping center, you've seen a mall.

6. A bicycle can't stand alone–it's just two tired.

7. When she saw her first strands of gray hair, she thought she'd dye.

8. Those who get too big for their pants will be totally exposed in the end.

9. Always laugh when you can…it's cheap medicine.

PERSONAL NOTE: *The Ballinger Lions Golf team of Jason Battle, Bobby Broyles, Fred Harwell, and Ebb Grindstaff set a new record after four years of playing at Lady Bird Camp Golf Tournament in Fredericksburg by shooting a 59, earning 4th place on a draw!*

A-1, A-2, A-3

District 2-A

Some of the great leaders in the organization of the camp and thereafter have been noted below and recognized as such:

To The Lions of District 2-A, Texas:

Greetings,

There are many duties that fall to my lot as Director-General of Lions International, which are extremely pleasant and give me a sense of warm satisfaction. But when, in the course of carrying out such duties, I, as a Texan, find myself in a position of extending greetings to fellow Texans, that pleasure is doubled.

Texas has never ceased exerting rich influence in the development of Lionism since the early days when the Association was first formed, and we are indeed grateful not only for the magnitude of Texas' contributions to our cause, but also for the manner in which their activities have served as an inspiration to others. Whenever the history of Lionism in general is written, Texas always looms large, and wherever the history of Texas Lionism is written, District 2-A is predominately present with an inspiring array of achievements. And, we know that as the years go by the future accomplishments of the Lions in District 2-A, will but add to an already glorious and impressive record.

We are proud of you, we are grateful for you, and we extend our warm personal greetings in the hope that the honor of service will be yours in abundance.

R. Roy Keaton, Director-General
April 6, 1959
Chicago, Illinois

TEXAS LIONISM PRIOR TO
THE FORMATION OF DISTRICT 2-A

Texas is truly the Birthplace of Lionism. Lions International came into official being in Texas at the first convention in October, 1917. This convention was held at the Adolphus Hotel (Dallas) and the name "Lion" was accepted as the name of our organization. In the 1920's we became truly International when the first clubs were organized in Canada. Illinois became District 1, because some preliminary work on a service club organization has been done in that state. Texas became District 2, and for a number of years one district governor served the whole state. The state was later divided into 5 sub-districts, and the world "Texas" was used to secure the names of the 5 sub-districts, namely 2-T, 2-E, 2-X, 2-A and 2-S. In later years, 2-S divided and became 2-S1, 2-S2 and 2-S3. Later 2-T divided, and in 1959 we became 15 sub-districts in Texas and will have 125 district governors. Texas has continuously had a Texan on the International Board of Directors—either as a director, or as an officer of Lions International.

District 2-A has always been an important district in Texas and in Lions International. District 2-A has worked together and its progress has been inspiring. R. Roy Keaton, Director-General of Lions International, organized many of the clubs of District 2-A and is highly respected by all Lions in this district.

The Host Club of San Antonio was one of the first clubs of Lions International, and it is my information it was called a Lions club prior to the first Convention held in Dallas in 1917, and thus it has the slogan "Birthplace of Lionism."

Many men have served Lionism from District 2-A and many have held an official office and many have served in the ranks, and all made their contributions to the great spirit of Lionism which prevails in our District 2-A. It has always been said of District 2-A that it works as a solid unit and that it takes care of its own.

It would be impossible in the space allotted to give a compete history of Texas Lionism prior to the formation of District 2-A, but in summation I would like to point out that Texas, from the inception of Lions International, has always occupied a prominent place in the affairs of Lions

International, and through its continued leadership and merited the trust and confidence of Lions all over the world.

—*by Herb C. Petry*

Governor William L. Dugger	1930-31
Governor N. H. Pierce	1931-32
Governor Charles H. Nixon	1932-33
Governor Arthur E. Biard	1933-34
Governor Lorimer Brown	1934-35
Governor H. V. Stokes	1935-36
Governor Murray A. Winn	1936-37
Governor Jack Bonner	1937-38
Governor Will Collins	1938-39
Governor Orville Cox	1939-40
Governor Roy Davenport	1940-41
Governor J. Andrew Smith	1941-42
Governor Ernest C. Hill	1942-43
Governor Hugh Hackelman	1943-44
Governor Herb C. Petry	1944-45
Governor J. E. Wilkins	1945-46
Governor E. C. Grindstaff	1946-47
Governor Frank Robertson	1947-48
Governor Jack Wiech	1948-49
Governor Robert E. Price	1949-50
Governor G. S. McCreless	1950-51
Governor Dr. A. Lewis Kline	1951-52
Governor Jack B. Wright	1952-53
Governor Judge J. L. Mogford	1953-54
Governor George H. Jones	1954-55
Governor Al Schmid	1955-56
Governor John Painter	1956-57
Governor Neil Mathena	1957-58
Governor Leonard Johnson	1958-59

Not only in 2-A have we had so many capable state secretaries that included Marlowe Fisher who was State Secretary from 1946-1958.

District 2-A and 2-A1, which is my District, District 2-A2 which is the San Antonio area and Mike Butler's District, and District 2-A3 which goes down to the valley and is Ray Hughston's District all had some outstanding District Governors and leaders and secretaries. I know many names will be missed, but it is not because we haven't tried. Sometimes our memories do not carry us to the train track and on the right road when we need it the most. Lytle H. Blankenship in 1981-82 is truly a faithful new member of our International Association, as is his wife, Margaret L. Blankenship who is President of the 2-A2 Lionesses was elected at their convention in Laredo. They were in the process of growing, and under the direction of Margaret that became true. Some of the modern leaders of T. J. Tijerina and wife, Juanita also were active in all affairs of A-2.

Organization of The Crippled Children's Camp

The idea of establishing a Lions Camp For Crippled Children originated with a group of Lions of the Kerrville club. At first it was proposed that such a camp be operated as a project of District 2-A. After a thorough study, the district cabinet authorized District Governor Jack Wiech to invite the other seven Lions Districts of Texas to join 2-A to make the camp the first Texas Lions statewide project. Acceptance of the idea was by no means immediate. However, on March 12, 1949, at Brownsville, five other district governors joined Wiech in signing the Charter of Texas Lions League for Crippled Children, Inc., the stated purpose of which was "To support, maintain and conduct, without charge, a crippled children's camp wherein crippled children from all parts of the state may receive supervised rehabilitation training." Jack Wiech became the League's first president, and he was reelected for three consecutive terms.

Many problems were to be met before the Crippled Children's Camp became a reality. At the meeting of the Board of Directors of Lions International held in New York in July, 1949, approval of the project was obtained and permission granted to the use of the Lions emblem by the League. In searching for a site for the camp, it was learned that a beautiful tract of hillside land belonging to the Federal Government located adjacent to the Veteran's Administration Hospital at Legion had been declared surplus property. The League made application therefore, and on August 1, 1950, contracted with the Federal Security administrator for the purchase of the tract. One of the conditions of the contract required that the League, within six months, have available not less than $100,000 earmarked for the construction of necessary facilities on the site. The League's finance campaign was launched on September 12, 1950, with a radio broadcast from Austin by Lions Allan Shivers, Herb C. Petry, Jr. and Jack Wiech. The first $100,000 came hard, but the deadline was met, and construction of the first two bunkhouses commenced.

As more and more Lions learned the true facts about their Crippled Children's Camp and the League, enthusiasm for its progress and expansion mounted steadily, and when construction of the specially-designed buildings and facilities got underway, Lions of Texas truly opened their hearts and their pocketbooks. Success was assured. The greatest day for Lionism in Texas since the original International Convention which convened in Dallas on October 8, 1917, was the day the Texas Lions Crippled children's Camp was formally opened and dedicated on July 3, 1953.
—*by Jack Wiech*

Operation of the Crippled Childrens' Camp

Three outstanding features mark the present day function of the Texas Lions Camp for Crippled Children: 1) the rapid growth in camp attendance with 3,539 handicapped children finding fun and confidence in the six camping sessions; 2) the consistent and well-organized building program, resulting in 15 permanent structures at the present time with additions and other buildings in the planning stage; 3) the enlargement of our services to become a year-round center with the addition of the Adjustment Training Center for the Adult Blind.

The camp proudly took its first shaky steps toward success in the summer of 1953. Our camp at that time had 5 buildings, including just two bunkhouses, and we accommodated 236 boys and girls. In 1958, we accommodated 743. These boys and girls have come from all parts of Texas, and attend the camp for a two-week period without charge. In 1856, the building which was originally envisioned was completed. At that time, we had the Admonition Building, six bunk houses, the Jack B.

Wright Memorial Chapel, the Arts and Crafts Building, the Dining Hall and Kitchen, the Infirmary, the Caretaker's Residence, the Amphitheatre, the Swimming Pool, and the Recreation building. But it was evident to the Texas Lions League that to continue our growth we must also continue our building program. In 1957, a two-wing infirmary and a duplex for married members of the staff were added. The old infirmary was converted into a program office and parts of it are used for staff housing.

In 1957, with a substantial investment of over $700,000 in lands and improvements, the league began exploring the possibilities of extending the services of the camp and using its facilities on a full-time basis. The result was the Adjustment Center for the Adult Blind, a rehabilitation program which returns back into society with confidence and cheer those who have lost their sight. This program is entirely separate from our summer camping program, but is parallel in its realm of service.

The camp has never closed since it opened its doors beckon wide throughout the year to visitors and thousands of Lions and their guests have personally inspected our camp. The camp has received countless donations of equipment, but its program of continuing service is based on membership dues, active and life memberships, memorials and club contributions.

The camp is dedicated to the idea that all children, despite their handicaps, have a right to a happy childhood and to the teachings of blind adults and things needed for day-to-day living. By continuing to serve such youngsters and adults, by consistently maintaining our building program and by constantly exploring new fields of service, the Texas Lions Camp for Crippled Children shall be a shining reflection of the good hearts and generous hands of the Lions of Texas.

—by Frank Robertson and Camp Staff

DISTRICT 2-A1 HISTORY

THE PAST

District 2-A1 was formed in 1959 from the northern 24 counties of the old District 2-A. J. W. (Bill) Jones from the San Angelo Downtown Lions Club was elected the first District Governor at its inception. There were 54 clubs with 2,800 members. The San Angelo Southside Lions Club was the first to be chartered in this new district with the East Angelo Lions Club as their sponsor.

The history of the first eight years of District 2-A1 is contained in *Texas Lions: 1917-67* by Julian C. Hyer. Those were the formative years for this district and the first eight governors are shown below. Governor Ebb Grindstaff would continue his leadership role in Lionism, becoming International Director in 1972 and International President in 1982. At the conclusion of Governor Palmer's year, the district had grown to 63 clubs and 3,092 members.

GOVERNORS

1959-60	J. W. Jones	1963-64	Louis Carothers
1960-61	Cecil Bridges	1964-65	E. J. "Ebb" Grindstaff
1961-62	J. T. Jones	1965-66	George M. Thompson
1962-63	David M. Ellis	1966-67	Harvey J. Palmer

Other highlights of these formative years were:

1. In addition to chartering a new club its first year, Lion David M. Ellis (who would later become a District Governor) was recognized for bringing in 40 new members.

2. During the second year (1960-61), five new clubs were chartered: Buchanan Dam, May, Kingsland, Sonora Westside and Ozona Southside.

3. Two clubs received international recognition during 1961-62: Midland Downtown as the third largest club in all of Lions International and Goldthwaite for membership gain.

4. District Governor David M. (Doc) Ellis (1962-63 was recognized by International for having brought in 200 members.

5. Lion Louis N. Carothers served as Governor in 1963-64. During his year, the district had every International officer (except 1st Vice President) at one of the cabinet meetings.

6. 1964-65 was the year for Lion Ebb Grindstaff to serve as District Governor. It was the first time a father and son had served as District Governor in our global organization, or in the entire Lions Clubs International organization. His father, Judge E. C. Grindstaff was governor of District 2-A1 in 1945-47. At the time Ebb became District Governor, there were 3 clubs that had not even met in 18 months; therefore Ebb dropped them in 1964 and still had a plus in membership in 1964-68, which we all thought was a pretty good accomplishment for our District at that time.

7. 1965-66 was another banner year for District 2-A1 under the leadership of Lion George M. Thompson. Four new clubs were charted: Sweetwater Evening, Bronte Evening, Eldorado Eastside and Menard. Seven clubs won the Melvin Jones Award.

8. 1966-67 was the 50th year of Lionism and the 8th for District 2-A1. Lion Harvey Palmer served as Governor. Two new clubs were chartered. For the second year in a row, District 2-A1 won the Melvin Jones Award for membership gain.

THE SECOND FIFTY YEARS
1967-2017

The second fifty years of Lionism for District 2-A1 began with J. Marvin Allen from the San Angelo Downtown Lions Club serving as Governor. His first act of service (following in the footsteps of some of his predecessors) was to charter two new clubs: Colorado City and Coleman Evening. The district was off to a good start as shown by the following year-to-year history:

1968-1969 Lion Connor Scott of the Brownwood Lions Club was elected District Governor. During his term, two clubs were chartered: Hill Country

Lions of Junction and Sand Springs. During his year as Governor, a Texas Lion, David A. Evans was installed as International President. Governor Scott ended his year with 66 clubs.

1969-1970 Lion A. E. Prugel of the Sonora Lions Club served as District Governor. Two clubs were dropped during the year and the membership decreased from 3,180 to 2,987. The Melvin Jones Award was earned by five clubs: Brownwood, Brownwood Evening, Early, San Angelo East Angelo and Sonora.

1970-1971 Lion Harry C. Wisehart, Jr. of the Junction Lions Club served as District Governor. Two clubs earned the Melvin Jones Award: Midland Downtown and San Angelo Southside. One club—Midkiff—withdrew its charter. Redistricting of the State had been a topic for several years and was brought to a vote at the State Council of Governors and it failed to pass.

1971-1972 Lion Homer J. Hodge of the Winters Lions Club served as District Governor. The greatest achievement during Governor Hodge's year, with the able assistance of Lion Leonard Hanson and Lion Ewart Phillips, was the organization and chartering of the Lions Eye Bank for District 2-A1. Three new clubs were chartered: Midland Tall City, San Angelo North Angelo and San Angelo Northwest. During this year PDG Ebb Grindstaff was elected to the office of International Director and became a candidate for the office of Third Vice President of Lions International. PDG Ebb eventually went through the chairs and reached the highest office as President of Lions International. Governor Hodge received the 100% District Governors Award, the District Governors Extension Award and the District Governors Award for 5% Membership Growth. He also received a Commendation Award Certificate for Leadership Contribution. Governor Hodge, of 2-A1, designed a commemorative " 3 in a Row" lapel pin honoring the District's 3 consecutive years of winning the Melvin Jones Award in 1966-67-68 under the leadership of PDGs George Thompson, Harvey Palmer and J. Marvin Allen.

1972-1973 Lion Ewart E. Phillips of the Brownwood Lions Club served as District Governor. At the first Cabinet meeting, the District Eye Bank Directors were incorporated into the Governor's cabinet as full voting members. The district was realigned in to five regions instead of four, and 10 zones. Membership increased in 1973 after a brief decline in 1972. Membership at the end of June 1973 was 3,150 versus 3,105 at the beginning of 1972. Two clubs lost their charters, Melvin and Junction Hill Country. Two Leo clubs were organized, one sponsored by 5 clubs in Midland and the other by the San Angelo Southside Lions Club. Colorado City Lions Club celebrated their 50th anniversary on July 22, 1972. International Director Ebb Grindstaff presented a 50-Year Charter Monarch Award to Past President Lewis B. Elliot. The Bronte Noon Lions Club celebrated its 25th anniversary on November 9, 1972 and the San Angelo Northwest Lions Club was chartered on August 19, 1972. More than 500 persons were in attendance as San Angelo gained its seventh club. Seven clubs won the Melvin Jones Award that year.

1973-1974 Lion T.N. (Tip) Nipp of the Midland Westside Lions Club served as District Governor. Onc new club was chartered, the Webb Spring Lions Club in Big Spring. Initially membership decreased by 101 but recovered 80 new members to end the year with 3127 members. During October, five clubs celebrated their 25th anniversaries, Eden, Miles, Paint Rock, Rowena and Talpa. The San Angelo Downtown Lions Club and the Winters Lions Club each celebrated their 50th anniversary. Two Leo Clubs were added, Winters Leo Club with 65 members and a Leo Club sponsored by the newly charted Webb Spring Club of Big Spring. At the Mid-Winter Conference in Sweetwater on January 18, 1974, International Director Ebb Grindstaff's name was submitted as a candidate for the Texas Lions Hall of Fame to the Council of Governors. Governor Nipp received the 100% District Governors Award and a certificate from Lions International.

1974-1975 Lion Jim Lemons of the Big Spring Downtown Lions Club served as District Governor. The year ended with a total of 65 clubs and 3233 members. The North Concho Lions Club and Paint Rock Lions Clubs were placed on status quo. On April 4, 1975, Eola Lions Club sponsored by the Rowena Lions Club was organized with 42 members. On May 14, 1975, Paint Rock Lions Club was reorganized with 21 members. Governor Lemons was awarded the 100% District Governors Award. Four clubs won the Founders Award, Brady, Colorado City Downtown, Midland Eastside and the San Saba Lions Clubs. At the International Convention held in Dallas, Governor Lemons was presented with the first place award for the best District pin in Lionism for the year 1974-75. PDG Homer Hodge designed the pin.

1975-1976 Lion Paul A. Bozeman of the Midland Evening Lions Club served as District Governor. The North Concho Lions Club was dropped, however many members transferred to the newly organized Grape Creek Community Lions Club. New clubs were organized in Mereta, Ballinger Breakfast, Wingate, Talpa Centennial, Garden City and the Concho Valley AG. Lion Fiveash was awarded the Lions International Service Award for his work in reorganizing the Mertzon Lions Club. At the end of Governor Bozeman's year the district membership stood at 3459 and 71 clubs. Governor Bozeman received the 100% District Governors Award and the International Extension Award. Five Clubs won the Founders Award, Mertzon, San Angelo Sundown, Greenwood, Reagan County and Sonora.

1976-1977 Lion Russell Devore of the Big Spring Evening Lions Club served as District Governor. During the year, the District cabinet voted to create the position of Lt. Governor beginning the year 1977-78. Three new clubs were chartered, Blanket, Richland Springs and Westbrook.

1977-1978 Lion Julian E. McLean of the Sweetwater Lions Club served as District Governor. At the District Convention, the voting delegates voted to create the position of Lt. Governor beginning in the year 1977-78. However, Governor McLean was unsuccessful in securing a candidate. The new cabinet position will appear on the ballot at the next convention. An "Ebb Tide" Finance campaign was organized to help Past International Director Ebb Grindstaff in his race for Third Vice President of Lions International. The problem of member retention continued to be a problem during this year, both for the District and in the nation as a whole. Four clubs were dropped, Buchanan Dam, Ozona Southside and two others. Membership was down to 3289 a net loss of 50 members. The final newsletter of June 1978 contained the following quote from Governor McLean. "I have sought answers all year to our membership retention problem, but it still defies a solution. We must not give up, however".

1978-1979   Lion Harland B. Brancel of the San Angelo Sundown Lions Club served as District Governor. Lion C. E. McCain of the Midland Southside Lions Club was elected the first Lt. Governor. Unfortunately Lt Governor C. E. McCain did not meet the requirements and eligibility rules for Lt Governor as prescribed by the by laws of Lions International, which stated that the qualifications for the position were the same as for District Governor. Therefore, the position of Lt. Governor remained open for the 1978-79 year. A committee consisting of PDG Paul Bozeman and PDG J. E. McLean was organized to set guidelines for the office of Lt. Governor. The report was made and after discussion, was adopted   The District hosted the State Eye Bank Association this year and Lion Leonard Hanson was elected President. The Buchanan Dam Club was reorganized on October 23, 1978 and the Ozona Southside Club which had been dropped was granted a new charter. A new Lioness Club, the East Angelo Lioness Club was organized. Another Lioness Club, the San Angelo North Lioness, already in operation, had its officers installed in January 1978. Past International Director Everett "Ebb" Grindstaff was elected to the office of Third Vice President of Lions International.

1979-1980   Lion Ben High from the Sweetwater Lions Club served as District Governor. Lion Glendon Westbrook of the San Angelo East Angelo Lions Club served as the first official Lt. Governor. At the 1st Cabinet meeting Governor High outlined a tentative format for the annual District Club contest to encourage member and club participation in District projects. The Sweetwater Lions Club celebrated their 50th anniversary on September 16, 1979 and the Brownwood Lions Club celebrated their 60th anniversary on October 30, 1979. During the year three clubs were dropped, San Angelo Grape Creek, Eola, and Richland Springs leaving a total of 69 clubs. San Angelo was selected as the site for the 1981 Convention. The district membership was 3245 members, a net loss of 8 members for the year.

1980-1981   Lion Glendon Westbrook of the San Angelo East Angelo Lions Club served as District Governor. The San Angelo East Angelo Lions Club sponsored a young blind man, Don McCurcheon, to go to training and received a Leader dog at the Leader Dogs for the Blind School in Rochester, Michigan. The Stanton Evening Lions Club was charted in July 1980. In

January of 1981, the San Angelo Sunset Lions Club was chartered, followed by the Lake Brownwood Lions Club. On June 1, 1981, Colorado City Lions Club was chartered. The 64th International Convention was held in Phoenix, Arizona on June 16-19, 1980. Second Vice President Ebb Grindstaff was elected as First Vice President of the International Association of Lions Clubs. Governor Westbrook was the Parade Chairman for the Texas unit. Colorful bands from Sonora High School and an All-Star band from District 2-A1 won third place in the Uniformed Marching Unit category. There was net gain of 114 members at the end of Governor Westbrook's term, second in Texas membership gain, and 13th overall in the USA and Canada. Governor Westbrook received the District Governor's Extension Award for his efforts.

1981-1982 Lion Russell McMeans of the Stanton Lions Club served as Governor. Serving as Lt. Governor was Lion George Weis from the Midland Downtown Lions Club. During Governor McMeans term two clubs were chartered, Water Valley-Grape Creek Lions Club and Mertzon-Irion County Lions Club. Two new Lionesses clubs were formed, Midland Tall City and San Angelo Southside. The Big Spring Webb Lions Club was reorganized. Governor McMeans received the 100% Governor's Award and six outstanding International President's awards. Lion E. J. "Ebb" Grindstaff was elected as President of the International Association of Lions at the International Convention in Atlanta, Georgia on June 30, 1982.

1982-1983 Lion George F. Weis of the Midland Downtown Lions Club served as Governor. Serving as Lt. Governor was Lion C. E. McCain from the Midland Downtown Lions Club. Governor Weis earned the 100% District Governors Award. The Midland Northside Lions Club was chartered and the Midland Downtown Lions Club celebrated their 35th anniversary. Governor Weis had the honor of serving as Council Chairman with the International President of the Lions Club Association.

1983-1984 Lion C. E McCain of the Midland Downtown Lions Club served as District Governor. Serving as Lt. Governor was Lion Oscar Cook of the San Angelo 'Downtown Lions Club. During Governor McCain's year the Texas State Convention was held in Midland, Texas. PDG George

'Thompson was elected to the Texas Lions Hall of Fame and PDG Homer Hodge received the Melvin Jones Fellow. The year ended with 71, a loss of 1 and 1 Club on Status Quo. The Midland Suburban Lions Club was chartered on February 21, 1984. San Angelo Downtown celebrated its 60th anniversary on Sept. 6, 1983. Governor McCain won the 100% District Governors Award.

1984-1985   Lion Oscar Cook of the San Angelo Downtown Lions Club served as District Governor. Serving as Lt. Governor was Lion George M. Beard of the Winters Lions Club. Celebration night for the newest Lioness Club, Midland Suburban, was held on August 14, 1984. District 2-A1 sent 38 handicapped children and 17 diabetic children to the Lions Children's Camp in Kerrville. The Midland Downtown Lioness Club was chartered on August 24, 1985 for a total of nine Lioness clubs in the district. The Brady Lions Club celebrated their 50th year on July 25, 1985. The year ended with 3323 members and 73 clubs.

1985-1986   Lion George M. Beard of the Ballinger Noon Lions Club served as District Governor. Serving as Lt. Governor was Lion Leonard Hanson of the Midland Suburban Lions Club. The City of Sweetwater was hit by a devastating tornado on April 19.1986. The two Lions clubs in Sweetwater received a grant of $5000.00 to aid the victims. The Christoval Lions Club was charted on July 20, 1985. Grape Creek Lions Club was chartered on June 30, 1986 and a new Lioness Club was chartered in Colorado City. The year ended with 3200 members and 71 clubs, a loss of two clubs.

1986-1987   Lion Leonard Hanson of the Midland Suburban Lions Club served as District Governor. Serving as Lt. Governor was Lion Cecil Templeton of the San Angelo Downtown Lions Club. A terrible car-truck accident in Winters on August 24, 1986, claimed the lives of four women and critically injured PDG George Beard's wife, Ruthie. She succumbed to her injuries on February 7. 1987. Lion PDG Carl O. Hyde was nominee for the Texas Lions Hall of Fame. On April 20, 1987 the Howard County Lioness Club, sponsored by the Big Spring Lions Club was certified. On May 9, 1987 the Llano Evening Lions Club sponsored by the Buchanan Dam Lions Club was chartered. Governor Hanson was presented the International

President's Award. At the end of Governor Hanson's term, the membership was 3,063 members, 68 clubs and 10 Lioness Clubs.

1987-1988 Lion Cecil Templeton of the San Angelo Downtown Lions Club served as District Governor. Serving as Lt. Governor was Lion Morris Hulsey of the Midland Downtown Lions Club. Governor Templeton was the first Governor of District 2-A1 to have lady Lions in the Lions organization. The vote to include women in the organization was passed in Taipei, Taiwan, Republic of China in July 1987. The first Lady Lion to be installed by Governor Templeton was Lion Sarah Rycroft of the Sweetwater Noon Lions Club. In January 1988, Lt Governor Morris Hulsey announced that he would not be a candidate for District Governor for 1988-89. Lion J. E. Barrington of the Midland Westside Lions Club announced that he would accept the Governor's office for 1988-89. He was elected. One new Lioness Club, the Runnels County Lioness was formed in Ballinger. The Early Lions Club celebrated its 30th anniversary. Celebrating their 60th anniversaries were Sonora, Ballinger Noon and Midland Downtown. Governor Templeton was awarded the 100% District Governor's Awards, the Everett J. Grindstaff State "Keep 'Em" Award and the International Leadership Award.

1988-1989 Lion J. E. Barrington of the Midland Westside Lions Club served as District Governor. No Lt. Governor was elected until the 2nd Cabinet meeting held in Llano, Texas when Lion Bob Noyes of the Big Spring Lions Club was appointed. The Concho Valley Lions Club was chartered ion January 21, 1989. The Ballinger Noon Lions Club celebrated their 60th anniversary on January 12, 1989. Two blind persons from the district received Leader Dogs, one from Midland and the other from San Angelo. Midland Westside Lions Club celebrated their 35th anniversary and the San Angelo Downtown Lions Club celebrated their 65th anniversary. On May 27, 1989, a special Appointment meeting was held in San Angelo. All cabinet members and PDG's were invited. The attending Lions voted to recommend to Lions International that Lt. Governor Lion Bob Noyes be appointed as District Governor for the year 1989-1990. The request was approved and Lion Noyes was given the appointment.

1989-1990   Lion Bob Noyes from the Big Spring Evening Lions Cub served as District Governor. Lion Ernest Barbee of the Midland Downtown Lions Club was selected by the District Cabinet to be the Lt. Governor after obtaining approval from Lions International. Governor Bob was the first Governor of District 2-A to have Lady Lions on the Executive Board with the appointment of 1st Lady Lion Jan Noyes as Cabinet Secretary and Lion Suncha Christensen as the Cabinet Treasurer and Lion Vera Westbrook as the Membership co-chairperson. At the District Convention held on April 27-28 1990, the Lions selected Lion Ernest Barbee as the Governor elect. Lion Paul Palmer of the Early Lions Club became the Lt. Governor elect. At the Convention, a District Diabetes Awareness Essay contest and a Drug Speech contest for high school students was held for the first time. The first annual Peace Poster Contest was also held. PDG Conner Scott was the nominee for the Texas Lions Hall of Fame.

At the Texas State Conference held in Wichita Falls, Texas on June 7-10, 1990, the District 2-A1 Queen was selected as the State Queen. On July 1, 1989 the membership was 2710 in 67 clubs, with 12 Lioness Clubs with 210 members. Several Lions clubs began accepting ladies and increased their membership. By July 1, 1990, however, membership had dropped to 2623 in 66 clubs, a continuing trend not only in the District and State but also nationwide. Governor Bob was instrumental in promoting club growth with the acceptance of Lady Lion members. He also promoted combining the Texas Lions State Office and the Texas Lions Foundation as one. This would promote a central location and authority to the Foundation. The Webb Lions Club was re-instated from Status Quo. The Eden Lions Club lost their charter. The Lake Brownwood Lioness Club was also dropped but the members joined the Lake Brownwood Lions Club. The Midland Sub-urban Lioness Club was dropped but many members joined the Midland Suburban Lions Club. Governor Noyes was awarded the 100% District Governors Award.

1990-1991   Lion Ernest Barbee of the Midland Downtown Lions Club served as District Governor. Serving as Lt. Governor was Lion Paul Palmer of the Early Lions Club. The Westbrook Lions Club was chartered. Governor Barbee received the International Leadership Award, the Governor's

Retention Award, 100% District Governors Award and a Melvin Jones Fellow Award. The starting membership for his year was 2,612 with 67 clubs.

1991-1992 Lion Paul Palmer of the Early Lions Club served as District Governor. Serving as Lt. Governor was Lion Bill Leach of the San Angelo Downtown Lions Club. Governor Paul announced his "Special District Project" for 1991-92. He proposed that the Lions Clubs in District 2-A1 fund and build a 2400 sq. ft. concrete block building in Cuidad Acuna, Mexico. This building will be the home of the Lions Health Clinic of Cuidad Acuna. Dr. Stephen Kelly of Brownwood will assist Lion Paul, Lion Doug Hill and other interested Lions in this project. On completion this clinic will be the site for free eye examinations, eye surgeries and other services performed by Dr. Kelly and others on a volunteer basis. A request was made to LCIF for a $50,000 grant for the Sight First building project in Cuidad Acuna. This grant was approved by LCIF as a "Sight First Project". In January of 1992, Governor Paul, his wife Dale and Lion Doug Hill traveled to Acuna to observe Dr. Kelly and staff to perform 24 cataract surgeries. They also delivered more than 1600 pairs of recycled eyeglasses. PDG Oscar Cook was appointed the District 2-A1 Lioness Chairman and he urged all Lioness Clubs to convert to Lions Clubs before June 30, 1992 as requested by Lions International. Three new clubs were chartered, Three Rivers Lions Club, Concho Pearl Lions Club (formerly the San Angelo East Angelo Lioness Club) and the Blackwell Lions Club. Midland Tall City Lions Club celebrated their 20th anniversary on November 30, 1991. On April 12, 1992, the District was saddened to learn of the death of PDG E.C. Grindstaff of the Ballinger Lions Club. He had been a Lion for 57 years and was the father of PIP E. J. "Ebb" Grindstaff. The ground breaking ceremony for the Lions Health Clinic building in Cuidad Acuna, Mexico was held on Friday, May 22, 1992. Governor Paul was the principle speaker and laid the first stone for the structure. At the end of Governor Paul's year, the number of clubs had increased from 67 to 69 and the membership increased to 2678, a net gain of 66 members. Big Spring Webb Lions Club dropped their charter that year.

1992-1993 Lion Bill Leach of the San Angelo Downtown Lions Club served as District Governor. Serving as Lt. Governor was Lion Henry

Goulet of the Midland Northside Lions Club. The 1992-93 year began with 2648 members but at the end of December the membership had declined to 2627 and 2578 by the end of June 1993. Three District clubs, Ballinger Noon, San Angelo Downtown and Midland Downtown received the Campaign Sight First Top 5 Honor patch for leading the district with the highest per capita contributions. The Coleman Evening Lions Club celebrated its 25th anniversary. The Texas Lions Sight First recycling center is located in District 2-A1. The Midland Downtown Lions Club was appointed to receive, process and distribute eyeglasses for the Sight First Program.

1993-1994 Lion Henry Goulet of the Midland Northside Lions Club served as District Governor. Serving as Lt. Governor was Lion Jim Wilks of the Sweetwater Downtown Lions Club. Governor Goulet served on the Eye Bank Board simultaneously with his duties as District Governor and had a part in moving the Eye Bank to San Angelo.

1994-1995 Lion Jim Wilks of the Sweetwater Downtown Lions Club served as District Governor. Serving as Lt. Governor was Lion John Hancock of the San Angelo Downtown Lions Club. At the beginning of the year there were 65 clubs and 2623 members in the district. There were four inactive clubs with a combined membership of 63. The Brownwood Lions Club celebrated its 75th anniversary and the Rowena Lions Club was reorganized with 17 members. San Angelo experienced a devastating wind and rain storm on May 28, 1995. Several homes received extensive roof and structural damage. In June LCIF provided a $5000.00 emergency grant and the Texas Lions Foundation granted $2000.00. At the District Convention Governor Wilks received the Inter-national Presidents Citation along with PDG's Verschel Smith, Paul Palmer and Leonard Hanson. Governor Wilks, PDG Leonard Hanson, Lions Tandee Curlee, Lewis Elliot, Harold Gilbert, Weldon Barton and Bill Collins all received their Melvin Jones Fellow Awards. Final membership at the end of June 1995 was 2578, a net loss of 10 members.

1995-1996 Lion John Hancock of the San Angelo Downtown Lions Club served as District Governor. Serving as Lt. Governor was Lion Ike Fitzgerald of the Midland Downtown Lions Club. The year began with 2578 members. The San Angelo Westside Lions Club was the first club to make a 300% donation to all the District supported charities. In October 1995 Governor Hancock introduced Campaign 2000, a new project implemented by the Texas Lions Camp to improve and expand its facilities to meet the goal of being able to accommodate 2000 children annually by the year 2000. In October Dr. O. H. Chandler of the Ballinger Noon Lions Club was honored for 60 years of humanitarian service and was presented with a Melvin Jones Fellow from his club. Also in October, Governor John had the honor of inducting the "Oldest" new member in the world into Lionism. Lion Maggie Cook, age 95, became a member of the Lake Brownwood Lions Club and she said her entire life had been in service to others. Through the Sight First Campaign, 140 million dollars was raised to fight the war against blindness. The San Angelo Downtown Club became a 400% contributor to the District supported charities. The San Angelo East Angelo Lions Club was the first club in the district to present a check for $3400.00 to Campaign 2000. On April 1, 1996, Debra Tijerina became the first coordinator-technician for the District 2-A1 Eye Bank.

1996-1997 Lion Ike Fitzgerald of the Midland Downtown Lions Club served as District Governor. Serving as Vice District Governor (a name change from International) was Lion Joan Caldwell of the San Angelo Concho Pearl Lions Club. Lion Joan was the first woman Lion from District 2-A1 to be elected to this office. Governor Ike wore several hats during his term, that of Governor, construction chairman of the Eyeglass Recycling building, eyeglass coordinator and he spearheaded the adult clinic for the State of Texas. In May 1996, at the State Convention in Houston, PDG Paul Palmer was selected to be in the Texas Hall of Fame. The Midland Downtown Lions Club raised $84,000 and received a $75,000 grant from LCIF for the MD-2 Eyeglass Recycling Center and the Midland Downtown Lions' Activity building.

1997-1998 Lion Joan Caldwell of the San Angelo Concho Pearl Lions Club became the first woman from District 2-A1 to serve as District Governor. Serving as Vice District Governor was Lion George Costlow of the Stanton Noon Lions Club. During this year the Colorado City Lions Club celebrated its 75 anniversary. The San Angelo Eyeglass Recycling Center celebrated the processing of 250,000 pairs of glasses. PDG Ike Fitzgerald was awarded one of the top ten International Awards for "Understanding and Cooperation". There are only ten given each year and this year just two were given to recipients in the U.S.A. and PDG Ike was one of them. On February 28, 1998 the Acuna Clinic celebrated its 5th anniversary. At the District Convention PDG Ike Fitzgerald was presented with the International Presidents Award, Lion Larry Evans of the San Angelo Southwest Lions Club was presented with the District 2-A1 Lion of the Year plaque for his work with handicapped children and adults and Lion Bill Caldwell of the San Angelo Southwest Lions Club was presented with a Texas Fellow plaque. The District began the year with 2386 members and ended with 2,323 members, a net loss of 63.

1998-1999 Lion George Costlow of the Stanton Noon Lions Club served as District Governor. Serving as Vice District Governor was Lion Robert "Bob" Edwards of the Midland Westside Lions Club. Governor George also served on the Eye Bank Board. The Texas Lions Camp celebrated its 50th anniversary on March 12, 1999. At the District Convention, Presidential Certificates of Appreciation were given to Lion Sabino Garcia of the San Angelo Southside Lions Club and Lion Denisa Marston of the Midland Westside Lions Club.

1999-2000 Lion Robert "Bob" Edwards of the Midland Westside Lions Club served as District Governor. Serving as Vice District Governor was Lion Alvin "Al" Owen of the San Angelo Downtown Lions Club. Governor Bob said we went screaming and howling into the computer sage. The District purchased a computer and for the first time dues billing was computerized. On Monday, July 6, 1999, following the Convention, Governor Bob started his year by visiting in Big Spring with Lions Youth Exchange students. On July 8th he attended the 15th anniversary and installation of the Midland Suburban Lions Club. At the District Convention held in San Angelo, Lion Denisa Marston reported that the Midland Eyeglass Recycling Center had served 56 adults in Big Spring, Midland and San Angelo areas who were fitted with glasses. Approximately 30,000 glasses were process for locations in LaMesa, Colorado City and San Angelo. The MTI Photo Scanner was utilized in Big Spring for young children with eye problems.

At the second cabinet meeting, PDG Paul Palmer reported that from July 1998 to June 1999, a total of 1,357 patients were treated at the Acuna Clinic. 71 cataract surgeries were performed, 854 pairs of glasses fitted and 432 patients received general medical care. Sweetwater Lions Club celebrated its 50th anniversary on October 2, 1999. The District was saddened to hear of the sudden and unexpected death of Elizabeth Owen, the wife of Vice District Governor Al Owen. In true Lions Spirit, Elizabeth Owen donated her corneal tissue to the District 2-A1 Eye Bank. Through her generosity, two persons received the gift of sight. The State Convention was held in San Angelo, Texas on May 18-19, 2000 as the State Council chair was PDG John Hancock of the San Angelo Downtown Lions Club. The Convention was attended by 460 Lions and guests. Mrs. Carole Henson from the Leader Dogs For the Blind gave a presentation on the puppy program.

2000-2001 Lion Alvin Z. "Al" Owen of the San Angelo Downtown Lions Club served as District Governor. Serving as Vice District Governor was Lion Sabino Garcia of the San Angelo Southside Lions Club. Governor Al's first official trip was to the International Convention in Hawaii where he was installed as District Governor. After the Convention, Governor Al married his fiancée, Billie Dye, on a cruise ship. At the 2nd cabinet meeting, four members of the Amistad Lions Club from Cuidad Acuna, Mexico were presented with a grant check for $20,000 from LCIF to purchase new equipment for the Acuna Eye Clinic. At the Mid-Winter Conference, PDG Paul Palmer received the "Top Ten International Understanding and Cooperation Award. Lion Denisa Marston and PDG Paul Palmer received the International Presidents Certificate of Appreciation Award. This year the District had two individuals enrolled at the Lions World Service for the Blind School in Little Rock, Arkansas. Governor Al received the International Presidents Leadership Award.

2001-2002 Lion Sabino Garcia from the San Angelo Southside Lions Club served as District Governor. Serving as Vice District Governor was Lion Virgil Polocek from the Sonora Downtown Lions Club.

2002-2003 Lion Virgil Polocek from the Sonora Downtown Lions Club served as District Governor. Serving as Vice District Governor was Lion Melvin Felch from the Brownwood Lions Club.

2003-2004 Lion Melvin Felch of the Brownwood Lions Club served as District Governor. Serving as Vice District Governor was Lion Joyce Downie of the San Angelo Concho Pearl Lions Club. The Sonora Downtown Lions Club celebrated its 75th anniversary. District 2-1 had 60 Lions Clubs at the beginning of the year. In July the San Angelo Southwest Lions Club dropped their charter followed by Westbrook, Llano Evening and Midland Southside. At the 1st cabinet meeting in Mason, Texas the question of raising the District dues was brought up and discussed. On April 11, 2004 Governor Felch and his wife, Mary Beth traveled to Midland to greet International President T.S. Lee who came to Midland to tour the Texas Lions Eyeglass Recycling Center. The next morning, breakfast was served at the Recycling Center and tours were given at the facility. That evening the Governor and his wife attended the 75th anniversary of the Ballinger Noon Lion Club. On May 4, 2004 Governor Melvin attended the 75th anniversary and installation of officers of the Big Spring Downtown Lions Club at the District Convention a dues increase passed raising the District dues to $6.00 a year. On June 1, 2004, the Winters Lions Club celebrated its 80th anniversary. At the International Convention held in Detroit, Michigan PID Jimmy Ross was elected to the office of Second Vice President of Lions International.

2004-2005 Lion Joyce Downie of the San Angelo Concho Pearl Lions Club served as District Governor. Serving as Vice District Governor was Lion Zac Gray of the Brady Lions Club. At the District Convention held in San Angelo, Texas, Governor Joyce presented PIP Ebb Grindstaff with his 50 year chevron and PDG Ike Fitzgerald was chosen to be inducted into the Texas Lions Hall of Fame. The District lost four PDG's that year, PDG Oscar Cook of San Angelo, TX. PDG Leonard Hanson, PDG J.E. Barrington of Midland, TX, and PDG Homer Hodge of Winters TX. PDG Paul Palmer was presented a beautiful figurine for his special work done at the Acuna Clinic. International Presidents awards were presented to Lion Dorothy Cook for PDG Oscar Cook, IPDG Melvin Felch and Lion Ron Downie for his work on the District Newsletter. At the State Convention in Waco, Texas, Governor Joyce had the honor of presenting PDG Ike Fitzgerald with the Texas Lion Hall of Fame medal. Governor Joyce was also presented with the International Leadership Medal by PIP Brian Stephenson.

2005-2006 Lion Zac Gray of the Brady Lions Club served as District Governor. Serving as Vice District Governor was Lion Marshall Twombly of the San Angelo Downtown Lions Club. The membership goals for this year were to have one more member in each club than last year. At the 1st Cabinet meeting, Lion Brigitte Rogers made an announcement that on June 18, 2005, Texas Governor Rick Perry signed Senate bill 24 into law that the Eye Banks has a donor registration bank. Records will be sent to the donor bank in Houston, Texas for a permanent record to be available when anyone becomes deceased and wishes their eyes, tissue, or organs to be donated. This replaces the donor card on the back of your driver's license. Also at the meeting Lions were encouraged to go the International Convention in New Orleans, La. in order to support PID Jimmy Ross for International President. At the 2nd Cabinet meeting PDG Jim Wilks was charged with the job of writing the constitution and by-laws for District 2-A1 to be presented at the Mid-Winter Conference in January of 2006. It was announced that the International Convention will be held in Boston, Massachusetts on June 30 to July 4, 2006 instead of New Orleans due to Hurricane Katrina. There will be a reception for International First Vice President Jimmy Ross. PDG Sabine Garcia gave an informative report on the Acuna Eye Clinic and reported that an anonymous individual had donated $15,000.00 to the clinic to complete the building. It is to be finished in February 2006. At the District Convention the new District 2-A! Constitution and by-laws passed overwhelmingly. The State resolution concerning the Texas Lions Eyeglass Recycling Center would be determined at the State Convention in Abilene, Texas.

2006-2007 Lion Marshall Twombly of the San Angelo Downtown Lions Club served as District Governor. Serving as Vice District Governor was Lion James Price of the Kingsland Lions Club. Governor Twombly's goal this year was to strengthen the clubs in the district. At the 1st Cabinet meeting Governor Twombly made several changes in an effort to get more participation in district activities. In order to reduce the expenses and time required to attend cabinet meetings, Governor Twombly implemented the one day cabinet meeting. He also announced changes to the District Club Contest. Since the 2006-2007 Council of Governors elected to have a state

Outstanding Youth contest instead of a state Queens contest, Governor Twombly has chosen to replace the District Queens contest with a District Outstanding Youth contest. This contest to be held at the Mid-Winter Conference. Finalists selected at the Mid-Winter Conference compete at the District Convention. At the District Convention, all Lions present vote for the Outstanding Youth contest winner.

2007-2008 Lion James Price of the Kingsland Lions Club served as District Governor. Serving as Vice District Governor was Lion David Hoopman of the Midland Northside Lions Club. District Governor James was unable to attend the International Convention in Chicago to be sworn in because he was diagnosed with bladder cancer soon after being elected District Governor. He underwent surgery, chemo and bladder reconstruction and was unable to be at his first cabinet meeting. At the first cabinet meeting PID Mike Butler presented International Leadership medals to PDG Jim Wilks, PDG Zac Gray and PDG Marshall Twombly. Governor Price was able to conduct the rest of his cabinet meetings and his District Convention.

2008-2009 Lion David Hoopman of the Midland Northside Lions Club served as District Governor. Serving as Vice District Governor was Lion Roy Landry of the San Angelo Downtown Lions Club. At this time Lions International had introduced the position of 2nd Vice District Governor and Lion Don Draper of the Lake Brownwood Lions Club served in that position. At the Mid-Winter Conference amendments to the District Constitution and By-Laws were presented to be voted on at the District Convention. At the District Convention those amendments were passed by the voting Lions.

2009-2010 Lion Roy Landry of the San Angelo Downtown Lions Club served as District Governor. Serving as 1st Vice District Governor was Lion Don Draper of the Lake Brownwood Lions Club and 2nd District Governor Lion Lee Sigler of the Brown County Lions Club. At the conclusion of the District Convention held in San Angelo, Texas, District Governor Elect Lion Don Draper resigned the position of District Governor for 2010-2011. Governor Roy ended his year with a plus 43 in membership. This is the first plus in 28 years. 3 clubs were chartered during the year, Ozona Lions Club, San Saba Lions Club and Concho Valley Law Enforcement Lions Club. Governor Roy received the Presidential Award for fulfilling the Service Mission of Lions Clubs and the MD-2 Award for Plus Membership. His home club, the San Angelo Downtown Lions Club, presented Governor Roy with the Melvin Jones Award and the Lion of the Year Award. PDG Roy moved here from another district, but has performed in this district as if her were born in this district. As this is being written he is working in Brownwood with PDG Ronnie Martin and PDGs Leon and Nancy Van Alstine in attempt to reserve the Brownwood Lions. Roy loves golf and is a regular at Bentwood Country Club in San Angelo.

2010-2011 PDG Al Owen was approved by Lions Clubs International after courageously agreeing to serve as District Governor again. Serving as 1st Vice District Governor was Lion Lee Sigler of the Brown County Lions Club and serving as 2nd Vice District Governor was Lion Tom Blasé of the Midland Downtown Lions Club. At Governor Al's first cabinet meeting he inducted his wife Billie into the San Angelo Downtown Lions Club. During the meeting the Midland Downtown Lions Club announced that they had donated 2 golf carts to the Texas Lions Camp. At the 2nd Cabinet meeting it was announced that this year all Lions Clubs must file income tax reports. PDG Jim Wilks was instrumental in getting the Endowment Fund started at the Texas Lions Camp. At the Mid-Winter Conference, PIP Ebb Grindstaff was congratulated for receiving the highest citizen award given by the Governor of South Carolina. Presidential Certificates of Commendation were given to IPDG Roy Landry, PDG Joyce Downie, PDG Marshall Twombly, Lion Marie Bryan and Lion Jim Calvert. PDG Joyce Downie was selected to be inducted into the Texas Lions Hall of Fame at the State Convention in Houston, Texas. At the District Convention a resolution was presented to merge the San Angelo North Angelo Lions Club and the San Angelo Northwest Lions Club and the resulting name will be the San Angelo North By Northwest Lions Club. This merger was approved by Lions International. At the State Convention Governor Al had the honor of inducting PDG Joyce Downie into the Texas Lions Hall of Fame.

2011-2012 Lion Lee Sigler of the Brown County Lions Club served as District Governor. Serving as 1st Vice District Governor was Lion Tom Blasé of the Midland Downtown Lions Club. There was no 2nd Vice District Governor at this time. During the year the Kingsland Lions Club celebrated its 50th anniversary.

At the first Cabinet meeting, a resolution was presented by the San Angelo Downtown Lions Club supporting Lion Frank Berthold as 2nd Vice District Governor. The election was held at the Mid-Winter Conference and Lion Frank Berthold was elected 2nd Vice District Governor. The Mereta Lions Club turned in their charter. At the District Convention Lions International Awards were presented to Lion Russell Livingston and 1st VDG Tom Blasé for completing the Guiding Lions certification and PCC John Hancock and PDG Roy Landry for starting new clubs.

2012-2013 Lion Tom Blasé of the Midland Downtown Lions Club served as District Governor. Serving as 1st Vice District Governor was Lion Frank Berthold of the San Angelo Downtown Lions Club. Acting 2nd Vice District Governor was Lion John Gammill of the Mason Lions Club. Lion John could not serve until he fulfilled the requirement of being a Zone Chair for 6 months. On January 12, 2013 a special Cabinet meeting was held to appoint Lion John Gammill officially as 2nd Vice District Governor. The district started 2 new clubs—the Lady Lions Club of San Angelo and the Santa Anna Lions Club and was plus 34 in membership. At the 2nd Cabinet meeting International Certificates were presented to Lions Mark and Carole Brown of the East Angelo Lions Club and Lions Don and Kathy McConnell of the Midland Westside Lions Club. At the District Convention, the keynote speakers were Texas's own Past International Presidents, Jimmy Ross and Ebb Grindstaff. This convention had over 125 in attendance, the largest crowd in many years.

2013-2014 Lion Frank Berthold of the San Angelo Downtown Lions Club served as District Governor. Serving as 1st Vice District Governor was Lion John Gammill of the Mason Lions Club and serving as 2nd Vice District Governor was Lion A. J. Dolle of the Concho County Lions Club. This was the year that District 2-1 elected a Council Chair for 2015-2016 and PDG Tom Blasé was elected to that position. For the first time ever, the

MD-2 State Convention was held on a Carnival cruise ship from
May 15-19, 2014. During the year, the San Angelo North By Northwest
honored their Club Secretary Ron Downie with a Melvin Jones Fellow
Award. At the Mid-Winter Conference, the name of PDG Al Owen was
chosen to be inducted into the Texas Lions Hall of fame at the MD-2
State Convention. At the District Convention, International President's
certificates were presented to Lion Jerry Hale of the San Angelo Westside
Lions Club, Lion Joe Guerro from the San Angelo Downtown Lions Club,
Lion Bill Holubec from the San Angelo East Angelo Lions Club, Lion Joel
Kuykendall from the Mason Lions Club and Larry Walker of the San
Angelo North By Northwest Lions Club. International Leadership Awards
were presented to 1st VDG John Gammill and DG Frank Berthold.

GOVERNORS FROM 1967-2014

1967-68	J. Marvin Allen	1990-91	Ernie Barbee
1968-69	Connor S. Scott	1991-92	Paul Palmer
1968-69	Verschel Smith (2T1)	1992-93	W.J. Bill Leach
1969-70	A. E. Prugel	1993-94	Henry Goulet
1970-71	Harry C. Wisehart	1994-95	Jim Wilks
1970-71	Robert F. Levo (2T2)	1995-96	John Hancock
1971-72	Homer J. Hodge	1996-97	Ike Fitzgerald
1972-73	Ewart Phillips	1997-98	Joan Caldwell
1973-74	T.H."Tom" Nipp	1998-99	George Costlow
1974-75	Jim Lemons	1999-2000	Robert "Bob"Edwards
1975-76	Paul Boseman	2000-01	Alvin Z. "Al" Owen
1976-77	Russell Devore	2001-02	Sabino Garcia
1977-78	Julian E. McLean	2002-03	Virgil Polocek
1978-79	Harlan Brancel	2003-04	Melvin Felch
1979-80	Ben High	2004-05	Joyce Downie
1980-81	Glendon Westbrook	2005-06	Zac Gray
1981-82	Russell McMeans	2006-07	Marshall Twombly
1982-83	George F. Weiss	2007-08	James Price
1983-84	C. E. McCain	2008-09	David Hoopman
1984-95	Oscar W. Cook	2009-10	Roy Landry
1985-86	George Beard	2010-11	Alvin Z. Owen

1986-87	Leonard Hanson	2011-12	Lee Sigler
1987-88	Cecil Templeton	2012-13	Tom Blasé
1988-89	J. E. Barrington	2013-14	Frank Berthold
1989-90	Robert L. "Bob" Noyes	2014-15	A.J. Dolle

TEXAS LIONS HALL OF FAME

Texas has been blessed with Lions who have provided yeoman service in many civic and humanitarian ways to help the less fortunate and to make our communities a better place to live. Many of these Lions have been recognized for other service and honored by being inducted into the Texas Lions Hall of Fame. District 2-A1 is proud to having the following Lions receive such an honor:

1974	Everett J. "Ebb" Grindstaff–Ballinger
1975	D. Sebley Riley–Big Spring
1981	Roy A. Minear–Midland
1987	Carl O. Hyde–Midland
1990	Connor S. Scott–Brownwood
1993	Leonard Hanson–Midland
1996	Paul Palmer–Early
1999	Harlan Brancel–San Angelo
2000	E.F.(Tripp) Triplett–(2T3)
2002	Verschel Smith–Sweetwater
2005	Ike Fitzgerald–Midland
2008	James L. Wilks–Sweetwater
2011	Joyce Downie–San Angelo
2013	Alvin Z. Owen–San Angelo

NEW CLUBS

Club growth has been a hallmark of Lionistic activity during these past 50 years. District 2-A1 currently has the following new clubs that have been chartered since July 1, 1967:

1968 Coleman Evening
1971 Midland Tall City
1972 San Angelo North By Northwest

1976 Ballinger Breakfast, Blanket, Garden City and Wingate
1980 Lake Brownwood
1982 Mertzon-Irion County
1983 Midland Northside
1984 Midland Suburban
1992 San Angelo Concho Pearl
2009 Concho County
2011 Concho Valley Law Enforcement
2012 Santa Anna
2013 San Angelo Lady Lions

HIGHLIGHTS

District 2-A1 has been fortunate to have Governors, clubs and members who were willing and able to work collectively on humanitarian projects that are beyond the capabilities of individual clubs. Following are some notable examples:

DISTRICT 2-A1 EYE BANK

The District 2-A1 Eye Bank was the vision of Lion Homer Hodge and became a reality in 1972 during his year as Governor. This was a time in the history of our country when the cornea transplant procedure had been perfected, and there was a great need for donor eyes. Initial emphasis was on securing donors and had 700 signed donor cards the first year. Over 3000 cards were secured before its practice was discontinued in favor of other methods of getting volunteers. Lions Leonard Hanson, Ewart Phillips and Paul Palmer were strong supporters of this effort during their year as Governor and throughout their Lionistic experience. Leonard's wife, Lion Shirley Hanson served as office secretary for many years when the office was in Midland. Several Lions became proficient at transporting corneas (this was a very rigidly controlled process) from the enucleation site to the transplant location. It was during this time that the District 2-A1 Eye Bank became a member of the Eye Bank Association of Texas, and Leonard Hanson served as Vice President and later President. During 1995-96 time frame, the Eye Bank was relocated to San Angelo and became fully accredited to preform enucleations and other procedures. Debra Tijerina was the first enucleator- technician on the staff while still headquartered in San Angelo. Today, it is a joint operation with District 2-T3 and District 2-A1 under the name 'Western Texas Lions Eye Bank Alliance'. From a vision came a reality.

ACUNA CLINIC OF DISTRICT 2-A1

The clinic in Acuña, Mexico, was a vision of the District Governor in early 1992. District Governor Paul Palmer learned of an Ophthalmologist in Brownwood that was going to Acuña annually to perform cataract surgery on people in northern Mexico. At that time, Dr. Steven Kelly was working out of a Sunday School room in a small Baptist church. The conditions were poor and pretty primitive. DG Palmer believed if we could partner with the Lions of Acuña and get all 60 clubs in District 2-A1 behind the project, we could build a clinic that would be suitable for performing eye surgery, eye exams, and fitting glasses. The Amistad Lions Club of Acuña aided in securing the land, and with a grant from Lions Clubs International and private donations, a very nice clinic was built on the northeast side of town. Medical equipment was donated by Dr. Kelly from Brownwood and Shannon Hospital in San Angelo. Dr. Cleve Kirkland from San Angelo joined Dr. Kelly in supporting the clinic. Dr. Kelly's mission was in February and Dr. Kirkland's mission was in October. Since opening, the equipment has been upgraded and we now have a clinic providing eye care, dental care and some general medical care in the facility. Improvements and upgrades are an ongoing effort.

In 1992, a complete set of recycled glasses was sent to the Acuña clinic. Since that time more than 9,000 pair of glasses have been given to needy people. Glasses are added to the set, from the stock in San Angelo, as they are dispensed to ensure glasses are on hand to fit the needs of those that come into the clinic for help. Each medical mission (about three per year) averages 10 to 12 cataract surgeries and 100 to 130 pair of glasses fitted. The supporting optometrist in Acuña (Dr. Gustavo Vela) also sees patients and fits glasses at the clinic in between times the U.S. doctors are there. The clinic is operated by the Acuña Amistad Lions Club and is financed jointly by them and the clubs in District 2-A1. The District has a non-profit organization that oversees the finances. All of the services of the clinic are free to the Mexicans and they come from all over northern Mexico for help.

Midland Downtown Lions and Eyeglass Recycling

A history of Texas Lionism would not be complete without a discussion of the contributions of the Midland Downtown Lions. In the first 50 years, as it grew to one of the largest clubs in the world, Midland Downtown was very involved in the International scene. Past District Governors Carl Hyde and Roy Minear were routinely part of the Credentials Committee at the International Conventions, and the club's band was world-renown, performing at several International Conventions. The club also built and operated a zoo with a small railroad around it in Midland.

However, their contributions to the second 50 years have made a much larger impact. In the early 1980s, the club built a park and a fire museum, refurbishing and preserving some of Midland's first fire engines. Then in the mid-1980s, Lion Ike Fitzgerald (now PDG) became tired of shipping countless pairs of glasses to New York, where valuable frames were turned into cash for the non-Lion distributor. What glasses were left were shipped overseas, with no process to help distribute them to the needy. Lion Ike decided they could put the same glasses to better use at home. Midland was in the midst of an oil recession, and cash raised from selling the precious metals in the frames allowed the club to increase its eyeglass budget, allowing the club to help many more children obtain glasses.

At the same time, Lion Dr. Norman Gould, an optometrist and Downtown Lion member, asked the club to not ship the remaining glasses to New York. Instead, and with the help of club members, he taught them how to read, sanitize and bag the glasses for him to take on a mission trip. The trip was successful. Upon his return, he and PDG Fitzgerald got together and developed a system to process and distribute used glasses to adults in need, while making sure the Lions did not cross the line of prescribing glasses. With a 400-member club behind them, recycling used glasses for adults began in Texas. Over time, word spread beyond Midland. Glasses started pouring into Midland to process, while mission groups came to Midland to learn how to do the same thing as they went to other countries.

During the same period, Midland Downtown Lions obtained a local landmark—the Howard Hodge Movie Theater—and remodeled it into their clubhouse and recycling center. The theater had been part of a family theater business owned by Howard Hodge and his brother, 2A1's own PDG Homer Hodge from Winters, Texas.

By the time Sight First came along in 1990, the Midland Downtown Lions were processing thousands of pairs per month, and thus became one of Lions International's first three Eyeglass Recycling Centers. Over the next few years, the Midland Center became an integral part in helping LCI develop centers around the world. Their training classes have trained thousands of Lions and other mission groups, and provided them with millions of pairs of glasses to take on their trips.

During this time, Lions from across the State started helping in the collection and sorting processes and became major contributors to the growth of the center. Eventually the involvement of Lions from across the state and the magnitude of the project within LCI's Sight First program prompted the MD2 Council of Governors to adopt the program as a Texas Lions State project. Under the direction of the CEO, PDG Ike Fitzgerald, the Center received its 501(c)3 designation, and the name was changed to the Texas Lions Eyeglass Recycling Center (TLERC). Lions International's Sight First program provided several grants over the years to develop and enlarge the facilities, to buy equipment, to fund mission trips, and most recently, to buy state-of-the-art lens-making equipment. In 2010, TLERC bought its own building, as it had outgrown the Midland Downtown building. In 2013, a bunkhouse was added, so that volunteers could come from around the state and work at the center, and so that students coming to the monthly training classes would have a place to stay.

Since becoming part of Sight First in 1992, a major thrust has been to develop similar satellite centers. Lion Tom Mills, an optician from Big Spring, Texas helped develop a training program to teach Lions Clubs how to run their own screening lanes and place used glasses on those in need in their hometowns, eliminating the need for annual mission trips to these areas. With the help of Midland Downtown Lion Francis McDonald, PID

Marshall Cooper from Lubbock (the Center's LCl liaison) and many other Lions from around the State, including PIP Jimmy Ross, the TLERC team developed 13 such satellite centers in Central America, South America, Mexico and Africa, not to mention three others in Texas. Once a center establishes a recycling distribution program, the team—under the direction of Lion Mills—returns and helps them set up a lens-making program to make new glasses for children.

Another innovative program that has been highly successful is the use of prison inmates to read, sanitize and bag used glasses. This provides a way for those who are incarcerated to do something positive for the community, and in many cases teaches them a useful trade. TLERC uses a prison in Big Spring, and a satellite center in San Angelo (also District 2Al) uses a prison in Eden, Texas.

Through the vision of PDG Ike Fitzgerald, and under the direction of Lion Tom Mills, TLERC has developed a children's program, making new glasses for children for just a few dollars per pair. TLERC has never advocated putting used glasses on children. Clubs can send prescriptions to the center from anywhere in the State, and in a couple of days, Lion Hayden Minton (Midland Downtown) will send them a new pair of glasses. With its computerized equipment, the lab is capable of making several dozen pair per day.

After successfully seeing the establishment of the children's program and the installation of the bunkhouse, PDG Ike Fitzgerald retired as CEO, dedicating almost 30 years of his life to this project. Lion Dr. Norman Gould still does eye exams on needy children in his office at TLERC once a week during the school year. Lion Tom Mills still heads up a monthly screening in Midland helping those in need to obtain recycled glasses. Entering the next century, under the direction of CEO PDG Carolyn Keskitalo, TLERC hopes to expand its training programs into South America, enabling them to set up their own centers. In addition, they are looking at ways to set up optometry schools in South America to help them develop their own industry, a dream of Lion Dr. Tulsi Singh, another Midland Downtown Lion.

THE FUTURE

Lionism in Texas and District 2-A1 has a proud past, with a record of service to our fellow man and to its communities. The need for such service is greater today than it has ever been before. In that environment, as we look forward to the two remaining years in this half century, we are confident that we will have a bright future.

DISTRICT 2-A2 of Multiple District 2
1959 to present
International Association of Lions Clubs

Background

Our story begins in 1915 when San Antonio was the largest city in Texas, boasting a population of almost 120,000.

It was in the summer of the year 1915 that a Dr. Wood, Dr. Frederick Terrell, Sam Weller, and other prominent businessmen of that day, gathered together and organized a businessmen's club which was named "LIONS CLUB". The first meeting was held at the Odd Fellows Hall and a charter was secured from the Secretary of the State of Texas, and thus the FIRST LIONS CLUB IN THE WORLD was born. Dr. Frederick Terrell was elected the first President.

During the early days, our founders labored under many difficulties. It was in 1916 that the Club changed its name to "CITY CLUB", and Dr. Terrell continued as President. Affiliated with no national or international association, the group wielded only a small influence in San Antonio but was among those contacted by Melvin Jones, the founder of Lionism, when he began forming a national association of similar clubs in 1916. When, by 1917, the work of forming a national association was completed, the new national service institution selected the name "LIONS CLUB", already used by the small club in San Antonio, as the designation under which it would work.

At once, the Lions Club of San Antonio was formed officially with 21 charter members and affiliated with the national organization. Thus it became one of the 23 officially recognized Founder Clubs of Lionism. William Stiles, a partner in the Piper and Stiles Insurance Agency, was elected the first President after joining Lions International. In its affairs, the Lions Club of San Antonio quickly adopted a pattern to which it has adhered throughout the years: charitable, social, and fundraising functions.

The foregoing was taken from a program at the Luncheon Meeting of the Founder Lions Club of San Antonio on Wednesday, June 19, 1963, presented by Lion Deed L. Vest and the script writer was Lion Henry Simms.

Current Make-Up

Today, the 63 clubs that make up District 2-A2 continue in the traditions established by the Founder Lions those 100 years ago. The motto of the International Association of Lions Clubs, "WE SERVE", is no better illustrated than by the Lions clubs of the 21 Counties in the Hill Country and in Southwest Texas that make up District 2-A2.

In 2015, District 2-A2 clubs serve the following Texas counties: Atascosa, Bandera, Bexar, Dimmit, Edwards, Frio, Gillespie, Kendall, Kerr, Kinney, La Salle, Live Oak, Maverick, McMullen, Medina, Real, Uvalde, Val Verde, Webb, Wilson and Zavala.

Current District 2-A2 Clubs by Charter Date

1256 SAN ANTONIO FOUNDER 01/17/1919 (Actual Club beginning 1915)
1245 LAREDO NOON HOST 03/03/1922
1224 DEL RIO HOST 03/05/1928
1279 UVALDE 06/28/1928
1233 FREDERICKSBURG 07/08/1929
1237 HONDO 03/06/1940
1216 CARRIZO SPRINGS 03/07/1940
1258 SAN ANTONIO ALAMO HEIGHTS 10/25/1940
1228 DILLEY 01/23/1941
1263 SAN ANTONIO HARLANDALE 03/23/1942
1265 SAN ANTONIO HIGHLAND PARK 03/26/1942
1232 FLORESVILLE 10/19/1944
1240 KERRVILLE HOST 09/24/1946
1248 LEAKEY 03/11/1948
1278 UTOPIA 03/19/1948
1251 PLEASANTON 05/19/1948
1234 GEORGE WEST 06/28/1948
1275 THREE RIVERS 07/08/1948
1276 TILDEN 07/13/1948
1274 SOMERSET 08/12/1948
1227 DHANIS 11/23/1948
1223 CONVERSE 03/11/1949

1218 CENTER POINT 04/14/1949
1225 DEL RIO SAN FELIPE 04/22/1949
1219 COMFORT 10/06/1949
1215 BRUNI 03/24/1950
1236 HELOTES 07/28/1950
1222 CRYSTAL CITY 03/05/1951
1269 SAN ANTONIO NORTHWEST 03/22/1951
1273 SAN ANTONIO WEST SIDE 07/17/1951
1226 DEVINE 04/24/1952
1214 BRACKETTVILLE 01/11/1954
1266 SAN ANTONIO HIGHLAND HILLS 10/16/1956
1268 SAN ANTONIO NORTHSIDE 11/05/1956
1241 KERRVILLE HEART 0'THE HILLS 04/24/1967
1257 SAN ANTONIO CENTRAL PARK 05/23/1969
1230 EAGLE PASS EVENING 10/21/1969
1252 POTEET 01/15/1970
1247 LA VERNIA 04/13/1971
31779 SAN ANTONIO WINDCREST 03/02/1976
32878 PEARSALL 10/29/1976
34603 SAN ANTONIO EDGEWOOD 11/07/1977
38415 SAN ANTONIO NORTH S A HILLS 05/13/1980
39336 SAN ANTONIO ALAMO CITY 01/31/1981
41774 BEXAR CNTY CHINA GROVE AREA 08/11/1982
45052 KERRVILLE SUNRISE 06/28/1985
50070 SABINAL 12/30/1989
50526 EAGLE PASS BORDER 05/10/1990
52514 SCHERTZ-CIBOLO BUFFALO VALLEY 02/18/1992
55869 SAN ANTONIO ALAMO POSTAL 06/22/1994
62315 NATALIA 08/24/1999
82366 SAN ANTONIO REGION 20 05/18/2004
97837 OUR LADY OF THE LAKE UNIVERSITY Campus 10/16/2006
103855 SAN ANTONIO HILL COUNTRY RETREAT 10/23/2008
106212 SAN ANTONIO AREA FAMILY 08/06/2009
106251 SAN ANTONIO FIRST LADIES 08/12/2009
111410 SAN ANTONIO LIGHTHOUSE 06/20/2011

116846 SAN ANTONIO UNIVERSITY OF INCARNATE WORD
Campus 05/14/2012
118634 SAN ANTONIO KELLY FIELD AREA 01/31/2013
119413 STOCKDALE 05/21/2013
120433 CASTROVILLE 09/27/2013
121730 COTULLA 03/28/2014
123307 SAN ANTONIO ROADRUNNERS Campus 10/08/2014

Leadership

The character and success of every great organization is a reflection of the caliber of its leadership. District 2-A2 has had great fortune in having great Lion leaders step forward throughout its history to steadily guide the District as its Governor. From various walks of life, these Texas Lions having proven themselves servant leaders in their Clubs and as District Committee Chairs, Zone Chairs or Region Chairs elected by their peers. They have nurtured and enhanced existing programs, and have expanded the abilities of their fellow members to be beacons of service in their individual communities. Those who have served as District Governor since the International Association formed District 2-A2 in 1959 are:

1959-60	Joseph P. Puig, Laredo
1960-61	J. Andrew Smith, San Antonio
1961-62	A.C. Schwethelm, Comfort
1962-63	George Willems, Carrizo Springs
1963-64	John D. Palmer, San Antonio
1964-65	T.L. "Les" Bourland, Converse
1965-66	Harold B. White, Eagle Pass
1966-67	Dr. Clyde R. Nail, San Antonio
1967-68	Bob Nunley, Sabinal
1968-69	James Ward, San Antonio
1969-70	Fred Standard, Eagle Pass
1970-71	Bert Slater, San Antonio
1971-72	Joseph C. Strange, San Antonio
1972-73	Edwin J. Blume, Kerrville
1973-74	Calvert Fain, San Antonio

1974-75	William J. Tyler, San Antonio
1975-76	A.J. Armstrong, Carrizo Springs
1976-77	James S. Long, Del Rio
1977-78	Rolando Perez, Eagle Pass
1978-79	Don E. Backer, Boerne
1979-80	Joe Yorfino, San Antonio
1980-81	Mike Butler, Leon Valley
1981-82	Dr. Lytle Blankenship, Uvalde
1982-83	John Petry, Carrizo Springs
1983-84	Rey H. Costa, San Antonio
1984-85	Harley Halstead, San Antonio
1985-86	Nick Sanchez, Laredo
1986-87	George Strickland, San Antonio
1987-88	Dick Alphin, San Antonio
1988-89	Ernest "TJ" Tijerina, Del Rio
1989-90	Manny Zamora, San Antonio
1990-91	Steve Bepko, San Antonio
1991-92	Kevin Dinnin, San Antonio
1992-93	John Kimbrough, San Antonio
1993-94	Michael Rourke, San Antonio
1994-95	Kenneth Riley, San Antonio
1995-96	Christopher Lloyd, Kerrville
1996-97	Hugh Scott, Leakey
1997-98	Carroll Albright, Schertz-Cibolo
1998-99	Herbert Morris, San Antonio
1999-2000	Allen McGillivery, Del Rio
2000-01	Patricia Carroll, China Grove
2001-02	Marvin Koenig, Converse
2002-03	Callaway Lawson, Universal City
2003-04	Juan "Johnny" Olivares, Del Rio
2004-05	Saul Lopez, San Antonio
2005-06	Dr. John Seale, Del Rio
2006-07	Raymond Conner, San Antonio
2007-08	Warren Weir, San Antonio
2008-09	Amado "Manny" Carrillo, Del Rio

2009-10	Glenn Burns, San Antonio
2010-11	John Cole, Del Rio
2011-12	Howard "Howie" Marbach, Converse
2012-13	Richard Keilholz, San Antonio
2013-14	Roderick "Rod" Chisholm, San Antonio
2014-15	Sam E. Pantusa, San Antonio
2015-16	Jim Weed, Converse
2016-17	John Lee, Kerrville
2017-18	Donald Kirchhoff, Comfort

Leadership at the State Organization Level

A number of those that have served as District Governor of 2-A2 answered the call to serve as leaders within the Texas State Organization using their experience to add to the success of the larger areas of service. They include:

Council of Governors – Executive Officers

Council Chairman:

1969-70	Fred Standard, Eagle Pass
1984-85	Rey H. Costa, San Antonio
2000-01	Michael Rourke, San Antonio
2016-17	Ernesto "TJ" Tijerina, Del Rio

Vice Council Chair:

1992-93	John Kimbrough, San Antonio
2003-04	Juan "Johnny" Olivares, Del Rio
2005-06	Dr. John Seale, Del Rio
2014-15	Sam E. Pantusa, San Antonio

Council Treasurer:

1974-75	William J. Tyler, San Antonio
1980-81	Mike Butler, Leon Valley • Texas Lions Camp President
2012-13	Patricia Carroll, China Grove • Texas Lions Foundation Chair 1994-95; 1995-96 John Kimbrough, San Antonio 2012-13;
2014-15	Dr. John Seale, Del Rio

Leadership at the International Level

M. P. "Mike" Butler, Kerrville was elected to serve a two-year term as a Director of The International Association of Lions Clubs at the Association's 67th annual convention held in San Francisco, California in July 1984.

Among many other International level appointments since serving as Director, PID Mike has served as Chairperson of the Global Membership Team for 2008-09.

Past International Director, J. Andrew Smith joined the Founder Lions Club of San Antonio in June 1928. "Andy" Smith served as President of the Lions Club of San Antonio in 1940-1941. He was District Governor of District 2-A2 for two separate terms—1960-61 and 1941-42. Then, Andy Smith was elected Chairman of the Executive Council of the International Board of Governors and officially recognized as a Past Director of Lions International during the year Everett J. "Ebb" Grindstaff was President. During his 52 years of Lionism, he has always supported the activities of the club for the blind and crippled with his time, energies and talent.

Leadership at the HIGHEST LEVEL

DISTRICT 2-A2 • FAVORITE SON • PIP HERB C. PETRY, JR.

Herb C. Petry, Jr., Carrizo Springs, Texas, was elected President of The International Association of Lions Clubs at the International Convention held in Chicago, Illinois in July 1950—having previously served as International Third, Second and First Vice-President, and as a Director. He has served four consecutive years as Chairman of the Board of International Relations. He is a Charter and Master Key member of the Carrizo Springs Lions Club and has held the offices of Zone Chairman, Deputy District Governor and Governor in District 2-A. President Petry is a graduate of Westmoorland College and the University of Texas, from which he received his law degree. He is now a successful businessman and attorney, heading his own firm of Petry and Dean. He is the president of the Dimmit County Bar Association, and is a member of the State Bar Association of Texas and the American Bar Association. He is also a director of the Union State Bank of Carrizo Springs. President Petry is a steward in the Methodist Church and is also active in community affairs. He and his wife, Josephine, have two sons, Boothe and John.

An inspiration to all who have been Lions of 2-A2 and surely to all in the future who will serve in Clubs of 2-A2.

OBITUARY
Herbert C. Petry, Past International President, 1950-51

Herbert C. Petry, who served as Past International President, 1950-51, passed away September 25, 1992. Past President Petry had been a Lion since 1940, when he became a charter member of the Carrizo Springs, Texas Lions Club. He served as club president, district governor and as international director in 1945-47. He was elected International President at the 34th International Convention held in Chicago, Illinois, in June 1950. , International President Rohit C. Mehta appointed Past International President Everett J. "Ebb" Grindstaff to represent the association at funeral services. Past President Petry is survived by his wife, Josephine, and two sons.
—THE LION • DECEMBER 1992/JANUARY 1993

On April 21, 1989, District 2-A2 established the Herb C. Petry Fellow Award and later expanded the significance of the recognition associated with such a distinction to elevate a recipient to become a Member of the District 2-A2 Herb C. Petry Hall of Fame.

Those recognized as Members of the Herb C. Petry Hall of Fame include:

M. P. Mike Butler	Rey H. Costa	Dr. Lytle Blankenship
Mel Smith	Michael Rourke	Dick Alphin
Jim Blocklinger	Juan "Johnny" Olivares	Ernesto "TJ" Tijerina
Juan "Ray" Castillo	Dr. John Seale	John Kimbrough
W.E. "Curly" Williams	Margaret Blankenship	William "Bill" Mechler
Sam E. Pantusa	Carl Gibbs	Bill Barker
Frank Bartlett	Patricia "Pat" Carroll	Henry Simms
LaJuana Newnam-Leus	M.D. "Mac" McCain	John Cole

Special Recognition

District 2-A2 Members of the MD-2, Texas Hall of Fame

1972	Herb C. Petry	1973	Frank Robertson
1982	G. S. Sealie McCreless	1985	Rey H. Costa
1986	M.P. Mike Butler	1988	"Zot" Zottarelli
1991	Sidney Schwartz	1994	Dr. Lytle Blankenship
1997	Mel Smith	2000	Michael Rourke
2003	Dick Alphin	2006	Jim Blocklinger
2009	John Kimbrough	2012	Ernesto "TJ" Tijerina

District 2-A2 Common Areas of Service

Lions of District 2-A2 are dedicated as all Lions are to identifying needs in their communities and to work to satisfy those needs. We provide Christmas and Thanksgiving to many who would not have those occasions. We help the homeless and those who may have suffered some natural disaster or other tragic situation. We help in cases of special needs children and when particular disease has afflicted families.

We are proud of two very special ways that our Lions have come together to serve. One is through the establishment on our Human Needs Board which combines the efforts of multiple clubs when the need is too large for one. The other is through our Hearing Board which has worked for years to provide audio screening services to children and adults in our communities. This Board offers our clubs assistance with providing hearing aids to those that cannot afford them. But for over 20 years the Hearing Board has screened thousands of children each year, a service which is very beneficial to proper learning.

Texas Lions Camp

The Lions of District 2-A2 have a very special place in their heart for the Texas Lions Camp since it came about as: "The idea for the Camp originated with Jack Roe and the Kerrville Lions Club. District 2-A Governor Jack Wiech encouraged the incoming eight district governors for 1948-49 to think of the camp as a statewide project and to promote it in their districts." - *The Doors are Always Open: A Short History of the Texas Lions Camp.*

Through the 1970s to the present, 2-A2 Lions sponsor 140 children on average each year to Camp and enjoy work days each year to get it spruced up to welcome kids and families. Because it is our home territory, 2-A2 Lions love to be at Camp, both on Sunday welcoming events and especially at Friday night awards ceremonies.

TLERC

2-A2 Lions are actively engaged in collection of used eyeglasses for recycling at Texas Lions Eyeglass Recycling Center. A Leader in District 2-A2 in this cause is Lion Mac McCain who serves as a Director of TLERC and who is personally responsible for the collection and transport of the used glasses to Midland. Lion Mac does not stop with collection because he has been a leader in the actual distribution of the recycled glasses. For years, Lion Mac, assisted by his lovely wife, Lion Durene actively helped to open and equip eye clinics to be operated by Lions in small towns and "colonias" across our border in Mexico. Lion Mac has been an inspiration to many.

Services for Youth

2-A2 Lions are active in all areas that serve our youth and are engaged in many ways to serve specific needs in our communities from health and wellness to sports activities and to serve to support education. Many Clubs participate in the LCI Peace Poster Contest and many work to encourage participation in Opportunities for Youth Contests.

We are most proud of our involvement in the LEO Program and in 2014 under the Leadership of Lion Lee Gonen, we formed our own LEO District. Through the LEO District members of all LEO Clubs share ideas, work together on projects and interact with the State LEO organization. We are proud that we have made the connection between LEOs that has allowed our 3 Campus Lions Club to now have feeder programs at UTSA, UIW and OLLU.

District 2-A2 Special Areas of Service

All Lions throughout the world are committed to serving others as their motto, "We Serve" explains. Because the Founders of the International Association took on the challenge laid before them in 1925 by Helen Keller to become "Knights of the Blind", Lions have always had their primary cause as that of helping the blind and visually impaired. Lions and their Clubs serve the visually impaired in many, many ways. But the most dynamic way that Lions of District 2-A2 carry out the mission to help the visually impaired is through their 501(C)3, Lions Sight Research Foundation, which is dedicated to supporting research into diseases which impair vision or even cause blindness. And to complement that work, the LSRF helps Lions in the 21 counties of District 2-A2 to provide a variety of needed vision services.

The varied entities of service that have been created by the Lions Sight Research Foundation which was formed in 1982, include the LSRF Research Center—a partnership with the Department of Ophthalmology of the University of Texas Health Science Center in San Antonio, made up of: the Lions Pathology Lab, a premier pathology laboratory in the Southwest; the Lions Surgical Skills Lab, an ophthalmic surgeon training facility; and the Lion Gene Eberlin Clinical Research and Imaging Facility, a Lions clinical facility in support of work and housed at the Texas Diabetes Institute.

Vision-related programs of the LSRF include: the Lions Low Vision and Rehabilitation Center, staffed and housed at UTHSC; the Mobile Eye Screening Unit, a mobile platform used by Lions to conduct vision screening services in their communities. Since its initiation, this program has served over 70,000 individuals in District 2-A2 counties and has lead thousands of people to seek further examination by eye care specialists. In addition, this service has been the first step in recognition of symptoms and needed treatment of glaucoma. PDG Chris Lloyd is the MESU Manager, and in that capacity drives the bus and visits with each person screened to explain the individual findings and recommend referrals when called for. PDG Chris has personally been on board for all screening events, except for two, as those 70,000 individuals were screened. LSRF also includes the KidSight Vision Screening Program, begun in 2012 and chaired by Lion Janie Garza. This vision screening program serves children ages 6 months and older. Lion volunteers are trained and certified to State of Texas standards and conduct these screenings to provide early detection of parameters that may be out of standard criteria. Of the hundreds of children screened, 16-20% are typically referred for further examination.

PET Project - Personal Energy Transportation

A special area of service which began in 2004 as a project of members of the San Antonio Northside Lions Club is the "PET Project" (which stands for Personal Energy Transportation). PET is a three-wheeled, all-terrain wheelchair, operated by hand power. Built by volunteers, PETs are delivered at no cost to people in developing countries who have lost the use of their legs due to birth defects, polio, diabetes, spinal cord injuries, landmines or war. The PET Shop in San Antonio works in conjunction with other shops that have Lion volunteers in College Station, Austin and the Rio Grande Valley, and have delivered PETs to Central America and to Lions who distribute them in India. Lion Tom Martin is the leader of our group at the San Antonio Shop located on Nakoma Avenue near the San Antonio Airport.

One very interesting sidelight to this project came about as Lion PET volunteers presented the project at the Council of Governors Meeting in Kerrville in 2010. Because of that presentation and three other visits to District 2-S4, a collaborative effort between PET Lions and the Dole Fruit Co. came about through introductions made by the Freeport Lions Club. This partnership lead to our being able to transport PETs at no cost using Dole cargo containers heading back empty after having delivered fruit to U.S. locations from Central America. Utilizing the Dole containers allows for the shipping of 160 units at a time. That affords us the chance to make a difference in the lives of 160 individuals and their families.

The San Antonio PET Shop also works directly with Lions in Del Rio to distribute PETs, when possible, to needy individuals in Mexico that are helped by the Lions of Mexico.

Membership and Membership Growth

Because membership and growth are the lifeblood of our organization, we work diligently to continue to add hearts and hands and ideas by inviting those that want to make a difference.

Since District 2-A2 was formed, the number of clubs in our District has reached a high of 74 in the mid '70s and has always maintained at a minimum of 55. Membership reached its peak in 1982-83 under the Governorship of Lion John Petry when it neared 3,000 members.

Changing lifestyles and changes in cultural priorities over the past 20 years has been a detriment to all service organizations. We are dedicated to the idea that our best public relations effort lies at our root, that of being of service to others. In all ways possible, we work to have success in our clubs by striving to remind each other that we must be in touch with the reasons that our fellow members have joined us. And that answer is always that they enjoy personal satisfaction in being of service. So, we work to maintain an atmosphere that encourages them to be successful in their goal to help others. Our Motto is WE SERVE and HAVE FUN DOING IT!

We look for imaginative ways to grow. We recently invited a struggling club to relocate its meetings to the San Antonio Lighthouse for the Blind, a facility that manufactures a multitude of products for the military and for office supply markets. This facility was started in the early 1930s through the efforts of our SA Founder Lions Club and nearly all that are employed there are visually-impaired or blind. Today, we have 35 new Lions from the workforce at the Lighthouse, and a new way to serve has been born.

Miscellaneous Articles

We have asked Past District Governors from District 2-A2 for input to supplement the foregoing.

PDG Rod Chisholm, 2013-2014: ABOUT THE S.A. FOUNDER LIONS

Our story began in 1915 when San Antonio was the largest city in Texas, boasting a population of almost 120,000. Our club was organized by Mr. E.A. Hicks. Our Charter Banquet was held at the Gunter Hotel on October 8, 1915 with 53 members in attendance. Our Charter bore the name "San Antonio Den of the Royal Order of Lions." The Den's objective was various forms of civic improvement such as paving the street in front of the Alamo, encouraging the construction of sidewalks downtown etc. Mr. Hicks had, one month before, organized a Royal Order in El Paso...but that club subsequently folded.

Early on, the relationship between the San Antonio Den and the Indiana Headquarters was disrupted upon receipt of the Charter documents for the Royal Order of Lions whereupon it was discovered that the Royal Order was in truth a secretive "fraternal" organization, considered savory...thus by 1916, many left the organization. In came Dr. William Perry Woods, a prominent medical surgeon in Evansville, Indiana. In consultation with Mr. Hicks, Dr. Woods proposed that those clubs who resented the fraternal aspects would form a new organization. Thus, on October 24, 1916, the International Association of Lions Clubs was incorporated in Evansville, Indiana.

In the summer of 1917, Dr. Woods sent out invitations to 33 Southern clubs to join him in October of 1917 in Dallas, at the Adolphus Hotel. The San Antonio Club received its invitation, bur because of the World War I effort, was unable to send a representative. It nevertheless elected to support the outcome of the meeting. Dr. Woods, the Founding Father of Lionism, was subsequently elected to be the first President of the International Association at the Dallas Convention and the San Antonio club became a part of the newly incorporated association. Of all the clubs invited to the Dallas Convention, the San Antonio Club had (and still has) the earliest date of organization as a Lions Club.

Through the years, the San Antonio Club has distinguished itself in service, to wit:

1917 - The Club sold War Bonds, sent cigarettes to the boys overseas, conducted clothes drives

1921 - Received authorization to organize Clubs in Mexico...Mexico City joined in 1924 after being sponsored by the San Antonio Club.

1921 - Established the Better Business Bureau.

1922 - Formed the San Antonio Conservation Society to preserve historic landmarks.

1924 - Raised $10,000 to purchase Lions Field, near Brackenridge Park, and deeded it to the City

1925 - Featured speaker: John Philip Sousa..

1926 - Featured speaker: Colonel William "Billy" Mitchell.

1927 - Featured speaker: Melvin Jones.

1934 - The Club's "committee for the Blind" got the city to pass the "white cane" protection laws.

1936 - During the depression, the Club purchased a cow for $50 for the Protestant Orphans Home.

1943 - During World War II, organized Blood Drives, raised money for Brooke General Hospital and sold $156,000 in War Bonds.

1944 - Organized a Lions vs Optimist baseball game and raised $5,500 net! Donated this money to pay for 2 eye surgeries, 62 pairs of glasses, 200 walking canes.

1946 - Raised $250,000 to finance the Lighthouse for the Blind, distributed 4 pocket-sized Braille typewriters.

1948 - Sponsored 12 new clubs in the district!

1948 - The Lighthouse moved into their new factory - the Club raised over $36,000.

1950 - District 2-A had become the largest in the world. $200,000 of pledgeswere raised for the project called the Texas Lions Club for Crippled Children in Kerrville.

1953 - TLC was dedicated as a living monument to all Texas Lions. Our Club added $8,000.

1954 - First service was held at the Jack B. Wright Memorial Chapel at the TLC, named after our past president.

Each and every year thereafter, the Founders Lions Club has supported guide dogs, eyeglasses, eye surgery, youth programs, continued support to the Lighthouse, the TLC, the Lions Sight Research Foundation, special charities, disaster relief, scholarships.

Featured speakers continued to visit our club, such as Ronald Reagan, Senator John Tower, Congressman Henry B. Gonzalez, Al Hirt, many San Antonio Mayors, Bexar County Judges, Council Members, Chiefs of Police and Fire Departments, Military Commanding Generals from the many bases in San Antonio, Church leaders from many faiths, Professional and amateur athletes, Media personalities, Entertainers, FBI Leaders to name but a few. The Founders Club is famous for the many speakers that attend each and every meeting - that's 99 years and counting...or said another way, we've had in excess of 5,000 quality speakers over the years! One such visit was the gentleman from the Secret Service who was in charge of combating counterfeit money dealers. During his talk, he distributed about 15 different pieces of counterfeit currencies to pass around. When the money was gathered up after the talk, people joked that he might get something LESS than the original 15—when, in fact, he got back 16 bills back! Someone slipped in a genuine $1 bill as a joke.

Our long-time Tail Twister, Louis Rodriguez, served in that capacity for over half a century! He set the standard for Lions International.

Each and every year, the Founders Club has continued to serve. We are proud of our heritage but also proud to have so many other Lions Clubs join us in our crusade of service.

We started our history in the Gunter Hotel almost 100 years ago. We have recently moved our meeting place to the Petroleum Club for lunch (1st and 3rd Wednesday at 11:30 a.m.). All Lions are welcome to visit us at our meetings, all we ask is to RSVP so that we can extend a proper welcome.

PDG Lytle Blankenship, Ph.D., 1981-82:

My year as governor was hampered somewhat by professional responsibilities since I was serving a two-year term as President of The Wildlife Society our international organization of wildlife scientists as well as developing and leading in a Wildlife Management Workshop in India. Probably the most beneficial successes, besides having a plus membership, during my year occurred as a result of three task forces I appointed. These task forces were appointed to solve ongoing issues in the District. At least they seemed to be issues critical to the progress of Lionism in our District.

Task Force 1 – Related to the Ear (Hearing) Board

Among some inadequacies, the major issue confronting the Committee was that some members were using Committee budget to pay for trip expenses, and miscellaneous items. Such practice seemed legal by the Current Constitution. To solve any inequities, I appointed PDG Mike Butler to head up a Task Force to review the Constitution and propose changes as necessary to the District. This was done with success.

Task Force 2 - Related to the Human Needs Board

Lion John Stacey, Founder Lions Club was Chairman of the Benevolence Committee of the Founders Club. He came to me with this complaint. "The Founders Lions Club is the only Lions Club with a telephone listing in the San Antonio Directory, so we get all the requests for assistance from not only San Antonio, but often from outside the city. We cannot handle all such requests." Consequently, I set up a District-wide Human Needs Committee with Lion Sid Schwartz as chairman. This committee operated as such until established as a 501c-3 Board (under DG George Strickland I believe).

Task Force 3 - Southwest Texas Eye Bank

As long as I was a Lion, it seemed all I heard about was the problems between the Hospital Administrator and the District pertaining to the Eye Bank. I was never quite sure what the problems were, so when I became Governor, the first thing I did was to set up a Task Force with PDG James Long as Chairman. The assignment was to study the Lions relationship to Sight Conservation and to come back with the best way for District 2-A2 to spend its time and resources on Sight Conservation. After several months, the Task Force returned with three alternatives, one of them being to remain with the Southwest Eye Bank, At the annual meeting between the District's Sight Conservation Committee and the Baptist Hospital representatives at the hospital in SanAntonio, it became obvious from the remarks of the Administrator that the hospital did not really need the assistance of Lions in collecting eye tissue. After further discussion, I informed the Administrator that we would sever relations. The question then was what would the District do for sight conservation? At that meeting was Dr. Wick VanHeuven, the new Head of Department of Ophthalmology for the University of Texas Health Science Center in San Antonio, fresh out of New York He turned to me and said, "Why don't the Lions become involved in research?" As a research scientist myself, this was right up my alley. Dr. Van Heuven and I met a couple of times at his office to further discuss the idea of a relationship between the Lions and the University. Since my term was fast closing, I had to leave the idea with incoming Governor, John Petry, who followed through with Governor-Elect Rey Costa to finalize the beginning of the Lions Sight and Tissue Foundation. Otherwise, I carried on the normal functions of a District Governor. As a member of the Council of Governors, I was elected as Vice-Chairman by the other Governors. At the close of the Wildlife Management Workshop at the Kahna National Park in India, Margaret and I were guests of my Twin Governor, Lion Dr. David Kung and his wife Kitty in Taipei, Tawain.

Task Force 4 – Unbeknowing Lytle by Everett J. "Ebb" Grindstaff

A longtime friend and associate has been traveling around the world like myself, but in different circles. Dr. Lytle H. Blankenship has written the book, *Trails That Lead Somewhere* that describes his life from early childhood, "In the Beginning" (some people will find this humorous), as that is one of my bylines. Lytle came from a family of 14 children during the Depression, but our paths met in Lionism in Uvalde in A-2 as he traveled in the Southwest on Indian reservations, but mostly in South America and the African trails. *Trails That Lead Somewhere* is the name of the book published by Outskirtspress and describes a man that has traveled many miles, has a dog at his side as his best friend, but naturally does not include his charming wife, Margaret who has traveled with him and taken care of him during these last years because of his physical impairment. During this time, he was always "a good neighbor" or "a good Samaritan", and as far as I would say in Lionism, "a global humanitarian" and one of the best friends I ever had.

PDG John Kimbrough, 1992-1993

MY year (1992-93) was noted for:

1. Starting the Stride for Sight program for the district, which at the time, and may still be, the only district-wide fundraiser in the world.
2. Having the second largest membership growth in the state and it was the first time in a long time that the district had back-to-back growth years.
3. It was an informational year, as the chairman of each of the district's programs explained their program at a cabinet meetings (i.e. Human Needs). Ed Flood came to one and gave an overview of the Texas Lions Foundation.
4. Developing new people to take leadership roles in the district. We had a mix of about half "old heads" and half people who had never led in the district.

PDG John Seale, DVM, 2005-2006

Certainly starting the first online district newsletter for 2-A2 was significant, as was having a cabinet meeting at UTSA Health Science Center so that the Lions of 2-A2 could tour both our Sight Research Center AND our Low Vision Center was important. It's the old story of a picture is worth a thousand words. You can hear about it indefinitely, but it really doesn't mean anything until you can see and experience it.

On a more personal note, there are two things that come to mind. The first one is that at the necrology service at the MD-2 convention. I started the ceremony whereby the Governor and all 2-A2 PDGs stand when the roll is called for the deceased PDGs and above from 2-A2. To me, this is a sign of respect for those who have crossed over. No other district does this. The second thing that I started is the passing of the gavel that we normally do at our district convention to recognize those who have walked this path before and also give their support to the incoming Governor.

PDG Amadeo "Manny" Carrillo, 2008-2009

1. Started branching out to Clubs that had never sponsored a District Convention to sponsor one.
2. Asked and received approval from LSRF's Board to give Lion Sight Research Foundation Fellows to Clubs that donated $1,000 or more to Stride for Sight campaign. Raised $18,000 at the Mid-Winter Convention once the idea was introduced.
3. Started the idea of clubs sponsoring District College Scholarships.
4. Had MERLO training go back to "basics". Training leaned more towards Club Officer and District Chairperson responsibilities.
5. Combined District Governor Lunch and Night banquets into one function, saving time and money for those members in attendance.
6. Introduced the idea of having the "Memorial Service" as an agenda item during the District Convention general meeting.
7. -30 Members the 1st of June 2009, started informing the Clubs where the District stood on Membership, end result +3.
8. Our council approved and started the Texas Lions Camp Endowment Campaign.
9. Our District ending up raising $77,311 for CSF II.
10. As a fun fundraiser, had the 1st DG Phantom Ball and a symbolic S4S walk during the DG Convention. (Both yielded excellent results)

11. In 2009, had the second ever Council of Governors Meeting in Del Rio. T.J. Tijerina had the first in 1989.
12. Starting in 2009, had the PDG Association start buying "memorial bricks" at the TLC for those PDs who passed away.
13. PDG Johnny Olivares and I amended the District's Constitution and By-Laws in 2010 in order to keep any excess funds within the District, better explain DG Chairperson responsibilities/duties and to have it coincide with the State and LCI's constitution. (This action monetarily aided incoming DGs and also added in the 2nd VDG.)

The Council of 2000-2001 and group of governors need to be recognized, along with their Council Chairmen, Michael and Liz Rourke in their year as Chairmen of the Council. This group of Governors were all recognized as 100% Governors, which has not been done again to-date, but the most significant part of that year was that they were the only Council to be recognized as a group with the presidential medals that were presented to each of them, allowing them to be part of the effort that year.

DISTRICT 2-A3 HISTORY

The growth of Lionism in Texas resulted in the restructuring of Texas Multiple District 2 at the Lions Clubs International Convention in 1959, the division of District 2-A to form Sub-District 2-A3, and an increase of Multiple District 2 to 15 sub-districts. Fourteen of the current 58 District 2-A3 Lions Clubs were active in 1959. The McAllen Lions Club—chartered October 25, 1923—is the oldest of these clubs. District 2-A3 covers 14 counties in deep South Texas, and extends from Rockport to Sinton, Freer to Zapata, and Los Fresnos to Brownsville. Since the first District Governor Buster Shely (1959-1960), the District has had 57 District Governors—five of whom are women, including the current District Governor, Lion Enedina Vela.

District 2-A3's heritage includes many outstanding Lions. The District is extremely proud to have been the home of PDG Jack Wiech, who spear-headed efforts to establish the Texas Lions Camp during his tenure as District Governor of District 2-A (1948-1949), and who served as Texas Lions Camp President from 1949 until 1952. The Texas Lions Camp Administration Building was dedicated as the "Jack and Elizabeth Wiech Building", and the "Jack Wiech Fellow" was created to recognize his service. The District is also proud of the leadership provided to the Camp by PDG Roy Davis (1984-1985) and PDG Richard "Rick" Talbert (2006-2007), Weslaco Lions Club, who both had the honor of serving as Presidents of the Camp. In addition, the District is the home of Past International Directors Ray Hughston, Brownsville Downtown Lions Club (1990-1992), and Conrado "Connie" de la Garza, Harlingen Lions Club (2000-2002).These outstanding Past International Directors, along with PDG Roy Davis were recognized as Lions Clubs International Ambassadors of Good Will.

The District is proud of the following 13 recipients of the Texas Hall of Fame Award: PDG Jack Wiech; PID Ray Hughston; Brownsville Down-town; PID Connie de la Garza, Harlingen; PDG Roy Davis, Weslaco; PDG Alfred Rogers, Donna; PDG Leroy Cornelius, Portland; Lion Orville Harris, Corpus Christi Southside; Lion Burt Diebel, Alice Evening; PDG Richard Talbert, Weslaco; PCC David "Ike" Boling, Rockport; PDG William Mannix, Corpus Christi Downtown; PDG Glynn Kaigler, Portland; Lion George Jackson, Corpus Christi Industrial; and PDG Dr. Clayton Roth,

Aransas Pass. Nineteen special Lions have been recipients of the unique District 2-A3 Ray Hughston Humanitarian Award, created in 1996 to honor PID Ray Hughston's many years of service to Lionism and the Texas Lions Camp. This award to recognize the demonstration of high ideals of service to others has been presented to: PID Ray Hughston; PDG Roy Davis; PDG Jack Wiech; PDG Glynn Kaigler; PDG William Mannix; Lion Jesse Guzman; Lion Gene Olszewski; PDG Richard Talbert; PDG Leroy Cornelius; PDG Carolyn Keskitalo; PDG Joe Trevino; PDG Norman Stradley; Lion Bill Flatters; Lion Lynde Todd; Lion Betty Moore; PDG Helen Muse; Lion Wally Bunton; Lion Robert Janik and PDG Buz Sawyer.

Proud of its past, the District is looking forward to future service, growth in membership through the efforts of many Lions, sponsorship of LEO Clubs, and implementation of Helen Keller's challenge to be "Knights of the Blind in the crusade against darkness" through its support of the Lions Clubs International Campaign Sight First, participation in the Lions Eye Bank of Texas, eyesight screening of many young children through the Spot Pedia Vision project, ongoing eyeglasses recycling and donation of eye examinations and eyeglasses.

INTERLUDE

Some other activities or situations might should be mentioned which would be of some humor to some people and there is a serious part to part of it also:

The most embarrassing moment in my travels happened in ENGLAND at a convention where there were about 400 people and they were all having a good time, a very good time. Prior to the speech, I added more fuel to the fire as I had the high privilege of meeting the Mayor of that particular city. I got through the ceremony about the Mayor with his long chain that went down below his waist, all his metals and so forth, and we also met the Duke and Duchess of Winchester. The Duke happened to be the richest young man in the world under 30 years of age, and had a beautiful 19-year old Duchess as his wife. Then I said and what a pleasure it was to meet the "Duke and Doochess" of Westminster. The crowd went wild, and there was no place for me to go behind stage or otherwise, so I just took it with a smile upon my face, but they were gracious after the meeting.

One of the most impressive activities that I saw performed was blind bowling in JOHANNESBURG, SOUTH AFRICA, while we were at the meeting of the Board.

The hottest day in the whole world was spent in MOROCCO at *118 degrees*, and of course it was with a small fan. The Mayor and I were in suits and they served hot tea for nourishment (I guess it was to keep us alive and to keep us from not fainting).

The name of the people that we had to provide for the City behind the Hardin-Simmons Cowboy White Horses were a group of people known as the "Pooper-Scoopers," and as you can imagine, they had their little cans and brooms and they went along behind the horses and scooped the poop and disposed of it properly. Fortunately, because of these scoopers, we were able to meet all the regulations of MONTREAL in 1979. The chief scooper was none other than J. T. (Difficult to name him as he has always been a dedicated Lion that performed in any manner asked.)

S-1, S-2, S-3, S-4, S-5

Lionism in District 2-S1

The International Association of Lions Clubs officially formed in October 1917, and Texas was named as District 4. In 1921, District 4 (Texas) was designated as Multiple District 2 at the International Convention held in Oakland, California. At the 1930 Convention held in Austin, the following Districts—2T, 2E, 2X, 2A, and 2S—were designated. District 2S consisted of 55 counties over 48,888 square miles.

District 2-S1

- In 1942, District 2S was divided into three Districts: 2-S1, 2-S2 and 2-S3.
- Two District 2-S1 Clubs were represented at the first International Convention and were designated as Founder Lions Clubs—the Beaumont and Port Arthur Founder Lions Clubs.
- District 2-S1 Governor, W. C. Steinhagen of Beaumont was serving in 1942-43 when District 2-S1 came about.
- Since the birth of Lions in 1917 thru 2015 (98 Years of Service), some of the recorded information was as follows:
  —In 1917, Texas Lions 1 District (District 4 was all of Texas), 12 Clubs, 360 Members.
  —In 1921, District 4 became District 2. In 1930, District 2 became District 2S, and in 1942, District 2S became District 2-S1. W. C. Steinhagen of Beaumont, served as the first District Governor of 2-S1.
  —In 1967, Texas Lions (known as MD-2), 15 Districts, 904 Clubs, 40,062 members.
  —Today in MD-2 (October 31, 2014), there are 16 Districts, 901 Clubs, 26,146 Members.

First State Conventions

The first State Convention was held in Beaumont (now District 2-S1) on June 8, 1922. The seventh State Convention was also held in Beaumont.

The 2011 State Convention held in Beaumont was a memorable convention headed by Council Chairman Stump Weatherford of Orange and District 2-S1 Governor James Browning of Carthage.

Service of the Lions of District 2-S1

District 2-S1 has had 83 District Governors, and all have served the clubs and District well. Twenty-one of the District Governors has had a plus in membership during their year of service (from 1959-2011).

District S-1 is proud to have 16 Texas Hall of Fame Lions, and has had two International Directors—Judge Joe Fisher, 1972-1973 and Marshall Cooper, 1993-1995 respectively.

The District has been represented by two Past Presidents of the Texas Lions Camp that chartered in 1949. PDG Robert E. Price from Port Arthur, served from 1967-68, and PDG S. R. Moe Cully from Nederland served from 1991-92. Many other Lions have served representing the District as State Committee Chairs over the years.

Many of the clubs participate in cooking for one of the work days at TLC over many years. Other District projects have been serving the Hearing Impaired, sight screenings on a regular basis each year and glasses, sponsoring children to TLC and disaster relief, just to name a few. Many Clubs of District 2-S1 do a great "Service" in their local communities.

Over the years, we have supported our International Family Members of the past and present and must be thankful of a grateful humanitarian organization like Lions Clubs International.

We also remember and salute the Lion who is considered the father of Lionism, Melvin Jones for his vision and dedication.

"It Is Great To Be A Lion In District 2-S1"

Compiled by PDG S. R. Moe Cully

History of District 2-S2

Any recent history, that is, from 1967 forward has to be rooted in the vison of Lions in the 1930s–1960s. For it was during that 30-year time frame that actions were taken by Lions following their visions that are still being acted upon today. The actions of Lions like Jack Wiech, J. B. Wooldridge, Don Buckalew, Gordon Dotson, William Adams, J. H. Stevens, Ray Elliot and H. O. Helm in the founding of The Texas Lions Camp, Lions Eye Bank of Texas and Lighthouse of Houston are still having impact on the lives of men, women and children within what is now District 2-S2. Let me give you a few highlights of these organizations.

District 2-S2 has a history of supporting the Texas Lions Camp. For over 25 years, we have had 100% of our clubs contribute funds to the Texas Lions Camp. One of our PDGs—George Connor—developed a special relationship with the school nurses of Houston Independent School District. PDG George is known to have loaded nurses onto a bus and taken them to Camp just to impress them as to the benefits of sending children to camp. PDG George had a list of 17 different sources of potential campers—from nurses, doctors, PTAs to medical associations. He sent Christmas cards to former campers still eligible to attend camp. In 1980, Lion Bob Dowden began a "Wild Game Dinner" using meat from game—deer, ducks, geese-whatever hunters had shot. The LaPorte and South Houston Lions Clubs did the cooking and meal preparation. The event was held at the Knights of Columbus Hall in Pasadena. Funds raised from this event were earmarked for the Texas Lions Camp. Lion Bob has since passed away, but the tradition of a dinner in the District specifically for Texas Lions Camp continues. The event has been named "The Bob Dowden Dinner" in honor of its founder. The two elected directors to the TLC from District 2-S2 chair the event. The menu is not wild game, but fun is had by all.

The Lions Eye Bank of Texas was the vision of Lions J. B. Wooldridge, Don Buckalew, Gordon Dotson, William Adams, J. H. Stevens, Ray Elliot and H. O. Helm.

The purpose, as stated in the By-Laws of the LEBT was:
1) "To foster and develop an Eye Bank in the State of Texas for the use of hospitals, physicians, and eye research in the restoration of sight of persons now blind or partially blind."

2) "To devise and carry out the ways and means necessary to aid the blind and visually-impaired citizens of the State of Texas in finding the causes of blindness, thereby promoting a program of prevention, corrections and improvement of impaired sight."

The LEBT began in District 2-S2, but expanded to include District 2-S4 in 1974. In 1975, District 2-S1 was added to the area included in LEBT. In 1992, District 2-A3 was included to complete our current area covered. Working with the Baylor College of Medicine, the LEBT serves a receiving, processing, research and distribution laboratory for eye tissue. Lions help inform the public about the benefits of eye donations, corneal transplantation, eye research and promote donor registry.

Unfortunately, much of the history of the Lighthouse and the Lions is oral; however, the following are some observations:

Although the Lighthouse was officially founded in 1939, services to persons with visual impairments can be traced back to 1925. The Dandelions—the Women's Auxiliary to the Lions Clubs—established a sewing club for persons who were blind, and helped to find a sales outlet for the work of blind individuals.

When the Lighthouse opened in 1939 (called the Harris County Association for the Blind), Lions donated money for sewing machines to make various textiles.

In 1945, the Lighthouse acquired it first permanent home. The Lions purchased a Lutheran Church building at 1658 Westheimer.

In 1952 and 1965, Lions in partnership with KPRC-TV, held telethons to raise matching funds for the buildings at 3530 Dallas. Matching funds were used to secure Federal grants for the construction of these buildings.

Several Lions have served as Lighthouse board chairman. These include Ray Elliott, Tom Elliott and James Anderson, Jr. in addition, the By-Laws call for three permanent director positions for Lions. Two Lion representatives and the District Governor. In addition, there have been several Lions who were elected to the board apart from their Lions membership. These include among others Albert Wong, Vernon Carmichael and Truett Childre.

Lions started an annual Christmas Shopping Trip for Lighthouse clients in the late 1980s. The Lions offered volunteer assistance for the Lighthouse annual Beeping Easter Egg Hunt, and have provided financial and volunteer support to the Lighthouse Dragon Boat Racing Team. Lions have contributed funds for many programs and equipment purchases over the past 25 years.

The Lighthouse continues to recognize the support of the Lions.

Sight First Grant
Harris County Low Vision Project

In 2014, the Center for Visual Rehabilitation Robert Cizik Clinic was the recipient of a 2014 SightFirst Grant. The Houston Sports Lions Club submitted the grant proposal. The project is aimed at increasing awareness by providing education and addressing barriers to accessing comprehensive low vision care. Currently the clinic serves 1,800 new low vision patients a year. The grant of $164,645, plus an additional $20,000 from the Hermann Eye Fund has helped in the following activities:

- Low Vision Education Day programs
- Creation of a "Loaner library" of commonly used low vision aides
- Group educational programs
- Monthly support groups
- 'Training the trainers' of mechanisms used to improve awareness of low vision services amongst the general public and the visually-impaired population.

Our district formed a Presidents and Secretaries Council (PSC) some-time around 1960. The purpose is to provide a forum to allow the exchange of ideas and news concerning the Lions Clubs and District 2-S2. The PSC may also be utilized to discuss methods to assist those clubs that are having difficulty with membership, finances and other areas. The PSC continues today as an opportunity for clubs officers to meet, share information and learn through various training activities.

In 1963-64, Lion Don A. Buckalew was elected as the youngest (29 years old) District Governor in our District. He still holds that record. PDG Don became an elected International Director 1974–1976. PID Don also served as a Lions Club International Board Committee appointee during 1980-1981, 1983-1984 and again in 1993-1994.

District 2-S2 also supplied another Lion as an elected International Director—PID C. Howard Leverett, Jr. PID Howard served as an ID from 1986-1988. Howard also served as Chairman of the Council of Governors in the early 1980s, and he and his Council were very influential because of their dedicated work in not only the election of Ebb Grindstaff as International President, but also of accomplishing their business at hand in the least amount of time.

District 2-S2 has always had a spirit of generosity (or better known as "Lionism"), starting back in the 1930s when Lions raised funds for the start of the Lighthouse of Houston, and continuing through the years. In 1969, Lions of the District raised $27,000 to help victims of Hurricane Camille. In the early 1970s, leaders in the District established the District's Humanitarian Relief Fund, designed to help District clubs aid others through matching grants.

Some random notes regarding our District:

Our District established the District Hall of Fame in 1994. The first honoree was PDG E. H. "Eddie" Munger.

Lion Kay Burke became the first woman Lion in our District on August 1, 1987. In 2003-04, Kay was the first woman to be placed in the District Hall of Fame.

In 1997, the PDGs of District 2-S2 began awarding the Distinguished Achievement Award to Lions in the District for service to Lions and community.

Our first female District Governor was PDG Melba Buado, 2003-2004.

History District 2-S3
1967-2016

Compiled from a variety of sources, including information from personal recollections, several District 2-S3 PDGs, past District directories, program/project managers, publications, historical archives and District Lions

Origins

Two delegates, Harry Reasonover and C.W.A. MacCormack from the Austin Lions Club were present at the organizing Convention held at the Adolphus Hotel in Dallas, Texas from October 8-11, 1917.

History/Timeline

1917   One District

1930   District 2-S

1942   District 2-S3

1967   Capital City Lions Club Chartered by CC E.B. "Tex" Mayer (Sponsor, West Austin) as first predominately African-American club in the world.

1987   Lion Bessie Hinkle (South Austin Lions Club) became first female member of District 2-S3

1989   Last year before District split:
        S3 **126** Lions clubs and **23** Lioness clubs

1990   First year of S3 and S5, 16 Districts in MD2S3:
        62 Lions clubs and **11** Lioness clubs

State Leadership from District 2-S3

1966-1967   Council Chair/PDG E.B. "Tex" Mayer

1981-1982   Council Chair/PDG Dr. L. Don Mayer

1996-1997   Council Chair PDG Lin Rose

2012-2013   Council Chair PDG Dennis Heitkamp

Awards/Recognitions

Harry Reasonover Award Upon the death of Charter Lion Harry Reasonover, one of two members of the Austin Lions Club to attend as delegates to the Organizing Convention in Dallas in 1917, the West Austin Lions Club proposed that the District memorialize Lion Harry's legacy of involvement and service by establishing a District award and naming it for him. The Cabinet accepted the recommendation and developed criteria for the award, which was first presented in 1961. The annual award recognizes a deserving Lion who has consistently displayed a high level of service to the District over a period of several years. It is the highest and most prestigious individual award given by the District. Nominations are submitted by the club, and selection is made by a confidential committee appointed by the District Governor. The award is sponsored and presented by the West Austin Lions Club.

Gold Spur Award Presented to a Lion in recognition of outstanding service during the current year. Nominations are submitted by the club and selection is made by a confidential committee appointed by the District Governor.

Silver Spur Award Presented to a Lion in recognition of outstanding service in first year of membership. Nominations are submitted by the club and selection is made by a confidential committee appointed by the District Governor.

Hall of Honor Award Presented to an outstanding Lion and selected by the District Governor.

C.W.A. MacCormack Award Presented to a club for outstanding service. Selection is made by the District Governor based on a review of Club Activity Reports. The award is sponsored and presented by the Austin Founder Lions Club in memory of the other member of the Club to attend as a delegate to the 1917 Organizing Convention.

District Projects
1974 – Lone Star Lions Eye Bank
Eye-banking began in District 2-S3 in the early 1970s, when a young physician named Richard E. Nieman came to Austin to set up his ophthalmology practice. He took his idea of beginning an Eye Bank to the Austin Lions Club (now the Austin Downtown Founder Lions Club) and quickly won their support. Led by the efforts of Legacy Lion PDG Willie Kocurek and

others, the District established an Eye Bank in 1974. The Lions District 2-S3 Eye Bank was housed in Seton Medical Center in Austin, where it remained for 23 years. When the District was divided in 1989, the newly-formed District continued its support of the Eye Bank, and its name was changed to the Lions Eye Bank of 2-S3 and 2-S5. Later, when the District 2-X3 Eye Bank merged into the Eye Bank, the name was again changed to the Lions Eye Bank of Central Texas.

As the Eye Bank's services expanded and Seton was unable to provide additional space, the Eye Bank sought out other locations. St. David's Medical Center was its next home. That arrangement lasted for a few years, until it became evident that the Eye Bank needed a permanent home in order to provide stability and continued growth with an increased level of services. In 2000, the Eye Bank purchased and renovated a former residence in Manor, Texas. The Eye Bank moved into the new facility in 2001. Its name changed in 2004 to Lone Star Lions Eye Bank.

1970s and 1980s – Zone Chairman Forum

For several years, the District hosted a very successful and educational Zone Chairman Forum in Austin. The event was primarily the result of Lion Ed Skypala's conviction that the Zone Chair position was the most important link in the Lions organization. Many current and developing Zone Chairs received extensive training during these sessions. In response to travel concerns, the Forums were hosted around the state for several years before being discontinued.

1997 – Texas Lions Camp Equestrian Center

Since its inception at Texas Lions Camp, the Equestrian Program has demonstrated its value as an aid to children with disabilities. Unfortunately, the open arena was difficult to manage because of inclement weather— primarily rain and relentless summer sun. In 1997, the Camp developed a proposal to cover the arena, and District 2-S3 accepted the challenge as a District project.

Initially, 2-S3 located and donated an actual disassembled structure and provided the funds to erect the structure over the arena; however, erecting a steel structure without plans or possibly all pieces proved to be too risky to proceed. With the concurrence of the District, the donated building was sold for scrap by the Camp and the proceeds were added to the funds already donated. An economical alternative was then found with a vendor that could erect a prefabricated structure for the same or lesser price. Additional funds were raised by the Lions of District 2-S3, and the metal pavilion-style cover was erected in time for the first camping session in 1998. The resulting structure has provided campers of all ability levels the opportunity to learn about the care of horses, and enables campers the opportunity to ride horseback even on rainy days or overly-hot conditions.

1999 - Mobile Health Screening Unit

Led by the vision and work of Lion Jodie Polk of the San Marcos Lions Club, the District established a Mobile Health Screening Unit (MHSU). The MHSU provided access to vision, hearing, and diabetes screening at community fairs, health fairs and other venues where the public gathered. Initial funding for the fully-equipped van and hauling vehicle was provided by Lions in the District, and corporate sponsorships from partnerships with HEB and McCoy's Building Supply. For many years, the unit traveled to locations in the District where it was staffed by trained local Lions Club members who set up and offered services staffed to the public. Unfortunately, expenses of operation, storage and replacement of equipment—coupled with declining financial sponsorship—resulted in diminished effectiveness, and ultimately forced the MHSU to downsize. In 2013, the District decided to discontinue the program.

2009 - KidSight Vision Screening

A new opportunity for needed service was adopted by the District in 2009, when Lion Dr. Sam Johnson proposed the establishment of an Early Childhood Vision Screening program. The District adopted the program and purchased one vision screening unit in 2009. The program was very successful, but was limited by the number of screenings that could be conducted each year. Following the introduction of new equipment which could effectively be operated by non-professionals, and the desire to expand services, the District revamped the program in 2012. The result is a vibrant and growing Kid Sight Vision Screening program that provides vision screening services to children across the District.

Conventions

International – The District has been well-represented with delegates, along with participation in the International Parade (with Lion J. P. Kirksey organizing the Texas Delegation in many of the parades). Probably the most memorable was the impressive display of pride for our incoming International President E. J. "Ebb" Grindstaff (and wife Jay) at the 1982 Convention held in Atlanta, Georgia. More than 200 Texas delegates marched, displayed Texas Flags, sang and chanted throughout the entire parade route. Much to the dismay of the local parade staff, the delegation halted at the reviewing stand, where Lion J. P. Kirksey led a "big Texas Howdy" to our International President.

State – The District hosted two very successful State Conventions in Austin: in 1997 at the Austin Renaissance Hotel with Council Chair Lin Rose and Chair Lion J. P. Kirksey, and in 2013 at the Austin Airport Hilton with Council Chair Dennis Heitkamp and DG J. P. Kirksey.

District – There have been many memorable District Conventions at the Villa Capri Motor Hotel in Austin, Hilton College Station, and the Seguin Convention Center. Before 1990, it was common to have more than 400 in attendance.

Notable Club Projects and Achievements

Wimberley – Market Days at Lions Field

Wimberley hosts the oldest outdoor market in the Texas Hill Country, and the second-largest in the state. Market Days has been an institution in Wimberley since 1964, when the first market was held on the town Square. The Market grew from a few trucks that first day, until there was no more room around the Square to handle all the vendors and visitors. By this time, the Wimberley Lions Club had assumed management and organization of the project. In 1972, they had the foresight to purchase property on RR 2325 and moved the Market to its current location at Lions Field. Through the years, the Wimberley Lions Club, along with the growing ranks of Market Day vendors, have worked together to improve the field— making Market Days the shopper's paradise that it has become. Nearly 500 booths offer goods for buyers to explore.

Wimberley Lions sponsor all of the food booths and offer plenty of options, including BBQ plates and sandwiches, grilled sausages, breakfast tacos, hot dogs and hamburgers. All profits from Market Day booth rentals, concessions and parking are donated back to local, state and worldwide charities, scholarships and community projects.

Taylor Lions – Leader Dog for the Blind Top Dog

For many years, the Taylor Lions Club has actively supported the Leader Dog Program, and has been a member of the Top Dog Club in recognition of their annual contribution of $5,000 or more. In 2014, the Club was one of the top 10 Top Dog Clubs in the US.

San Marcos Lions – Tube Rental

The Tube Rental and River Shuttle are fundraising projects of the San Marcos Lions Club. The Tube Rental is located in City Park. Proceeds from this and other projects allow the Lions Clubs to support over 100 charities, and provide educational opportunities for students.

The tube rental project originally began during the 1970s out of a cattle truck with a portable air compressor and recycled automotive tubes. The project rented 20-40 tubes a day beginning at about 10:00 am on the weekends from a truck parked behind Joe's Crab Shack on the San Marcos River. The project has grown to 800-850 rentals a day—making this program the single largest fundraising event of the San Marcos Lions Club. The program currently operates out of a multipurpose building in City Park, and each year, students from Bobcat Build and other volunteers work with Lions to get the Tube Rental ready for a season of fun on the San Marcos River.

Buda Country Fair and Weiner Dog Races

Since its inception in 1996, this annual country fair has become an extremely popular spring event—beginning with a Pet Parade, crowning of the best dressed Weiner Dog, followed by the now nationally-known "Wiener Dog Races". The event has grown so popular in recent years that the Buda Weiner Dog Races now attract around 400 racers each year (that's 1,600 very short legs). Although Buda claims the trademarked status of "Wiener

Dog Capital of Texas," a significant number of the dogs are out-of-towners (and out-of-staters).

With qualifying races on Saturday and Sunday, the highlight is the run for the roses Sunday afternoon. Participants come from all over the country for this exciting event. In addition to the races, the Buda Lions Club sponsors the Buda Country Fair which consists of a BBQ Cook-off, Tolbert-sanctioned Chili Cook-off on Saturday, dessert bake-off and live auction, and the crowning of the best-dressed dog. The chili cookers compete for points that qualify them for the world-famous Terlingua International Chili Championship. There is live entertainment throughout the weekend, along with food booths and arts and craft vendors. Proceeds from this annual spring event are donated back to local, state and worldwide charities, scholarships and community projects.

Remembrances of District Governors

It was noted that Tom B. Ward was a District Governor in 2-E1 from Breckenridge, Texas until he moved to Austin, where his daughter, Ann lived and was a contributing member of the Austin Founders Club.

1980-1981
Under DG Don L. Mayer's leadership, the District achieved the District Membership Growth Award for 350+ net gain in membership and the District Extension Award for net gain of nine clubs. Both awards were presented in recognition of the greatest net gain in membership and clubs for North and South America!

Before the start of his year, DG Don successfully convinced LCI to allow the District Governor to conduct official Club visits at scheduled Zone meetings. That allowed DG Don to meet his work obligations in his private practice, while still meeting his Club visit requirements for more than 100 clubs. The results were very satisfactory, and significantly increased attendance at Zone meetings all over the District.

2003-2004
One of DG Dennis Heitkamp's major goals for the year was to achieve a positive growth in net membership. With hard work, focus, leadership and

dedication, the goal was achieved. For the first time in a number of years the District ended the year with +36 Lions. When DG Dennis served as Council Chair of MD2 in 2012-2013, the Council adopted a goal for MD-2 to end the Lion year with a positive membership growth, which had not been achieved for several years. Again, with hard work, focus, leadership and dedication, the goal was achieved with +237 Lions.

2010-2011

One of DG Mike Smith's goals for the year was to continue the involvement of women Lions in the District. Under his leadership, the District achieved an increase in membership of women in our Lions clubs for the second consecutive year. The District also led MD2 with the largest number of Leos and Leo clubs.

2011-2012

During DG Gary Cocanougher's year, a disaster struck in the District which brought together many Lions—not only from this District but other Districts as well. Beginning on September 2, 2011, massive wildfires broke out in the Central Texas area, and thousands of lives were changed because of the devastation of the wildfires. Pflugerville, Leander/Cedar Park, and Steiner Ranch were impacted. Spicewood and Bastrop received the most extensive damage. Lions from all over the District and the state began contributing resources through their clubs. The District applied for (and received) a $2,000 emergency grant from Texas Lions Foundation which was used to purchase $25 gift cards for the Spicewood Lions Club to distribute to victims in their area. A $10,000 grant from LCI was also received. In Smithville, a collection center was set up, and District 2-S5 Governor Andy Gonzales also received a $10,000 grant from LCI. Working together, Lions of Texas overcame this tragedy and showed what Lionism is all about.

2012-2013

In DG J. P. Kirksey's year, the Early Childhood Vision Screening program was expanded and reenergized with new leadership, a new philosophy of service, a new name–KidSight Vision Screening– and new equipment. The Spot vision screening instrument was adopted as the standard for all clubs, and a cost-sharing program was established for clubs to purchase Spot instruments to be owned and insured by the District. In 2015, the District had seven machines for use by all clubs at events hosted by the club, with more machines planned.

After experiencing four consecutive years of membership decline, DG J. P. challenged the clubs to reverse the trend. Clubs accepted the challenge, and the District experienced a positive net membership gain for the year.

A new era of Lionism in District 2-S3 was initiated with the organization of the first successful Campus Club–the Lions Club at the University of Texas. Under the leadership of enthusiastic President Jee Ho Kang, the club held their charter night in September 2012 with more than 100 members as charter members. PIP Jimmy Ross congratulated the club and encouraged the new Lions to excel. Accepting that challenge, the Club continues to thrive with regular service projects and involvement by all members. In 2015, another Campus Club was organized at Texas State University in San Marcos.

Notable Events

On January 18, 2016, the Austin Founder Lions Club celebrated 100 years of Service Through Lionism. A gala, held in the Bob Bullock Texas State History Museum on January 9, featured Immediate Past International President Joe Preston as the keynote speaker. PIP Preston noted that the Austin club was the first to celebrate their centennial and congratulated the club on its long history and legacy of service.

District Governors

1966-1967	E. B. "Tex" Mayer* – La Grange Noon
1967-1968	Roland Dansby – Bryan Noon
1968-1969	Dexter Anderson* – Eagle Lake Noon
1969-1970	Charlie Briggs III – Bryan Breakfast
1970-1971	William J. "Bill" Kolodzie – New Braunfels Noon
1971-1972	David Kahlich – Weimer
1972-1973	William H. "Bill" Raschke* – Austin Founder
1973-1974	Freddie Wolters* – College Station Noon
1974-1975	Harold Love* – Rockdale
1975-1976	Joe Al Picone – Brenham Evening
1976-1977	Julius Stephens* - Lockhart

1977-1978	Marvin J. Nite* – San Marcos
1978-1979	Mark Anderson – Eagle Lake Noon
1979-1980	J. L. Akridge* – Georgetown Evening
1980-1981	Dr. L. Donald Mayer – La Grange Noon
1981-1982	Gordon B. Richardson - Caldwell
1982-1983	Lindall C. "Lin" Rose – New Braunfels Evening
1983-1984	Dr. Jay Williams* – College Station Noon
1984-1985	Jack W. Wise* – New Braunfels Noon
1985-1986	David H. Slider* – Austin North Austin
1986-1987	Joe Robinson* - Kyle
1987-1988	Ralph Henry* – Navasota
1988-1989	W. E. "Webe" Ray* - Bulverde
1989	**District 2-S3 split and District 2-S5 was formed; Texas now has 16 Districts**

District 2-S3

1989-1990	Leo Ogea – Rockdale
1990-1991	G. W. McConico* – Austin Capitol City
1991-1992	James T. "Tom" Lokey* – Austin Founder
1992-1993	Roy H. Byars* - Blanco
1993-1994	Dr. W. C. "Bill" Daniels – San Marcos
1994-1995	Charles Hampton – Austin West Austin
1995-1996	Melvin Chambers* – Austin Capitol City
1996-1997	Fred Novak* – Spring Branch-Bulverde
1997-1998	William T. "Bill" Phillips – New Braunfels Evening
1998-1999	Thomas "Tom" Galbreath* - Rockdale
1999-2000	George Sotack* – Spring Branch-Bulverde
2000-2001	J. Elwood Arnold * - Balcones
2001-2002	Ron Knott – San Marcos Noon
2002-2003	Dr. Morris Treadwell* – Austin West Austin
2003-2004	Dennis Heitkamp – New Braunfels Noon
2004-2005	LuNan Ogea* – Rockdale
2005-2006	Gilbert "Gil" Burrell – Manor
2006-2007	Angela "Angie" Nicholson – Liberty Hill
2007-2008	Lester Stockhorst – New Braunfels Noon
2008-2009	Charles Handrick – Buda

2009-2010   Larry Nicholson – Liberty Hill

2010-2011   Michael "Mike" Smith – New Braunfels Breakfast

2011-2012   Gary Cocanougher – Georgetown Noon

2012-2013   James. P. "J.P." Kirksey – Austin Founder

2013-2014   Frank Kinald – Georgetown Evening

2014-2015   Len Heimer – New Braunfels Noon

2015-2016   Michael "Mike" Smith – New Braunfels Breakfast

2016-2017   John Lyon - Wimberley

Deceased

TEXAS LIONS HALL OF FAME

1972   PID E. B. "Tex" Mayer * - La Grange Noon

1978   PDG Joe Parr *

1980   PDG Joe Franks *

1982   PDG Robert Konnecke * - Seguin

1985   PDG Dexter Anderson * - Eagle Lake

1989   PCC Lindall C Rose - New Braunfels Evening

1992   PDG Willie Kocurek * - Austin Founder

1995   PDG Jack Wise * - New Braunfels

1998   PDG Roy Byars * - Blanco

2001   PDG Bill Kolodzie - New Braunfels

2004   PDG JL Akridge * - Georgetown Evening

2007   Lion J P Kirksey - Austin Founder

2010   PDG Dr. Bill Daniels - San Marcos

2013   CC Dennis Heitkamp - New Braunfels

Deceased

Compiled by Lion PDG J. P. Kirksey
March 24, 2015

A Brief History of District 2S4

At the beginning of 2014-15 year, there were 82 clubs in District 2S4, with a total of 2,464 members. The first club was the Galveston Lions Club, chartered on January 26, 1922. Four other clubs were chartered in the 1920s: Victoria, Wharton, Yoakum and Angleton. Six new clubs were added in the 1930s: Woodsboro, Rosenberg, Alvin, Cuero, Texas City and Yorktown. One of the Texas City charter members is still active in the club.

Twenty clubs were chartered in the 1940s—half while World War II was going on. These were Bay City, Hallettsville, East Bernard, Sugar Land, Dickinson, Port Lavaca, El Campo, Freeport Host, Sweeny, Lake Jackson, Needville, Brazoria, LaMarque, Boling, Goliad, Pearland, Refugio, Edna, Palacios and First Capital West Columbia.

Only five clubs were formed in the 1950s. These were Victoria Boulevard, Louise, League City, Galveston West End, and Stafford-Missouri City. The 1960s showed a spurt of growth again with eight new clubs: Texas City Noon, Santa Fe, Rosenberg-Fort Bend, Port Lavaca Noonday, Ganado, Angleton Noon, Austwell-Tivoli and League City Evening. At this point in history, there were 44 of the 82 Lion's clubs which still exist today.

Only eight more clubs were formed before the new millennium. In the 1970s, two new clubs were born—Brazosport Evening and Missouri Blueridge. The 1980s were better with the addition of four new clubs: Texas City Mainland, Bay City Evening, Manvel and Brazosport Breakfast. New club formations slipped again in the 1990s with only two new clubs: Skidmore-Tynan and Baycliff-San Leon Bayside.

In the new millennium, District Governors wanted to grow the district and greatly increase the number of new clubs. There was also a lot of emphasis placed on retaining older clubs. Several went from town-to-town, knocking on doors and talking to businesses. The results were staggering. In the 2000s, eight new clubs were formed: Moulton, Pearland-Silverlake, Fulshear-Simonton, Friendswood, Galveston West Beach, Seadrift, Port O'Connor and Beeville. Since 2010, 22 new clubs have been formed, and the decade is only half over! These new clubs include: Hitchcock, Alvin Noon, Pearland West, Matagorda, Dickinson Noon, Shiner, Bolivar Peninsula, Blessing Eflm, Bloomington-Placedo, Kemah, El Campo Lady,

Victoria Downtown, Bayou Vista, Van Vlek, Brazosport Lady Noon, Bay City Lady, Clute, Sargent, Surfside, Richmond, Freeport-Brazosport Noon and Hitchcock Noon. Hitchcock Noon is our newest Lions club, chartered on June 23, 2014.

History of District 2-S5

PREFACE
Lionism comes to Texas!

It began in 2-S-3 with the formation of the Austin Founders Club on January 18, 1916 prior to the first Lions Convention held in Dallas on October 8, 1917. "The International Association of Lions Clubs". Illinois was designated District 1 in honor of Founder Melvin Jones (his home state). Texas was designated District 2 and continued to operate that way until 1930, when the "S" from TEXAS was added. At that time, District S2 was the third largest of 5 districts representing 53 counties and 48,888 square miles.

Texas' District S2 boasted of four Founder Clubs—Austin, Houston, Beaumont and Port Arthur—each of which had representatives at the memorable Dallas Convention in 1917.

In the first few years, the State Convention was held in cities in those areas—Houston (second and eighth) and Beaumont (fourth and seventh). Then in 1943, as a war-time economy measure, the work was divided into districts 2-S1, 2-S2 and 2-S3—continuing that way until the 1959 "grand rearrangement" of the entire state when District 2-S4 was added. That division continued until 1989, when District 2-S3, with approximately 125 clubs, was divided into two districts—basically east and west—and District 2-S5 was created. The eastern portion became 2-S5 and the western portion remained 2-S3.

Chartered on August 26 1923, the oldest club in District 2-S5 is the Bryan Lions Club, commonly referred to as Bryan Noon Lions. Lions Clubs International Founder and Secretary General, Melvin Jones, attended their 25th Anniversary in 1949. Julian C. Hyer, International President 1931, spoke at their 50th Anniversary in 1973.

District 2-S5 has benefited greatly from the service and contributions of six living PDGs and others who have passed away who served as District Governors in S-3 before our district became 2-S5. Those PDGs have remained active throughout the years and served the district in many capacities, including cabinet members, committee and convention chairmen, zone chairmen, members of the boards of the Texas Lions Camp and Lone Star Lions Eye Bank, and as trusted advisors.

Those still with us include PDG Charlie Briggs, PDG David Kahlich, PDG PID Joe Al Picone, PDG Mark Anderson, PDG Don Mayer and PDG Gordon Richardson. Several of these distinguished PDGs have been inducted into the Texas Lions Hall of Fame. Here is biographical information on some of them.

PDG Charlie P. Briggs-2-S3, 1969-70

Joined the Calvert Lions Club in April 1956 and was President in 1959-60 and served as Secretary for 8 years, served on the District 2-S3 Cabinet as Zone Chairman (twice), Deputy District Governor (twice), District Tail Twister, elected in a contested race as Deputy District Governor At Large in1968. As District Governor 1969, was installed in Tokyo, Japan, at the first International Convention held in the Far East, and named State Treasurer by the Council of Governors. During his year, organized two clubs, including the first non-hearing club, Ephitha, in Austin. International President Dick Bryan was speaker at the Charter Night in his only visit to Texas that year. Led the Texas Lions in collecting over $32,000, which was sent to the Lions of Mississippi for their rebuilding projects after Hurricane Camille and visited all 74 clubs plus numerous trips around the state working for PDG E.B. Tex Mayer, who was elected International Director at the Lions International Convention in 1970.

Lion Briggs holds a Membership Advancement Key for sponsoring new members, Five Extension Awards for organizing new clubs, including Bryan Breakfast in which he is currently a Charter Member, the Harry Reasonover Award for Outstanding Lion in 2-S3, and the Lions International Presidents Award from IP Ebb Grindstaff for his work in the election of Lion Ebb. He continued to work, helping to originate the first District Trading Pin in 2-S3 and with his wife, Mary Kathryn, designed over 20 District and State trading pins. Served from District 2-S3 and 2-S5 on the Long Range Committee at the Lions Camp in Kerrville, and as Chairman, helped develop a Master Plan for improvements and expansion of the camp.

PDG David E. Kahlich

Joined the Weimar Lions Club in December 1955, sponsored by Lion Jim Hluchanek. My first service project was working with Lion Jim to get electric power to a farm house for a blind lady and her daughter to give them safer living conditions. Lion Jim continued to mentor me for many years. I was elected club secretary for 1956-57 and attended my first District Convention in Galveston in May 1957. We were in District 2-S-2 at this time, and Weimar Lions were moved to District 2-S-3 in 1959, and in 1989 became part of District 2-S-5. I have been in three Districts and have never moved. This has been due to the growth of Lionism in our area. I have served as Zone Chairman, Deputy District Governor, and Deputy District Governor at Large before being elected District Governor in 1971-72 and I was Treasurer for our Council of Governors. Our Council designed a new Texas Lion Uniform for members and their spouses. Orders and payment were sent to me and then forwarded to Imperial Costumes of Dallas via Council Chairman Wally Franklin also of Dallas. The price was $15.00 plus postage and handling. This vest design is still being used today. A white western cut long long sleeve shirt and khaki pants with either black boots or shoes completed the uniform. White plastic western hats were furnished to all parade participants in Mexico City (1972). Our Lionesses wore the same vest over a white long sleeve sheath dress made from a Simplicity Pattern. Dress length to be at the middle of the knee and white walking shoes completed the uniform.

The 1972 Mid-Winter Conference was held at the Ramada Inn of College Station. Dr. Jack Williams, President of Texas A&M was the speaker. His topic was a review of the book "Lessons of History". Pre-registration was $4.50 per person and attendance was high. Bill Scott and Freddie Wolters were co-chairman. District 2-S-3 had the largest Mid-Winter conference of the fifteen Districts in Texas.

The District Convention that year and many other conventions were held at the Villa Capri Hotel in Austin (now a parking lot for the President LBJ Library).

The Lions year 1971-72 for 2-S-3 started with 82 clubs and three new Clubs were Chartered – Bryan Breakfast, Grimes County, and Carmine.

This qualified me for the 100% District Governor Award.

PDG Kahlich was active in Lion Ebb Grindstaff's campaign for International Director at the Mexico City International Convention in 1972. He also supported International Director Ebb's campaign for International President in 1979 in Canada. In Lions year 1971, PDG Kahlich installed Lion Joe Al Picone as President of the Brenham Evening Lions Club; then, in 1975, supported Lion Joe Al for Governor, and supported him again in 2011 in Seattle when he ran for International Director for Texas.

Since 1970, PDG Kahlich has worked with Texas Lions Camp to provide a summer experience for diabetic and disabled children by serving on the Camp Improvement committee, chairing the committee for 10 of those years. He was appointed to an ad hoc committee of three members in 1991 to develop a master plan for the camp. This plan was adopted in 1992, funded by CAMPaign 2000 (2.5 million), and Phase I and II completed in May 2000. PDG Kahlich was elected to the Camp's executive board in 1994, and served as President 1999-2000. Texas Lions Camp has served over 65,000 handicapped children since 1953. PDG Kahlich is presently a Permanent Director of the Camp and serves on the Finance and Security Committees.

PDG Kahlich showed his dedication and commitment to the 2-S3 Eye Bank by serving as its 6th President, and by serving as Secretary and President of the Eye Bank Association of Texas. In 1979 he was recognized for his efforts by District 2-S-3 with the Harry Reasonover Award, the highest honor the district bestows on a Lion.

PDG Kahlich was inducted into the Texas Lions Hall of Fame in the year 2000.

PID Joe Al Picone

A Lion since 1966 in the Brenham Evening Lions Club, he has held many offices within the association, including club president, district governor in 1975-76, council chair 1998-99, state membership chair and state Campus club chair. While Lt Governor in 1974-75, he was instrumental in forming the Lions Eye Bank of Dist. 2-S3 and was a charter director and 1st Vice President. He also served as a member of the host committee for the Ft. Worth, Texas Forum, Chair of the Texas Lions Long-Range Planning Committee, Chair of the Texas Lions Camp By-Laws Committee and president of the Past District Governors Association.

In recognition of his service to the association, he has received numerous awards including the 100% District Governor Award, Harry Reasonover Award 1981-82, two International President's Certificates of Appreciation, four International President's Medals, an International President's Leadership Award, the Supreme Extension Award for 11 new Lions clubs, the Global Membership Key Award for sponsoring over 250 new Lions, and the Ambassador of Goodwill Award, the highest honor the association gives to its members. He was also inducted into the Texas Lions Hall of Fame and is a 15 diamond Progressive Melvin Jones Fellow, a progressive Jack Wiech Fellow, a Texas Lions Fellow and a Celeste and Harrison Shepherd Fellow. In addition to his Lions activities, PID Picone is active in numerous professional and community organizations, including serving as Chair of the City Planning and Zoning Commission. He has also served as president of the Board of City Development, and the Washington County Chamber of Commerce. He was inducted into the Brenham High School Hall of Fame and the Blinn College Hall of Fame, and was a graduate of Baylor University. In 2013 he retired as President of the Blinn College Foundation.

He has received numerous honors, including the Washington County Man of the Year Award and being named to the Phi Theta Kappa International Hall of Honor and the Brenham Maifest Hall of Fame.

Joe Al Picone, from Brenham, Texas was the first Council Chairman elected from Dist. 2-S5 in 1998-99 and was elected to serve a two-year term as a director of Lions Clubs International at the association's 94th International Convention held in Seattle, Washington July 4-8, 2011 becoming District 2-S5's first International Director. Past International Director Picone and his wife, Merle, also a Lion, have two sons and one granddaughter.

PDG Don Mayer

Served as MD-2 Council Chairman in 1981-82 while our district was still a part of 2-S3 while the District grew to 110 clubs which called for a division of the District, and in 1992 was a Board Appointee by President Rohit Mehta.

District 2-S5, 1989 - 2015

Lion Clarence Wolfshohl was the first District Governor of the newly-created district 2-S5. The officers and members had been reorganized into a brand new district much smaller than the one they had been a part of before. Membership is very important to the Lions of Texas, and having gone from being the largest district in the state to one much smaller did not set well with Governor Wolfshohl, Past District Governor Freddie Wolters and others, so they set out to make a change.

Under their leadership, District 2-S5 quickly grew, and within a very short time our district became "King of the Hill" in membership once again (and remained there for many years thereafter).

1989 – 1990

Clarence Wolfshohl of the Giddings Breakfast Lions Club served as Governor. Clarence Wolfshohl, PDG was inducted into the Texas Lions Hall of Fame in 2012. As a new Lion, PDG Wolfshohl developed the concept of being "Dedicated to Growth for Strength in Service" which has had a lasting mark on District 2-S5 and Lions Clubs International. He was well qualified to receive this honor.

In 1980, Lion Wolfshohl was invited to join the Giddings Club. Lions had made an impression on Clarence as a child when a family tragedy saw Lions in his home community provide much-needed help to his family.

In 1981, Clarence became a charter member of the Giddings Breakfast Lions Club, and in 1982 he became Club President, and from 1983-89 served as Club Secretary.

During this time frame, what is now District 2-S5 was a part of District 2-S3. From1984-89, Clarence served as Zone Chair, Deputy District Governor and Lieutenant Governor. As Zone Chair, he structured the Zone meetings around membership, with District leaders emphasizing membership at each meeting and all Lions gatherings. This structure resulted in a net gain in membership both years he served as Zone Chair.

As District Governor, he set a goal of making District 2-S5 the leading

District in membership within five years. Extension meetings were held around the District, with Zone Chairs and Club Officers stressing membership. The District rallied around the slogan, "Dedicated to Growth for Strength in Service" and it was a great year. Looking back, there was an increase of 322 members within the District adding nine new clubs. Forty-seven Presidents received the 100% Presidents Award. District 2-S5 ended the year with the largest membership in the state, retaining that status most of the years.

Through the years, Clarence has been honored for his dedication to Lionism, receiving the Club Lion of the Year, E.B. "Tex" Mayer Award, PDG Association Membership and Extension Awards, Zone Chair and Deputy District Governor Membership Awards, International Leadership and International Presidents Award, 100% District Governor, Supreme Extension Award and Senior Master Key Award. Lion Clarence Wofshohl is truly an outstanding Lion and Leader in District 2-S5 and Multiple District 2.

1990 – 1991
Clinton Blezinger of the Industry West End Lions Club served as Governor.

1991 – 1992
Felix W. Meyers (deceased) of the of the Navasota and Madisonville Lions Clubs served as Governor.

1992 – 1993
Elden W. Korenek (deceased) of the Wallis Lions Club served as Governor.

1993 – 1994
Lee Boyd Montgomery (deceased) of the Seguin Noon Lions Club served as Governor.

1994 – 1995
Ron Gay of the College Station Noon Lions Club served as Governor.

1995 – 1996
Ray Criswell (deceased) of the Bryan Breakfast Lions Club served as Governor.

1996 – 1997
Alan Schulke served as Governor.

1997 – 1998
Michael R. Morgan of the Giddings Breakfast Lions Club served as Governor, and also served as membership chairman of the MD2—traveling to all the Districts with his enthusiasm and dedication—even though he had two daughters in high school, one playing basketball and a good one also.

1998 – 1999
Jessie Bryan of the Caldwell Burleson County Lions Club served as District Governor and was the first woman Governor in our district. She was a good one and is still active, and comes to all State meetings and only the sixth in MD-2. Lion Jessie served as Council Secretary during her year on the MD-2 Council. District 2-S5 had a plus in membership that year and organized one new club.

Pat Beavers served as Secretary, Lynne Matcek served as Treasurer. Lion Ron Heinemeyer served as Vice-Governor. The state convention was in College Station, Texas at the Hilton Hotel. PDG Joe Al Picone, also of District 2-S5, served as Council Chairman.

PDG Bryan has served the Lions of Texas in many capacities and received numerous awards for her service. She has served as State Chairman for Leader Dogs for the Blind, served two terms as Texas Lions Foundation Trustee. She has also been a Texas Lions Camp Director.

Her many awards include: A Jack Wiech Fellowship and a brick at the Texas Lions Camp, a Texas Lions Foundation Fellow, a Life Member of the Past District Governor's Association of Texas, the Ed Flood Award, the International Leadership Award from PIP Frank Moore, the President's Award from PIP Barry Palmer, and numerous Lone Star Lions Eye Bank awards.

1999 – 2000
Ron Heinemeyer of the Seguin Noon Lions Club served as the District Governor with Danny Zitterich from La Grange serving as Vice Governor. Jim Johnson served as Cabinet Secretary and James Vordenbaum served as District 2-S5 Treasurer; both from Seguin.

The 1999-2000 International President was James E. "Jim" Ervin from Albany, Georgia whose international theme for the year was; "Each One Reach One". District 2-S5, through the district theme; "DO IT" made a real effort to improve membership growth in 1999-2000. We were fairly successful by having a positive 90 in net membership growth and forming and chartering a new club in Waelder, known as the Waelder New Millenium Lions Club. "DO IT" was the district pin to reflect the district's effort to get things done.

In this Lions year, our district, along with Lions throughout the state of Texas, celebrated the 50th anniversary of the Texas Lions Camp that was chartered in 1949. IP Jim Ervin, in August of 1999, as part of the 50th celebration; dedicated the new swimming pool and miniature golf course at Texas Lions Camp.

PID Ray Hughston from Brownsville, Texas, was our keynote speaker at our Mid-winter Conference in Giddings, Texas. Our 2-S5 District Convention, held in Seguin, with keynote speaker PID Joseph Marcheggiani from Carmel, Indiana.

PDG David E. Kahlich, Weimar Lions Club, was inducted into the Texas Lions Hall of Fame at our state convention in May 2000 in San Angelo, Texas.

Seguin Noon Lions celebrated their club's 60th anniversary on March 9, 2000.

A new Leos Club was formed by the Brenham Evening Lions Club on April 19, 2000.

Lion Mel Grones, Seguin Sunrise Lions, was presented the E.B. "Tex" Mayer Award—the top recognition to an individual Lion Member in District 2-S5.

The Robert E. Koennecke award is presented annually to the Lions Club in the district that is judged to have rendered the greatest service and carried out the most effective activities in the community. The club selected in 2-S5 in 1999-2000 was the Sheridan Lions Club.

It was indeed a pleasure and rewarding to have served as 2-S5 District Governor in 1999-2000 – PDG Ron Heinemeyer.

PDG PCC Heinemeyer was inducted into the Texas Lions Hall of Fame in 2009.

Here is his nomination letter:

RON HEINEMEYER, PDGPast District Governor Ron Heinemeyer has lived the Lions Motto; "We Serve", in many areas of his life including his community, church, school, family and lionistic activities. He is well qualified to receive this honor. Lion Heinemeyer joined the Seguin Evening Lions Club as a Charter member in 1965. Later he transferred to the Seguin Noon Club where he continues his Lions work today.

He has served both clubs in many offices and capacities; including Committee Chairs, Director, Vice-President, President and Past President. While President of the Evening Club, a new Club was Chartered in McQueeney and a Leo Club was Chartered in the Seguin High School. As President of both Clubs, Lion Ron was awarded the 100% President Award for progress made during the year. He is a leader who plans well and goes a bit extra to ensure success.

At the District level, Lion Ron has served in many capacities. Some of these roles include Zone 1-A and Region 1 Chair, Co-Chaired two Mid-Winter Conferences, Co-Chaired two District Conventions, served as District Diabetes Chair, District Leadership Chair and currently serves as District Extension Chair. Unofficially, he has mentored many Seguin area Lions as they prepare to assume new leadership roles in the District.

During the 1999-2000 Lions year, Lion Heinemeyer served as District Governor for District 2-S5. The District motto reflected his enthusiasm for Lionism and the urgency to implement programs and procedures to reach more people. The motto was "Do It". Meaning if it would improve Lionism —"Do It". A well-planned year resulted in a net gain of 90+ members in the District. For his leadership, he received the 100% District Governors Award, Lions International Leadership Award and the Lions Clubs International Founders Membership Growth Award.

Lion Ron has represented 2-S5 as a trustee of the Texas Lions Foundation, member of the Long Range Planning Committee and is in a 3 year term as MD-2 Extension Chair.

PDG Ron is a Melvin Jones Fellow, Texas Lions Foundation Fellow and a Life Member of Texas Lions Camp and Lone Star Lions Eye Bank. LION RON HEINEMEYER IS TRULY AN OUTSTANDING LION AND LEADER IN DISTRICT 2-S5 AND MULTIPLE DISTRICT 2

2000 – 2001

Danny "Zee" Zitterich of the LaGrange Noon Lions Club served as Governor, and is still active at all meetings of the District and State.

2001 – 2002

Uel Stockard of the Bryan Noon Lions Club served as Governor. The motto for the year was "The Year of the Club."

Based on strong research, the year's plan centered around the fact that "Voluntary Organizations Have A Life Cycle." Two approaches to extending the "Life Cycle" of a voluntary organization were included in training, Zone meetings, Mid-Winter Conference, Newsletter articles, etc. The two actions include, (1) Bring new members into the organization or (2) change the program of work for the organization. Both efforts are successful when the organizations plan of work included projects of interest to the membership (not just a small percent of the group). The Cabinet budget funds for Andy Rodriquez, the Retention Chair, to obtain and prepare materials for training and use by Club Leadership.

The Lions Year began with 2,817 members in 69 Lions Clubs. In May 2002, the Aggieland Lions Club was chartered as the first Collegiate Club in District 2-S5. Seven new Zone Chairs were recruited and new Chairs were included in leadership roles on the District Cabinet.

The year concluded with a few less members, but with new leadership and a different way to view retention.

2002 – 2003

Edward "Edd" Kelarek (deceased) of the Hilltop Lakes Lions Club served as Governor. Pat Beavers of Caldwell served as Vice District Governor.

2003 – 2004

Pat Beavers of Caldwell served as District Governor and Myron Koehler of Bryan served as Vice District Governor.

2004 – 2005

Myron Koehler (deceased) of the Bryan Breakfast Lions Club served as Governor and Waldo Dalchau served as Vice District Governor. John Rauser of College Station served as District Secretary/Newsletter Editor and Lori Eike of Bryan served as District Treasurer. The theme that year was "Success Through Teamwork".

2005 – 2006

Waldo Dalchau of Brenham served as District Governor, with Charles Villeneuve serving as Vice District Governor. Dr. Wilfred Dietrich of Brenham served as District Secretary and Gregory Carll served as District Treasurer. The theme that year was "Never Stand Still".

It was during this year that District 2-S5 was trying to implement the MERL (Membership, Extension, Retention, and Leadership) theory within our district structure. Although the concept had been available for several years, there hadn't been enough information from LCI to lend guidance toward its introduction into our District's organization. Similarly, previous district leaders had been reluctant to embrace the notion…thinking it would not come to fruition and it would merely "go away".

The newly-installed DG had just gone through the process of appointing new members to the MERL Team for 3-year terms and everyone was wanting to know what they were supposed to do and when they were supposed to do it. The DG's dilemma was simple, he had:

1. Limited knowledge of the MERL concept because the previous leadership failed to embrace it, thus, nobody had taken the time to learn and understand it

2. Lions in positions of leadership who were seeking direction and guidance. Especially those who had just made a 3-year commitment…the MERL Team

3. Many complaints about how terrible training sessions had been in previous years and how grassroots Lions felt like it was a waste of their time to attend training. And, attendance at training sessions was extremely low.

4. Other cabinet officers, Region and Zone Chairs included, complaining that there was little to no training for their positions and wanted more direction and guidance

5. Previous Leadership Chairmen chose PDGs to train secretaries, treasurers and presidents because of the PDG name, not because of their ability to train or expertise in the subject to be trained. And, probably most pressing, LCI was issuing directives and warnings

that ALL reporting would have to be done "online" by the end of the year…snail mail reporting, MMRs and most correspondence would become "a thing of the past".

Governor Dalchau decided that to move forward and grow, we were in need of a team effort. So, being an ex-basketball coach, he went back to his roots of coaching and assembled a group from which he would form a "Winning Team" that could tackle all the challenges identified above.

A meeting was called in August of that year that included; the DG and VDG, MERL Chairs, Region Chairs, Zone Chairs and others whose experience might be beneficial to this assembly. The meeting was held in "roundtable" fashion and designed to encourage input and share ideas. We broached the subjects of:

1. Embracing the MERL concept because it wasn't operating as a team

2. Ineptness of current training

3. Needs in training and information dissemination

4. District's capabilities and resources

The group decided:

1. There were many areas of interest (MERL, Officers, Reporting) receiving little to no training and that existing training was grossly inadequate because of trainer limitations

2. LCI was introducing more and more information, training and expectations through technology which wasn't being used or implemented by district leaders

3. LCI had higher expectations of club secretaries and treasurers, especially in the technology area

4. There needed to be a higher degree of understanding and implementation of the MERL concept at the club level

5. Grassroots Lions were seeking to be "fed" in a more professional manner by qualified, experienced trainers…they wanted a higher level of substance for their commitment of attendance at training.

Immediately after brainstorming about the problems, solutions began to materialize from those gathered. District leaders and members of the cabinet asked, "Why can't we employ technology into our meetings by making presentations on PowerPoint to encourage the use of technology tools like a projector, laptop and PowerPoint?" They concluded that an added bonus would be how much money we could save on printing minutes, reports, etc. The idea was implemented and continues today.

The Leadership Chairman, Lion Andy Rodriguez, asked what courses should be taught and a long list of ideas emerged. Armed with that information, he was able to direct his attention toward the question, "How can we achieve these goals?" He wrote a plan to include these steps:

1. Developed a District Training Team by identifying potential trainers by asking district and club leaders

    a. Who's doing the best job in officer positions?

    b. Who is tech-savvy?

    c. Who trains or teaches for a living?

    d. Which of the potential trainers has the time and resources to assist the district's needs and efforts?

2. Identified and targeted potential trainers geographically so they would be spread throughout the district to keep driving distances to a minimum.

3. Sought and identified resources needed for training

    a. No-cost facilities with ample space and breakout rooms

    b. Equipment that could be borrowed

        i.   Laptops

        ii. Projectors

        iii. Screens

        iv. Easels

4. Developed training modules based on LCI materials and guidelines that would satisfy the wish list of training topics

5. Set "Spring Training" dates for district and club officers

6. Set other training dates in conjunction with other district meetings

7. Set a date for "Fall Training" to develop Certified Guiding Lions

8. Implemented the plan

There was NO money in the budget for this Leadership plan. The team begged and borrowed anything and everything we could. However, armed with the fantastic success and results of the Training Team and high attendance at training sessions, the Leadership Chairman submitted a budget proposal to enhance the program even further, and $500 was placed in the budget to buy equipment and pay for class materials the next year. The following year, $750 was budgeted and that same amount was budgeted for the next couple of years, allowing us to purchase more equipment, while continuing to cover the cost of class materials.

This year, the District Governor wanted to focus the team's efforts in an area that required a little more funding, so the budget line item was increased to $1,000. That focus was so successful that we will be able to decrease the line item to probably $500 for this coming year because we have purchased the equipment we needed in previous years, and there isn't any large effort requiring more money. The only expenditures required this coming year will be for class materials.

In other words, we made equipment purchases over several years to develop and grow our program. Now we don't need a large budget because it has already been developed. The only time we need extra funding is when there are "special" training essentials.

In a nutshell, "If you run your district like a business, you need funding to operate the business and train your employees to realize bigger and better results." The amount of your investment, whether it is money, time or other resources, will directly impact your ROI (Return On Investment). As the old saying goes, "You have to spend money to make money." In our situation, you have to spend money to achieve higher results in Lions education, Lions community service and Lions membership.

Lion Rodriguez recruited and trained experienced Lions to serve on the new training team. The new concept was not fully implemented until the following Lions year, but the effort continued with the full support of the new District Governor, Dr. Floyd Golan.

That year, Region 5 Chair John Rauser of the College Station Noon Lions Club, along with others in the area, committed to building a Habitat House. Lion Rauser received approval from Governor Dalchau and the district cabinet to apply for a grant from LCIF. At that time matching grants for up to one-half the cost of a house were made available if a qualifying family included one or more handicapped persons.

The Lions in the Aggieland, Bryan Breakfast, Bryan Evening, Bryan Noon, College Station Morning and College Station Noon Clubs contributed the funding to meet the matching portion of the grant and it was approved by the International Board of Directors.

On the day construction of the house began, Governor Dalchau attended the "Wall Raising" and offered congratulatory remarks to the new homeowners and the Lions participating in the funding and construction of the house.

All of the participating clubs took part in the wall raising and then took individual responsibility for different phases of construction. One club installed the drywall, and another installed the outdoor siding, another floor tile, and so on until the house was completed. The Aggieland Campus Club put on the finishing touches by planting the shrubbery and laying sod.

All of the participating clubs were represented on the day the keys were presented to the new owners.

After the family moved in, Lion Rauser went to visit them and noted that although the house was clean and well-kept, the furniture was in terrible condition. The husband, Mr. Bradford, was wheelchair bound and could not get his chair close enough to the dining table to enjoy a meal with the family.

The bed that Mr. and Mrs. Bradford slept on consisted of several ragged old mattresses stacked one on top of another.

The College Station Noon Club raised some additional funding, took the Bradford family furniture-shopping, and helped deliver and set up the new (used) furniture.

2006 – 2007

Charles Villeneuve of Seguin served as District Governor and Dr. Floyd Golan, of College Station, served as Vice District Governor. The Governor's theme was "We Serve – Together".

We finished the year with approximately 58 or 59 clubs and 2,475 Lions on the rolls. We started one new club, Geronimo Lions Club, just north of Seguin. Their actual Charter Night celebration was not until during the early administration of Floyd Golan. We had no major catastrophes to deal with that year. The year started with the International Convention in Boston which ended with the awesome performance of the Boston Pops Orchestra performing on July 4th over the Charles River – truly unbelievable! This was also the year that we saw a Texan installed as the International President of Lions Clubs International, Jimmy Ross from Quitique, Texas.

The year was marked by a steady maintenance of total membership and great projects throughout the district.

This was the year, which was initiated by DG Waldo Dalchau, that we saw the first team approach to training of club officers throughout the district. This was led by future DG Andy Rodriguez before the days of the current GLT concept. This idea caught on in other areas of the state and Andy Rodriguez has taken it to new heights. Great job, Andy!

2007 – 2008

Dr. Floyd A. Golan, College Station Noon Lions Club, served as District Governor. His Vice-District Governor was John Rauser, also of College Station Noon. DG Golan's Secretary was Lion John Simmang. Cabinet Treasurer was Lion Eric R. Wylie. The theme for the year was "Serving with Impact".

One of the significant events that happened during the 2007-08 Lions year was the implementation of a Leadership Development Committee, chaired by Lion Andy Rodriguez. The formation of this committee came as a result of a meeting with 2005-2006 District Governor Waldo Dalachau, 2006-2007, District Governor Charles Villeneuve and Lion Andy Rodriguez (Governor 2010-2011) and Vice-Governor Golan. These Lions determined to move District 2S-5 into the electronic era. As can be seen in the following paragraph, a plan was developed and put into action.

Lions International was making remarks Lions would need to be connected to the internet. They were going to do away with use of paper reporting forms. Lion Andy developed training sessions for Presidents, Secretaries, Treasurers and Board members. Our District began the year with about 25 percent of District clubs using internet. By the end of the 2007-2008 year, the District clubs had moved up to the 75% level of use. The following year the clubs nearly reached the 100% level.

Near the end of the 2007-08 year, information became available that all tax exempt organizations would be required to file a 1099 with the IRS, regardless of club income.

This became an item that Lions Andy's Leadership committee spent time in 2008-2009 getting all clubs ready to file the necessary paperwork with the IRS.

2008 – 2009

The 2008 – 2009 Lions year was led by District Governor John Rauser of the College Station Noon Lions Club, and Vice District Governor Lewis Simpson of the New Baden Camp Creek Lions Club. Lion Michael Bolton served as District Secretary and Lion Rosie Van Booven served as District Treasurer.

Lion Andy Rodriguez produced the district directories and helped design the Governor's pin.

The theme that year was "Serving together with pride" and throughout the year, the Governor's message was to encourage men and women to join together in service.

Hurricane Ike struck the Texas coast on September 13, 2008, killing 84 people and causing $19.3 billion in damage. Most of the district 2-S5 area was spared heavy damage, other than widespread utility outages and minor flooding. Lions throughout the district joined in service to their communities. One example is the Lions Club of Franklin. Their community was without power for several days and they organized a community cookout where people could bring food that would have otherwise spoiled and cook it on community grills set up by the Lions.

The Gonzales Lions led an effort to send food to the hurricane-stricken region. They contacted the local HEB Food Store and Kitchen Pride Mushroom Farms with an idea to collect and transport food. The HEB store agreed to assembled $20-$50 bags of food and kept them at the check-out counters with a simple sign...BUY THIS BAG OF FOOD FOR HURRICANE VICTIMS. Kitchen Pride Mushroom Farms donated the use of one of their delivery tractor-trailer rigs and driver to deliver the goods to the hurricane-affected area. Local patrons of the store, while shopping for their food needs, could add a bag of "hurricane groceries" to their bill. The idea received an overwhelming response. Customers didn't just buy the prepared bags...they were walking into the store and asking if they could buy pallets of food and water. The local newspaper and radio station got on board with advertising the day of the event, and folks began filling the trailer moments after the HEB store opened their doors for business that day. By early afternoon, the truck was fully loaded and was sent to a drop-off point in Houston where Texas Emergency Management officials requested the delivery.

Many other clubs in the district stepped up and served the needs of their communities. Some of the stories were never told, but no one was looking for rewards or recognition. The Lions of 2-S5 just did what Lions do. However, the Lions of District 2-S5 may have provided their most outstanding service by joining with Lions in the hardest hit areas to provide immediate emergency relief to the victims of the hurricane.

Governor Rauser was in Canada attending the USA Canada forum when he received a call From Lion Joe Franks in Giddings informing him that areas along the coast were in desperate need of assistance. Lion Franks had already spoken with PID Marshall Cooper about obtaining a TLF grant of $2,000 to aid the Lions in the southern districts. Governor Rauser contacted PID Cooper to secure the grant, then reached out to District 2-S4 Governor Howard Clayton to see what assistance was needed. Governor Clayton's only way of communicating was by his cell phone that he was able to charge from the power outlet in his car. Governor Clayton explained that he had received approval for a $10,000 LCIF disaster assistance grant, but had no way of using the money to purchase needed supplies, because everything in his area was shut down and they were completely cut off. They had no place to buy fuel or any of the necessary supplies.

Governor Rauser sent out a call for help to all of the 2-S5 clubs and a trailer load of bottled water, packaged food, diapers, baby food and baby supplies, along with feminine hygiene products, were soon on their way to Dickenson—paid for by contributions from Lions clubs and led by Vice District Governor Lewis Simpson and Lion Joe Franks. The Bellville Lions Club raised almost $20,000. They, too loaded a trailer and took it to the coast. Their effort was led by Lions Newton Boriack and Ernie Koy. Governor Clayton reimbursed some of the "grant eligible" expenses after he received the funding, but the contributions from the Lions of District 2-S5 were a gift given to help those in need and far exceeded his $10,000.

Once VDG Lewis Simpson got started helping the citizens of the coastal areas, there was no stopping him. His daughter was a member of a club in the Galveston area at that time, and the two of them teamed up with the Zone Chair and made numerous trips to that area to deliver water, food, clothing and other needed supplies.

Lions Ed and Deloris Mardis, along with Lion Nancy Ryan and her husband of the Hilltop Lakes Lions Club spent many days working at a shelter in the Galveston area helping to feed victims and relief workers.

Shortly after returning from Canada, the Governor was contacted by Lion Jason James, a member of the Bryan Evening Lions Club whose parents lived in Bridge City. Lion James asked if something could be done to help the children whose homes had been damaged by the winds and flooding. The families were being helped with emergency supplies, clothing, etc. but the children had lost all of their personal belongings, and parents were unable to address their needs because of all the other things they had to deal with. Governor Rauser contacted Lion Meredith Franks and asked if she would like to help organize a toy drive for the children of Bridge City. She was on it before she could even hang up the phone. Lion Meredith put the touch on the Lions of Giddings and local businesses, and in just a couple of days, had a rental truck full of toys ready to go. Lions from Giddings, College Station, Hilltop Lakes and other cities in 2-S5 pitched in. By the following Saturday morning, there was a convoy of Lions with toys on their way to Bridge City to deliver them.

District 2-S1 Governor Harold Yost was ill at the time, so PDG Stump Weatherford and VDG Charles Tarver were contacted and they arranged a location from which to distribute the toys—enlisting local Lions to help. The day before we left, Governor Rauser received a call from Lion Don Bailey of College Station whose wife, Nita, wanted to donate her collection of stuffed toys. We had been instructed to give only new toys, but she was so touched by the need of these children that Governor Rauser accepted a giant lawn and leaf bag full of them and took them along, not knowing what he was going to do with them.

The Bridge City Lions had publicized our coming and made arrangements for us to set up in front of the Chamber of Commerce Building. It had a circular drive out front and parents' were directed to drive through. Lion Meredith had sorted the toys by sex and age, and when a car pulled in to the driveway, someone would shout out "Girl 9" or "Boy 7" and a volunteer would pull the appropriate toy from the stack and present it to a very delighted child (and grateful, often tearful, parent). As it turned out, the collection of stuffed animals was by far the most popular with the smaller children. Those kids had been so traumatized by having their homes and possessions destroyed that they really needed something personal they could hold on to, and that is exactly what they did. Immediately upon receiving the stuffed toy, they put whatever else they had aside and hugged it tightly to their chest. Obviously, the toy was going to be sleeping with them that night and for several nights to come. It was the most rewarding experience I have ever had.

Later that year, a fire struck the Smithville area. It was minor compared to the fire that would come a few years later, but the Lions of Smithville worked to assist the victims and we were able to obtain another TLF grant to help with the relief effort.

I received a letter from the Zone Chair that VDG Simpson worked with thanking me and the Lions of District 2-S5 for coming to the aid of those so desperately in need of help. I carried that letter with me to every club visit I made throughout the remainder of the year and read it to the members there, so that they could know how greatly their efforts were appreciated and share the pride that I felt in being a Lion.

At the state convention that year when Lions from around the state were gathered for the last big meeting of the year, accolades and awards were presented to the District Governors who served in the areas hardest hit by the hurricane, but there was no mention made of District 2-S5.

When PDG Stump Weatherford took the podium to accept the award for District 2-S1, he said "You are rewarding the wrong people. The Lions of 2-S5 are the ones that should be rewarded. They came to our aid when we needed help. They went to other districts with food, water and the things that were needed the most and worked alongside us to help our communities. They reached out to help other districts and I don't think that has ever been done before." I was never so proud. We didn't have a plus in membership that year, but no one can tell me that we didn't have a good year. The men and women of District 2-S5 had truly served together. It had nothing to do with my leadership, and I actually had a very small part in it. It was just the character and nature of our Lions doing what Lions do. —PDG John Rauser

2009 – 2010

This Lions year was led by District Governor Lewis Simpson of the New Baden Camp Creek Lions Club, 1VDG Vicky Murray of the Giddings New Horizons Lions Club and 2VDG Andy Rodriguez of the Gonzales Noon Lions Club. Sherrie Hopkins of the Bryan Noon Club served as District Secretary and Don Bailey of the College Station Noon Club served as District Treasurer.

2010 – 2011

The 2010 – 2011 Lions year was led by District Governor Vicky Murray of the Giddings New Horizons Lions Club, 1VDG Andy Rodriguez of the Gonzales Noon Lions Club and 2VDG Ernie Koy of the Bellville Lions Club. Lion Sherrie Hopkins served as Cabinet Secretary and Lion Nicole McCoy served as Cabinet Treasurer.

District Governor Vicky served on the Council of Governors as the Council Treasurer.

The Washington County Ladies Lions Club was chartered during the year with 92 members.

The District Convention was held at Blinn College in Brenham, TX.

We were honored to have International Director Robert G. Smith as our convention speaker. Lion Michael Bolton was awarded the PDG Award for his outstanding and dedicated service over the years to District 2-S5. Lion Wesley Rodriguez, District Leo Chairman, and Lion Dr. Kenneth Gottwald, District Leadership Chairman, GLT District Coordinator and Zone Chairman were presented with the International President's Letter of Commendation for their outstanding service. The Robert Koennecke Award was presented to the New Baden Evening Lions Club and the E.B. "Tex" Mayer Award was presented to Lion Mark Ulrich of the LaGrange Noon Lions Club.

For her service as Governor, Lion Vicky received an International Leadership award, Governor's Extension award, District Family Growth award and the District Governor's Excellence award. She also received the 100% District Governors award from the Texas Lions Camp.

Governor Vicky took office at The International Convention in Sidney Australia. At her first cabinet meeting she sang 'Beacon of Hope', which was President Sid Scruggs theme for the year.

2011 -2012

The 2011–2012 Lions year was led by District Governor Andy Rodriguez of the Gonzales Noon Lions Club, 1VDG Ernie Koy of the Bellville Lions Club and 2VDG Danny Stribling of the College Station Noon lions Club. Lion Sherry Hopkins served as District Secretary and Lion Julie Fairchild served as District Treasurer.

Joe Al Picone, from Brenham, Texas was elected to serve a two-year term as a director of Lions Clubs International at the association's 94th International Convention held in Seattle, Washington July 4-8, 2011 becoming district 2-S5's first International Director.

Significant-sized wildfires started in Bastrop County on Labor Day 2011. One of the worst was in the Smithville/Bastrop area officially named the Bastrop Complex Fire. Governor Rodriguez received a disaster assistance grant from LCIF, and District 2-S5 was recognized in the "Lion" magazine for providing assistance to many residents that were affected by the fire. Article from that issue follows here:

The LION, March 2012

Fire and Faith
Texas Disaster Ignites Service

by Mary O. Parker, photos by Mary Parker

Smithville, with its deep Czech roots, is a tight-knit community located at the edge of the Lost Pines region of central Texas. There, I'd raised a family, led Cub Scouts, and once owned a bookstore. And there during a long, brutal September the second worst wildfire in U.S. history turned lives upside down.

Sparked by downed power lines and propelled by a perfect storm of drought, wind and heat, the Bastrop Complex Fires raged for 26 days. The blazes tore through dozens of rural neighborhoods and destroyed miles of rare loblolly pine ecosystem. The fire ultimately consumed 1,664 structures and 34,068 acres. The blaze came within four miles of the city limits, and nearly 40 of my friends lost homes.

Burnt towers meant days of no cell service and mounting anxiety. To stem the worry, residents combed the Smithville Recreation Center to seek information about friends and loved ones. At the fire's peak, 500 evacuees and countless pets found refuge here.

I helped oversee the Smithville Distribution Center, a couple of blocks from the rec center. Evacuees, and later, those who'd lost everything, came for necessities. In a three week period, our center served over 4,200 fire-affected folks. To put that into perspective, that's more than the entire population of Smithville.

As the weeks went by and the separate fires raged ever greater, eventually drawn toward one another, we residents too, drew together emotionally. At the same time, we also breathlessly raced from one dire need to the next.

With all that breathless racing, I didn't realize until later just how many "racers" belonged to Lions clubs.

Once I connected the dots, the picture formed made this non-Lion's jaw drop. In a crisis heavy with volunteerism, Lion activity consistently outweighed it all.

My connect-the-dots drawing begins with Joe Franks, president of the

Giddings Lions Club.

On Labor Day, Franks headed to Paige, a tiny community at the fire's northeastern edge. There, he immediately spearheaded efforts to feed evacuees and firefighters. "We got to Paige on Monday. Red Cross got there on Thursday," Franks says.

Twenty miles away, Charley Baugh, Giddings Lions Club treasurer, checked out the scene back in Smithville, now four miles from the fire's southeastern edge, where he discovered 120 evacuees needing meals.

Baugh recalls, "I'd just walked out of the rec center in Smithville and called Joe. He'd just walked out of the community center in Paige. We each had a frog in our throat, but we got it together and went on. I told him, 'We need this and this,' and he said, 'Go. Get it.' He didn't question me."

Behind the scenes, Andy Rodriguez, Governor of District 2-S5 and a member of the Gonzales Noon Lions Club, worked at rounding up funding. Ultimately, he says, thanks to grants and generous club contributions, approximately $25,000 went toward relief efforts. That figure includes $10,000 from Lions Club International Foundation (LCIF).

Rodriguez says, "With LCIF 100 percent of your dollar goes into relief efforts, no administration costs. Well, I put in for the grant at 9:45 and by 10:43, 58 minutes later, it was approved. Now that's cutting out bureaucracy!"

Those of us volunteering at the Smithville Distribution Center came to appreciate that lack of bureaucracy. While donations poured in, no one knew exact needs until the moment arrived. To wit: by week two we had plenty of pillows–a shortage the first week–but folks desperate to sort through ashes and uncover what the fire had left behind lacked trash cans, gloves, rakes, shovels and hoses needed to do the job. For those who still had homes but with smoke damage, we needed vinegar. So we made a wish list.

Now to my connect-the-dots picture add Amberley Palmer of the Smithville Noon Lions Club. Palmer asked us, "What do you need?" We gave her our list, not really believing she meant to go out and buy all that stuff. Who actually does that? Well, we soon found out: Lions, that's who. And not just once, not twice. Every single day for nearly three weeks, Palmer posed her question and Lions delivered.

Palmer's involvement began with a call to Rodriguez, who told her to check in with Joe Franks. "When I talked to Joe, he said, 'Go buy what you need. It doesn't matter how much you spend, just let me know if it goes over $500. Do you understand?' I said, 'Yes,' not really understanding." She laughs, remembering. "I think he asked me that three or four times in the course of our short conversation. I had to get a check from Charley [Baugh] and even though we'd never even met before, Charley just handed me a blank check."

Franks explains, "I think 'faith' is a good word here". With faith in Rodriguez, who assured him the district would reimburse the club, he says, "I was telling [Baugh and Palmer] to spend money, and I didn't have the money to spend."

On September 6, just two days after sparks ignited, the Texas Lions Foundation awarded the Giddings Lions Club $2,000, thanks in part to efforts of Charles Villeneuve, a 2-S5 past District Governor.

"But that went really quickly," states Baugh, who ultimately wrote 24 fire-related checks totaling nearly $9,000, "We were the front lines." Items purchased included mattresses, eyeglasses, food, cleaning supplies, school supplies and, of course, those items on our lists.

Lisa Gonzales of the Smithville Noon Lions accompanied Palmer as she shopped with our first list. Before I knew she belonged to Lions, I'd seen Gonzales, an insurance agent with fire-related claims tripling her workload, come in regularly collecting necessities for dazed clients.

"Some just couldn't do it, so I'd do it for them," she shrugs. When the City of Smithville insisted center volunteers take a Sunday off, Gonzales co-managed the center for a day so the doors would remain open.

Week two, volunteer Meredith Franks joined us, her spunky personality engendering easy rapport. After connecting with a woman who talked of returning to work but having lost her make-up to fire, Franks showed up the next day with a basket full of make-up. Another day, a set of cookware came with her but left "with a woman who likes to cook and who'd lost everything," says Franks.

Chatting one day, I shared my amazement at how the Lions kept fulfilling our wish lists. Franks' response? "Oh, yeah, I know. I'm a Lion." She'd been in on it from day one! In fact, she's not only president of the Giddings New Horizons Lions Club but also Joe Franks' wife.

After I'd worked days with Cherrie Pullium, a key player in the Smithville Distribution Center, I discovered she's not only a Lion but also Leo adviser for the Smithville club. Pullium housed evacuees, solicited donations, organized warehouses and assisted fire victims. "I did what needed to be done," she states, simply.

Ironically, the last Lion I uncovered I had "raced" with the most. Sheila Tamble of the Smithville Noon Lions coordinated all aspects of Smithville's fire-related efforts including working with FEMA. Not only that, but Tamble's Facebook post suggesting they create a distribution center lured Pullium to Main Street at 4 a.m. on Sept. 5 to get the whole thing started.

I suspect, as the smoke continues dissipating, I'll discover more Lions who "raced" beside me during those crazy times since it's clear to me now that when disaster strikes, Lions do, too. What's also clear is how many parts they play. As Joe Franks notes, "Our role changed over time from relief to taking food and medicine to taking trash cans."

What doesn't change, stresses DG Rodriguez, whom I met when he delivered a load of those trash cans, is the role Lions can and should play in situations like the Bastrop Complex Fires. "We found out where we fit through this. It's in that short-period time between when disaster strikes and when the long-term recovery organizations like Salvation Army and Red Cross come in."

Or as my connect-the-dots would read if it formed words: "A Lion helps those in need and helps them right now."

2012 – 2013

The 2012 – 2013 Lions year was led by District Governor Ernie Koy of the Bellville Lions Club, 1VDG Danny Stribling of the College Station Noon Lions Club and 2VDG Thom Holt of the College Station Noon Lions Club. Lion Robert Fait served as District Secretary and Lion Robert Herridge served as District Treasurer.

Throughout the year, efforts to foster strong communication among members were emphasized. Michael Bolton worked to enhance the District 2-S5 website. Lion Fait facilitated the design and publication of a Directory and Calendar. Lion David Morley served as the editor of a monthly newsletter that was distributed to Lions in District 2-S5 throughout the year. International President, Wayne A. Madden, promoted the theme "In a

World of Service." Zone Chair reports at the Cabinet meetings in Industry, La Grange, Brenham and Bellville defined various projects that illustrated a dedication to service by all District 2-S5 clubs. Lions across the District joined in partnering with public schools in The Reading Action Program (RAP).

District Governor Koy recognized many Lions for service at the District Convention that was held at Concordia Hall in Bellville on May 4, 2013. Appreciation gifts for the various individuals included donations to Lions Charities.

Lion Koy, a former professional football player, adopted the slogan, "Keep The Ball Rolling!"

The year was highlighted by positive interaction among Lions who worked together to demonstrate the WE SERVE motto in both attitude and in action. Lions "kept the ball rolling" throughout the year as they served the citizens and communities in District 2-S5.

PIP Bill Biggs was the speaker for the 50th anniversary.

2013 – 2014

The 2013 - 2014 Lions year was led by District Governor Danny Stribling, 1VDG Thom Holt and 2VDG Jim Fox.

PDG John Rauser served as District Secretary and Judy Nixon as the District Treasurer. Throughout the year, Governor Stribling challenged Lions to "Be the Miracle" which served as the governor›s theme throughout the year. The year started with over 100 attending the first cabinet meeting in Smithville. The Giddings Lions hosted the second cabinet meeting. Council Chair Lewis Gardner was in attendance and gave remarks to the attendees. The Mid-Winter conference was hosted by the Caldwell Lions and chaired by Lion Judy Richardson. The conference program featured the "Not Ready for Prime Time Players" presenting the play "Death of a Lions Club". PDG Mike Morgan was the Keynote speaker. The District Convention was held at the Pridgeon Center in Franklin and chaired by Lion John Nichols. Past International Director Donal Knipp of Ausasse, Missouri served as the Convention›s Keynote address. Throughout the convention, Master of Ceremonies Lion Don Dickenson read a list of "Miracles" that Lions across the district had performed during the year. Governor Stribling closed the convention by thanking the Lions for stepping up and accepting his challenge to "Be the Miracle.» The wonderful year ended with an incredible State Convention that Lions will be talking about for years—a Caribbean cruise! Past International President Bill Biggs served as the Convention›s keynote speaker.

2014 – 2015

The 2014–2015 Lions year was led by District Governor Thom Holt of the College Station Noon Lions Club, 1VDG Jim Fox of the Weimar Lions Club and 2VDG Michael Smalley of the LaGrange Noon Lions Club. PDG John Rauser served as District Secretary and Lion Judy Nixon served as District Treasurer.

Our District Objective is the "Share the Miracle" of Lionism. Our strategy for achieving this objective is to have "Fun, Fellowship and Follow-up". Our Midwinter Conference in College Station broke recent attendance records and featured a Tail-twister competition, a Leadership Panel and Professor Michael Wesson from the Mays School at Texas A&M speaking on Generations in the Work Place and Organizations - or, as I liked to refer to the talk, "How to communicate with your Children and Grandchildren. As of St. Patrick's Day we are positive 42 members in our retention and club growth and are set to work 2-4 new or branch clubs in March and April. Our District Convention is set for 10-11 April and PID Scott Storms will be our Speaker. Our District will host the State Convention in College Station Texas May 21-23. The theme is centered on "grass-roots" Lionism.

This effort was jointly accomplished by the Past District Governors of 2-S5 and compiled by our Cabinet Secretary PDG John Rauser at my request. Any compliments go his way, and concerns or complaints come my way.

Fair winds,
Lion Thom
Governor District 2-S5

District 2-S5 Hall of Fame Members

PID E.B. "Tex" Mayer	1972
PDG P.C. Franks	1980
PDG Robert Koennecke	1982
PDG Dexter Anderson	1985
PDG Freddie Wolters	1991
PDG Mark Anderson	1994
PID Joe Al Picone	1997
PDG David Kahlich	2000
Lion Gerry Chandler Criswell (Chair)	2003
PDG Uel Stockard	2006
PDG Ron Heinemeyer	2009
PDG Clarence Wolfshawl	2012
PDG Charles Villeneuve	2015

Ebb and Jay Grindstaff at 2014 Lions International Campaign in Toronto • 2014

Judge Grindstaff and Ebb • 1960

Ebb Grindstaff celebrates on horseback in a 1964 Lions Parade.

Ebb Grindstaff with Judge Brian Stevenson

Ebb Grindstaff (left) meets Egyptian President, Anwar Sadat on a visit to Egypt.

Ebb Grindstaff (center) with Israel's Prime Minister, Menachem Begin (second from right) • 1980

Everett J. "Ebb" Grindstaff, second left, Immediate Past President of Lions Clubs International, receives the 1983 American Diabetes Association Distinguished Service Award from Joseph H. Davis, left, ADA vice Chairman of the board, during the national voluntary health organization's 43rd annual meeting in San Antonio, Texas. Also pictured are ADA board member Dexter Anderson, second right, and Alfred Hodder, president of Medical Alert Foundation International.

The Juvenile Diabetes Foundation International awarded its Humanitarian Award to Everett J. "Ebb" Grindstaff, Immediate Past President of Lions Clubs International. Grindstaff, pictured here with Todd Duffy, Houston JDF poster boy, and Jacqueline Colville, Past President of JDF International, inaugerated an international Diabetes Education and Awareness Program for Lions Clubs during his 1982-83 presidential term.

*President Reagan,
Nancy Reagan,
Jay Grindstaff and
Ebb Grindstaff*

*Ebb and Jay
Grindstaff
present gifts to
Pope John Paul II
during their visit
to Rome.*

THE WHITE HOUSE

WASHINGTON

December 27, 1982

Dear Mr. Grindstaff:

It was a real pleasure to meet you in my office and
to have the opportunity to discuss the International
Association of Lions' Clubs "War on Drugs." Both
Nancy and I are deeply grateful to you and your
membership for your dedicated efforts in making
Drug Abuse Awareness a priority for Lions International in 155 countries.

Sincerely,

Ronald Reagan

Mr. Everett Grindstaff
President
International Association
 of Lions' Clubs
Post Office Box 576
Ballinger, Texas 76821

President George H. W. Bush and Ebb Grindstaff

Ebb Grindstaff and his grandson, Will Grindstaff

To Mr. Everett J. Ebb,

Thank you for your support of the Republican National Committee. Together we can build a better, safer, more prosperous future for America.

Warmest Regards,

Another Past International President form the great State of Texas is Jimmy Ross, who served in 2006-2007.

PIP Ross is pictured here in Boston, presenting his inaugural speech after his election on July 4, 2006.

The Ross family (L to R) Daughter and son-in-law, Janet and Josh Brook; daughters Julie Ross and Sammie-Dee Ross; Jimmy and Velda Ross at the 2003 Texas State Convention.

Jimmy and Velda Ross in Detroit 2004 when Jimmy ran for LCI's Second Vice President.

Jimmy and Velda Ross on stage in Boston, right after he became the 90th President of Lions Club International.

*Pictured (L to R)
Sammie-Dee Ross,
Velda &
Jimmy, Julie Ross*

Detroit 2004

*(L to R) Jimmy went in as President in Boston. Pictured (L to R) are Sammie-Dee
and husband Cory Varnell; Jimmy & Velda Ross, Julie Ross, Janet Brooks, granddaughter Braylee Brooks, Josh Brooks.*

International Officers

Chairman of the Board of Directors, **J. Andrew Smith** served from 1962 to 1963 by appointment. Because of his service as Chairman of the Board of Directors, he was confirmed by International President, Everett J. "Ebb" Grindstaff.

Past International President, **Dave Evans**, along with wife Betty, served from 1967 to 1968.

Past International Director, **E.B. "Tex" Mayer**, along with his wife, Nell, served from 1970 to 1972.

Past International Director, **Everett J. "Ebb" Grindstaff**, along with wife Jay, served from 1972 to 1974. In addition, Ebb Grindstaff also served as Past International President from 1982 to 1983.

Past International Director, **Don Buckalew**, along with wife Dale, served from 1974-1976. Don was later married to Elaine.

Past International Director, **Edwin H. Flood**, along with wife Ann, served from 1976-1978.

Past International Director, **Mike Butler**, served from 1984-1986, along with wife Annette who is now deceased, later married to Sheryl Sterling Butler, whose father was a District Governor that served in the Beaumont area.

Past International Director, **Howard Leverett Jr.**, along with wife Sue, served from 1986 to 1988.

Past International Director, **Ray Hughston** from District A-3, along with wife Norma who is now deceased, later married to Noralee, served in 1992. Past International Director, Marshall Cooper, along with wife Wanda, served from 1993 to 1995.

Past International Director, **Conrado "Connie" de la Garza**, along with his wife Lisa, served from 2000 to 2002 in District 2-A3. Connie was also a former Mayor of the City of Harlingen.

Past International President, **Jimmy Ross** from District T-1, along with wife Velda, served from 2006 to 2007.

Past International Director, **Beverly Stebbins**, along with husband Ed who was a Past District Governor, served from 2008 to 2010. She was the first woman in Texas to serve as an International Director.

Past International Director, **Joe Al Picone**, along with wife Merle, served from 2012 to 2014.

Joe Childers was born between Ballinger and Abilene, was a lawyer by profession, but a businessman by trade. Joe served as District Governor in both Texas and Colorado. In July 1956, he was elected to a two-year term as International Director in Colorado, where he spent most of his adult life in Durango, Colorado.

International Director **Sam Lindsey** was elected Director at the Convention in Japan in 2016.

(L to R) PID Mike Butler, PID Marshall Cooper, PID Joe Al Picone, ID Sam Lindsey, youngest DG from Texas and PID Don Buckalew, PIP Jimmy Ross and PIP Everett J. "Ebb" Grindstaff sign the Centennial resolution written by PIP Grindstaff at the Texas Senate Chambers in early 2017.

J. Andrew Smith

J. Andrew Smith joined the Founder Lions Club of San Antonio in June 1928. Known as "Andy," Smith served as President of the club from 1940-1941. He was District Governor of District 2-A2 for two separate terms in 1960-1961 and 1941-1942. He was then elected Chairman of the Executive Council of the International Board of Governors, and was officially recognized as a Past Director of Lions International during the year Ebb Grindstaff was President.

During his 52 years of Lionism, Andy always supported the activities of the club for the blind and crippled with his time, energies and talent.

Dave Evans

It is certainly worthy of mention that David A. Evans was elected President of our Association at the beginning of the second 50 years of Lionism in Texas. Dave took office as President in 1968-1969, and his story is best told in his own history in his letters to Texans.

My Texas Lions History
by David A. Evans

It started on April 16, 1947 at 9:12 a.m. with a roar that could be heard for 100 miles and that shattered windows as far away as Houston. A sudden explosion of the freight ship "Grand Camp," laden with ammonium nitrate to be used for fertilizer, exploded and killed 502 people in the harbor in my hometown of Texas City.

At that time, I was a member of a volunteer rescue squad. Out of the 23 members of this squad, I and one other person were then the only ones left alive. The volunteer fire department suffered the same fate, with all being killed, with the exception of the Fire Chief who was out of town.

All this may seem to you to be far removed from Lionism, but was actually my start at a Lion, even though I was not to become a member for another four years. I saw the way that the Lions Club in Texas City went into action, even though the five top officers of the club had been killed in the explosion, I saw how the Lions from all over the world started to send money and supplies to the local club for use in this disaster. I saw how men who had their own businesses to run, their own families to look after, worked night and day for those people whom they did not even know. I wondered to myself, 'What kind of man is this that would do all these things without expecting anything in return? What kind of people do we have in this world, who would send money to a little community that they had never heard of before to help those in need?'

I decided that I must find out what made these people tick, and if possible, become one of them. I soon learned that the only way to get into a Lions Club was to be invited, and this invitation did not come until January 1951. So needless to say, when the invitation did come, I was ready!

And there are many people who become members of a Lions club, and never become Lions. Fortunately, soon after my business as a builder, I was given the assignment to work on a project of erecting a monument to those Lions who were killed during the explosion four years earlier. I was so enthusiastic about the project, I did it single-handedly, even though I was not the chairman, and there were eight other members on the committee. Three days later, I reported to the club that the project had been finished, they could hardly believe it was true. So, I did become a Lion, shortly after becoming a member, and I feel that I have been a Lion ever since.

I continued to be happy to serve on committees, to work for the community, to work our fund-raising project, as a member of the Minstrel Show, to expect nothing in return, until one year I found myself nominated for a Director of the club. I won the election, served for two years as a Director, and all went well until the following year when I was elected "Tail-Twister."

My enthusiasm for the position soon caused me problems. I was thrown out of the Club on several occasions, and soon found that there were two members of the club who did not believe in fines. In my persistence to fine these members, I found myself involved in a hot argument that caused me to offer my resignation from the club. Because of good friends who came to me and insisted that the organization was gibber than these two men who did not like to go along with the rules, I was persuaded to stay in the club, and the following year was elected Third Vice-President.

Anticipating that it would take me at least three years to become President of the Club, I was really surprised when I was nominated for President the following year in a field of three candidates. I won the election. I became the first member of my Club to jump from third Vice-President to President.

As President, I tried a new experience in appointing members of the club who had been members for many years, but had never shown any inclination to work as chairmen of certain committees. To the surprise of all those in the club, these people who had not worked in the past suddenly came alive and made some of the finest Lions in our entire club. Most of these members are still in the club today.

I went from President to Zone Chairman to Deputy District Governor. When the state was divided into 15 districts, and the area where I lived was made into the new District 2 S-4, I became a candidate for District Governor. Having no opposition to the post, I won very handily.

After serving as District Governor, the following year I decided to become a candidate for International Director. To add many other things that confronted me at the time, we had a visit from an old sister called "Carla." This hurricane brought 13 feet of water across the seawall in Texas City, and deposited two feet of water, mud, soot, chemicals and raw sewage in our home. Not to be outdone by any wet lade, we immediately set about cleaning up and rebuilding, while at the same time, campaigning for the nomination within the state.

Having an opponent who was very well-known, I found that getting the nomination was not an easy task. But at the last convention held in Amarillo, it was finally confirmed that I had received the nomination. We went on to Nice, France to campaign on the international level. We were fortunate in having only nine candidates for eight positions, and I won the office of International Director.

The following January, after being elected as Director, the Dallas-Fort Worth Lions held a banquet in our honor. At this banquet it was decided that we would again try to get the International Convention to Dallas. In the next three months, we carefully laid our plans, contacted our known friends on the Board, gathered our ammunition, and in April, we headed to the Board meeting in Tokyo.

All the Board members assembled in Vancouver, British Columbia. At this point, we presented every Director and Past President with a Texas Stetson (hat). When we got off the plane in Tokyo, it looked like a meeting of the Southwestern Cattlemen's Association. From the time we left Vancouver, we had the situation well in hand. The night before we were to vote on the convention site, the Board attended a cocktail party hosted by the Atlantic City Convention Bureau. Even their convention manager conceded that we would win. When the vote was taken the next morning, the vote was so overwhelming for Dallas that they would not announce the three votes that we did not receive.

I served two years as International Director, and then announced my candidacy for Third Vice-President. This was probably one of the most enjoyable experiences of my entire Lionistic career, running for this office at the Los Angeles Convention.

To sum up the Los Angeles Convention, I refer to the letter I wrote immediately after my return from Los Angeles:

Texas City, Texas
August 1, 1965

My dear Texas Lions,

THEY SAID IT COULDN'T BE DONE, but you and all the other Lions of Texas joined ranks and won the greatest victory ever for the Texas Lions. I felt as they must have felt on that day of April 21 many years back when they unfurled the Lone Star Flag at San Jacinto.

This was not a grudge fight, and we were not trying to vindicate anything. We won with dignity maintaining our self-respect and the respect of others along the way. We won because we had an excellent campaign manager in R. A. "Lip" Lipscomb. He is one of the greatest men I have ever known and his devotion to Lionism is unquestionable. His wife, Irene...there are not enough adjectives to describe Betty's and my feeling toward her. In Spanish I would call her, "mi princesa Simpatico." She and Lip are our dearest friends and have won the respect of all Lions they have met, from the Past Presidents of Lion International to the newest Lion.

Then there was our advisor, Past International President, Judge Julien C. Hyer. He talked to me like a father, directed me like a coach, counseled me like a judge and advised me and our organization to a victory. What more could you ask of any man? He was our inside man and did a terrific job for Texas.

And Herb Petry, in his subtle way acting mostly behind the scenes during the early stages of the campaign did an outstanding job of molding and so-lidifying our State into one united front, always being there when we needed him.

International Counselor, Don Buckalew of Conroe, and my neighbor Lon Charles Barre, flew out with us and it befell their lot to be the peons and do all the work until reinforcements arrived. They accepted the responsibility without looking back and attacked the multitude of problems with usual Texas Lionistic vigor.

One lone reinforcement appeared on the scene Saturday. This was International Counsellor Charles Carruth of Andrews. Most of you remember him as our Chairman of the Council for 1963-64. Charlie flew his own plane to California and spent half a day trying to locate Los Angeles through the smog. No sooner had he landed, he and Don set up an assembly line putting our banners together. International Counsellor Charlie "Clem" Daniels of Norton, Virginia (no relation to Jack) joined our "peace corps" project and set out to hang the banners in the different hotels. He headed for the airport area and Hollywood while Charles Barre and his two sons John and Herbie invaded the Biltmore (which housed all Governors and Governors-elect). It didn't take us long to find out that Los Angeles had some sort of ordinance against such banners unless they are flame proofed. Even though our banners were of a weight heavy enough to be exempt we couldn't convince the hotel managers.

Not to be outdone by this unfriendly approach taken by the hotels District Governor Bill Stein took the venetian blind cord, tied it to one of the banners and let it down the outside of his hotel room. The hotels eventually relented and by Wednesday morning we had the city covered like a heavy snow.

Don Buckalew (a Chevrolet dealer) was elected to be the chauffeur and we immediately dispatched him to North Hollywood to pick up a new Pontiac station wagon that had been made available to us through the generosity of the Pontiac division of General Motors. On his return to the hotel, Don installed a Texas flag on each front fender and from that moment on we owned the city.

On Sunday, Abe Houston, our Convention Chairman arrived at the International Hotel and started setting up his control center. NASA could learn some things from Abe on his operation of this center. It was highly organized with contacts into each hotel and motel where Texas were staying.

International Counselor John Painter and ZotZottarelli were also on the scene early, getting their committees into shape. They traveled halfway across California to find a tank of helium to fill the balloons. They missed most of the Wednesday morning convention session getting ready for the parade on Wednesday night. Man, what a parade...Zot and his committee were really clicking. The California TV stations televised the first two hours of the pa-

rade and most of that two hours was taken by Texas. The narrator of the TV show would say after each Texas band passed, "well, this concludes the Texas Part," after about the sixth band had passed he was heard to say, "My gosh, they brought the whole State with them."

These wonderful people stood there for over an hour before the magic moment came. When it did, there is only one way to adequately describe it and this is to use Arby Verbage, "All hell broke loose." I have never seen a demonstration like this before. We were allowed only 15 minutes and it took longer than that just to get out Texans through. Betty and I were on the stage and from our vantage point it was an impressive sight. I'm not ashamed to admit that more than once I had to brush away the tears. I was never before so proud of my Texans and never more proud to be a Texan. Our daughter Tanya insisted on marching in the demonstration and did fine for the first few minutes, but after that pent-up emotion came through. Visualize a little girl of 13 marching placard in one hand and wiping tears that were flowing copiously, with the other. Our neighbor girl Shirley Zenthoefer had gone with the band to California and had lost a toenail in a little accident but was marching in the demonstration, quite a feat I would say. No stone was left unturned, everything was perfect. International Counsellor Don Buckalew came upon the stage and presented to Betty, Texas yellow roses. Lip and Dick were standing with us. Julien and Herb escorted us to the center of the stage. John Painter and his committee had the demonstration organized so well that no once was the procession stopped.

Thursday afternoon we spent visiting caucuses, pigeon-holing delegate, entertaining the leaders and once or twice sitting down and pulling our shoes off. Thursday night was "Florida Night" and the Sports Arena. They present-ed a fine show (so I'm told, I slept through most of it) and our new President and his wife were radiating enthusiasm. One of the funny things of the night was when one of the helium-filled balloons, shaped like a clown's head (that was released during the morning demonstration) floated down from the ceiling and drifted to within 18 inches of the microphone during the perfor-mance of the Four Saints. It appeared as if the balloon had joined in the sing-ing. Of course these balloons had printed on them "EVANS FOR THIRD" and we were accused of having them radio controlled.

Saturday was a big day for Texas. Everyone was out early to vote and most all the Texas delegates voted, not all, but a good percentage. Former Vice-President Richard Nixon spoke on the Vietnam problem and was well received.

Then came the big moment for us, the announcement of the new Third Vice-President. And once again John Painter's crew took over the Sports Arena and an even better and larger demonstration, than before, took place.

When the tooting of horns, the beating of drums, the clash of symbols, the shouts of joy and the shuffle of feet had finally died down, the past president of the Rio Piedras Lions Club of Puerto Rico presented to Kermit Agee the New President of the Texas City Loins Club the banner of the Third Vice-President. It was a wonderful, thrilling moment for all of us and all of Texas. It was made possible by the united efforts of all Texas Lions. I am proud of you and I commend each and every one of you.

We captured many prizes in the parade. The Texas City Band won second place which is more than the top honor considering our State had a candidate.

The White Oak Band was terrific and came up with the fourth prize. The Texas A&I Band won first place in the adult division. Jacksboro and Carthage both took honors in baton twirling.

The entire group form the International family stood as the strains of "The Eyes of Texas" reverberated up and down Hollywood Blvd., an act never before witnessed by any lion.

Thursday morning broke through the smog-laden valley even before Wednesday night had ended. Being the morning for the Texas Breakfast, which as being held 18 miles away at the International Hotel we had to leave the Statler early and fight the peak traffic hour to be on hand for the greatest breakfast ever held. There were over 430 District Governors and their wives there. We had a good representation of the International family there, we had "millions" of Texans there. We had a total of 1,053 people at this breakfast, and all-time record for the size of any State breakfast. The Midland Lions Club Bank was on hand to help awaken those still asleep with their wonderful renditions. They were followed by the Lamesa "Slumtown Symfunny" composed of Lions and business leaders of Lamesa. What a great impression these two groups made, not only at the Texas breakfast, but at every function where they appeared.

International Counsellor Bert Belcher of Seagraves was in charge of *this entertainment and he was covering more places, at more time, with less groups than seems possible. Bert is the kind of Lion that can do the impossible.*

While we were on the subject of breakfasts, I must mention the terrific job done by Past International Director Dick Self of Dallas. Dick was, among other things, also in charge of the speakers' bureau for all breakfasts. He had this organized down to the last detail and left nothing to be desired. He met with each speaker, coached him in the things to do, provided him with all the ammunition he needed, and sent him in his way...but... it didn't stop there. Dick was up each morning long before breakfast time checking to see that the assigned speaker was up and ready to go. After giving each of them a pep talk, he would then turn his efforts toward other duties for the day. He watched these breakfasts so closely that when "yours truly" did not show up at the Kansas breakfast as scheduled he was there in my place without any advance warning. What a great, dedicated and devoted Lion this man is and that also apples to his wife, Louise.

Following the Texas breakfast we all (some 3,500 Texans) converged on the Los Angeles Memorial Sports Arena to await the nominations. As usual the program was running late and our group was getting restless. Can you imagine some 3,500 Texas men, women, and children, nine large bands and States like Pennsylvania and Oklahoma wanting to join us, all bunched up behind a rope waiting to let off their steam? One shot and they would have stampeded through the walls of the arena.

The District Governors of 1962-63 took the initial step and laid the ground work. The Governors of 1963-64 picked it up and got it off the ground and the Governors of 1964-65 carried it to victory. We owe a lot of these men and especially to the 1964-65 Governors who carried a double load. Mt hat is off to them all.

To the International Counsellors Association who lent their support and contributed greatly to our success, to the Governors with whom I served in 1959-60 who worked so hard, to the District Chairmen of each District, to the Promote Texas Chairmen and especially to International Counsellors Charles Davis who handled this fund in such a fine manner. To the campaign Committees in Los Angeles under the great leadership of International Counsellor Abe Houston to men like Buckalew, Carruth, Barre, Palmer, Painter, Zottarrelli, Redmon, Puig, Schwartz, Kelly, Cornett, J.T. Jones,

Nelson, Carrington, Dyer, Belcher, Houston, to the Governor-elect who performed like troupers, to many, many others that I would like to mention by name if space permitted but my thanks to you as much as to everyone else. To Dick and Louise Self, to Lip and Irene, two great past Directors who served so willingly, so tirelessly and so efficiently; to Julien Hyer, my advisor, my confidant, my dear friend and to his sweet wife, Agnes; to Herb Petry who was near when I needed him, who lifted me up when I was down and to beautiful Jo; to all Texas Lions, their ladies, their children; to the Paris, Andrews, Jacksboro, Carthage, White Oak, Harper, Texas A&I, and the Texas City Banks, to the Midland Lions Band, the Slumtown Eymfunny and the Castleberry Choir.

To all my friends both mentioned and unmentioned herein from Berry and me we say thank and God bless you. May you carry Texas Lionism to greater heights than ever before.

Sincerely,
David A. Evans, Third Vice-President

At the convention in Los Angeles, one of the bands that went to the convention was from Harper, Texas, now the home of Trish Wilson, Development Director of Camp Operations at the Texas Lions Camp. It was during this time as you will note in the letters that Don Buckalew and some other District Governors were referred to as International Counsellors, which was the case in 1963, but in 1964 at the time I became Governor, they changed the name to District Governor. I and others for that one year could be known as International Counsellors and District Governors, which did not make that much difference, since we were all proud to be in that position whatever we were called.

It is worthy of note that one of the International Counsellors or District Governors Don Buckalew from Conroe and one of the stalwart campaigners during the Evans years later became Past International Director in 1974. In addition, he had to be one of the youngest District Governors in the association upon his election at the age of 29.

E.B. "Tex" Mayer

E.B. (Tex) Mayer was a businessman and rancher from La Grange, Texas—my closest friend, past International Director of Lions Club International, a true confidante, and one of the most loyal individuals I've ever known.

Elected International Director at the Lions International Convention in 1970, PDG E.B. "Tex" Mayer, was one of the great International Directors of Texas, and he served our Association with distinction as Director from 1970-1972, and continued to serve many different capacities—Leadership, Extension and a loyal member of the Texas Delegation throughout history of Lionism in Texas. He was also the father of Past District Governor Don Mayer, an orthodontist in La Grange, who, in his District 2A reached a record of 110 clubs, which required a split by the clubs which pleased Lions Clubs International.

Membership is very important and a lot has been written about it. We cannot mention membership or extension without mentioning Past International Director Tex Mayer, as he's one of the best Lions for extension, and one of the best extension people that we've had in the State of Texas. Tex was able to organize clubs in every mall and by-way—from Austin to Houston and otherwise—and by doing so, he helped Lionism grow in the late '70s and early '80s to its greatest heights. Tex and Nell had the Dairy Mart in La Grange from which (along with his famous consolidated smokehouse) he was always taking German summer sausage and tenderloin to all board meetings to give directors a taste of Texas.

I always thought Tex would run for president of the Lions Clubs International, as he was certainly qualified and was financially independent, but he told me at the state convention in 1974 in Waco that he was not going to run, but that he would support me and work for me wholeheartedly, which he did. His wife Nell was beside Jay and me in every move, as well as was their son, Dr. Don Mayer. Don, a member of the Texas Longhorn fan club at the University of Texas, and Tex Mayer, an avid graduate of Texas A&M, might have both been surprised when Matthew Mayer became a member of the Baylor University band, where he attended school as a freshman.

It was a coincidence that Dr. Don Mayer and J. P. Kirksey were in the Longhorn Band (I cannot take sides because of Baylor), but J. P. is now active in the Austin area and attended many conventions by flying with Moton Crockett, a very successful businessman in Austin and a great Lion. I am certain that great Lion PDG Willie Kocurek will be mentioned in their district history; who also graduated from Texas Law School at the age of 83 and practiced in Austin.

Everett J. "Ebb" Grindstaff

Everett J. "Ebb" Grindstaff of Ballinger, Texas was elected President of Lions Club International at the Association's 65th annual convention held in Atlanta, Georgia in July 1982.

A Lion since 1954, and currently a member of the Ballinger Noon Lions Club, PIP Grindstaff has held numerous offices—including club President, District Governor and Past President of the Texas Lions League for Crippled Children. He has also chaired several committees at Lions' conventions, serving a two-year term as a member of the Association's Board of Directors from 1972-74.

For his efforts on behalf of the Association, he has received 17 International President Awards, two Extension Awards and teh Ambassador of Good Will Award—the highest honor given to members by the Association. He is also a Melvin Jones Fellow, a Jack Weich Fellow of the Texas Lions Camp, and a Texas Lions Foundation Fellow. In addition, PIP Grindstaff received the Juvenile Diabetes Foundation's 1983 Humanitarian Award for his work in helping diabetics worldwide, and received the highest award given by the American Diabetes Association—the Dr. Charles Best Award—in 1984.

In addition to his Lion activities, PIP Grindstaff is a Life Fellow of the Texas Bar Foundation, past Chairman of the Upper Colorado River Authority, Life Member Counselor of Baylor University Law School, past Director of the State Bar of Texas, past President of the Ballinger Chamber of Commerce, and past District Chairman and past District Commissioner of the Tri-Rivers District of Concho Valley Council of the Boy Scouts of America.

Ebb and his wife, Jay have two children and four grandchildren.

Don Buckalew

Don's involvement in Texas Lions history is spread throughout this book—in Dave Evans' tenure, in Ebb Grindstaff's tenure, and in all of the campaigns of nearly all of the past officers.

He joined the Magnolia Lions Club in 1956 at the age of 22, when he graduated from Baylor University. He transferred to the Tomball Lions Club in 1957 and served as President of the club from 1959-1960.

Dave then transferred to the Humble Lions Club in 1960, where he served as District Governor in 1963-1964 at the age of 29.

He once again transferred to the Conroe Noon Lions Club in 1965.

PID David Evans from Texas City asked Don to be a part of his campaign for Lions Clubs International Third Vice-President in 1964-1965. This was an exciting time for Texas Lions, and a fantastic experience, as Dave was elected Third Vice-President in 1965. Don was a part of Dave's MD-2 team that assisted him as he advanced through the chairs to become President of the International Association in 1968-1969. Don has many stories of his experiences in being a part of Texas Lionism and Lions Clubs International during the Dave Evans era.

Don Buckalew served as Chairman for the two (2) MD-2 International Director campaigns—E. B. "Tex" Mayer in 1970 and Ebb Grindstaff in 1972, and served Lions as Past District Governor to Dave Evans, Tex Mayer and Ebb Grindstaff.

Don Buckalew was elected to the Lions Club International Board of Directors in 1974 at San Francisco, California. As an elected Director, he served on the Finance and Headquarters Operation Committee, becoming its chairman in 1975-1976. Don also served on the International Constitution and By-Laws Committee as a Board Committee Appointee three times in 1980-1981, 1983-1984, and 1993-1994.

In 1979, Don was Chairman of the campaign to elect Ebb Grindstaff to Third Vice President of Lions Clubs International. During Ebb's rise through the chairs to becoming President, Don served on several USA/Canada Lions Forums Committees. He served as Chairman of two forums—Denver, Colorado in 1981 and Louisville, Kentucky in 1982.

As is evident, Don was always available for service from a young age (and of course from his education at Baylor along with Jo Al and Ebb.) He was a very successful car dealer in Conroe and the surrounding area, and he was called upon because of his financial business acumen and for his desire to "get things done."

One of his other involvements was a large and very active Houston Livestock Association, which was time-consuming as a Board Member and President. This was a BIG job each and every year, and restricted Don's involvement at the February Council Meeting. However, this organization provided hundreds of scholarships for young people all over the state as far reaching as Ballinger, Texas (a great surprise when one of our young people told about Don presenting a $10,000 scholarship to her several years ago).

As mentioned before, and as can be seen in many places in this book, he was campaigner, politician and statesman during the entire 50 years because of his dedication to service. There is not another one more capable or distinctive than Don.

Thanks, Don.

Edwin H. Flood

Edwin H. "Ed" Flood and his wife Ann were an integral part of the team. Past International Director Ed's service was in the Foundation, along with Marshall Cooper. Ed took the "Bull by the Horns". His only problem with Marshall was that Marshall had to quit going to Lubbock because of Ed's driving.

Prior to the convention in Honolulu, Hawaii, where I went as President of Lions Clubs International, I have made at least four or five trips to Australia since I was director in 1973. During the last trip or two, I kept running across the Mint program in Australia, and the fine program in Publicity and Public Relations that they had in order to raise funds for different activities of the Lions. They even had a film and a lot of publicity about same, and I was so impressed by this that I brought it to the Lions of Texas at the convention in Honolulu.

As far as I know, this is the first time that we actually had a vote on a project—anything but politics—at the International Convention as far as the state of Texas is concerned. However, this was so important that we needed to have the opportunity for the Lions of Australia to present this program to us, and also to take action at that particular time. As a result, we had a special meeting after the presentation, and the Lions of Texas adopted this program as a statewide project...the Mint program began.

After that, John Petry actually drew up the constitution and by-laws for the Texas Lions Foundation. After a great deal of research, we were able to talk to Past International Director Flood to take on the financial end of this program, which he did, as well as the publicity of same. The program began and grew into quite a fundraising project for different projects for Lions in Texas.

The idea of a Foundation owned by and for the benefit of the Lions of Texas was the foresight of PID Edwin H. Flood of Amarillo. Lion Ed was successful in selling the idea to the 1983-84 Council of Governors. This Council approved the Articles of Incorporation and the Texas Lions ratified it at their 1984 State Convention.

A preliminary meeting of the Foundation was held in Kerrville the first weekend of August 1984. The first organizational meeting of the Foundation was held in San Antonio on November 3, 1984, where the Constitution and By-Laws were adopted, and PID Flood was elected the first Chairman. PID Flood carried the Articles of Incorporation to Austin, and the Articles were approved by the Secretary of State on December 4, 1984. The Constitution and By-Laws were ratified by the Texas Lions at their 1985 State Convention.

Ed was the first chairman and then Executive Director Emeritus of the Texas Lions Foundation until his death in July 2012.

Mike Butler

In 1988, Texas put forth their #1 candidate, Mike Butler—who qualified for Third Vice President at that particular time—and sent him to Denver, Colorado.

TEXAS SENDS MIKE BUTLER
TO SAN FRANCISCO

Texas Lion Mike Butler went to San Francisco as a candidate, and came home a full-fledged International Director in 1984 (serving through 1986). Butler seemed "to be an instant hit"—the remark made by those who spearheaded his International Convention Campaign. Of course, there were some very prominent Texas Lions that had paved the way—those that had served as our International Officers in the past.

Director Butler assumed a very heavy responsibility—a tradition of great men of quality—unequaled in Lions International, men from Texas who have guided this organization since that first meeting in Dallas in 1917. We just want to say, "Good luck, Mike. The eyes of Texas are upon you."

"Let a Butler serve you" was successful for Mike Butler here in Texas, as he used this slogan in his race for Director. No one would deny that there were prominent (and quite formidable) opponents who stood as candidates with Butler for Director. It is an honor simply to be nominated for this high office.

As the slogan denotes, "Much more truth than fiction," since it is an office of service, we are sure that Director Mike will never lose sight of the fact that service—especially service to those he serves, the Lions of Texas—is why he now occupies this high office.

At that particular time, Ray Costa was Governor of 2-A2 and was serving on the 1984-85 Council of Chairmen. Of course, Texas Lions Camp continued to be a full-fledged project of Texas Lions who were bracing for their Texas-sized celebration in late November 1984. The celebration included a Longhorn Parade down Main Street and a rawhide ribbon-cutting that officially opened a new hotel. Saturday night saw an Old West costume ball, where guests feasted from the unique cuisine honoring the

Hill Country's heritage. Tastebuds were tantalized by rattlesnake paté, blackbuck antelope in Aspic, escargot, sweet and sour axis deer, and whole roast suckling pig.

As has been mentioned, one of the greatest Texas Lions in the second half of this century of Lionism is Mike Butler from Kerrville, Texas—who, along with his lovely wife, Annette helped entertain every leader throughout the years from 1970s on that came to Texas to their home in Kerrville. He always had a wonderful knack for serving food, and the right food for all occasions. It was certainly appreciated and meant a lot to their guests. As can be seen from his resumé below, Mike has been very active in Lions' affairs, and has been of great assistance to state secretaries and all other Lions that have come into Kerrville on Lions' business. He participated in all Texas Lions Zone Forums, and over 20 U.S./Canada Lions Forums since they began in 1969—making six or seven presentations at those Forums. Unfortunately, he lost his wife Annette to illness. It was a great loss to not only Mike and his family, but also to the Lions in Texas. He was later very fortunate to meet and marry Sheryl Sterling Butler, who is a Lion, and whose father was a Lion for 64 years. He served as District Governor and was very astute in all Lion affairs. Sheryl has continued both her father's and the Butler family's efforts to this day.

RESUME OF M. P. "MIKE" BUTLER

Joined Leon Valley Lions Club in March 1974.
Served Leon Valley Lions as 2nd and 1st Vice President (1975-76 / 1976-77)
Leon Valley Lion/Lioness Liaison (1976-77)
100% President Leon Valley Lions (1977-78)
District Lioness Liaison (1976-77)
District Leo Chairman (1977-78)
District Zone Chairman (1978-79)
District 2-A2 Lt. Governor (1979-80)
100% District 2-A2 Governor (1980-81)
State Treasurer (1980-81)
Received District Governor Extension Award for 3 new clubs (1980-81)

Received Extension Award for Leo Club sponsorship (1980-81)
Received several International President's Award over the years
Received Ambassador of Goodwill Award from International President
"Ebb" Grindstaff (1982-83)
Past District Governor's Association Tail Twister (1981-82 / 1982-83)
Received District Extension Award (1983-84)
Holder of Senior Master Key (effective 1/84)
Chairman of S.A. Host Committee for International Directors Board
Meeting (1983)
Charter Member of Texas Lions Camp Century Club
Life Member of Texas Lions Camp
Transferred to Kerrville Host Club in 1982
Recipient of a Melvin Jones Fellow
Voted "Lion of the Year" by Leon Valley Lions Club (1980-81)
Member Saint Paul Methodist Church – Kerrville, Texas
Past Cub Scout Master – Helotes, Texas
Past member of the P.T.O. of Helotes
Past member of the P.T.A. in San Antonio
Coached Pop Warner Football – San Antonio
Coached Little Dribblers Basketball – Kerrville
Member of Kerrville Area Chamber of Commerce
Supporter and Life Member of Girlstown, U.S.A.
Voted "Business Person of the Week" in Kerrville (October 1983)
Member of American Concrete Insitute of America
Owns and operates MPB, Inc.

Mike has three children, eight grandchildren and nine great-grand-children. Tragically, he lost his son, Jerry in an auto accident in 1985.

The continuing saga of one of the great leaders of Lionism during the last 25 years has been nearly a full-time job for Mike Butler. Why? He believes in service in all phases of Lionism, including, but not limited to his involvement in:

1. Constitutional expert from his training provided by Past International President, Herb Petry, and from serving on the Committee as Chairman.

2. A speaker at anniversaries, any Lions' meeting, District and State Conventions, and many places outside of Texas and the U.S., due to his popularity.

3. Group leader at Forums in MD 2-A at the U.S./Canada Lions Forums throughout the world of Lionism on "Get 'em and Keep 'em" (membership and extension).

4. Adviser to the Council of Governors before, during and after their meetings.

In addition to his many activities in Texas, and on the Board, he has traveled to many different states in America and all over the world. He can be of no greater service to Lionism than in the manner that he is presently offering as a leader and an adviser to the Lions of Texas. THERE IS NO GREATER LION THAT HAS GIVEN MORE IN SHARING THE VISION OF SERVICE THAN MIKE BUTLER. Thanks, Mike!

Howard Leverett

Howard Leverett, a Houston native, was the state's Council Chairman in 1988. Howard, along with his wife Sue, was not only a popular Council Chairman, but also a very effective one who led the Lions of Texas to great membership gains. In fact, he was probably the leader of one of the best all-around Councils in Texas.

One of the great things that the Lions of Texas did was to create an "elite" uniform—including chaps, spurs, cowboy boots, Hawaiian shirts, a Texas vest and a Western hat. You have to know Howard to know that he was a large person, and another name used for him was "Heavy Levy". He wore his elite uniform at Lions conventions, and at one convention, for some odd reason, his chaps began to work their way down and were about to come off by the time Howard and his peers reached the reviewing stand. All of the Governors and Lions hollered to keep his chaps up, becoming the mantra of Howard's Council, *"Keep your chaps up!"*

Howard established a rule at Council meetings that it was would be efficient, but to the point, in order that meetings would be finished before noon each time. However, one of the Council meetings finished about 10:30 a.m., and the Council had done everything they intended to do. As they were sauntering out after the Council meeting, Past International President Herb C. Petry, Jr. showed up. Herb said, "Ya'll taking a coffee break, or what?" We said, "No, sir, we're through." And he said, "No, you're not. I haven't talked to you yet." We replied, "Yes, Sir, we have already adjourned this meeting and we're not going back to start another one." Past President Herb was a bit upset with the Council, but on the other hand, was pleased to know that that they had taken care of their business and were ready to go on to other items that needed their attention. Thank you, Howard for your services as a District Governor, and also as one of our state's outstanding Council Chairmen.

Ray Hughston

by "Ebb" Grindstaff with assistance from PID Bev Stebbins and
PDG/Chairman-Elect of the Council of Governors for 2017-18, Richard Talbert

Lion Ray Hughston of the Brownsville Downtown Lions Club first joined Lionism in 1948 and continues to serve to this day. Lion Ray served District 2-A3 as District Governor in 1984-85, and served as Council Chair for MD-2 in 1985-86. Thereafter, Ray served as an International Director for Lions Club International from 1990-92 as the first serving International Director from District 2-A3. In addition to receiving the Ambassador of Good Will from Lions International, District 2-A3 not only designated him for induction to the Texas Lions Hall of Fame in 1986, but also established the Ray Hughston Humanitarian Award in his honor in 1996, and names an outstanding Lion serving in the District each year.

While PID Ray's service to Lions International and District 2-A3 has been long-standing and exemplary, his true love in Lionism can be found in Kerrville at the Texas Lions Camp. If there is one that had more love for the Camp than Ray Hughston, other than his mentor noted below, he has not appeared on the scene. One of the reasons for this, besides the children attending the Camp, is Past District Governor Jack Wiech—also a member of the Brownsville Downtown Lion Club and PID's Ray's mentor in Lionism. PDG Jack, a lawyer by trade, did not originate the idea of the Camp, but is credited with taking the ball and running with it to have the Camp established as the preeminent project in all of Texas Lionism in 1949. PDG Jack served as the initial President of the Camp from 1949–1953, and attended 100 consecutive Camp Board meetings during his service to the Camp. The Camp honored PDG Jack by designating its highest honor as the Jack Wiech Award and naming the Administration Building after Jack and Elizabeth Wiech.

PID Ray's love for the Camp is easily seen in what became known as the "Crazy Ray and Skinny Bones Bike Ride" from College Station, Texas to San Diego, California (a distance of 1,412 miles) in 1999 (at which time Crazy Ray was 72 years old, and Skinny Bones was not exactly skinny). Skinny

Bones is otherwise known as PDG Ed Stebbins, husband of PID Beverly Stebbins, and served as President of the Camp in 2001-2002.

PID Bev tells the story in a very clever, clear and touching way in the following passage:

"The Texas Lions Camp"

The Texas Lions Camp has been the "crown jewel" project for Lions across Texas for many years. Officially charted or created in 1949, it would celebrate 50 years of serving the children of Texas in 1999. A major Texas Lions Camp devotee, Past International Director Ray Hughston, had a dream—a plan for highlighting that 50-year anniversary in a special way. His plan was for a bicycle ride from the State Convention in College Station, Texas, to the Lions International Convention in San Diego, California. In February 1998 in Kerrville, he challenged PDG Ed Stebbins—a member of the TLC Executive Committee—to join him in riding from College Station to San Diego. Never one to turn down a challenge, PDG Ed agreed. PID Ray recruited PCC Lin Rose (2-S3) to be Wagonmaster of the caravan. Ray scouted out the route and decided on locations for daily stops across Texas, New Mexico, Arizona and California. Motorhomes and other RVs would provide the housing and support for the riders across the country. Riders received pledges and donations for the Camp, some based on dollars per miles ridden. Five or six bike riders rode the distance from College Station to San Diego, including PID "Crazy Ray" and PDG "Skinny Bones" Ed Stebbins. Other riders rode short segments between stops (i.e. from College Station to Caldwell, or east of El Paso to downtown El Paso).

The ride took approximately one month, with daily rest stops at the RV Parks which PID Ray had located in advance. Starting out from the Bush Library on the Texas A&M campus on May 23, they went through Caldwell and Dime Top, stopping for the first night at the home of PDG Mike Morgan in Giddings. From Giddings to Austin—where they received a send-off from Governor George Bush—then on to New Braunfels and to Boerne by way of the edge of San Antonio, the riders were supported by local Lions. From Boerne on to Kerrville and the sendoff from the Camp, neither rain nor heat nor hills everywhere could keep the riders from reaching Junction. Texas is NOT flat level country, as the riders would gladly testify. Each day when the riders called it a day, local Lions took good care of them when it came to food. Barbeque was the most common food, but not always. No one went hungry. On across Texas to El Paso meant the riders covered about half their ride. The distance across west Texas (2-A1 and 2-T3) was hot and dry, and hills turned into mountains.

Spending the night at an RV Park just east of El Paso set the stage for one of the big events of the ride—the stalwart riders were joined by many T3 Lions to into downtown El Paso to the Old Train Station. Some of the local cyclists were riding vintage bikes that had not been ridden for years. Even the support vehicles, RVs and motorhomes (which usually drove ahead to the next rest stop) made the trek into El Paso to the Old Train Station—on a Monday morning during rush hour traffic. It was a harrowing experience and there were some close calls getting on and off the main road, but it was unforgettable.

From downtown El Paso, the riders and caravan spent the night in Anthony, just west of El Paso. El Paso Lions provided a memorable evening dinner and entertainment before the "do or die" core of riders headed into New Mexico and points west.

It certainly did not get any cooler or easier as the troop crossed southern New Mexico, including stops in Las Cruces, Deming and Lordsburg. Arizona presented several challenges, but the Wild West riders peddled westward. If west Texas is hot and dry and NOT flat, New Mexico and Arizona proved not to be any different, maybe even more harsh. Texas Canyon in Arizona was a major challenge, going up peddling hard, followed by coasting down with brakes on. Some of the RV parks where the entire entourage stopped for the night or a rest day were very nice, but some were...well...on a scale of one to 10, they were a one or two. The trailers and motorhomes provided COOL rest each day—unless the electricity went off at the park (some of the group had generators, but some did not).

If Texas Canyon in Arizona was a challenge, Incopah Peak in California was almost the nemesis of the "never say quit" riders from Texas. After crossing Incopah Peak, it was downhill "sorta" into southern California. "San Diego or Bust" was now San Diego reached!

The stalwart five or six riders who had completed the entire trek rode their bicycles into the Pacific ocean in San Diego, and in the LCI parade. The event, which was a fundraiser for the Texas Lions Camp, raised $150,000. "Skinny Bones" Stebbins had some doubters who had pledged $1 per mile, because they never dreamed he would ride the distance in Texas, much less to San Diego! Those pledge checks represented thousands of dollars.

A trip that took about a month going west only took a couple of days returning back home, with bicycles on racks and at least four wheels replacing two wheels as exclusive means of transportation.

(Note: I became DG in San Diego in 1999 attending DGE School as soon as we reached San Diego)

It is, among other reasons, PID Ray's long and continuous commitment to service to others through Lions International and the Texas Lions Camp that I write this with a great deal of respect.

Marshall Cooper

In 1964, I moved to Whiteface, Texas to run a girls home called "Girlstown, USA." The first day I was on the job, the Superintendent of schools came out to my office and said, "You WILL join the Lions Club." He didn't say "Will you," he said "You WILL." He said, "Anybody who is anybody in this community is in the Lions Club." So the next Monday, I joined the Lions Club. That was in 1964, and I have been a Lion ever since. I have 100% attendance ever since that time and have enjoyed my Lionistic years.

I was elected District Governor in 1980, and served in 1980-81 and was installed in Chicago. Our President was Bill Chandler. There were only 15 Texas Governors at that time. We had a really good group of Governors, and we had a lot of training. Our Council Chairman was C. Howard Leverett from Houston. Howard was a very good Council Chairman, a good teacher, a trainer and he didn't put up with a lot of guff from us, even though he had a tough bunch to work with. Some of our Governors were Lynn Cherry, Glendon Westbrook from San Angelo, Bill Melton from Dallas, and Bruce Rickerd from Carthage.

I remember one of the things we had over at District Governor-elect School was a Past President from Oklahoma was one of our speakers. Our theme that year was "Touch a Life with Hope," and our theme song was "It's a Small World" with a few changes in words to fit Lionism. We all faced the problem of membership and we were challenged to not drop anybody during the year and to try and increase our membership; by the end of the year, we were exactly even. We had not lost any members, we had not gained any members, and the way we did that was to build two new clubs which took care of the numbers that had dropped during that time. You've got to have at least one or two new clubs in order to break even.

One of the great things we did at the next International Convention was to have an "Elite" uniform. We had chaps, spurs, cowboy boots, Hawaii shirts and a Texas vest, and a western hat. Howard Leverett (a big rotund fellow) had on chaps that began to work their way down and were about to come off about the time we approached the reviewing stand, and we all hollered at him to keep his chaps up. This became our mantra, "Keep your chaps up!"

I recall at one of our Council Meetings that we had finished early—we got in, took care of our business, did everything we needed to do, and we broke and we were through for the morning—and as we went out, Past International President Herb C. Petry, Jr. showed up. Herb said, "Y'all taking a coffee break or what?" We said, "No, sir, we're through." And he said, "No, you're not. I haven't talked to you yet." We said, "Yes sir, we have already adjourned this meeting and we're not going back to start another one." Past President Herb was a little bit upset with us, but on the other hand, I think he was pleased that we got in, took care of business, got it over with, and didn't do a lot of extra BS. That was the kind of leader Howard Leverett was for us.

Mike Butler was in that group as a representative. At that time, he lived in San Antonio, but moved to Kerrville about the same time and was a member of the Kerrville Host Lions Club.

We continued our work, and I was very interested in the Lions Camp because I had worked with kids for a long time. As a result, I served on the Texas Lions Camp Board and worked my way through the chairs. I was President of the Texas Lions Camp around 1987, somewhere along there. I had a great experience and a great run with the Texas Lions Camp, and still serve on that Board as a Past President. I also make the meeting and go to the committee meetings. I served on the Public Relations Committee. We've seen lots of improvements in the Lions Camp over those years and have seen it grow with the facilities and the services that are provided. There were a lot of interesting things that happened during the time that I was serving on the Executive Committee. The Lubbock Lions Club built the swimming pool. Then they found out it wasn't big enough, and we needed a way for the kids to take a wheelchair and go down into the water; in a wheelchair especially designed to stay in the water. They would put them in there and roll them around. So the Lions Club built the second swimming pool, and Ron Betenbough, who was my Lieutenant Governor(in those days we called them Lieutenant Governors) the next year when they finished the pool. As they dedicated the pool, they threw Governor Ron Betenbough into the pool—christening it (and him) real well.

We've been very active with the camp through the years. Professionally, I was running children's homes during the time I've been serving as a Lion. I did that for about 46 years. Girlstown at Whiteface, then I went to Beaumont. I started out at West Texas Boys Ranch in the early 50s, '54-'55, somewhere along in there, and then in 1964 I went to Girlstown. In 1987, I left Girlstown, after 23 years to the day, moved over to Beaumont, Texas, where I had been offered a job. The Director of Boys Haven had tragically suffered a heart attack and died while he was standing in line at the airport. They were then in need of a Director, and because I had a license, they were hounding me and knew I didn't have a job, so I finally went down and interviewed and went to work for them in '87 and stayed there for 13 years, then moved back to Lubbock. I moved to Lubbock, (close to Whiteface) and joined the Lubbock South Plains Lions Club. I've had a very good experience in that club—a good club about 60 members strong. Wanda became secretary of the club and we've enjoyed being over there. Their big projects are selling roses and Christmas wreaths, and we also do a lot with the Boys and Girls Clubs and other activities there in the Lubbock area.

In 1987, when we were still living in Beaumont, some folks in Lionism started talking to me about running for International Director—something I had never had any inkling to do and not real concerned about doing it. In the early 1990s, several came and talked to me about it. I said, "Okay, I might as well try it," so I started campaigning for an International Director position.

I had an opponent from the College Station Noon Lions Club, fellow by the name of Freddy Walter, a Past District Governor. He and I ran the race in Texas and when it all boiled down, I won the race by one vote. It's hard to tell me that one vote doesn't matter, because that one vote gave me the opportunity to serve as an International Director.

My first year, I served with Jim Coffey as my President and learned a lot that year. Jim was a good President to work with and we had some good opportunities. We had a board meeting in Columbus, Ohio, one in Puerto Rico, and one in Vienna, Austria.

The next year, our President was Pino Grimaldi. Pino was from Italy. We had a board meeting in Rome. I had an audience with the Pope—that was a very impressive situation for an old Baptist boy from West Texas to be able to have an audience with the Pope. He was a tremendous individual. That was Pope John Paul II. He greeted each one of the Lions that was on the Board in their native language. A brilliant man, and it was very impressive. We got to tour the Sistine Chapel and we were able to see a lot of Rome. We went to a Family Night in Rome and Pino got up to make his Presidential speech. The Board was there, along with probably 300 Italian Lions. Pino got up and talked for about 30 minutes in Italian and then said, "For those board members who do not speak Italian, would you like for me to now give my speech in English?" Of course, we all said, "No, we know what you said!" We didn't tell him that though, we just told him no. That was quite an experience, the Italian Lions were very gracious. We were very warmly welcomed. They drank a lot of wine and smoked a lot of cigarettes during that banquet, which lasted about four and a half hours, but we had a great time there. I went over to Vienna when we went to the board meeting again. Then I went over to Salzburg and saw where they filmed the "Sound of Music" and rode the train over and back. We got in a sandstorm and then a snowstorm over in Halsburg, but we had a great experience. We got to travel to a number of places that we would have never otherwise gotten to go.

Only two Directors a year get to go to Alaska, because there are only two districts in Alaska. I was lucky enough to get to be one of those one year. That was quite an experience. I got to do a lot of traveling. We certainly enjoyed our time as we traveled a good bit. We were gone every weekend (except for Christmas and Easter, when we opted to stay home) on speaking engagements for the two years we were on the board, and one year after.

We served with some great people. Out of our group of International Board members, we served with people who became Vice Presidents or Presidents. We served with Jim Ervin, from Georgia; J. Frank Moore from Alabama; and Al Brandel from New York. These guys went on to be President. Out of our group, T. S. Lee became President. We had a great group during the two years we were on the Board. They were great Lions, some of them progressed quite well and became leaders of our association. The experience we had there was tremendous.

We got to travel places that we would never get to travel. When you are in the childcare business, like Wanda and I were, you didn't make much money. The people who ran those facilities and who paid the bills thought that if you work with children, you ought to work for free. So the salaries were not good. We could never, had it not been for Lions, have traveled to the places that we went. We rocked along and enjoyed being in Lionism. We worked hard to get Jimmy Ross elected, and when Jimmy was elected to the International President's position, I was appointed to the board. One of the board meetings was in Beijing, China, and that's another place I would never have been able to travel to without that position. We also had a board meeting, of course, in San Antonio.

We got to travel a good bit. Jimmy asked me to go to every one of the Eyeglass Recycling Centers in the United States and Canada and give him a report on what they were doing and how they were doing it. That was a great experience. Once again, from everything we saw, Indiana had more of the recycled glasses and probably handled more glasses than anybody else, but their facility was just controlled chaos. Their warehouse was very unorganized, and so full you couldn't walk through it, but they handled a lot of glasses and most of it was with volunteer help. They had maybe one or two paid people. Texas was second, and we were coming up the line. Our facilities were much better. We added on and did a lot of things with it. That was a really tremendous experience to get to go to all of those facilities in the U.S. and Canada. There has been more added since that time that we have not seen, but I have talked to many of those people.

I have been able to go to Mexico on a number of eyeglass recycling training missions. What we would do is take a group of trained Lions and most Past Governors. My first trip was with Sue Fitzgerald as our leader, because Ike's mother was very ill. As a matter of fact, I think she passed away while we were down in Nicaragua. We went down there and spent a week. We had some good training and good experience. We would go into those facilities and train a minimum of 20 Lions on how to place recycled glasses that had been catalogued, how to obtain a near refractive status of the eye, how to run the auto refractor, how to do the enzometer, how to use the glaucoma tonometer, and how to get their near prescriptions. We took the necessary equipment with us, then we would leave it with Lions in those places. I learned a whole lot. The bug will get you and you will want to go back and do it again, as I did. I think I wound up with 11 different missions which included Mexico, Nicaragua, Guatemala and Honduras, (our favorite).

We went to Honduras a number of times. We would go into San Pedro Sula on the plane and have a great time. One of the reasons we went into San Pedro Sula was because we could fly from Houston directly there. From there we could take buses and travel to different places in Honduras and had some tremendous experiences there. One evening, after working all day, we went to a dedication of a church that one of the Lions was involved in. We were sitting in the back with the dedication and the music and the speaker speaking, and the biggest hog you've ever seen in your whole life came walking in the front doors and went from one side of the church to the other. They had a door on each side of the podium and the pulpit. This big old hog came walking in one door, walked across the church and walked right back out. Nobody seemed to notice, except for those of us who were not accustomed to that sort of thing. Then about 10 minutes later, here comes the biggest dog you've ever seen—mangy, scroungy-looking dog. He comes in and instead of going all the way across, he comes in and goes down the middle aisle. He checks everything and everybody out, then goes on out the back door. That was kind of a new experience for us. They were just building the church and it didn't have any real doors or windows in it. That was one of the side events we saw. We stopped on the way to that church and got some plantains, or little small bananas, and they were very tasty. It was really quite an experience.

We had a lot of good experiences on some of those trips. We did find an ice cream store in San Pedro Sula that one of the Lions owned. We did a training there for a week, and for the first few evenings, the owner of the ice cream store would take us to his shop and the ice cream would be free. After about the third day, he decided we might break him if he kept that up, so he told us that we had to pay for our own ice cream. But it was worth it. They had some of the finest coconut ice cream I've ever eaten anywhere. It was very good. One evening the people that worked there got tired of us eating so much ice cream that they said it was time for them to close. They told us they were going to close and leave, and for us to just make sure the door locked behind us. They just left us there, we ate some more ice cream, and then we left.

The Eyeglass Recycling Program is an outstanding program, and I really have gotten into that. In Lubbock, when Terrell Thompson was our District Governor, he asked his Council and the District Cabinet to vote to support a Recycling Program in Lubbock. We worked on that for about four to six months. Then somebody said, "Why don't you do something for the kids?" So we talked to a group of optometrists in town that belonged to a group called South Plains Eye Care Services. We talked to them and got about five or six of them to volunteer. We set up a clinic with a complete doctor's office in a Lubbock Children's Health Clinic where the doctors would examine the kids. We also got the school nurses to work with us on this, and if the school nurses recommended the kids, we would provide glasses for them.

Each of the Lions in our district would provide $2.00 per member per year, and that would keep us in bind with the lenses we needed. We would bring the kids in where a doctor examined them, then let the kids pick out the frames they wanted. We would then send the frames and prescription to Midland where they would make the glasses, then send them back to us. We've gotten right at 2,000 pairs since December 10, 2010. We have been very successful with that program thanks to a lot of the Lions help (and some non-Lions help). We have a couple whose son-in-law is a Lion, and they got interested in this because they wanted to learn and go on missions to Peru with us, so they helped us with the supplies and glasses that go to Peru.

We've been enjoying that program just as much as anything else. When we set up the Foundation and the 501(c)3, instead of the Board of Directors, for the operation of the Texas Lions Eyeglass Recycling Center, there were about three of us that set up the by-laws, and all the things we needed to incorporate to get our 501(c)3 for the Center.

Ike Fitzgerald, Frances McDonald and myself wrote all of it up and got it ready to go. We got it passed through the Council of Governors, and that was when Tut Tawwater was Council Chairman. Then we started operating as our own 501(c)3. We moved the operation of the Center from the Midland Downtown Lions Club building, which, by the way, was purchased by the Texas Lions Eyeglass Recycling Center, but we were running out of room. We didn't have the facilities, warehouse space and so forth. Midland Suburban Lions Club made a deal with the Texas Lions Eyeglass Recycling Center, and we bought their building. They had a big warehouse (that had at one time been a tile shop) and four or five acres of land. We set up there and have been operating very successfully since that time. I got elected as treasurer of that board; Claude Durham from Livingston was chairman. Ron Knott from New Braunfels was vice-chairman; Carolyn Keskitalo was one of our officers, along with Bob Edwards who was the office manager and warehouse manager for a while, with Ike serving as CEO. Things rocked along pretty good, then we had some internal problems and Carolyn Keskitalo became our CEO. Ike was having some problems with dementia. After his wife, Sue passed away, he spent a lot of time at the Center, working really hard, and then the dementia situation kind of hit. It became really hard for him, and he obviously couldn't run it anymore.

Ron Knott is our chairman at this point. Officers have been elected and things are going well. We have a lot of work to do, and we continue to do that work. Housing became a real problem whenever we would have people come in for three or four days to train from all over the country, and from foreign countries—such as Mexico and Africa—so they could go back to wherever they live and put on recycled glasses, how to read them, separate them and do the things that need to be done. We had the oil boom hit Midland, and we couldn't get people to come in because it would cost them about $200 a night per room, which nobody could afford, and if you could afford one, you couldn't find one because the oil companies were taking them all up. We borrowed some money from Ike Fitzgerald and bought a bunkhouse. When we got the bunkhouse installed, it would sleep 16. There were four bedrooms with bunk beds in each of those, along with a bathroom and a closet. In the middle of the bunkhouse was a kitchen and dining room-type facility. We have some good training and good experiences. We start the training on the third Thursday of each month. We start on Thursday with Thursday and Friday training, then on Saturday, we have a hands-on clinic with the adults.

Our licensed Optician and lab person is Tom Mills. He and one of the Lions in Midland—Hayden Mitton—make the glasses. Tom taught Hayden how to do all of it. With the adults, we use recycled glasses, unless we can't find a certain one, and then Tom will make them a pair of glasses. We started having a children's clinic, and Dr. Gould was doing the clinic in the Downtown Midland Lions building, but he decided to move out to the Recycling Center, where we built him a doctor's office and put in the equipment it needed. He then started seeing kids there. On Thursdays, they do a clinic for kids that are referred from school nurses. Dr. Gould examines them, then the kids pick out their frames and the lab makes them. They're usually ready by the next day, and the kids come back and pick up their glasses. That's a new program, but it's doing very well. We were able to get an article in the Midland Magazine that they put out in the hotels and businesses and offices. We've had some good coverage from that.

Conrado "Connie" de la Garza

Lion C. "Connie" de la Garza of the Harlingen Lions Club first joined Lionism in 1968, and continues to serve to this day with 44 years of perfect attendance. Lion Connie served District 2-A3 as District Governor in 1992-1993, and thereafter served as MD-2 Membership Chair. He was the very first Hispanic to serve as an International Director from Texas for Lions Club International from 1999-2001, when he was elected in San Diego California at the 82nd International Convention—the same year that Past International Director "Crazy" Ray Hughston and Past District Governor Ed "Skinny Bones" Stebbins rode bicycles from College Station, Texas to San Diego, California.

Connie has received three International Leadership Awards and two Extension Awards, and District 2-A3 inducted him in to the Texas Lions Hall of Fame in 2001.

During his tenure, he encouraged all Lions to be "MAD" Lions—that is to **Make A D**ifference in this world through extending membership opportunities to others, and through living the Lions Motto of "We Serve." Lion Connie is also a Melvin Jones Fellow, a Jack Wiech Fellow of the Texas Lions Camp, and a Texas Lions Fellow of the Texas Lions Foundation.

In addition to his service to Lionism, Connie served the City of Harlingen as Mayor for six years, served 12 years on the Board of Regents for Texas State Technical College (with the last four as Chairman of the Board), and has served on numerous other civic committees and boards. Lion Connie also had the privilege of serving on the Inaugural Committees for both Texas Governors—George W. Bush in 1999, and Rick Perry in 2003.

Past Director Connie continues to encourage all Lions to be MAD Lions.

Jimmy Ross

In the late 1950s, my father was a charter president of a club in Beaumont where I attended high school, so I had a working knowledge of what Lions were all about and this was actually a philosophy of our family, giving, being a part, doing things.

I went to West Texas A&M for my undergraduate and the University of Arizona for graduate work. While in Lubbock working in public relations (at the High Plains Underground Water Conservation District). The attorney that I was working with, Don Rafting, invited me to come to a Lions Club meeting and that's when I joined the South Plains Lions Club. After I worked for Governor Preston Smith and after he was out of office, I came back to the local area and moved to Quitaque where I purchased a ranch. A local banker invited me to join the Quitaque Lions Club. Two weeks later I was elected third vice-president, and I was glad, because any time I am a part of any organization, I want to lead it. The philosophy of my family was, "If you're a part of it, lead it." A year later the second vice-presidents decided that they did not want to serve as president, so I went in as president. The bells and whistles went off and it felt like the club was dead. That was a concern of mine. The attendance of our club at that time was around nine to 11 members.

Over the next several months, we did many things to develop the club and the excitement in town. At the end of that year, our average attendance was forty-four. Then, I was asked to serve as a zone chairman. At the first meeting I had with the governor he asked me if I would be a candidate for lieutenant governor and I ran and was successful. Before I was lieutenant governor, my first convention after serving as a President and Zone Chairman, was the International Convention in Dallas. Thereafter, I became Governor and my district led the state in membership and extension. Later I was elected Council Chairman. I told my governors at that time that I would assist them in organizing as many clubs as they would take care of and we would go out and organize clubs. By the August meeting we had sixteen clubs and it created an excitement not only in Texas but outside the State.

In 2002, under the direction of President Kay Fukushima, I gave membership and extension seminars to every group of the new District Governors.

During subsequent years, I was invited to organize clubs on 6 continents. By this time, I had organized over 500 clubs and was recognized as organizing more clubs and bringing in more charter members than anyone.

As President (2006-2007), I wanted a simple, yet powerful theme that encompassed what we do and chose "WE SERVE." I also called for a paradigm shift, making the clubs the center of importance and focusing on making us a family organization, both for men and women and boys and girls, with an eye to the future for recruiting new members from younger generations.

I also pushed to expand the scope of Lions and encourage the organization to think in broader terms, such as working in conjunction with our state department on projects throughout the world. Other areas where I encouraged new thinking included moving away from having a Presidential Program every year to having a Lions Clubs International Program with a standard yearly theme of "WE SERVE" in order to promote continuity from president to president. I am also proud of the fact that I pushed the organization to take an analytical and expanded examination of expenditures and look for cost-cutting areas, such as using a video conference instead of extensive travel, and working in sync with large corporations and private donors to financially streamline the organization.

Whenever my father and I would be driving back to Kerrville, we had many opportunities to stop and visit with the President in Ballinger. President Ebb was always a good friend of my father and myself, and we really appreciate him. Not only when my father and I would go through, but when other Lions from district 2-T1 would go through, we would stop by his office. It was always a very nice meeting and he was always cordial and always very, very helpful. An officer, President Kusiak from Maryland, invited me to come to his district, and with his assistance, we organized eight clubs in a short few days and we also put members in clubs.

While a first year director, I was in Brazil with Augustin Soliva and as I traveled I would make speeches in Spanish. Sometimes it was called "Spanglish" but different dialects have a different way of speaking Spanish so it was interesting, but it was always entertaining because they would be glad to come up and explain to me how I misspoke. They invited me and others to the White House to discuss how they were going to get people off of welfare. At that time, many of the Lions of Texas had a lot of friends who could assist people in giving jobs.

While second vice-president, I organized some clubs in Arizona when I got the call from the Executive Committee telling me that I had been endorsed to be the second vice-president. Before I was endorsed that year I had virtually been in three or four different continents organizing clubs. I was very fortunate as an officer to work with some other outstanding officers, starting with President Dr. Tae Sup Lee. It was great to be able to work with them, and the staff of the headquarters was extremely strong and extremely good and they were able to work with me very closely and it was a joy.

As president I did not feel like a dictator, as I felt like we had a board of directors who came together to make decisions. It was truly a joy, I never felt pressure of any kind. It was just a real warm feeling all around as an officer. It was probably one of the easiest jobs that I've ever had to do. Then I was elected president and one of our first visits was to the White House, when George Bush was the president and we had a steak dinner. There were probably 400 people there, and 12 were introduced. Velda and I were two of the 12, so I felt very honored to be able to be a part of that. I presented Stetson hats to the White House and presented one to President Bush. We actually met with many presidents of many different countries including the Pope and the royal family of Japan. We had high tea with them and I presented hats. While presenting a hat to a prime minister of China, he said, "My father had a Stetson, and I have one now." In Taiwan, the president who received the hat said, "Wow! I have a hat. Where are my boots?" So I had some boots made and sent to him.

We were fortunate to give the 10,000,000th dose of medicine that kills parasites to keep a person from becoming blind in Africa. We went into one location and we pulled into a large courtyard with 200 girls ages 14-20 sitting there. I waved to them and then we went upstairs and there were babies on the floor. There were pens set up all around a large room about 100x200 feet. The pens were like what you would keep goats in and they had one pen that was full of babies wrapped in swaddling clothes. They had AIDS and these were their children but they also had AIDS. We had no medication for them, but we tried to teach them some kind of profession, like sewing, so that they could make some money before they and their babies died.

When we walked out in front of those girls onto a little stage, their eyes were hollow. The girls had no expression on their faces. As I remember, it was one of the most difficult speeches and one of the most devastating facts that I had ever, ever, ever have been around. I was able to witness and help take bandages off a lady's eye who had never seen her children. They were gathered around her bed as the doctors pulled the bandages off from the surgery that she was able to have due to Lions efforts. She was able to open her eyes and see her children.

There was an occasion in New Zealand, not as emotional, but serious for me. They wanted to see me ride a horse, and so I said fine. I looked at the horse and could tell the way he was standing he was not comfortable to saddle, or was not comfortable with anyone around it. They were there to see me get thrown off. I had two options. One, turn and walk away and let them laugh, or ride the horse. I caught ahold of the bridle and pulled it around right up against the side of the horse and then I got on. When I lifted the horses head, it turned its head around and it started bucking. It bucked for over 100 yards. But I did not get thrown off. They said get on this horse we want to take a picture of somebody who can ride, but the bad part was there was a lady there who wanted to ride a horse. She got on the bronc that they had brought for me to ride and was thrown off and she was hurt very badly and had to go to the hospital.

My theme was "We serve" because it was not about me, it was about the association. During the campaign, Lions continued what was known as a "Taste of Texas". When we went to the convention, we brought food from all over Texas and served it to the convention Lions so they could have a "Taste of Texas". Pat Carroll did a great job with the "Taste of Texas" and she did it on her own. I just asked her and she said she would. I was very, very proud of it, and that's why it is so nice being from Texas because we have the pride.

My campaign chairman was Beverly Stebbins. I was criticized by many people who said a lady never had been the campaign chairman, but Beverly

Stebbins did a great job. I appointed PID Beverly Stebbins, PID Marshall Cooper, and PID Mike Butler to my board and they did a great job for me. They were able to be my eyes and ears as my appointees.

As president we were in the Sight First Program. That was a very, very rewarding opportunity. I was able to stand and speak all around the world and raise money for SightFirst 1, and then also be able to give a little direction for SightFirst 2, because we as Lions in the past had not been doing anything with refractive error (glasses that correct this refractory error). There are so many people in the world that have refractive error as a challenge, so we were able to get refractive error available to us. It also gave Vice Presidents, Presidents and Chairmen of the Foundation the ability to be able to set policy and to be able to know and see and understand where the money was going and how it was being used; and to be able to appreciate the World Health Organization and what they were able to bring to the table. In the very beginning, some people had some misconceptions, like who are they and telling us how to spend our money, but they were not telling us how to spend their money. They were advising us of what they saw and they did an outstanding job and I really developed some outstanding friendships with them because they are some of the best people I know. Also as chairman I was able to spend two weeks with Former President Jimmy Carter and Past District Governor Jimmy Carter in Africa, flying from location to location and we were helping to develop Lionism and also to be able to understand what the needs were and to be able to sit and discuss with the government leaders of Africa some of the challenges that they really had and were not wanting to see. We are, the world is saying, developing the eyeglass industry, the Lions are assisting eyeglass recycling people and all the teams, such as Past International Director Marshall Cooper and Past District Governor Ike Fitzgerald and everyone that has been doing it for so long in an attempt to carry eyeglass recycling to a higher level where we assist the people to make their own glasses. (This concept is continued in detail under the Recycling Center in Midland.) This is a great need in Africa and they are actually, at this moment, taking grant applications to LCIF to be able to assist in the recycling programs' development. Development of things in Africa are ongoing and they are not moving at the speed I would like, but they are still moving.

Capitol Hill Day Association is a meeting to have the Presidents in Washington, D.C. and I am the chairman of Capitol Hill Day, a new position that has just been started and the first visit is going to be in 2015 or soon thereafter. It will be primarily directors and we are going to be visiting our legislators. The program is in such an early stage of development.

What is going to be happening over the next few weeks in 2015, is legislation is going to be introduced. The Lions Alert Program began my year as President and is what we do whenever there is a disaster. The program is to train the governors, the district and have them prepared whenever a disaster does occur. We need to be there cooking breakfast for them or whatever to help them facilitate it in the proper manner, proper receipts, and proper records because many times the governor has no idea what or how or where to do it and to work with other agencies involved.

Beverly Stebbins

Four Important Episodes in My Memory of Lionism in Texas

Note: I joined a Lions Club officially in June 1992 just before the end of my husband Ed's year as District Governor of District 2-E2. At that time I had about 15 years of Lionistic experience by osmosis—being the wife of an active Lion leader in 2-E2 and MD 2. I have always thought those 15 years of observing, listening and learning about Texas Lionism gave me a head start in becoming a leader in not only my club, but also my district and the state. For that I shall always be grateful.

As the song says "Memories.....pressed between the pages of my mind" reflect events or episodes that I feel have been important over the past quarter century of Texas Lionism.

EPISODE 1: Election that led to a Major Voting Procedure Change

Texas has always played a major role in Lions Clubs International, and has always done so with its own flair. An example of this is the manner in which Texas Lions vote on Multiple District Issues, including endorsement for International Offices. For many years before the 1991-1992 International Director Candidacy Campaign, voting on Multiple District issues had been conducted by secret ballot at the individual district (16 after 1988) conventions. Those ballots had been counted at the district conventions and reported immediately to the State Secretary. At the Multiple District Convention, those results were reported and ratified by the voting delegates at that convention. Because the individual districts had conventions that spread over several weeks, it was possible to determine how any vote on any issue was going; hence, it was possible for the candidate campaigns to keep track of how the statewide voting was progressing. This endorsement campaign was between two Past District Governors who were both qualified and both well-known across Texas.

It was a hotly-contested race from beginning to end. The vote was very close as the district conventions occurred. As the race was drawing to an end, there were accusations of improprieties in the election process in some districts. This carried over to the Multiple District Convention in Amarillo in May 1992. When the original results—as reported by District Governors to the State Secretary—were reported to the convention by the Council of Governors, the outcome of the contest was ratified, but the controversy over the voting left scars and dissention across the districts. One thing became clear—some change needed to be made in the way voting was done to prevent this same divisive type of controversy from happening again. The incoming Council of Governors proceeded forward with constitutional changes in the process of counting of votes for Multiple District elections. The Lion delegates at individual district conventions would continue to vote on those MD issues, but the votes would be on separate duplicate ballots (from the district ballots) which would be put in boxes and sealed immediately after voting closed. One sealed box with the original copies would be sent to the State Secretary immediately following the election, and the other sealed box with duplicate ballots would be kept by the District Governor and brought to the State Convention. The Multiple District Election Committee would count the originals of the state ballots at the State Convention immediately before it began.

Because all District Governors brought the sealed box of duplicate ballots, if there was a question that arose, those duplicates could be opened. The results of the election would be reported and ratified at the state convention. This is the procedure that is followed at this time. There has been no major controversy in any election in MD-2 since the change prompted by the 1991-1992 ID contest.

EPISODE 2: Wild West Bicycle Ride
for Texas Lions Camp

The Texas Lions Camp has been the "crown jewel" project for Lions across Texas for many years. Officially chartered or created in 1949, it would celebrate 50 years of serving the children of Texas in 1999. A major Texas Lions Camp devotee, Past International Director Ray Hughston, had a dream—a plan for highlighting that 50-year anniversary in a special way. His plan was for a bicycle ride from the State Convention in College Station, Texas to the Lions International Convention in San Diego, California. In February 1998 in Kerrville, he challenged PDG Ed Stebbins—a member of the TLC Executive Committee—to join him in riding from College Station to San Diego. Never one to turn down a challenge, PDG Ed agreed. PID Ray recruited PCC Lin Rose (2-S3) to be Wagonmaster of the caravan. Ray scouted out the route and decided on locations for the daily stops across Texas, New Mexico, Arizona and California. Motorhomes and other RVs would provide the housing and support for the riders across the country. The riders received pledges and donations for the Camp, some based on dollars per miles ridden. Five or six bike riders rode the distance from College Station to San Diego, including PID "Crazy Ray" and PDG "Skinny Bones," Ed Stebbins. Other riders rode short segments between stops (i.e. from College Station to Caldwell, or from east of El Paso to downtown El Paso).

The ride took approximately one month, with daily rest stops at the RV Parks which PID Ray had located in advance. Starting out from the Bush Library on the Texas A&M campus on May 23, they went through Caldwell and Dime Top, stopping for the first night at the home of PDG Mike Morgan in Giddings. From Giddings to Austin, where they received a sendoff from Governor George Bush, then on to New Braunfels and to Boerne by way of the edge of San Antonio, the riders were supported by local Lions. From Boerne on to Kerrville and the sendoff from the Camp, neither rain nor heat nor hills everywhere could keep the riders from reaching Junction. Texas is NOT flat level country, as the riders would gladly testify. Each day when the riders had called it a day, local Lions took good care of them when it came to food. Barbeque was the most common food, but not always. No one went hungry. On across Texas to El Paso meant the riders had covered about half their ride. The distance across west Texas (2-A1 and 2-T3) was hot and dry, and hills turned into mountains.

Spending the night at an RV Park just east of El Paso set the stage for one of the big events on the ride—the stalwart riders were joined by many T3 Lions to ride into downtown El Paso to the Old Train Station. Some of the local cyclists were riding vintage bikes that had not been ridden for years. Even the support vehicles, RVs and motorhomes, which usually drove on ahead to the next rest stop, made the trek into El Paso to the Old Train Station—on a Monday morning during rush hour traffic. It was a harrowing experience and there were some close calls getting on and off the main road, but it was unforgettable.

From downtown El Paso, the riders and caravan spent the night in Anthony, just west of El Paso. El Paso Lions provided a memorable evening dinner and entertainment before the "do or die" core of riders headed into New Mexico and points west.

It certainly did not get any cooler or easier as the troop crossed southern New Mexico, including stops in Las Cruces, Deming and Lordsburg. Arizona presented several challenges, but the Wild West riders peddled westward. If west Texas was hot and dry and NOT flat, New Mexico and Arizona proved not to be any different, maybe harsher. Texas Canyon in Arizona was a major challenge going up peddling hard followed by coasting down with brakes on. Some of the RV Parks where the entire entourage stopped for the nights or a rest day were very nice but some were----well on a scale of 1to10,they were a 1or 2. The trailers and motorhomes provided COOL rest each day----unless the electricity went off at the park (some of the group had generators but some did not).

In Arizona, the troupe took time off to see Cochise's Stronghold and Tombstone. Tucson was a bit of a problem because officials would not allow the riders to ride on the shoulder of 1-10. They wanted the riders to detour through residential streets with local traffic. This was the only place where all the bikes were placed on the sag-wagon to move from east of Tucson to west of Tucson where they could again ride the shoulder. Back to peddling from then on. The Chuck Wagon RV had mechanical problems in Arizona and had to be left behind. Never fear---no one starved. Other support personnel picked up the slack and the group carried on. There was plenty of spaghetti provided by the Arizona Lions who were told the riders need carbs more than protein.

If Texas Canyon in Arizona was a challenge, lncopah Peak in California was almost the nemesis of the "Never say quit" riders from Texas.

After crossing lncopah Peak, it was downhill "sorta" into southern California. "San Diego or Bust" was now San Diego Reached.

The stalwart 5 or 6 riders who had completed the entire trek rode their bicycles into the Pacific Ocean in San Diego and in the LCI Parade. The event which was a fundraiser for the Texas Lions Camp raised $150,000 for the camp. "Skinny Bones" Stebbins had some doubters who had pledged $1a mile because they never dreamed he would ride the distance in Texas much less to San Diego. Those pledge checks represented thousands of dollars. A trip that took about a month going west only took a couple days returning back home with bicycles on racks and at least 4 wheels replacing 2 wheels as exclusive means of transportation. PDG Ed served as President of the Texas Lions Camp in 2001-2002. (NOTE: 1 became DG in San Diego in 1999 attending DGE School as soon as we reached San Diego.)

EPISODE 3: Campaign for a Texan to be President of LCI

Everett "Ebb" Grindstaff from Ballinger, Texas had been President of Lions International in 1982-1983. There had not been another President from Texas since. PID Jimmy Ross (1996-98) decided to seek the office going through the chairs from International Second Vice President. His campaign opened in August 2001when the MD-2 Council of Governors opened the state for someone to seek the endorsement of Texas Lions to run for 2nd VP. The campaign continued full steam ahead from August 2001until the International Convention in Detroit in 2004. The 2001-2002 year was a campaign within Texas to gain the endorsement from the Lions of Texas. Gaining momentum after the August 2001 Council meeting in Kerrville, Jimmy Ross campaigned across Texas while his campaign workers "beat the drum" in all 16 districts to get a large voter turnout at the district conventions in the Spring of 2002. Ross Rangers denim shirts, baseball caps, and JR badges joined JR boot pins as popular campaign attire and paraphernalia. Ross Rangers Clubs sported banner patches indicating financial support of Jimmy's candidacy. After the 2002 MD-2 Convention when it became official, Jimmy had the endorsement from the Lions of Texas. The plan was to actually run in 2004 in Detroit, but he went to the 2002 LCI Convention in Osaka, Japan as the endorsed candidate from Texas. Jimmy campaigned across the US and parts of the world over the next two years. The Lions of Texas continued to support his candidacy with enthusiasm across the state as plans were under way for a big Texas-style campaign in Detroit.

The highlight of the Detroit campaign was the outdoor "Taste of Texas" event like no one had seen before. Lions came from Texas with their barbeque smokers and their Tex-Mex offerings, as well as culinary treats from Texas' other ethnic groups. Not to be forgotten were desserts, including Blue Bell Ice Cream. The table decorations and the music all reflected Texas, and it all was an indication of how much the Texas Lions supported JR's campaign. All Lions at the convention were invited to attend this Texas picnic. The Texas presence in the parade earlier in the week included Ross's Rangers in denim shirts, joining the elite corps and the marchers in standard Texas Lion attire. Texas flags flew high and proud in the Michigan sky. There was a campaign rally every evening, both as a Pep Rally and as an information source for Texas Lions about the next day's schedule.

Campaign signs were joined by bluebonnet flower giveaways urging Lion delegates from around the world to vote for Jimmy Ross for 2nd V.P. Many Texas Lions were involved in the Detroit campaign—from those campaigning with materials at the Convention, to the representatives going to delegation meetings of other Multiple Districts to urge them to vote for JR, to the ones chauffeuring Jimmy and others and the ones who worked the campaign headquarters every day.

Of course, Jimmy Ross won and became 2nd V.P. Texas Lions celebrated with a private reception, as well as joining the Officers Reception for all the new officers. It was a proud time for Texas Lions knowing that JR would become the seventh International President from Texas in 2006. Now the campaign shifted to preparing for the big celebration in 2006. The JR campaign was geared up to have the 2006 convention in New Orleans. This included having the Officers Reception, which would be Texas' responsibility, at the New Orleans Aquarium instead of a hotel. In August 2005, Hurricane Katrina changed all that. Lions International had to move the 2006 convention to Boston; therefore, campaign plans had to change. Acquiring refunds for deposits made in New Orleans just before Katrina hit, and scrapping old plans and making new plans in Boston were priority items for the campaign. Unfortunately over the long run, some Texas Lions who had made plans to be in New Orleans (because it was a drivable distance) could not make the trip to Boston for the convention. Nevertheless, big plans were carried forward, because Texas wanted to show its pride in Jimmy. They brought the Hardin Simmons University Mounted Horses to lead the Texas Parade contingent. It was impressive, to say the least. Finally, Texas had another International President!

On President Ross' Board of Directors, in addition to Elected Directors and the Executive Officers, he selected nine Board Appointees from around the world. Included among the nine were three Texans—PID Mike Butler, PID Marshall Cooper, and PDG Beverly Stebbins. The October Board Meeting was in Beijing, China. This gave the Board members and spouses the opportunity to view one of the great landmarks of the world—the Great Wall—as well as the Imperial Palace and Tiananmen Square. China was beginning to rise in importance within the association, after years of being outside the association. In addition to working on the business of the association, this trip allowed the board to see Lionism in action in China.

The March 2007 Board Meeting was held "deep in the Heart of Texas" in San Antonio. This allowed board members and spouses to experience Texas hospitality and flavor. A real rodeo and a dinner on the barges of the Riverwalk were followed by a farewell dinner at the top of the Hemisphere Tower. Again, the business of the association occupied the time and energy of the board members, while spouses enjoyed getting to know San Antonio. Beijing, China to San Antonio, Texas—what a contrast and testimony to the diversity of Lionism around the world.

President Ross' year came to a close in Chicago in 2007. At the International Convention, he was presented the keys to a 2007 Lincoln Town Car as a gift from the Lions of Texas.

EPISODE 4: Time to Elect another ID

Following Jimmy Ross' year as President, while he was serving as Immediate Past President, the Lions of Texas had another campaign within MD-2. This was a contest to endorse a candidate to seek the office of International Director. At the August 2007 Council of Governors Meeting in Kerrville, the campaign was officially opened, with four candidates vying to be the next International Director from Texas. At the November Council of Governors meeting in Temple, Past Council, Joe AI Picone withdrew from the contest because of health issues leaving three candidates: PCC Michael Rourke, PDG Hal Griffin and PDG Beverly Stebbins. All three campaigned across the state visiting local clubs and district meetings, as well as sending campaign materials to clubs and Lions in all 16 districts. When the votes were counted at the State Convention in Amarillo in May 2008, PDG Bev Stebbins was the victor. She would be the first woman in Texas to serve as International Director, when chosen in Bangkok to be one of seven Directors elected from the United States. From around the world, there were 17 directors elected, including three other women—Debra Wasserman from Minnesota, Ellis Suriyati Omar from Malaysia, and Rosane Teresiha Jahnke from Brazil. Among the second-year Directors on the 2008-2009 Board were two more women— Dana Biggs from California and Patti Hill from Canada. That meant there were six women Directors—the most to serve on a Board at one time as of that year.

From Bangkok in 2008, to Maui to New York to Minneapolis in 2009, Board meetings in 2008-2009 required being directly involved in the business of the association by serving on the Membership Committee, and working with other directors to shape the decisions regarding policies and procedures—including the creation of the GMT concept to replace the old MER (L) plan. Then, the next year from Minneapolis in 2009 to New Orleans to Hamburg Germany to Sydney Australia in 2010, the 2009-2010 Board meetings included again serving on the Membership Committee, as elements of the GMT continued to be developed, as well as the GLT. In addition, the development of the Second Vice District Governor joined other issues for discussion by the board. Through two years on the board as a Director, I had the opportunity to serve as an Ambassador of Lions International across about 35-40 states or multiple districts, attending conventions and encouraging Lions to continue their Lionistic work, while answering their questions and explaining the LCI program. For many Lions, their only exposure to the International Association is a visit from an International Director; therefore, it is very important that the Director represent the association well, and help every Lion know that he/she is very important.

Beginning in Amarillo in 1992 and ending in Amarillo in 2008, my memories of these episodes encompass a wide range of thoughts about why I feel so fortunate to be a Texas Lion. Because the Lions of District 2-E2 welcomed me so warmly into the family of Lions, I decided to become a Lion. Because my husband was so active in so many areas of Lionism, I acquired priceless knowledge and an awareness which gave me the courage and insight to seek leadership roles. Because Jimmy Ross had enough faith in me to have me as his Campaign Chairman, I gained additional knowledge and experience which gave me the confidence to move forward. AND because the Lions of Texas had enough confidence in me to elect me as their ID candidate, I was able to step into the International leadership arena. Our association is one of the most important elements for good in the world. Although it may not be perfect, we must work to ensure that Lions International continues into its second century carrying on the goals and ideals from its beginning—Service—the most important thing. I count myself so fortunate to be among the leadership that Texas has sent to our association. Thank you Ebb, Mike, Marshall, Joe AI, Ray, Don, Jimmy and Connie.

Joe Al Picone

A Lion since 1966 in the Brenham Evening Lions Club, Joe Al has held many offices within the association, including club president, district governor in 1975-76, council chair 1998-99, state membership chair and state Campus club chair. While Lt Governor in 1974-75, he was instrumental in forming the Lions Eye Bank of Dist. 2-S3 and was a charter director and 1st Vice President. He also served as a member of the host committee for the Ft. Worth, Texas Forum, chair of the Texas Lions Long-Range Planning Committee, chair of the Texas Lions Camp By-Laws Committee and president of the Past District Governors Association.

In recognition of his service to the association, he has received numerous awards including the 100% District Governor Award, Harry Reasonover Award 1981-82, two International President's Certificates of Appreciation, four International President's Medals, an International President's Leadership Award, the Supreme Extension Award for 11 new Lions clubs, the Global Membership Key Award for sponsoring over 250 new Lions, and the Ambassador of Goodwill Award, the highest honor the association gives to its members.

He was also inducted into the Texas Lions Hall of Fame and is a 15 diamond Progressive Melvin Jones Fellow, a progressive Jack Wiech Fellow, a Texas Lions Fellow and a Celeste and Harrison Shepherd Fellow. In addition to his Lions activities, PID Picone is active in numerous professional and community organizations, including serving as chair of the city Planning and Zoning Commission. He has also served as president of the Board of City Development, and the Washington County Chamber of Commerce. He was inducted into the Brenham High School Hall of Fame and the Blinn College Hall of Fame. In 2013 he retired as President of the Blinn College Foundation.

He has received numerous honors, including the Washington County Man of the Year Award and being named to the Phi Theta Kappa International Hall of Honor and the Brenham Maifest Hall of Fame.

Joe Al Picone was the first Council Chairman elected from Dist. 2-S5 in 1998-99 and was elected to serve a two-year term as a director of Lions

Clubs International at the association's 94th International Convention held in Seattle, Washington July 4-8, 2011 becoming District 2-S5's first International Director.

Past International Director Picone and his wife, Merle, also a Lion, have two sons and one granddaughter.

District Governor
1975-1976

Joe Al Picone was District Governor of 2-S3. Julius Stephens was Lieutenant Governor (as they were called at that time) with Wilfred Dietrich serving as Secretary-Treasurer. This being the United States Bi-Centennial Year, the official colors of the district were red-white-blue. A tremendous gala was staged at the Villa Capri in Austin for the Mid-Winter Conference with PDG Willie Kocurek as Chairman. Over 500 people attend this event highlighting the Bi-Centennial. PDG Bill Raschke was Extension Chairman and 6 new clubs were organized this year and the district experienced a membership gain of 139. Lion Don Buckalew was an International Director at this time as well. Lion Picone recalls the great mentoring he received during his early years as a Lion from Past International President, Ebb Grindstaff, PIDs Tex Mayer and Don Buckalew. One thing of particular interest was how different the Council of Governors meetings were at that time. Actually an incoming District Governor was not encouraged to attend council meetings until the Feb. before being elected District Governor. The meetings were held in a small room at the Inn of the Hills in Kerrville

International Director
2011-2013

On July 8, 2011, Lion Joe Al Picone was elected International Director of Lions Club International at the association's 94th International Convention in Seattle, Washington. Picone retired as President of the Blinn College Foundation. In addition, he is a member of the Brenham Evening Lions Club with 49 years perfect attendance and a past Council Chairman for the State of Texas.

As he recalls some of the highlights of his years as director from 2011-2013, he mentions some of the wonderful visits to International Board meetings and speaking at other district conventions.

The first board meeting of his term was held in Hong Kong with International President Tam where he served on the Membership Development Committee and the Audit Committee. Spending 11 days in China visiting Hong Kong, Shenzen for Lions World Sight Day, and Macau was most enjoyable and exciting. San Francisco was the sight of the 2nd wonderful board meeting. This was followed by 2 weeks at the 3rd board meeting in conjunction with the International Convention in Busan, Korea which was very interesting as well. The language barrier made for hard times communicating!

During his 2nd year on the board he was Chairman of the Audit Committee, Vice Chairman of Finance and Headquarters Committee, and a member of the Women's Task Force Committee. Three committees proved to be most interesting! The first board meeting of his 2nd year was held in Indianapolis, Indiana, where everyone enjoyed a wonderful time on the Indianapolis Speedway and Speedway Museum.

International Director Joe Al and Lion Merle will always remember the wonderful time at the April 2013 board meeting in Spain. They were extremely excited to spend a few days celebrating his birthday in Barcelona and at the awesome Sagrada Familia Basilica. In Spain, they were treated to a week in Marbella at the Gran Melia Resort on Costa del Sol. This was the most beautiful place they had visited and they thoroughly enjoyed touring Ronda, Spain at an elevation of 6,000 feet. Can you believe, he was awarded a Diploma for participating in the Paella Contest at Alabardero Beach Club!?

The final board meeting in Hamburg, Germany started off great with a visit to Berlin. However, the board meeting was very stressful since ID Picone did not vote as he was instructed on the issue of endorsing a candidate for 2nd VP of Lions International for election at the International Convention in Toronto, Canada. When PID Mike Butler was not selected as the endorsed candidate, he voted the way he thought the Lions of Texas would like and voted "no" on the endorsement. While he was not in the good graces of the International officers, he remains proud having stood up for the Lions of Texas. Friendships made with other directors from all over the world will last forever.

All the official visits as an International Director were outstanding. Of particular fondness was the visit he and Lion Merle made to Salt Lake City, Utah in November 2011. While there they were treated to the live performance of the Moorman Tabernacle Choir. They were escorted to special seats inside the Tabernacle where ID Joe Al was introduced over the airwaves with the words, "We are pleased to have the Lions Club International Director from Texas, Joe Al Picone in our audience." The performance was most moving with patriotic music celebrating Veterans Day.

Also in November 2011, he went to New York where he visited West Point and was privileged to go into Cadet Chapel and see the world's largest pipe organ and walk across the Hudson Gate Bridge on a cold and windy day.

Another memorable occasion was their visit to the district convention on the beautiful island of Bermuda in March 2012 with outstanding hosts. This first ever district convention on the island was held on a gorgeous resort.

On their visit to Colonial Heights, Virginia, they were given a complimentary stay in historic Williamsburg, Virginia touring Yorktown and Jamestown.

Of course, he will always remember spending two Januarys in cold Minnesota! Being in the snow and ice with temperatures of -10 degrees in Rochester, and the next January in Minneapolis proved to be very interesting for this warm-blooded Texan!

Then a much warmer treat was the convention in sunny Ft. Lauderdale, Florida in March 2013. Also in March 2013 while visiting the Lions in Canton, Ohio, they were treated to a tour of the Pro Football Hall of Fame. April 2013 took them to Manchester, Pennsylvania visiting the Amish country.

They became addicted to lobster with two visits in May 2013 in both Maine and New Hampshire. Joe Al says he had to fall off the lobster wagon when returning to Texas!

Their final visit was to the State Convention in Iowa with ID Judy Hankom. While it was sad to see these wonderful official visits as an International Director come to an end, they will always remember the many friends made in these outstanding and memorable visits. Seeing the wonderful work of Lions all over the world - living our Motto: We Serve - was truly an awesome adventure for both Joe Al and Merle. Being an elected director of Lions Clubs International was certainly a highlight in their lives. One thing they will not miss is the airline travel!

Joe Al and Merle say that they will always be indebted to the Lions of Texas for giving them the opportunity to represent them.

Interlude
Grandchildren and Names

The most significant example of individual esteem has to be that of grandparents with their own grandchildren. When I finally got to be a grandpa, I realized all those grandparents who talked about their grandchildren are not nearly as crazy as I thought.

But don't get yourself in the situation of the Louisiana woman whose grandson asked, "Grandmama, how old are you?" and she said, "Well, grandsons don't ask their grandmama how old they are." The next day, he asked, "Grandmama, how much do you weigh?" and the grandmother said, "Well, grandsons do not ask their grandmamas how much they weigh." And the next day he came back and said, "Grandmama, I'm not going to ask you how much you weigh and I'm not going to ask you how old you are, because I found your driver's license, and on the driver's license it said that you weigh 138 pounds and that you are 62 years old—and besides that, it says you got an F in sex."

My dad always said our name is so important to protect, but in another sense, we do not know the reason, because to us, our name seems very simple. Approximately 80% of the messages that I leave for someone else, or at the time that I make the initial call, there is always a question as to how to spell my name. We have seen and heard many versions—Grindstone, Grinstaff, Millwheel, and of course, one of the most infamous came from the lawyer that served on the state bar of directors—Richard Haynes, better known as "Racehorse," which I believe came from his track days in high school. Everyone called him "Racehorse," and he became more famous in later years as one of the top criminal defense lawyers for several people, most notable being Cullen Davis. However, at the time of our service together, we were playing golf at a course in Dallas. During that activity, Racehorse kept asking me, "Now, what is your name?" I think that I finally mentioned something about Grindstone and he said, "Well, I tell you what, I think that I'm just going to call you something I can remember, 'Crankshaft.'" Therefore, we can just add "Crankshaft" to the other names mentioned above, and he did call me "Crankshaft," as did a few of the other lawyers who heard him make that statement. One of the more famous name quotes was from Herb Caen, who was the morning line editor for the *San Francisco Chronicle*. In his column of May 27, 1983, this quote appeared, "*...Lurching on: Edwin Oviaft III of First Sutter Financial here has been in correspondence with the Ballinger, Texas law firm of Grindstaff, Grindstaff and Slimp, and challenges anyone to top that. Even our own Low, Ball and Lynch comes in a poor second...*" The mail still amazes me, as we have had "Grindstall, Grindfall and Limp" and all other such combinations. However, as long as they used us as lawyers or sent us business, we did not mind.

Sam H. Lindsey, Jr.
International Director
2016-2018

What an incredible journey from a brand-new Lion in November 1972 to being elected International Director at the 99th International Convention in Fukuoka, Japan in June 2016.

My Lion life began in Conroe, Texas as a new businessman in town, trying to become known. The principles of the accounting firm I worked for were both Rotarians, and asked me to consider joining a service club. Since there was already a CPA in the Conroe Rotary, I was inducted into the Conroe Noon Lions Club in November 1972. Little did I know that my life was going to be changed forever. And not just my life, but my wife Jodye's, too.

The Conroe Noon Lions Club was a welcoming club that provided new members opportunities to grow and become involved in service. Being a new member in a growing and vibrant Lions Club gave me an experience that many new members regrettably don't get to enjoy, but learning at an early time in my Lions career how clubs operate through proper committees and projects, how Board of Directors should manage the club, and the proper way to conduct elections has served me very well throughout my Lions journey.

So much in life seems to be governed by being at the right place at the right time. I believe that those intangibles were in full force as I was a new Lion in Conroe. The first intangible was that Don Buckalew, a Past District Governor and member of the Conroe Noon Lions Club was elected as an International Director in 1974. Being able to see from afar how International Directors interact was a great experience and learning tool. It reminds me that as Lion leaders, we never know who is watching from afar, and how we might influence leaders to come. The Conroe club also participated in most all of the District activities, so I was new Lion attending zone and district meetings, and in not too many years, Jodye and I attended our first International Convention in New Orleans. It was there that I discovered pin trading, and what a truly international organization that we really are.

While I probably did not realize what was happening, I was being influenced by Lions whom I considered to be truly outstanding leaders in our District. The first of these is Past International Director, Howard Leverett. PID Leverett was District Governor the year I served as President of the Conroe Noon Lions Club. His strength, dedication and quiet confidence helped pull the District together, and showed us all what leadership could do. The next year PID Leverett served as Council Chairman, and a few years later, campaigned for (and was elected an) International Director.

Also in the District were three Past Presidents of the Texas Lions Camp: PDG Eddie Munger, PDG Jimmy McPherson and PDG Fred Hamilton. These great Lions who had served the Texas Lions Camp for so many years, and with so much love, greatly influenced me and Jodye, and set us on a path to where the Texas Lions Camp changed our lives forever. Their grace, their dignity, and their dedication portrayed an example of what Lion leaders should be.

In 1973, the Conroe Noon Lions Club decided to organize a bus trip to the Texas Lions Camp. Fourteen couples went on the bus trip. We arrived on Saturday afternoon and intermingled with the children as they were having their activities. Jodye, myself and several others returned Sunday morning to attend their chapel service. We saw the children using sign language—signing to inspirational music along with the counselors. The impact on those children's lives cannot be described adequately, but Jodye and I knew that we would continue to be part of the Lions Camp from that day forward.

Using a campaign slogan of "Send Sam," the Lions of District 2-S2 elected me as a Director to the Texas Lions Camp from 1984-1986. After moving to District 2-X3, I was again elected to serve as a Texas Lions Camp Director from 1989-1991, using the same campaign slogan.

District 2-X3 Lions encouraged me to run for District Governor, and I served as Governor from 2006-2007—the same year that Texas' own Jimmy Ross served as International President of our association. While I served as Governor, I was the Council Representative to the Executive Committee of the Texas Lions Camp, was then elected as Secretary in August of 2007, and went on to serve as the 44th President of the Texas Lions Camp for the year 2012-2013.

Many Lions encouraged me to run for International Director, and I was endorsed by the Lions of Texas at the State Convention in College Station in August 2015. I was elected International Director at the 99th Convention in Fukuoka, Japan in June 2016.

The great honor of serving as an International Director reminds me that we are truly an international organization. While most of our District conventions are in the United States, board meetings and international conventions include interaction with Lions from all over the world. Serving on committees with directors from all of the constitutional areas where decisions are being made that affect Lions all over the world drives home the responsibility that comes with the office of International Director.

One of the greatest benefits of serving as an International Director is making friends all over the world. Just as the close association that comes from serving as Governors together, there is a significant bond that occurs from serving as Director with others elected for the same term as your own.

At the time of this writing, Jodye and I are in our first year of a two-year term of service. The experience is difficult to describe, but it exceeds all of our expectations. We would not have had this opportunity without the confluence of events that have happened throughout our Lion lives, and without the great support of more Lions than we could possibly name. To our many mentors, your lives of service have inspired me and so many more Lions. To the Lions of District 2-S2 and District 2-X3, thank you for your encouragement and support. To the Officers and Directors of the Texas Lions Camp, thank you for your dedication to the children that we serve together, and for your confidence in me to have the opportunity to lead our great Camp. And to the Lions of Texas, "Thank you" seems so inadequate, but your friendship, trust and overwhelming support has allowed me to serve in the same arena where so many giants from Texas have served. The many great leaders from Texas that include past presidents and past directors have served as examples to all of the Lions of Texas and the Lions of the world. My prayer is that my opportunity for service will be with honor and integrity, and always mindful that I was endorsed by the Lions of Texas to serve the Lions of the world!

Interlude
"Stump"

Some of the greatest smiles have resulted from the antics of "Stump." "Stump" is a Past District Governor and Past Council Chairman by the true name of L. E. "Stump" Weatherford, who happens to have a wife that gives him some credence to his other attributes. However, one of his attributes is not that of taking care of the protocol of some of our past officers. This was evidenced in Beaumont, Texas at the State Convention when Stump was Chairman of the Council of Governors, and in charge of the main speaker. He started his day off correctly on the day before the Convention when he transported the Speaker for the entire Convention, Past President Judge Brian Stevenson of Calgary, Canada, and myself to the golf course. We were both playing together with a couple of other Lions in the Golf Tournament. Stump did not play golf, but he took us to the golf course some mile or two from the hotel.

We enjoyed a wonderful game of golf—Brian and I—and because of the ability of the two golfers we were playing with, we actually won first place! The win carried no prize, but added a lot of credibility to our golf attributes. After that, we enjoyed a hamburger lunch at the County Club, then went outside to leave for the Convention hotel. Stump was nowhere in sight, nor did there seem to be anybody else that we knew in our group. However, we were very fortunate that a pickup came by and asked if we were going back to the hotel. We said we were, and they told us to jump into the back of the pickup. We took our clubs, shoes and dirty socks and put them in the back of the pickup—with six other bags of golf clubs, six pairs of shoes and 24 pairs of dirty socks. The only place left for us to sit was on top of the golf paraphernalia. Since there was no sign of Stump, we rode to the hotel on top of the golf clubs. For some reason, we did not know who to thank, because we did not know who brought us to the hotel (even though they were very kind in doing so). We later tried to find out who the driver of the pickup was. It took some nine months for that to happen. One of the Past Council Chairmen admitted that he had taken a picture, but had not produced the picture until that time. This picture was enlarged and now hangs on a wall in my office. Our esteemed Past International President requested an enlargement of it, as he wanted an example of "Texas Protocol" which was carried out, or attempted to be carried out, or forgotten to be carried out by our Council Chairman, Stump Weatherford. This has transgressed the annals of protocol of our Association to where it has been of some embarrassment in some circles. However, this seems to be the perfect spot to let everyone know that Stump did not take the picture, but Stump is an ever-present photographer at most State occasions, a lot of the District occasions, and at all the meetings in Kerrville. A smile always exists on each person's face as he takes a picture because we have to look at Stump's entirely bald head. Seriously, though, we take this time to thank you, Stump—not only for your service to Lionism—but for your special service as the non-elected (but recognized) photographer of the Lions of the State of Texas.

There are some attributes of Stump that you might not be aware of. First is that it was a good Convention, and his lovely bride, Dayle provided good hospitality and a very entertaining program. Secondly, Stump is completely bald and takes a lot of pictures, and you have to look at that bald head each time a picture is taken. However, over the course of years, Stump has taken all the official pictures of any Lions State function or any other function where he might be near. He not only takes a picture, but he provides whoever he takes a picture of with their picture. This is very thoughtful of him, and his pictures have graced our different scrapbooks for over 25 years. Stump has also taken some pictures for this book (and did the best that he could with the Collector and Collaborator), but it should be noted that L. E. "Stump" Weatherford is not only a humorous, Lion but a Lion that stands out, a Lion that is very humble and one who has taken his place in Texas History as one of the great Lions.

Past Council Chair "Stump" Weatherford was born and raised in Athens, Texas. He attended East Texas State University (now Texas A&M at Commerce) where he received a B.A. Degree in Photojournalism. He was transferred to Orange, Texas by the Safety Kleen Company in 1974. Shortly thereafter, he went to work at Orange's DuPont Sabine River Works. In 1978, he joined the Orange Lions Club where he has served as two-time president, and continues to serve as board member and tail-twister. In 1995, he was named Lion of the Year by his local club. He is also a Life Member of the Texas Lions Camp. In 2010-2011, Stump served District 2-S1 as Council Chair, and is presently serving as GLT Coordinator as well as President of the PDG Association. PCC Stump is seldom seen at any Lions function without his camera. He has been the MD-2 Lions official photographer for many years.

In recognition of his service to Lionism, Stump has received a Melvin Jones Fellow and a Jack Wiech Fellow. He has received an International President's Award, Leadership Award and numerous other Certificates of Appreciation.

Stump and his wife, Dayle, whom he married in 2010, are both active in their local community. Stump is a Life Ambassador with the Orange Chamber of Commerce, treasurer of his local chapter of the Texas Federation for the Blind, and a board member of the Lions Eye Bank of Texas. Both are active members of St. Mary Catholic Church. Together, they have six children, nine grandchildren and one great-granddaughter.

Stump's wife, Dayle, shares this anecdote about her husband: *"In 2001, Stump took me to my first MD-2 State Convention held in San Antonio. On Friday night, we went with a couple of young governors and their wives to a club to listen to some music. At the club, the music was deafening (what I call "head-banging" music) and everyone there was about half our age. I whispered to Stump that I was going to the ladies' room. I could not have been gone more than two minutes, but when I returned, the band was belting out 'Johnny B. Goode' and Stump was nowhere in sight. I looked up on the stage, and what to my wondering eyes should appear but Stump skipping across the stage, playing his air guitar and giving them the best Chuck Berry imitation you ever saw! When the contest was over, Stump was proclaimed the winner by applause. They handed him his prize, and as he exited the stage, all the young honeys in the club mobbed him. When he finally returned to me, he had red lipstick marks all over his bald head and he was holding up the prize he had won....two tickets to a concert to hear more head-banging music!"*

THANK YOU, "STUMP" FOR ALL YOUR SPECIAL VOLUNTEER SERVICES TO YOUR DISTRICT AND TO ALL LIONS OF TEXAS.

Campaign: Mexico and Montreal

Running for International Director of Lions Clubs International was a thrilling experience. Never did I have any idea that I would run for anything above District Governor of a Lions Club. Camp meetings were at the Inn of the Hills. All the Lions stayed at the Inn of the Hills from the day it opened through 2000 when the Council of Governors, because of the room situation, began to stay at the YO Motel.

I was President of the Texas Lions Camp in 1969 to 1971, and during that particular time, it seems that there were about 35-40 kids of age that were staying with their parents at the Inn of the Hills. Since I was President of the Camp, I had the top two (2) suites of the main building, and during our meetings, it seemed that the kids gravitated to these rooms and we only had one sponsor of these kids (who was unmarried at the time and a little bit older than those kids. That was Don Mayer, who later became a Past District Governor). He kind of looked after them and kept them in line if we needed some help.

This will be alluded to during the times that we talk about the programs, one of the programs that was initiated during that particular time. However, while standing under the arbor at the Inn of the Hills, Past District Governor Charlie Phillips said something about me running for International Director, which had never entered my mind. Anyway, this idea grew into fruition, and I was selected to run for International Director in 1972 on the heels of one of the greatest Lions of Texas, Past International Director Tex Mayer from LaGrange, Texas.

There was a hotly-contested race between Pat Whitaker from Hillsboro and PDG Everett J. Grindstaff (myself). We both had Hospitality Rooms at every Cabinet Meeting, Mid-Winter Conference and District Convention in the State until late March when his wife died suddenly from an illness, an unfortunate circumstance.

There were several candidates that were running, and one of those that was not selected by the group, but stayed in the race, was past Director Barry Cohen from Cape Town, South Africa, who was a dentist and who made the rounds and speaking and talking and was one of the ones that was elected. However, as far as my campaign was concerned, I was concerned about having the name "Ebb" on the ballot, because Grindstaff was an unusual name in some respects, and I wanted to try and have something that they would be sure and remember when they voted. The Lions of Texas were very innovative in coming up with ideas. They came up with a plastic Texas hat, and we ordered 1,000 of these, and we had a time getting those across the border (and received them only after we were in Mexico City). I went to the airport and finally obtained the hats. In addition, we had the "EbbTide" Campaign that was selected—we had boxes of Tide detergent with a sticker on them that read "Ride the EbbTide". In addition to putting the stickers on the boxes, we placed them on the Continental Hotel walls in Mexico City. We were successful in placing "Ebb" on the ballot because of the name 'Grindstaff', which was not easily remembered. However, after the campaign, we were taking the stickers down, but they would not come off the walls, so I was very anxious to check out of the hotel and head back to Texas as soon as we could.

Past International Director Don Buckalew played an important part in that campaign, as in all campaigns. Don was also one of the top leaders working with the campaign of Dave Evans from Texas City for International President, and a change in the leadership in the Lions Clubs International by the election of Bob McCullouch who assumed a leadership position for Lions International. Don was very good at finances, and at times he was one of those that stood up and was a little more vocal in whatever issue might be at hand, but he was logical in his approach, as are all good Baylor graduates. It was necessary that he set one or two of the higher campaign associates in their proper place in order to do what was proper to do, including the Council Chairman.

Mexico City was a very difficult place to get around. During one of the campaigns, I had the opportunity to go around the circle of the main part of Mexico City trying to reach the place where I was to speak. We had rented a couple of cars, but we had individuals from Texas driving, and we were not always successful in reaching the places we wanted to in time. However, we finally reached one place and I went into the room, there were about 300 people in the room and there did not seem to be enough seats. I was late but I went up front and found a seat in front of the podium, which was the only seat left. I turned to the person who was sitting next to me, and he appeared to be of Asian origin and asked him "How are you enjoying the convention?" No response. I had been stationed in Japan for a year, so I used a few Japanese words. Still no response. They then brought out the soup for the occasion so I tried by saying, "Soupee," and I still got no response. After determining the flavor, I said, "Chilee soupee" and still no response. After two or three more questions, I decided I was not going to make any progress in reaching this particular individual. However, after the meal, they called on the main speaker for the occasion and the guy sitting next to me got up, went behind the podium, and in very fluent English, delivered the main address. I was surprised about this, but I was even more surprised as he came around and he set down next to me, turned his face to me and said, "LIKEE SPEECHEE?"

This has always been one of my favorite stories, and I have recited this story many times throughout the global world of Lionism. As part of the delegation of Texas, we were directors at the time Dave Evans was running for International President, in which he was successful. I was in charge of the breakfast for the Texas delegation at the convention. We had over 1,000 Lions present at the breakfast at the convention in Los Angeles, California. At that particular time, Lionism in Texas continued on with a director every two years. I remember that after Tex Mayer, I was International Director, and then Don Buckalew was elected in San Francisco in 1974, and after that Ed Flood was elected Director in 1976. During that particular time, I had been approached, and was running, for Third Vice-President of Lions Clubs International. As result of the election of Ed, I did not run until 1979 in Montreal.

During the campaign for third vice-president, Bing Miller from Pennsylvania was also running. He dropped out of the campaign in March prior to the election for Third Vice-President, and I was successfully elected Third Vice-President in Montreal in 1979. We felt this was a good year for Texas, and it was a good year for us to run. The Lions of Texas were very supportive and the Lions of Ballinger, Texas were very supportive in that they sent the Ballinger High School Band to Montreal to march in the parade. The Hardin-Simmons Band was also there with their white horses during the parade. It was very difficult for us to raise $30,000 for the Ballinger Band in 1979. There were many different events that Lions put on, but one of the most unusual was that a large apple truck from Washington turned over near Ballinger. The insurance man, who happened to be a Rotarian, but a very good friend, convinced the company to allow Ballinger to have all the apples from the truck because they did not know whether they could sell them or not. We had all kinds of apples, sold all kinds of apples, and had all kinds of apple pies, and suppers and everything else. Everyone was nearly tired of the apples, but because of that we able to get over the hump and send our 80-piece band to Montreal.

Changes in Organization

Even though we have had losses in the last few years in membership, our place in history is solidified because of the fulfillment of needs and our service in humanitarian causes.

When I first was elected District Governor in 1964, I did not know (or have the opportunity to) meet the other 14 governors that I would be serving with during my year. In fact, I met the governors at the State Convention in Odessa, Texas in 1964 when Charlie Caruth was chairman. I also met the notable Don Buckalew, who later became an International Director. At that time, the districts did not pass along any funds as they do now. We used a telegraphic machine that caused us to use a lot of soap and water when we tried to put out a newsletter or any type of correspondence. I then proceeded to the International Convention in Toronto and met other governors throughout the world of Lionism at the Royal York Hotel, where we had our District Governors School (which was the Headquarters for the International Convention in 2014). When I walked into the hotel and went up to the room where the governors were meeting, I met two red-faced Lions men, Don Buckalew and Norm Dall from Chicago, also a Director, because of some issue that had wrongfully passed the Board of Directors.

Don was not only a whiz in finances, but knew how to proceed to the bottom of any controversy and give profound, logical reasons for or against that particular issue. Don was certainly a leader in my campaign in Mexico City in 1962 as International Director. Following my two years as Director, he became International Director in San Francisco. He was also an invaluable asset in my campaign in Montreal in 1979, and during the time that I was going through the chairs of President. In addition, he has been involved in each and every campaign of anyone on an International basis. More on this will be revealed in later pages.

Later, it became obvious that the governors did not have the time to be governors and do the other things that needed to be done as far as the organization was concerned, and the idea of Lieutenant Governors was conceived. Some of the best governors that we had during part of that period of time—people like Howard Leverett and Art Cook—did their jobs as governors and had great years as far as their other governors and district business were concerned. However, the term "Lieutenant Governor" was adopted by International and we had no choice in the matter.

Subsequently, it was decided that the Lieutenant Governor should be called the Vice Governor. Before we knew it, we had a First Vice Governor, a Second Vice Governor, a Third Vice Governor, a Chairman-Elect and a Chairman Elect-Elect. It appears now that we are quite organized. In fact, we may have over-organized, because we have not seen any significant growth or change in our organization as far as clubs and our membership is concerned. It does make for a full house at the meeting of the governors, but it is quite an expense, and it felt like in some circles that maybe that expense could be used for other projects. These changes were probably influenced mostly by the Europeans.

As a result, dues were raised with this money to be spent on membership and extension, and actually the result of this has yet to be seen. However, we look back during the late 70s, prior to the time that we reached 45,000 in May 1983, and we've found that good news was made of having some Past Governors or very qualified people to serve as membership and extension representatives. At one time prior to the time of my Presidency, we had three or four Past District Governors serving, and they paid their travel expenses and so much for each club organized. The best organizers of clubs are individuals who are doing other duties around the state as Lions. Not surprisingly, some people are built for extension, and some people are built for membership. Therefore, it varies, but when you have men like PID Tex Mayer, PID Jimmy Ross, PDG Ed Stebbins and others, you wonder what is the best program. We are looking for good men like this to help us build for the future. During the past couple of years, we have seen growth in our membership because of the special efforts of Mike Butler and others, as he was running for International Second Vice President and was able to inspire people to find new members, as he has been a driving force in new Clubs and members.

The major changes in the organization and philosophy of Lions Club International began in 1980-1982, and resulted in a split board voting in 1982 and 1983. There was a group of Lions that called themselves the

'Concerned Lions.' Even though they had some different ideas about different things, there was no animosity during my year as president when I had a split board. This was probably the last split board that the Association has had. It was mainly a matter of different philosophies and thoughts, and again, I would say that all these Lions were very good Lions and I could not have had a better board than we had that year. Because of that split, some ideas came up that were set forth and used in the changes.

I would mention that there were three members of my board that later became International Presidents—Donald Banker, William Woolard and Kajit Habanananda. However, I did have the strong support of my Second and Third Vice Presidents. We spent many nights into the early morning working out some of these philosophies and changes. There is no question that if we had not had Bert Mason and Joe Wroblewski, we would not have had success in making these changes. In fact, the ideas were supported by my appointments to the board by Past International President Bert Mason, PIP Joe Wroblewski, and PIP Sten Akestam for the next three years after I went out as Past President and Chairman of Lions Club International Foundation. My first year as Immediate Past International President was quite different from those serving now. Even though I had the First Melvin Jones Luncheon, then-President Jim Fowler would not let me leave the country on any Texas Lions or Lions Club International Foundation business because of the conflicts in the years before.

Theme

I always had in mind something about vision for the theme about how people cared and how they shared. I wanted to use the eye as part of that. The staff we had at International was responsible for coming up with the eye and 'Share the Vision of Service'. I thought it was very appropriate, as we are a service-minded organization, and we are people that share and want to share our vision. That vision has been shown and shared in so many ways through the entire history of Texas, but especially during the last 40 years.

Along with the theme and the ideas that we came up with, membership was important throughout the International Organization. We had a little "3" that would fit in the middle of a watch and you would still be able to tell what time it was. We gave that to all the District Governors, along with some to pass on to Lions. The purpose of the "3" was to help us remember "3 in 83". That was the goal that we had for each member—to bring in 3 new members. That was a goal that one would be reminded of every day, at least if he could tell time, regardless of what language or where he might be from.

It was my thought that the speech I might deliver at the beginning of the year should be one that would express my thoughts and views. This is difficult for some lawyers to do in a short manner, but it was necessary. I had all these ideas, but I could not get them together, until I spent a day and a half in Florida by the swimming pool. One of the greatest writers and speakers that I know of was Roy Keaton, who was a representative in Texas, later the Secretary of Lions International, and finally into the Directorship of Lions International (or what we might call a CEO). During that time in our Association, he and Herb Petry organized more Lions in more countries than anyone else. It was a period of great growth. They led Lions into a direction of growth in members and activities. In fact, I had been keeping Roy's article in a folder since I was a youngster in high school (after my dad became District Governor) in a folder entitled "Roy Rides Again." I still have that folder and information for the beginning of my thoughts and speeches. It was good, but some folks thought it was great, because for the first time, we had a monitor in front of the speaker that seemed to improve our supposed knowledge.

Council Chairs

Thanks to all the Texas Council Chairs who have served with distinction and dignity.

Year	District	Name	Email
74-75	2-E1	Irvin Hiller	*Deceased*
75-76	2-E2	Dub Horn	*Deceased*
76-77	2-T1	Jimmie Pigman	*Deceased*
77-78	2-T2	Art Cook	jncook_1@yahoo.com
78-79	2-T3	Lamar Dyess	*Deceased*
79-80	2-S1	Raymond Lewis	*Deceased*
80-81	2-S2	Howard Leverett	*Deceased*
81-82	2-S3	Don Mayer	donmayer@cvctx.com
82-83	2-S4	John Galsin	*Deceased*
83-84	2-A1	George Heis	*Deceased*
84-85	2-A2	Rey Costa	rcosta@satxrr.com
85-86	2-A3	Ray Hughston	rayhughston@att.net
86-87	2-X1	John Eads	jeads@dallascpas.com87-88
	2-X2	Herbert Daniels	*Deceased*
88-89	2-X3	Larry Freeman	*Deceased*
89-90	2-E1	Dwayne Spradlin	
90-91	2-E2	Jack Harris	*Deceased*
91-92	2-T1	Jimmy Ross	jmross@caprock-spur.com
92-93	2-T2	Tut Tawwater	*Deceased 2015*
93-94	2-T3	Francis "Frank" Leroux	fleroux@sbcglobal.net
94-95	2-S1	Tom Gann	tgann@lufkinrealestate.com
95-96	2-S2	Pat Brennan	phbrennan@consolidated.net
96-97	2-S3	Lin Rose	lionlin@sbcglobal.net
97-98	2-S4	Pete Rygaard	pwr1930@comcast.net
98-99	2-S5	Joe Al Picone	joepicone600@gmail.com
99-00	2-A1	John Hancock	han929@verizon.net
00-01	2-A2	Mike Rourke	pccmikemd2@sbcglobal.net
01-02	2-A3	Ike Boling	rockport125@aol.com

02-03	2-X1	Joe Montag	jlmpdg@tx.rr.com
03-04	2-X2	Carol French	clfrench@cablelynx.com
04-05	2-X3	Dick Robinson	rrobinson38@hot.rr.com
05-06	2-E1	C. Lee Smith	clsmith@web-runner.com
06-07	2-E2	Rick Stoorza	rickstoorza@hotmail.com
07-08	2-T1	Ray White	rayzoie@yahoo.com
08-09	2-T2	Bernie Gradel	bgradel@hugoreed.com
09-10	2-T3	Don Peppard	don@dpeppard.com
10-11	2-S1	Stump Weatherford	stumpwl@hotmail.com
11-12	2-S2	Barron Cagle	barroncagle@yahoo.com
12-13	2-S3	Dennis Heitkamp	Heitkamp@gvtc.com
13-14	2-S4	Lewis Gardner	pdglewisgardner@gmail.com
14-15	2-S5	Ronald Heinemeyer	ronheinemeyer@sbcglobal.net
15-16	2-A1	Tom Blasé	tomblasesr@gmail.com
16-17	2-A2	Ernesto "T.J." Tijerina	
17-18	2-A3	Rick Talbert	

Snowball Express
by Joe Al Picone

They say that you don't have to travel far to experience some of the best things in life. My story proves just that.

Snowball Express—WOW! What an awesome organization! As the newly-elected International Director in July 2011, I received a call from PDG Carolyn Dorman inviting me to be a part of Snowball Express in Dallas, Texas in December. Not knowing what to really expect, but having such respect for PDG Carolyn, I very enthusiastically accepted her kind invitation and blocked out other director visits so that Lion Merle and I could attend. I learned that Snowball is an organization to create hope and new memories for the children of our fallen heroes. American Airlines—a major sponsor—flies all over the United States that special day to pick up these children and their surviving mother or father to take them to Dallas for a wonderful experience. The Lions of Dallas, chaired by PDG Carolyn are the coordinators of the local events.

The first day, we got up very early, as I was to meet all 1,000 kids, their mothers and a few fathers as they arrived at the host hotel in downtown Dallas. It was extremely cold and windy on the sidewalk as we stood nervously to greet the first busload of these wonderful children. However, when the first bus, escorted by the North Texas Patriot Guard turned the corner, my heart began to warm. As the children exited the bus and greeted me with a big smile, a warm hug or a high-five, I realized the importance of family. As I saw some moms carrying babies in their arms, it became obvious that some of the fallen young men never had the chance to see their baby boy or girl. It made me very thankful for my children and granddaughter, and that we would all be together in a few weeks celebrating Christmas...but these children would never see their father or mother again. Even so, they were so excited, all smiles and full of energy and laughter as they anticipated the great experience in store for them. Here, they could be with other kids who have been through the same loss they've experienced, and talk with one another about their dads and moms and how they miss them. I later found that because some of these kids have had the Snowball experience for several years. This was a reunion for them to see their friends again. Many of the kids wore buttons with pictures of their dads, while some wore their dad's dog tags.

It was late in the evening when the final bus arrived. Even though we were tired and cold, we were so excited to be a part of this wonderful event. We then went to party with the kids.

The hotel was set up with ballrooms filled with games and snacks for the kids, while the adults had another area in which to socialize and meet others who have experienced the same tragedy in their lives. What was truly amazing was the ballroom set up by Neiman Marcus—decorated to be similar to their stores. It was full of extravagant gifts, and each child was given a shopping bag in which to place his/her selection of any item he/she would like to give his/her mother for Christmas. Choices included sweaters, coats, boots, robes, perfume and jewelry in addition to many other things. It was so exciting to see these little guys and gals looking around and trying to make their selection. Of course, Neiman Marcus employees were there, dressed in Christmas attire, to help them. Some of the little boys would fall on the floor when they smelled the perfume! They were told to not tell their moms what they selected, but of course some couldn't wait!

The next day, buses were loaded to take them to the American Airlines Center for an outstanding program. As they got off the bus, they walked a few blocks through lines with people waving American flags before they entered the arena. I remember one little boy with a T-shirt that read, "My Dad–My Hero." Another read, "I love you Dad–Rest in Peace." A race car driver was there with his car on which he had painted "Snowball Express". He told the kids that every race he is in is for them because of the sacrifice they have made. At the end of the program was the most moving event I have ever experienced. A young man sang "God Bless the USA." Just watching the mothers holding onto their children so tightly as everyone joined in the singing brought tears to your eyes. After the program, everyone went outside and released 15,000 red, white and blue balloons.

What a wonderful experience this was to work with so many dedicated Lions of Dallas in offering these children and their surviving family a real Christmas party. Lionism at its best!

Having such a meaningful experience, I immediately blocked my travel schedule in order to attend Snowball in Dallas in December 2012. Once again, as the first bus arrived, the tears began to flow from my eyes and my heart filled with pride as I again began greeting 1,000 kids and surviving family members. Those hugs and smiles will last a lifetime. This year, I was touched greatly by a particular young man, his younger sister and their mom from Little Rock, Arkansas when they arrived. Throughout the day, I kept running into them. I finally told him he was like a lucky penny, and had to explain what that meant! That night, we all walked several blocks to the ATandT Center where Snowball had been invited to light the Christmas tree. What an eventful evening this was—the program totally centered on these beautiful kids. I had the privilege to once again run into this family as the procession began at the hotel. As we walked, the mother told me of how her husband died, and about getting the call with the news. She said he was killed on top of a mountain, and for some reason, the helicopter crew would be unable to retrieve his body. His good friend told her he just couldn't leave him up there, so he carried him all the way down the mountain himself. She then told me that some months after that, that friend and her husband's team were all killed. She said she spent several days making trips to attend all their funerals, because she could never forget all they did for her husband.

I could never make contact with them after leaving, but will always remember that outstanding 11-year-old young man named 'Nathan'. It was truly heartwarming to see how he took care of his little sister. Before we left, I told him that his dad is so proud of him and how much he loves him, and that I love him and am also proud of him. I told him to continue as he is now, and he will always be a loving and caring person. Such a beautiful family with such memorable smiles and caring attitude after suffering such tragedy.

Many times we find that something truly touches our heart. And Snowball truly touched mine.

As I continued to travel and speak as an International Director, I often concluded my speeches by telling stories of my experience with Snowball Express, and relating that you don't have to travel far from home to experience the best. At one such address, the wife of a Past International President was in attendance, and she told me to please tell this story on every visit I make. Telling the Snowball story on many visits was most meaningful.

The words to one of my favorite songs are, "Make someone happy, make just one someone happy, and You will be happy, too." I know that all Lions participating in this event—myself included—are happy that we could make life just a little happier for some adorable children those few days in Dallas, Texas. It is great to be a Lion!

International Projects
2-A1 · Acuña, Mexico

Through the foresight of Past District Governor Paul Palmer and the Early Lions Club in Brownwood, Texas, a vision was born to create a clinic in Acuña, Mexico. Governor Paul announced his "Special District Project" for 1991-92. He proposed that the Lions Clubs in District 2-A1 fund and build a 2,400 square foot concrete block building in Ciudad Acuña, Mexico. This building would be the home of the Lions Health Clinic of Ciudad Acuña. Dr. Stephen Kelly of Brownwood assisted Lion Paul, Lion Doug Hill and other interested Lions with this project. Upon its completion, this clinic served as the site for free eye examinations, eye surgeries and other services performed by Dr. Kelly and others on a volunteer basis. A request was made to LCIF for a $50,000 grant for the Sight First building project in Ciudad Acuña. This grant was approved by LCIF as a "Sight First Project". The ground breaking ceremony for the Lions Health Clinic building in Ciudad Acuña, Mexico was held on May 22, 1992. Governor Paul was the principle speaker and laid the first stone for the structure. Many, many, many trips were made by Dr. Stephen Kelly and his staff during the construction, and also after the dedication of the building. Others involved, beside our own Past District Governor Sabino Garcia from San Angelo (that helped keep the clinic going during some difficult times), were Dr. Cleve Kirkland from San Angelo who joined Dr. Kelly in supporting the clinic.

District 2-A1 was proud of this project, because it was an International project, and it is still in existence as set out by Al Owen in the paragraphs hereafter, and his concerted efforts in seeing that eyeglasses and cataract surgeries were performed in an efficient and timely manner. Of course, it was natural for Al Owens to be involved in such a project, as he was a graduate of Baylor University, but all of these people and many, many more deserve our compliments and thanks which they receive by their service in the Acuña Clinic.

The clinic in Acuña was the vision of a District Governor in Brownwood in 1992. District Governor Paul Palmer learned of an Ophthalmologist in Brownwood that was going to Acuña annually to perform cataract surgery on patients in northern Mexico. At that time, Dr. Steven Kelly was working out of a Sunday School room in a small Baptist church. The conditions were poor and pretty primitive. DG Palmer believed that if we could partner with the Lions of Acuña and get all 60 clubs in District 2-A1 behind the project, we could build a clinic that would be suitable for performing eye surgery, eye exams and fitting glasses. The Amistad Lions Club of Acuña aided in securing the land. With a grant from Lions Clubs International and private donations, a very nice clinic was built on the northeast side of town. Medical equipment was donated by Dr. Kelly from Brownwood and Shannon Hospital in San Angelo. Dr. Cleve Kirkland from San Angelo joined Dr. Kelly in supporting the clinic. Dr. Kelly's mission was in February, and Dr. Kirkland's mission was in October. Since opening, the equipment has been upgraded and the clinic now provides eye care, dental care and some general medical care in the facility, with ongoing improvements and upgrades.

In 1992, a complete set of recycled glasses was sent to the Acuña clinic. Since then, more than 9,000 pair of glasses have been given to needy residents in the area. Glasses are added to the set from the stock in San Angelo, as they are dispensed to ensure glasses are on-hand to fit the needs of those that come into the clinic for help. Each medical mission (about three per year) averages 10-12 cataract surgeries and 100-130 pair of glasses fitted. The supporting Optometrist in Acuña, Dr. Gustavo Vela also sees patients and fits glasses at the clinic in-between times the U.S. doctors are there. The clinic is operated by the Acuña Amistad Lions Club, and is financed jointly by the club and other clubs in District 2-A1. The District has a non-profit organization that oversees the clinic's finances. All services of the clinic are free to Mexican citizens, and they travel from all over northern Mexico for help.

Club Project

LUBBOCK DOWNTOWN LIONS CLUB
GOES INTERNATIONAL

Due to the need for food, but especially because of the earthquake and tsunami relief in Asia, Breedlove Dehydrated Foods was established in Lubbock as a processor of surplus or unmarketable vegetables. The Breedlove facility is the only commercial-sized plant that is non-profit and engaged solely in humanitarian aid.

Items that Breedlove has provided are designed specifically for use for hunger relief—with products designed to be as effective as possible in terms of palatability, nutritional quality, cost per serving, and ease of transportation and storage. Breedlove has delivered over 350 million servings of food worldwide.

Breedlove's unique expertise provides concerned citizens and organizations with a dependable food resource. A $1.00 donation to Breedlove will sponsor 28 people with one serving of hot soup. With just that $1.00 donation, a family of four in need could eat a hot cup of soup every day for a whole week! Further, any one item described in the following proposal will cost less than 4 cents per serving.

After examination of the plan material by Past District Governor Art Cooke of Lubbock, a letter was directed to Peter Lynch, Director of Lions Clubs International Foundation (LCIF) and Dr. T. C. Louis, President, with information about Breedlove. Also in the letter was information about and Breedlove General Manager, David Fish's trip to earthquake and tsunami-stricken areas in January 2005 to assess damages and to observe the transportation of product.

A little history: An earthquake occurred off the coast of western Sumatra, Indonesia on Sunday, December 26, 2004. The tsunami sent large waves rushing to the shores of 13 countries, affecting 11 with extensive damages and massive loss of life, including Sri Lanka, Indonesia, Thailand, and India. The death toll from the high water was expected to exceed 150,000, with an expected homeless population of more than 5 million.

Severe damage to basic infrastructures (water lines, electricity, roads, public buildings), private property loss (homes, businesses, government buildings) was reported. The area's needs included the basic necessities of life (food, water, shelter), with the threat of disease looming due to the lack of proper resources to handle the dead. Many were injured, sick and in need of medical care, with thousands of children orphaned with the loss of one or more parents. Joblessness was widespread due to damages to business and infrastructure. The emotional toll on citizens, visitors and relief workers spread to 30 different countries.

The Lubbock Downtown Lions Club partnered with Breedlove and helped to provide funds to respond to earthquake and tsunami victims— along with partners from Samaritan's Purse, Heart to Heart International, Healing Hands International and Stop Hunger Now.

Samaritan's Purse is a humanitarian organization headed by Franklin Graham. Information on their organization can be found at www.samaritanspurse.org. Samaritan's Purse coordinates food distributions in Sri Lanka and the Aceh province of Sumatra, Indonesia.

Heart to Heart International is an organization whose background is based in medical relief. Information regarding this organization can be found at www.hearttoheart.org. Heart to Heart coordinates transportation and food distributions.

Breedlove Dehydrated Foods Product Information

The most popular product is a vegetable blend with a base of potatoes, with rice, carrots, onions and Textured Vegetable Protein (TVP) added. The vegetable blend product is provided to many clients in Mexico, and is the primary product delivered to the USAID agency for distribution through NGOs. Ordinarily, it is not flavored, with seasoning being left for local input to satisfy cultural preferences.

Breedlove also has a series of products based on lentils. One such product developed with USAID agency for India is a mix of lentils, rice, carrots and onion. Another variety of lentil products developed for Mexico has lentils, potatoes and TVP, as well as carrots and onions to provide a high protein mix.

In addition to these staple items, Breedlove has developed specialty items for therapeutic feeding in Mexico—including a dry fortified and flavored milk drink, and a fortified flavored oatmeal product which delivers a minimum of 30% RDA (Recommended Daily Allowance) for vitamins and minerals.

As a result, three to four container loads per week have been delivered to areas in need of 404 Lentil Blend and 504 Lentil Blend. This program has been a successful method of being of service to others.

Club Project

Lufkin Host Lions Club

One of the many outstanding Lions Clubs in Texas is the Lufkin Host Lions Club. The history and activities of this club have been attributed to many different members, but PDG Paul Mayberry and PDG and Council Chairman Tom Gann (a good Baylor man) have been two of its leaders. One of the main reasons for their ability to serve their community in such a fashion is the miniature train in Lufkin—a giant hit—and is exemplified in the *Lion Magazine* report by Pamela Mohr in 2007.

All Aboard! Miniature Train a Giant Hit
by Pamela Mohr · The Lion, May 2007

When Lufkin Host Lion George Thannisch was a medical resident at Hermann Hospital in Houston, he noticed that a nearby park was always filled with laughing children who enjoyed circling the grounds in a 16-gauge train. Moving to Lufkin in 1958 to begin his practice as a Pediatrician, Thannisch couldn't help but notice there was little for kids to do in the area.
He thought of Houston's miniature railroad, remembering how youngsters happily clamored to ride the train with their parents in town. His first thought was that Lions could install a similar train at nearby Lake Sam Rayburn, but then the local Ellen Trout Memorial Park built a zoo. The plans came together perfectly—a zoo and a train ride for families to enjoy together during one single outing. And through the years, as the zoo has grown, adding more animals and exhibits, so has Lions' dedication to expanding and improving on their railroad. Obviously, they make very good neighbors.
Lufkin Host Lions worked hard to create a destination that would serve a purpose as well as provide funds for their many service activities in the community. Thannisch says that their first train was purchased in 1969 from a Kiwanis club in Bristol, Tennessee. "When we first saw it, we knew we were looking at our train," he recalls. Tracks were purchased from several different

sources, including a similar venue in another Texas town and an old abandoned mine.

Host Lions set to work laying the track. It was a tough job. Thannisch remembers, "Many others joined in the project, and a few—such as my two sons, ages 8 and 11—were conscripted," he wryly explains. He notes that some volunteers became proficient in "Swearing at the work, and others at swearing at the foreman." Installed and officially opened to the public on July 4, 1970, the aptly-named Z and 00 Railroad was an immediate hit.

There was one problem, recalls Thannisch. "The little train had developed a bad habit. It did not like to stay on the track we had so lovingly built." Fortunately, it was not very heavy and we became adept at putting it back on the track – and wondering if it would complete the next run."

For a 25-cent fare, kids could ride the 30-inch train until a derailment nearly spelled disaster, reports Tom Gann, who was incoming 1983-84 president. Since the accident happened right before he took office, Gann knew Lions had to act immediately. "Luckily, no one was really hurt, but the small train was a different story. "The train was too old and had suffered too much major damage. I can still hear Lion Paul Mayberry saying, "It's time to either get in or get out of the train business. And it was time to make a decision, because the old tin and pole shed that stored the train had deteriorated, the tracks were old and not in good condition, and the locomotive and cars were just too old to get parts for anymore." The problem was, as Gann recalls, "We had no money available for any of those needs."

Necessity breeds invention, and Lion Mayberry worked behind the scenes to develop a finance plan within the Lufkin Host Lions Club and its individual members in the amount of $165,000, with no interest and a payback time of up to five years. "Those who could 'lend' us $100, $250, $500, $1,000, or $5,000 with no guarantee of return did just that," Gann relates, "And it worked."

The second time around, Lions hired a professional crew to do the tough job of installing wider tracks, and a contractor was hired to build a station modeled on an historic passenger station. Fares were raised to 75 cents to keep up with the times, and Lions established an escrow account for upkeep and replacement. The Polk Oil Company has supplied free fuel to Lions since Z and 00 was established.

A new 76-inch train was purchased and served the community until 2004, when brand new engine No. 337. was installed and the coach cars were refurbished. The new computer-controlled engine has all the bells and whistles, Lions report, including state of-the-art technology with electric fuel injection and emissions control. Costing more than $117,000, it was paid for in full with the money earned from railroad rides.

The club hires an engineer to run the railroad, which currently sells tickets for $1. An average of 70,000 passengers a year now loop around the tracks in three 1863-style coaches, pulled by the C. P Huntington authentic 1863 locomotive. Well over 1.5 million people have enjoyed the train since it first began operating.

Lion Keith Allred, a frequent rider when his 5-year old grandson Brian comes from Houston to visit, says that one of the things the little boy likes best when he comes to Lufkin is going to the zoo and riding the train. "The train is a key attraction for the zoo," Allred believes. "As the end of a school year approaches, the train has more traffic than it can handle. Elementary school classes plan their year-end trips to the Lufkin zoo, and it appears that they all want to ride the train," he added. "The train circles the zoo, then runs alongside the lake and then crosses a bridge that crosses one part of the lake. It takes a short trip into a wooded area, and then returns across the bridge to its depot. The length of the track is a little more than one mile and the ride lasts approximately eight minutes," Allred explains. "An interesting note is that there are signs posted in the lake water to beware of alligators. They are there; I've seen them several times."

Host Lions have built a train maintenance bar, pavilion, parking lot and a train depot that bears the name of Thannisch, whose desire to bring some fun into the lives of Lufkin's children resulted in a work in progress for more than 37 years. They also donate their time and money to the zoo, putting in an irrigation system fed by the lake, feeding Lions and being all-around helpful neighbors. They've even purchased a full-size van for the zoo.

A trip around the track also means a trip back in time for many parents, who once rode the miniature train with their own families as children. The Z and 00 may be built on a small scale, but it makes a pretty grand memory for those who ride its rails.

Another outstanding project of the Lufkin Lions Club is the Angelina Down Benefit Rodeo, with a strong history of being one of the top rodeos in the country.

One of the newest projects to the club is the Pine Woods Purgatory Bike Ride. All of the officers and directors should be commended for sharing the vision of service. We certainly appreciate the President of the Lufkin Host Lions Club this year—Kirk Mathis—along with Paul and Tom for furnishing us this information. I have had the opportunity to be there on several occasions and have observed their activities, not only for the community, but also in the manner in which they take care of business in their club and the leadership they provide. These wonderful people do wonderful work not only for the club, but also for Lions Clubs International.

Club Project

Conroe Noon Lions Club
Community Partners Program

In 2005, the Conroe Noon Lions Club discontinued an annual PRCA Rodeo and pre-rodeo kick-off dance and auction. To replace the rodeo in 2006, an innovative Community Partners Program was created. It has become the most successful fundraising effort in the club's history. For a one-time annual contribution at one of three specified dollar levels, an individual or business becomes a sponsor at every fundraising event held during the year. More importantly, the sponsor is recognized as a "partner" of the club in the community all year long through the club's numerous community service projects. In keeping with Lions Clubs sight conservation efforts, the current partnership levels are: Knights of the Blind ($1,500), Vision Ambassador ($1,000) and Sight Saver ($500). Solicitations for the annual Community Partners Program takes place in July and August of every year. The benefit to the club's partners is they are solicited only once for the entire year (and only need to write one check) rather than for every fundraiser throughout the year. The club also benefits with having the majority of its fundraising completed in the first couple of months of a new Lions' year. The Community Partners Program has increased participation at every fundraising event by three-fold or more. For example, there have typically been 60+ participants in the club's annual golf tournament prior to the Community Partners Program, but now there are 200+ participants over two flights at the annual golf tournament.

A "Dinner, Dance and Auction Gala" was an important part of our Community Partners Program, and an invitation to this event was included. The increased participation helped to drive auction prices even higher to add significant money to the overall success of this program.

Each year, the club holds a Community Partner Day Appreciation Lunch at a club meeting in June, where club members can express their appreciation to all the partners. From scholarship recipients to Texas Lions

Camp campers, the club showcases all of the various community service projects that were supported by the Community Partners through their annual donations. While Conroe Noon is one of the larger Lions clubs with approximately 300 members, the Community Partners Program can easily be scaled to an active Lions club of any size.

Conroe Noon Lions Club
Sight Conservation Program

Since its early days, Conroe Noon Lions Club has had a very active Sight Conservation Program. In cooperation with Conroe area ophthalmologists and optometrists, the club's eyeglass program has helped pay for eye exams and prescriptions glasses for needy school-aged children for many years.

In 2006, after many years of operation, the Texas Telecom Pioneer Recycling Center in Houston closed its doors. Prior to closing, several members of the Conroe Noon Lions Club worked with the Pioneers to continue the local eyeglass recycling effort, and the club's board of directors established the Conroe Noon Recycling Center to continue the recycling program. Club members and other community volunteers collect, sort, clean, repair and categorize used eyeglasses collected from Lions clubs, other service groups, and the general public within District 2-S2. On average, the facility will process approximately 120,000 of donated eyeglasses each year. Not only does the Recycling Center save glasses to be reused, it sends the scrap metal and plastic off for additional recycling. This in turn provides funds for the Center, and saves materials from being dumped in landfills. Since its inception, the Conroe Noon Recycling Center has provided over 260,000 eyeglasses, sunglasses and eyeglass cases via mission trips through numerous other charitable organizations. The distribution of these refurbished eyeglasses expands CNLC's Sight Conservation Program by restoring sight to people around the world via many vision mission trips.

In 2007, an eyeglass manufacturing facility became a reality for the club to provide more eyeglasses for more children. Area students are examined by participating ophthalmologists and optometrists. Prescriptions are forwarded to the CNLC eyeglass lab. The lab is operated by Lion volunteers who have received special training to operate the digital machines that cut lenses to prescription accuracy. Once the lenses are cut and checked for accuracy, they are mounted in new frames. These new eyeglasses are then returned to the eye clinics for a final student fitting and accuracy testing under the supervision of licensed professionals. Local school administrators, nursing staff, local ophthalmologists and optometrists work very closely with the club to achieve the program's high degree of success. On average, CNLC assists 160 students each year with new eyeglasses.

The club also added vision screenings to its sight conservation efforts. In the beginning, the club assisted District 2-S2 on a few screenings around the Houston area, using borrowed equipment. After purchasing an auto-refractor for acuity, and a tonometer to measure pressures for early signs of glaucoma, a new sight program began. The club has done vision screenings at area clinics, churches, public events, and assisted other Lions clubs in the area to do the same. In 2010, to better serve children, the club purchased a PediaVision machine. This piece of equipment has allowed the club to screen hundreds of school-aged children for early signs of sight issues. The efficiency and quickness of the camera gun provides a way to screen children in just a matter of seconds. Club members join with the Conroe Service League each October to screen preschool children for hearing and vision problems at some 20+ day care center in the Conroe area.

Additionally in 2010, the Conroe Noon Lions Club began assisting the Montgomery County Homeless Coalition by providing vision-related assistance. The club provides quarterly vision screenings, examinations, and glasses similar to that of the school program.

The Conroe Noon Lions Club Recycling Center provides an excellent backdrop to initiate new members to the Lions signature service projects for sight conservation. The club uses the center often for various meetings and events, further reinforcing the size and scope of the club's efforts.

How and Why 'Kids on the Lake' Began

In the early 1990s, Conroe Noon Lions Club member Ken Albertson visited the Huffman Lions, the club he originally joined in 1982. They were holding a fishing event for children on nearby Lake Houston. Lion Albertson was so impressed by the event that he came back to Conroe Noon to pitch the idea of conducting a similar event on Lake Conroe. Lion Ken teamed up with fellow member Lion Pat McPherson and came up with the first 'Kids on the Lake'—a fishing tournament for special needs children—in 1993.

Kids on the Lake is a one-day event that gives parents and their special needs child time to enjoy the beauty of the lake, the wonder of the great outdoors and the thrill of catching a "big one!" The first tournament had five children attend at the beautiful home of Lion Pat McPherson on Lake Conroe. This event has grown to average 50 child participants, with approximately 175 total attendees, including parents, guests and volunteers.

In recent years, with the Community Partnership of Entergy Corporation, Entergy's Lewis Creek Reservoir serves as the backdrop for Kids on the Lake. This private lake with a large pavilion, recreation area and fishing piers has proven to be the ideal location. The tournament accepts children ages 5-18 with physical, mental and visual impairments, and a parent or guardian must be present with each child. Club volunteers assist children with fishing, boat rides, games and loads of fun! Participants and parents are treated to a hamburger and hot dog lunch, and every child takes home a big fish trophy. Past President Morris Eickenhorst often told this story when he became a Lion: it was at Kids on the Lake when he was taking children out on his boat for a ride around the lake that a small boy looked up at him and said, "Mister, this is the best day of my life!"

Club Project

Killeen Evening Lions Park Project

This is a project that I had the opportunity to observe on one of my first visits to the Killeen Evening Lions Club that started about 20 years ago. Actually, the project probably began some time before then when the Club donated $250,000 to start the program. The Killeen Noon and the Killeen Evening Lions clubs both decided they needed to do something beneficial for the kids, and if the money could be given to the City (and would be matched by the City), it would be quite beneficial. However, that was not the case, as the next step was to the State of Texas, when the funding grew from $250,000 to $1 million very quickly.

The clubs then contacted businesses in the community and asked them to support or sponsor billboards, and the project grew from the $250,000 to $5 million dollars, and was really a program that was a benefit to the handicapped children of the community.

Also, during some of the early stages and during the time that Sergeant Major Dick Robinson was Governor, the group asked Lions Clubs International for support. Another $50,000 was added, and the City of Killeen matched that amount; therefore, their park has not only has playground equipment, but every ball field is of regular size and state teams are invited, and do come, to compete. Besides a softball field, they have four soccer fields—two complete and two under construction—and all this was done under the imagination of the Lions of Killeen, and has been of great benefit to the community.

DRUGS

There were three Lions that were the primary originators of the Lions campaign on the War on Drugs: PDG Lin Rose, Lion John Hall as grass-root Lion and PDG Bill Hudson. Lin was responsible for obtaining General Robert Risner as a known leader to assist in the campaign. General Risner joined the Lions club, later became the State Chairman, and was appointed by the Governor to lead the charge along with the Lions.

One of the greatest leaders in this drug program, and one who became a Lion because of his involvement in the Program of Texas, was Colonel Robinson Risner (better known as Robby Risner) who wrote the book, *The Passing of the Night: My Seven Years as a Prisoner of the North Vietnamese.* This book was a great inspiration because of his past history, and also because during the campaign, he became the Executive Director for the State of Texas War on Drugs (which became prominent because of the Lions of Texas). Colonel Risner's book had an immensely important story to tell about his involvement as a PO.W. which showed his reliance on God and the American way of life. His faith had been tried by fire, never failed, and he said, "Don't ever be ashamed of your faith or your wonderful heritage. Be proud of those things which make America great and which can, with our help, be even greater."

Colonel Risner was in our convention in Hawaii and spoke throughout Texas on the Lions War on Drugs. His most compelling story was that even after being subjected to the most brutal of torture, such as "the ropes," lake stocks, and every imaginable privation as his captors tried to break him and use him for propaganda. It was during this time that he told one of the most memorable days of his time in solitude and capture. One day when he looked through a small hole in his confinement, he was able to see one small blade of grass. This small blade of grass gave him more hope than he had ever had. For many years, he existed in a 7' cell, eating food hardly fit for consumption, among dirt and filth that we would not have raised pigs in. It was during this time that he prayed, "I cried, Lord, you promised grace to bear anything but this pain."

There were many District Leaders and thousands of grass-roots Lions. (General Risner and his one blade of grass, along with the West Texas Terrain was the impetus for my calling workers "grass roots workers"). In addition, there were many speeches made and many programs carried out in schools, and many speeches made to different clubs by different Lions all over Texas. We believe that a great dent was made in the trafficking and use of drugs because of these programs in Texas, and because of the fact that the Drug Program, along with the Diabetic Program, was introduced as an International Program in 1982. During visits by officers of the Association at that time, many meetings were held with a professional U.S. drug appointee. Many programs were coordinated; however, if it had not been for PDG Lin Rose, Lion John Hall and Lion General Risner, it would not have been successful. Another active participant was District Governor Bill Hudson, from Denton.

Here is what President Ronald Reagan thought at the time:

Dear Mr. Grindstaff,

It was a real pleasure to meet you in my office and to have the opportunity to discuss the International Association of Lions' Clubs "War on Drugs." Both Nancy and I are deeply grateful to you and your membership for your dedicated efforts in making Drug Abuse Awareness a priority for Lions International in 155 countries. This outstanding example of volunteerism is particularly heartening to Nancy and me, and I want to reaffirm our Administration's commitment to this critical human area. The support of Lions International can do a great deal to help combat the problems of drug abuse.

The special remembrances which you presented to me are truly appreciated. I am really going to enjoy the Western sculpture of "Pine Johnson and His Shadow Ole Brown," and the awards from Lions International mean more than I can say. Thank you and your colleagues very much for these generous expressions of your friendship.

Nancy and I wish you and your associates continued success with your wonderful work, and our warmest regards for a happy New Year.
Sincerely,
(signed) Ronald Reagan

A portion of the Lions Campaign on the War on Drugs is exemplified by a collection of pictures and ideas that John Hall (very humble, just as was PDG Lin Rose)—one of the most involved Lions on that program and other programs during the '70s and '80s—prepared and is quite a collection, especially because he never served in any office except as a grass roots Lion. Some of the items involved in this collection are as follows:

1. Challenging the Drug Culture
2. Drug Abuse, the Problem and Some Solutions
3. International Symposium on Drug Abuse – February 25, 1983
4. Keep Off the Grass
5. A message from Nancy Reagan, in an Article
6. Youth is Too Precious to Waste on Drugs
7. Art Linkletter Praises the Lions Art on Drugs, in an Article
8. Get America Off Drugs
9. Lions War on Drugs, Diabetes, Awareness—Keep Them and Share the Vision of Service All In One, Picture
10. Your Child Can Resist the Marijuana Culture
11. Involvement A Commitment: A Tradition
12. Lions Aid in Drug War
13. Lions Join in War Against Drugs
14. Local Lions Backing War on Drug Effort
15. Lion Members in Texas Join Against Drugs
16. Lions Combat Drugs
17. Lions Join the Battle
18. Lions Aid in Drug War
19. Taken from the Lions Magazine in one of my monthly articles "Root Out This Social Cancer"
20. While receiving the award in the White House from Nancy Reagan "Citizens Unite Against Drug Abuse"
21. Offer Youth a Share of the Vision
22. Challenge to Club Presidents by Jay and Ebb Grindstaff, First Vice-President Lions International "We Challenge You Lions War On Drugs"
23. Program Objectives
A. Expand our Vision for Sight Services

B. Offer our Youth a Share of the Vision
C. Keep 'em by Sharing the Vision
D. Three in Eighty-three (3 in '83)
E. On the front of the September 19, 1982 *Lions Magazine* "Challenging the Drug Culture" and "Nancy Reagan Recognizes Work of Lions, see page 12"
F. Get America Off Drugs
G. Keep off the Grass

ONE OF OUR HIGHEST AWARDS WAS THE VOLUNTEER CITATION FROM PRESIDENT RONALD REAGAN. THE CITATION READS:

The President's Volunteer Action Award
Citation
Established to recognize, inspire and encourage exemplary volunteer
achievements in communities throughout the United States
This Citation presented to Lions Clubs International
April 13, 1983
(signed) Ronald Reagan

Interlude

District 2-E2
First and Only: Who Killed J.R.?

Who would have thought that anyone would have a Charter Night at Billy Bob's Arena in Fort Worth, Texas? But Gib Lewis—then Speaker of the House—and Ebb rode out on horses (real cowboys dressed in suits and hats that did not properly fit). Both jumped off their horses and conducted the Charter Night for the new Lions Club.

WHO KILLED J.R.?

On my first flight to England aboard Braniff Airways, we rode in First Class. Before the flight began, I was talking to a lady in the front seat (we were in the second row of seats). She was a very lovely lady and a very good conversationalist. All at once, Jay punched me. I turned around, and there was "J. R." (Larry Hagman) of *Dallas* fame coming up the aisle in a robe and boots! He sat in the first seat, and I realized that I had been talking to J.R.'s wife, Maj. Our conversation quickly turned to boots between J. R. and me. He asked where I had my boots made, and I told him, "At Leddy's." He told me he had most of his made at Casey's in San Antonio, but he that owned a pair or two from Leddy's in Fort Worth. The reason we began our conversation was because of our introduction. He was familiar with the Grindstaff name because my uncle was a lawyer at Weatherford, and J. R.'s dad was a lawyer who was married at one time to Mary Martin (who was from Weatherford). Larry had visited Weatherford on occasion and knew the name because of the legal ties.

J. R. was also a jogger, and we had plans to both meet and jog in Hyde Park in London, but the plans did not work out—even though Larry did jog in London in Hyde Park, as his picture was in the paper the next day.

BOARD MEETINGS
1982-83

The first Board meeting of the 1982-83 Board was in Johannesburg, South Africa, which was not popular, with some people who thought that we were not using good judgment in having a possibly dangerous Board meeting. However, we needed to have a Board meeting in that area of the world. We had an excellent Board meeting, but then there was the plane crash of one of the planes as told by Bruce Murray, Past International Director from Canada and Chairman of the Executive Committee. He performed an excellent job in that position, and also was able to take command after the crash and look after the injured and emotionally-scarred individuals.

The first two planes arrived at Kruger Park from Johannesburg, and we arrived before dark. We went out in buses and were able to witness a lion kill, which was very unusual. The kill itself was certainly unusual. After that, it was dark and we went to a souvenir shop at Kruger Park. While in the shop, they called me and said that I needed to go back to the airport. I did not know why, until I arrived and they told me about the crash of one of the planes. At that particular time, they did not know the extent of the crash or the reason for it. The rest of that day and all night long, the officers of the Association, many of which were on the first plane, took their time to call all members of the families involved in the crash. I later went to the hospital in Johannesburg to meet the injured and be of assistance if/when called upon. Bruce Murray relates some of the details of the crash below, as we were very fortunate that no deaths occurred. All of the passengers were very fortunate that the plane did not go off the massive rock formation and down the sheer drops—likely to have caused more injuries and death.

Bruce relates: *A successful International Board of Directors meeting finished on October 11. Our International President, Lion Everett J. "Ebb" Grindstaff had made arrangements for Board members to visit and stay overnight at Kruger National Park—a famous wildlife park—recognized as one of South Africa's most treasured wildlife sanctuaries. ·Thursday morning* in a light rain with some fog, 3 planes were waiting to transport our Lions family. Two were loaded and departed, leaving the third plane made up of 27 of the Lions family and a crew of 3. The aircraft was owned by Calm Air, doing subcontract for Air Botswana as ordered by South African airlines. Our crew was made up of a pilot on his first flight of this nature, having just returned from the military, the recently-married co-pilot, and his wife serving as stewardess.

The Lions included three Past International Presidents and their wives. Past International President Herb Petry, Jr. was on the flight. The takeoff was uneventful ,and as we rose into the sky, rain continued and the fog became more pronounced—making land difficult or impossible to see.

(This part of this report has been made available with information given by the crew). An instrument indicated by its movement that we had approached the airport, even though unable to see due to fog. The crew made the aircraft turn to follow the instruments. As we descended, land became visible to the crew. The pilot took control and realized we did not have sufficient power or thrust to get us over Grauskoph Mountain, and so gave full power and directed the aircraft directly at trees on the side of the mountain. At the last moment he maneuvered the aircraft by dropping the tail, which hit the trees first (causing the loss of the tail), then the wings hit and were badly damaged and partially lost. At about the same time, a large limb came through the front of the aircraft between the two seats for the pilot and co-pilot and ended up through the baggage area, stopping next to first passenger seats.

At this point we continued bouncing along the ground. To our left was a large sheer drop, directly in front of us was a massive rock formation, and we skidded slightly to the right to the only open area to be seen. The cabin of the aircraft was in a chaotic state, with all seats off their moorings, and the cabinets and lavatory in the cabin as well.

There was a small fire, however, the pilot urged us to save the cockpit and the instruments which we were able to do. Evacuation of the aircraft was orderly, with no panic or hysteria being shown. Athough there were some with serious injuries, everyone cooperated. After 2-1/2 hours, a guide led all but 2 to a lodge, and then 2 hours later, 4 men arrived with equipment to carry our one member who was unable to walk.

That night, some were kept in the hospital in Skukuza, and the rest in a hotel. The skill and experience of the pilot was instrumental in our survival. The following day, we were returned to our hotel in Johannesburg by auto."

After the plane crash, Board members were disbursed to Port Elizabeth and a couple of other places in South Africa, other than the ending trip in Cape Town, where a large banquet was held.

Spring Board Meeting
1983

This Board meeting was split between Houston and San Antonio, which had really not been done previous to this, but it was to give Board members a double-taste of Texas, and to carry on the business of the Organization in addition thereto. At a Board meeting on the day that the reports to the entire Board are finished, they must be typed and presented to the Board for approval at the final Board meeting, which the staff performed.

On the day reports were being finished, buses left Houston for San Antonio, after seeing the Astrodome, the Rodeo and the Houston Fat Stock Show. San Antonio was where the balance of the Board meeting was to be held; however, there was one Texas Lion that was appointed to the Board by the name of E. B. "Tex" Mayer—one of the outstanding Directors from the State of Texas—and the one who had made arrangements for the Board to stop at (of all places) the "LaGrange Dairy Mart." It was just a regular Dairy Queen, or "Dairy Mart" as it was called in LaGrange, but Tex and Nell Mayer were the proud owners of the Dairy Mart, in addition to ownership of a large processing company. The entire Board enjoyed sandwiches, ice cream, and whatever was available for our noon meal (one of our cheaper meals, but one we still had to pay for, even though Tex was our host). It was a unique treat, to say the least, for many of the Board members from some of the larger cities of our country to be treated in such a manner.

On to Johnson City and the opportunity to tour the home of Lyndon B. Johnson and the park at Stonewall.

We were able to enjoy the Riverwalk in San Antonio as we finished our Board meeting, but it is unbelievable that during a year of different activities that we would have a rather unusual incident—we had a fire at the hotel where we were staying. Some of us that were on the 20th floor had to evacuate to the first floor in quick and orderly fashion, but fortunately, we were able to make this sudden change without any injuries or losses.

This ended our Board meetings for the year, except for the one in Hawaii (which was a very short one) prior to the Convention in Honolulu.

It was an important one, as we collected over $1 million of "blocked funds" from India through the efforts of our Treasurer, Elsa Vaintzettel, and PID Rohit Mehta.

It was a year of challenges, and a year in which the Board was split on some issues, but a year in which programs were presented and adopted (different from previous Boards of having a program for one year.) Programs in 1982-83 included the Diabetic Program, the Drug Program and Journey for Sight—all programs that still exist in our International organization—in existence since 1982-83. They exist because they were programs that were and needed on a global basis, and ones that addressed needs at that particular time. These grew into International programs that will maintain their longevity for many years to come, thanks to the Lions that made them possible.

Later, I was able to show the directors some approaches firsthand, because we had a board meeting in San Antonio-a split meeting (the only one I know of), but one that gave the directors a big taste of Texas—not only the big city of Houston and the rodeo, but also the downtown river area of San Antonio with a stop at the Dairy Mart in La Grange (from which along with his famous consolidated smokehouse, Tex Mayer was always taking German summer sausage and tenderloin to all Board meetings to give directors a taste of Texas).

Interlude

Hospitality Room: Mike and Marshall

When he was incoming President in Atlanta, Georgia, Ebb was receiving many gifts. As Marshall and I were in charge of his hospitality room from 1979-1983, and tasked with keeping everything in proper order, we received a gift in a box—kind of a sheet metal box—and as we got to looking at it, it was full of buttons, little buttons of different colors. You would plug it in, and a Lions' emblem lit up from within with colors coming through the buttons cut into the sides of the box. It would change different colors and would rotate around, showing red and green colors and eventually it would come back and you could tell it was a Lions' emblem. We tried to show it to incoming President Ebb, but he didn't have time to look at it. He didn't care one thing about it, so Marshall and I decided that we wanted him to see it. We hired the maintenance department in the Hilton Hotel in Atlanta to come up to his room. We hung up this fine piece of artwork that the Chinese delegation had given to our President, and we wanted him to view it, so we hung it in the bathroom—wiring it into the light switch. In the morning, when he decided to get up and go do his constitutional journey at the john, he turned around to turn the light switch on and was able to see by the light of a reflecting Lions emblem! He enjoyed (or so we thought) that view the whole time he was in the restroom that morning. He found that a quite unusual way to display his gifts, and we did hear about the way we displayed that particular gift later.

That's one of the stories about Everett J. "Ebb" Grindstaff's claim to fame as he came up through the Chairs. There are many things that happened in Atlanta. Mr. Cooper and I would love to tell you more stories.

As we got ready to check out, it was our job, as stated earlier, to be in charge of the hospitality room. We had to be sure there was food kept there and things of that nature, so we would go down to a delicatessen, where they would make us watermelon boats. We'd buy lunch meat and our wives would help us prepare all of it. We had food available constantly, and as people would come in to see the incoming President, we would offer them drinks, something to eat, and to greet the various different delegations. To keep all this, we had to keep it refrigerated, so I rented a 16-cubic foot refrigerator and had it smuggled up the hotel's back stairwell. I had to pay the bellman and some other people to get me up the elevator, but we got it up there! We had a 16-cubic foot refrigerator in a suite that Marshall and I had—in the center of the room—and when we got ready to leave, we told the lady at the front desk that ABC Rental (or whatever the local rental company's name was) would be picking up the refrigerator. She said, "Well, they don't have any refrigerators in the room." I said, Yes they do, it's a 16-foot." She said, "Oh no, the largest we have are just those little bitty chest refrigerators." I said, No, ma'am, there is a refrigerator up there, and they will want to lay claim to it, so I wanted you to know that it is upstairs." That was one of the ways we kept refrigeration going.

Because there was a corkage for all this, and of course we were trying to save the Lions of Texas' money, and as we talked about watermelons, there were watermelon rinds and watermelon boats. We didn't know what to do with them, so Marshall and I would take them two floors down to a linen closet and we'd leave them in that linen closet. We thought they'd find them pretty quick, but after about three days, you could start to smell those watermelons. Nobody ever claimed them, so we quit going to that one, and found another linen closet to hide more watermelons in.

Those are just *some* of the things we did. By the way, Marshall did smuggle 16 cases of Lone Star Beer across six 6 state lines for the cause. If he'd ever gotten caught with all that beer—smuggling across those state lines and not paying any taxes—this wouldn't be written.

The year 1982 was an exciting year of enjoying the hospitality in Grindstaff's room. We had many other stories we could tell, but those are probably two of the best ones.

Ebb Grindstaff recalls: "Mike, Annette, Marshall and Wanda were in charge of the Hospitality Rooms for Montreal in 1979 through 1983. They always had the best food, and everybody came up there and of course devoured the best food. They did a fantastic job, and either one of them could have been in the same spot I was, but Jay and I and all our family appreciated all they did for us in those and many other ways."

The 1950s and 1960s were really the growth years of Lions Clubs International. The 1980s—starting with our own Past President Grindstaff—

were really the heyday of Texas Lions. That's when we had our growth, and that's when we were affecting things throughout this great state. For example, through the leadership of Past President Grindstaff, we were able to become involved with the Texas War on Drugs, the start of the recognition of a drug problem, and the very start of an anti-drug program put on by the State of Texas. In November 1980, at the El Tropicana Hotel in San Antonio, President Grindstaff brought General Robbie Risner (head of the Texas War Drugs Program) to a Council of Governors meeting.After his presentation, the Lions of Texas picked up the banner of the Texas War on Drugs, and from that, the Drug Program expanded. In addition, due to Past President Grindstaff starting the "Grass Root" Lions, we were able to develop a program of speech contests. Our very first speech contest was called "Young Texans Speak Out Against Drugs". We were able to start the Drug Program, the Diabetic Program, and many of the programs that we see today. These were really started in the 1980s. That's the highlight, I think, when Texas Lionism was really placed on the map. We should be proud of all the people that led us through that time of growth. That's when we were highest in membership, and the highest in recognizable service throughout this country. I can remember that the Governor spoke at our State Convention in Dallas. We had a great deal of influence in those times, and that is something we should strive to regain.

Also during that time, we changed the method of operation of Lions Clubs International through our Executive Secretary and Administrator, Roy Schaetzel, Ebb Grindstaff, and the majority of the Board. We didn't have a new program every year, but we established during that year between 1982-83 what had already been established through the Board. Nobody knew what the program was going to be, except for Roy Schaetzel and President Ebb Grindstaff. It was all because of the Texas programs and the Lions of Texas that these were accomplished—both the Drug Contest and the Diabetic Contest. The Diabetic Contest has now ballooned into many different projects. These came at the beginning of 1982-83 when we started those particular programs. In 1982, we started Drug Program education. We also started education of diabetics which moved into the Juvenile Diabetics, (we had already been in the Juvenile Diabetics field in Texas since 1971). We then had the Journey for Sight, which was a means of fundraising with people such as Wayne Gretsky, who participated in this program of his own free choice in Canada, and at no charge. His hockey stick is in the annals of the Lions of Texas. From the Journey for Sight came such things as Ice Races on the rivers of Canada, motor races, bike races, and many other types of races.

Membership of Texas: 1983

In May of 1983, Texas reached 45,000 Lions for the first time in the history of the Association. It was only because of the hard work of Texas Lions that this was possible. We had membership meetings in Kerrville at least three times, every time we met. We always had the meetings on both nights, and sometimes during the day. Freddy Wolters was one of the enthusiastic membership Lions during these meetings. Even though he might have stepped on a few toes, he got the job done, along with the Lubbock Downtown Club, the Conroe Club, the Lufkin Club, and many other clubs I know that I am leaving out. Roy Davis in the Valley was a great help for the entire Valley (and Texas), as he already had a membership plan intact and he put it to use.

Our theme for membership was a simple one because membership is simple—"Get 'em and Keep 'em." Over 36 years later, they are now using "Ask 'em"...still simple. It will work if you will, but we must "Keep 'em" a phrase substituted for retention (a negative word to me).

It reminds me of the story of the man who was working with a spade in his garden, who hit some rocks and damaged the spade's tines. He took the spade to the blacksmith for repair, and when he returned, he asked the blacksmith if it would work. The blacksmith replied, "It will work if you will." That's what happened—Texas Lions worked and were enthusiastic.

Tons has been written on membership, but it takes a little bit of work itself. It is not a new problem, as my theme in 1964 when I was District Governor was "Stop Drops." Of course, extension played a large part in this growth, and we cannot mention membership or extension without mentioning Past International Director Tex Mayer. He's one of the best Lions, along with PDG Clarence Wolfshol of Giddings, who fell under the magic of Tex Mayer for Extension, and one of the best extension people that we've had in the State of Texas. I know that Bill Miller of Waco led in the number of clubs extended in 1982-83, which I believe to be 10. Then came Council Chairmen Art Cook, Howard Leverett and John Petry—fantastic in their capacities in leading Governors to heights unknown. Along with appointed member of the International Board, Dr. Don Mayer and Past Council Chairman and Past District Governor of La Grange, son of "Tex", who led his District to 110 Clubs—which required a split by the clubs, pleasing Lions Clubs International. We also had three part-time PDGs who worked in membership and extension. Ronnie Martin is the modern Membership and Extension Lion in Texas and other states.

We had some enthusiastic Lions that were willing to use special efforts to see that we completed our goals—always looking for ways of increasing our membership to the highest level at that time.

Membership in 1982-83 was the beginning of "Russell's Raiders", which was District Governor Russell Willis in 1983-84, who came from San Angelo and ended up as a Chamber of Commerce Manager in Weslaco and did a tremendous job in A-3. He had the highest membership in 1983-84. In addition, he also organized 10 clubs in that particular year. Our membership grew for a period of time because Lions put some effort into it.

One leader who had never been a District Governor was Joe Franks, a real fireball and motivator. The districts in that area were full of them—PDG Gordon Richardson and many folks we do not have room to mention such as PDG Michael Morgan, State Membership Chairman one year—they keep coming in flashes, but many are recognized in so many other ways. We have Sandy Griffin from Abilene, who trained numerous pups for Leader Dog, and her husband was PDG Hal Griffin who served loyally as District Governor, and was also on State and Global committees. Both of them in their respective capacities were a great influence on many Lions because of their enthusiasm and love of service to their fellow man, and both were responsible for new members. All the Lions of those years gave all they had.

Just like the story told by President Eisenhower when speaking to the National Press Club, "It reminds me of my boyhood days on a Kansas farm. An old farmer had a cow that we wanted to buy. We went over to visit him and asked about the cow's pedigree. The old farmer didn't know what pedigree meant, so we asked him about the cow's butterfat production. He told us that he hadn't any idea what it was. Finally, we asked him if he knew how many pounds of milk the cow produced each year. The farmer shook his head and said, 'I don't know. But she's an honest cow and she'll give you all the milk she has!' " Well, I'm like the old cow, I'll give you everything I have." These Lions gave all they had.

A Vision in Midland
is Helping the World to See

A history of Texas Lionism would not be complete without a discussion of the contributions of the Midland Downtown Lions. In its first 50 years as it grew to one of the largest clubs in the world, Midland Downtown was very involved in the International scene. Past District Governors Carl Hyde and Roy Minear were routinely part of the Credentials Committee at International Conventions, and the club's band was world-renown, performing at several International Conventions. The club also built and operated a zoo with a small railroad around it in Midland.

However, their contributions to the second 50 years have made a much larger impact. In the early 1980s, the club built a park and a fire museum, refurbishing and preserving some of Midland's first fire engines. In the mid-1980s, Lion Ike Fitzgerald (now PDG) became tired of shipping countless pairs of glasses to New York, where valuable frames were turned into cash for the non-Lion distributor—with what glasses were left shipped overseas with no process to help distribute them to the needy. He decided they could put the same glasses to better use at home. Midland was in the midst of an oil recession, and cash from selling the precious metals in the frames allowed the club to increase its eyeglass budget, thus allowing them to help many more children obtain glasses. At the same time, Lion Dr. Norman Gould—an Optometrist and Downtown Lion member—asked the club to not ship the remaining glasses to New York. Instead, and with the help of club members, he taught them how to read, sanitize and bag the glasses for him to take on a mission trip. The trip was successful, and upon his return, he and PDG Fitzgerald got together and developed a system to process and distribute used glasses to adults in need—while making sure that Lions did not cross the line of prescribing glasses. With a 400-member club behind them, recycling used glasses for adults began in Texas. Over time, word spread beyond Midland, and glasses started coming in to to process. Mission groups then came to Midland to learn how to do the same thing as they went to other countries.

During the same period, Midland Downtown Lions obtained a local landmark, the Howard Hodge Movie Theater, and remodeled it into their clubhouse and recycling center. The theater had been part of a family theater business owned by Howard Hodge and his brother, 2-A1's own PDG, Homer Hodge from Winters, Texas.

By the time "Sight First" came along in 1990, Midland Downtown Lions were processing thousands of pairs of eyeglasses per month, becoming one of Lions Club International's first three Eyeglass Recycling Centers. Over the next few years, the Midland Center became an integral part in helping LCI develop centers around the world. Midland's training classes have trained thousands of Lions and other mission groups, and have provided them with *millions* of pairs of glasses to take on their trips.

During this time, Lions from across the state started helping in the collection and sorting processes, and became major contributors to the growth of the center. Eventually, the involvement of Lions from across Texas, and the magnitude of the project within LCI's Sight First program prompted the MD2 Council of Governors to adopt the program as a Texas Lions state project. Under the direction of the Center's CEO, PDG Ike Fitzgerald, it received its 501(c)3 designation, and the name was changed to the Texas Lions Eyeglass Recycling Center (TLERC). Lions International's Sight First program provided several grants over the years to develop and enlarge the facility, to buy equipment, to fund mission trips, and most recently, to buy state-of-the-art lens-making equipment. In 2010, TLERC bought its own building, as it had outgrown the Midland Downtown building. In 2013, a bunkhouse was added, so that volunteers could come from around the state and work at the center, and so that students coming to monthly training classes would have a place to stay.

Since becoming part of Sight First in 1992, a major thrust has been to develop similar satellite centers. Lion Tom Mills, an optician from Big Spring, Texas helped develop a training program to teach Lions clubs how to run their own screening lanes, and to place used glasses on those in need in their hometowns—eliminating the need for annual mission trips to these areas. With the help of Midland Downtown Lion Francis McDonald, PID Marshall Cooper from Lubbock (the Center's LCI liaison) and many other Lions from around the state, including PIP Jimmy Ross, the TLERC team developed 13 satellite centers in Central America, South America, Mexico and Africa, not to mention three others in Texas. Once a center establishes a recycling distribution program, the team (under the direction of Lion Mills) returns to help them set up a lens-making program to make new glasses for children.

Another innovative program that has been highly successful is the use of prison inmates to read, sanitize and bag used glasses. This provides a way for those who are incarcerated to do something positive for the community, and in many cases teaches them a useful trade. TLERC uses a prison in Big Spring, and a satellite center in San Angelo (also District 2-A1) uses a prison in Eden, Texas.

Through the vision of PDG Ike Fitzgerald and under the direction of Lion Tom Mills, TLERC has developed a children's program, making new glasses for children for just a few dollars per pair (TLERC has never advocated putting used glasses on children). Clubs can send prescriptions to the center from anywhere in the state, and in a couple of days, Lion Hayden Minton (Midland Downtown) will send them a new pair of glasses. With its computerized equipment, the lab is capable of making several dozen pair per day.

After successfully seeing the establishment of the children's program and the installation of the bunkhouse, PDG Ike Fitzgerald retired as CEO, dedicating almost 30 years of his life to this project. Lion Dr. Norman Gould still provides eye exams for needy children in his office at TLERC once a week during the school year. Lion Tom Mills still leads a monthly screening in Midland to help those in need obtain recycled glasses.

Entering the next century, under the direction of CEO PDG Carolyn Keskitalo, TLERC hopes to expand its training programs into South America, thus enabling them to set up their own centers. In addition, they are looking at ways to set up optometry schools in South America to help them develop their own industry—a dream of Lion Dr. Tulsi Singh, another Midland Downtown Lion.

The roar of the Midland Lions is being felt worldwide. A 101-year-old man received a vision screening in a hot, dusty and extremely poor part of Mexico. His 80-year-old daughter nagged him to let the volunteers screen his vision and put on a pair of eyeglasses. "Once the glasses were put on his face, he turned to his daughter and put two fingers at her temple, and then ran his fingers along her jawline. The only way he could identify his daughter other than voice was by the shape of her face. He said that he had not seen his daughter's face in over 47 years, but now he could with the new glasses," recalled Carolyn Keskitalo. She witnessed that moment during a mission trip, and says that it's moments like those that give focus to what is taking place in Midland, Texas.

Midland is home to the Texas Eyeglass Recycling Center where 3.5 million eyeglasses are collected, processed, and distributed each year. There are only 18 centers worldwide, and one in Texas. All centers are part of the Lions Club International Vision Charities Program, which strives to prevent blindness through vision screenings, eyeglass recycling and production. It's a mission that began nearly 90 years ago when Helen Keller offered this challenge at the 1925 International Lions Convention, "I appeal to you Lions, you who have your sight, your hearing, you who are strong and brave and kind. Will you not constitute yourselves Knights of the Blind in this crusade against darkness?"

In Midland, that crusade gained momentum with the vision of the Ike Fitzgerald, a Downtown Lions Club member and former Midland fire fighter and Dr. Norman Gould O.D., a Midland optometrist. "I knew in advance I was going to need glasses for a mission trip in Belize. At that time, Lions clubs in Midland were collecting eyeglasses to recycle, but were shipping them off to other places to get repaired. I asked them to keep the used glasses here in Midland, because I knew I could fix them up in such a way that they could be useful. We read the prescriptions and bagged them in my office and took about 500 on the mission trip," says Dr. Gould. Upon his return, Dr. Gould met with his friend Fitzgerald, who helped design a system to collect glasses and keep them in Midland, instead of sending them away. "The first thing I had to figure out was how to process the glasses," explains Fitzgerald. "Whenever I was stumped, I would go to Dr. Gould for help. He told me that there were essentially only two types of glasses: single vision and bifocal."

Over time, the recycling process grew, and Lions Club International approached Fitzgerald about starting a recycling center in Midland. "Midland was a natural fit for the center since the program was so active there already with the tremendous hearts of Dr. Gould and Ike Fitzgerald," says Marshall Cooper, Texas Lions Eyeglass Recycling Center Board Member and former Lions Club International Director. "It's just a wonderful thing, what a pair of used eyeglasses can do," says Cooper, "I tell people all the time that if they aren't going to use their old glasses, donate them. There are people that can use them."

The Texas Lions Eyeglass Recycling Center opened in downtown Midland in 1992. Lions club satellite centers from across Texas and surrounding states collect used glasses and send them to Midland for processing. Past District Governor Bob Edwards and Lion Aubrey Linne have been of constant help and service in the everyday operation of the Recycling Center since its initial opening. Keskitalo is the CEO of the Texas Lions Eyeglass Recycling Center. "When we first get a box of used glasses, we go through them to check for broken parts and scratches. If they can be used, then we resort them into single vision and bifocal lines," says Keskitalo, "Used glasses are then sent to prisons in Eden and Big Spring, where prisoners have been trained on how to read prescriptions. Prisoners are given the opportunity to learn something and give back to the community. It's a very coveted job inside the prison. They are learning a skill that they can use on the outside."

Once lenses are read, they are bagged and stocked by their prescriptions. It's the catalog system Fitzgerald began several years ago, that is now used worldwide. "They tell me all the other centers are using it," Fitzgerald admits modestly and adds, "I simply showed our center and volunteers how to use it, but they're the ones who do all the work."

Once eyeglasses are ready for their new owner, TLERC completes requests for glasses for those in need. That need can be in Midland or thousands of miles away. "Church groups, medical groups, military service members and others will request glasses for their humanitarian missions," says Keskitalo, "On these global missions, volunteers give free vision screenings and help match patients with a used pair of eyeglasses that fits their prescription." However, adults are the only ones who can receive used eyeglasses. Children must receive a new pair of eyeglasses. "For the most part, adults know when they can't see correctly. Children's eyes are still forming and they may not be sure what is correct. They may have lost vision in their right eye, but vision in their left eye is good, so their brain says they can see just fine. It's just better to ensure that children can see properly by giving them brand new glasses," explains Keskitalo.

Volunteers on mission trips conduct vision screenings on children. Once they have the prescription and measurements they need, they can order a pair of glasses from their local Lions club. The order is then sent to Midland, where TLERC makes the glasses. "We have a state-of-the-art fully-automated laboratory that is licensed, so we can make glasses just like any retail store you may go to for your glasses, like Lens Crafters or Wal-Mart," says Keskitalo. TLERC's cost to make one pair of glasses is just $14 to $18, depending upon the prescription. That cost is never passed to a patient. It is paid for by various Lions club fundraisers.

Those in need overseas aren't the only ones getting a new perspective. Lions club volunteers offer vision screenings in schools, churches and day-cares. Screenings reveal whether or not a child needs glasses, and a referral is then made to a local doctor, like Dr. Gould. "The Lions club asks doctors like me to conduct low-cost eye exams for those in need, so we get glasses to those children whose parents couldn't afford them otherwise," says Dr. Gould.

However, most volunteers aren't doctors, and they must be trained on how to screen patients and use equipment. TLERC offers a three-day training. "People come from all over for this training. We just trained a priest from Italy and several people from England," says Keskitalo, "They are trained on auto refraction, tonometer, focometer, visual activity, fitting, adjusting glasses and so forth. On the third day, they put what they learned into action." The last day of training typically falls on the third Saturday of the month, where the community is invited to a free vision screening so that volunteers can get hands-on training with what they've learned.

"We have trained a lot of people in Midland. If we get an eyeglass program similar to the one in Midland in every country in the world, it would improve lives in third world countries like you could not imagine," says Lion Cooper.

Lions Club International and the TLERC have already helped set up a successful eyeglass recycling center in Mexico, and are focusing its reach in Central America. "We are now going to be concentrating on setting up centers there by taking what we've learned and have had success with in Mexico. We've got to train people all over the world to put glasses on children correctly. We have a new instrument called a 'spot' that gives you a valid refraction. It's easy to operate once we teach more people how to use it," says Fitzgerald.

By following the Lions club motto, "We Serve", Fitzgerald believes the efforts being made in Midland will continue to have a life-changing impact across the world. Keskitalo echoes that sentiment, "We never know where the used glasses come from or where they are going. We never know what someone saw through them, and we don't know what the new wearer is going to be able to see. We take a leap of faith knowing that someone will benefit."

It took supreme efforts and contact with Lions Club International for the guidance and funding for this momentous effort in a needed field, along with the efforts of so many dedicated Lions in Midland, including PDG Bob Edwards and Lion Aubrey Linne, who had been the Operations Officer and is now involved in children's screening, and is in charge of the Midland Lions club building after the move of the TLERC.

As Ebb Grindstaff recalled, "While in Sri Lanka on a Lions visit, Jay and I visited a Lions Project that covered three of our main thrusts: sight, diabetics, and drug education. While visiting, they asked that I place a pair of eyeglasses on a lady in another room. Never did I realize the effect that it would have on me. Walking in, she reminded me of my grandmother with a solid head of gray hair, the wonderful wrinkles of a grandmother's face, but such a sweet smile. As I placed the eyeglasses on her (recycled at one of our recycling centers, such as Midland), she looked up at me and then at the ceiling, looked around at other objects and people in the room, then glanced at some of the other projects being carried out in the next room. She then said the simple words that really have an impact from a small light, 'Now I can see.' Just think, you may have played a part of that one pair of glasses."

Texas Lions Eyeglass
Recycling Center Letter

November 1, 2014

Council of Governors and Fellow Lions,

In these times of different needs and many places in this world that have suffered great need, TLERC has had a larger amount of calls for recycled glasses. Mission teams have called on us to supply glasses in large numbers. Church teams requesting the most.

Some places that these mission teams have traveled to: Meteti Panama, Cotui Dominican Republic. Saltillo, Mexico as well as Alcapulco, Mexico. Sudan, Africa and two different locations in India. It has been said that recycled glasses are no longer needed but this has not shown to be the cases with us. 90,600 recycled glasses, sun glasses, and frames sent.

Standing clinics in Mexico, and Oklahoma plus in New Mexico on Tribal Lands, glasses have been shipped. They serve many people each week and month.

A new satellite was welcomed as part of TLERC in the Fort Worth area, District 2-E2. Shipments from Midland to the new satellite have been sent with more to follow.

Southwestern Motor Transport Company has proven to be a wonderful partner for TLERC. Each week two to three shipments of glasses, supplies and or equipment arrive. This company is very friendly and helpful. Glasses came from Kansas. Supplies came from New York, as well as from Lions all over Texas.

The children lab in Midland has served 110 requests since school started. Glasses arrive daily from clubs in Texas that are serving their schools and towns with good quality glasses. Lion Tom Mills, Mills Optical whose license runs the lab, and Lion

Haden Minton, donate between $14.00 and $18.00 per pair. TLERC will finish the frames free. Remember that this is a Children's eyeglass project. Please do not ask for adult glasses to be made.

Thanks to all the Districts, Clubs and Governors who remember us as part of the three Texas Charities. Ask your District Director to be a speaker at your club or cabinet meetings. Let us at TLERC serve you.

Submitted by: PDG Carolyn Keskitalo TLERC CEO

Texas Lions Foundation History and Growth

Prior to the convention in Honolulu, Hawaii, where I went out as President of Lions Clubs International, I have made at least four or five trips to Australia since I was director in 1973. During the last trip or two, I kept running across the Mint program in Australia, and the fine program in Publicity and Public Relations that they had in order to raise funds for different activities of the Lions. They even had a film and a lot of publicity about same, and I was so impressed by this that I brought it to the Lions of Texas at the convention in Honolulu.

As far as I know, this is the first time that we actually had a vote on a project, anything but politics, at the International Convention as far as the State of Texas is concerned. However, this was so important, that we needed to have the opportunity for the Lions of Australia to present this program to us, and also to take action at that particular time. As a result thereof, we had a special meeting after the presentation, and the Lions of Texas adopted this program as a statewide project and the Mint program began.

After that, John Petry actually drew up the constitution and by-laws for the Texas Lions Foundation, and after a great deal of research, we were able to talk to Past International Director Ed Flood to take on the financial end of this program, which he did as well as the publicity of same. The program began and grew into quite a fundraising project for different projects in the Lions of Texas.

The idea of a Foundation owned by and for the benefit of the Lions of Texas was the foresight of PID Edwin H. Flood of Amarillo. Lion Ed was successful in selling the idea to the 1983-84 Council of Governors. This Council of Governors approved the Articles of Incorporation and Texas Lions ratified it at their 1984 State Convention.

A preliminary meeting of the Foundation was held in Kerrville the first weekend of August 1984. The first organizational meeting of the Foundation was held in San Antonio on November 3, 1984, where the

Constitution and By-Laws were adopted, and PID Ed Flood was elected as its first Chairman. Ed Flood carried the Articles of Incorporation to Austin and the Articles were approved by the Secretary of State on December 4, 1984. The Constitution and By-Laws were ratified by the Texas Lions at their 1985 State Convention.

From the sale of mints, the Foundation continued to grow. When the sale of mints was discontinued, an amount in excess of $150,000 had been placed in the Trust Fund. The Foundation is structured so that only interest from the Trust Fund can be used for grants. The Constitution and By-Laws specifically state how this money can be spent. It states that the Trust Fund Corpus may not be spent for any purpose. Only the interest funds of the funds of the Foundation may be expended by the Board for grants by the Foundation for the following reasons:

1. To promote any charitable activities sponsored by the Lions of Texas
2. To support the Texas Lions Camp
3. To support any Lions International program
4. To help defray costs of any designated disaster
5. List of Grants Issued

PDG Bernie Gradel has performed yeoman service for the Foundation and all the District and State Projects.

Texas Lions Foundation

PROGRAMS

Texas Lions Foundation (TLF) is an organization committed to filling humanitarian needs throughout the State of Texas. As a public, non-profit, tax-exempt corporation, its purpose is to promote human welfare by careful application of contributed funds.

TLF concentrates its efforts in two areas: humanitarian services and disaster relief. The Foundation strives to support projects that, while falling into one of these two categories, also have long-term and farm reaching effects, and promote the objectives of the Texas Lions Foundation. Overall, the Foundation maintains a strong commitment to helping people achieve their own potential, and to implementing projects that make permanent and positive changes. Projects are favored that provide benefits to as many as possible.

HUMANITARIAN SERVICES - Humanitarian Service grants can be issued in support of a broad range of projects designed to fill diverse needs. In general, projects, designed to create or expand community programs or institutes preferred.

DISASTER RELIEF - Disaster Relief grants are made in responses to natural disaster that cause significant mortality, injury and property damage and loss.

Texas Lions Foundation
6005 99th Street
Lubbock, TX 79424-3823

Chief Operations Officer	**Asst. Chief Operations Officer**
PID Marshall W. Cooper	PDG Claude Durham
6005 99th Street	520 West Lake Drive
Lubbock, TX 79424-3823	Livingston, TX 77351-6027
H) 806-698-6489	H) 936-327-4645
F) 806-698-6491	F) 936-365-2999
C) 806-790-5051	C) 936-328-1688
email: pidmwc@msn.com	email: cdurham@livingston.net

Chairman
PDG Dr. John Seale
112 Saint Andrews Loop
Kerrville, TX 78028-8124
H) 830-896-1646
C) 830-329-6441
email: jseale@windstream.net

Vice Chairman
PDG Gill Burrell
PO Box 68
Manor, TX 78653-0068
H) 512-272-5100
email: gill007@earthlink.net

Treasurer
PDG Gladys Tramp
442 CR 4315
Lampasas, TX 76550
C) 254-238-2474
email: gtramp42@gmail.com

Secretary
PDG Claude Durham
520 West Lake Drive
Livingston, TX 77351-6027
H) 936-327-4645
F) 936-365-2999
C) 936-328-1688
email: cdurham@livingston.net

Texas Lions Foundation Chairmen

Year	Chairman	District
1983-1984	PID Edwin H. Flood	2-T1
1984-1985	PID Edwin H. Flood	2-T1
1985-1986	PDG Gerald Devault	2-T2
1986-1987	PDG Joe Parish	2-T3
1987-1988	PDG Jim Jones	2-T2
1988-1989	PDG Pat Waddle	2-E2
1989-1990	PDG Mark Anderson	2-S5
1990-1991	PDG Mark Anderson	2-S5
1991-1992	PDG Vernon Carmichael	2-S2
1992-1993	PDG Duane Howell	2-T2
1993-1994	PCC Jack A. Harris	2-E2
1994-1995	PCC Jack A. Harris	2-E2
1995-1996	PDG Julius Yellott	2-S2
1996-1997	PDG Jack Wise	2-S3
1997-1998	PDG Tut Tawwater	2-T2
1998-1999	PDG David "Ike" Boling	2-A3

Year	Chairman	District
1999-2000	PDG Oscar W. Cook	2-A1
2000-2001	PDG Felix Meyers	2-S5
2001-11/2001	PDG Felix Meyers	2-S5
11/2001-2002	PCC Irvin D. Hiler	2-E1
2002-2003	PDG Gid Terry	2-X2
2003-2004	PDG Gid Terry	2-X2
2004-2005	PDG John Kimbrough	2-A2
2005-2006	PDG John Kimbrough	2-A2
2006-2007	PDG Bernie Gradel, Jr.	2-T2
2007-2008	PDG Bernie Gradel, Jr.	2-T2
7/2008-12/2008	PDG Virgil A Polocek	2-A1
12/2008-2009	PDG Marcella V. Henke	2-S4
2009-2010	PDG Marcella V. Henke	2-S4
2010-2011	PDG Marcella V. Henke	2-S4
2011-2012	PDG Gary Linker	2-T2
2012-2013	PDG Gary Linker	2-T2
2013-2014	PDG Dr. John Seale	2-A2
2014-2015	PDG Dr. John Seale	2-A2

Partial List of Grants Issued

Date	District	Amount	Total grants to-date	Project
10/24/1994	2-S1	$2,000.00	$38,500.00	Flood Relief-Beaumont
5/30/1997	2-S3	$10,000.00	$67,700.00	Disaster Relief Tornado in Jarrell
6/30/1998	MD-2	$10,000.00	$85,983.00	Texas Lions Camp
11/19/1998	MD-2	$250.00	$107,733.00	American Diabetes Assn-Printing
8/1/2000	MD-2	$22,750.00	$145,983.00	Driscoll Children's Hospital for production of video: *Taking Diabetes to School*

Date	District	Amount	Total grants to-date	Project
8/8/2005	2-A1	$7,360.00	$225,948.00	Rowena Lions Club Fire Equipment Matching Funds
8/8/2005	2-A1	$12,500.00	$238,448.00	Rowena Lions Club Water System Matching Funds
12/9/2005	MD-2	$10,000.00	$250,448.00	Driscoll Children's Hospital Diabetes Education
5/3/2014	MD-2	$5,000.00	$410,158.00	TLC - Campers & Parents Diabetes Education Program

A total of $410,158.00 has been spent by the Texas Lions Foundation for Humanitarian Programs since its initiation, and this is quite another feat for the Texas Lions.

To the Council of Governors:

Good Morning! It may seem to you and many other Lions that the Texas Lions Foundation has been relatively inactive during the first six months of this Lions' year. This year is no different than most years when the first half of the year is slow and activity expands during the last six months (particularly the last three months) of the year. There have been no emergency grants given for the first six months because there have been no requests for assistance. I hope this is not the calm before the storm.

The Texas Lions Foundation has made a couple of presentations for $5,000 each. The first one was to the Texas Lions Camp for a pilot program designed to help teach parents of diabetic children. I understand the program has been well received. The second donation for $5,000 was given to the Texas Lions Centennial Committee to help fund the celebration in Dallas, Texas in 2017. The Texas Lions Foundation was one of the first to contribute to this project. Also, this afternoon, our Board of Trustees will be considering another Humanitarian Grant.

So far this year, we have received approximately $45,000 in donations which is about average. Donations are always better in the second half of the year. Our goal for this year is still $115,000 for the entire year.

The Foundation is still actively involved in working with representatives of the immediate past Council of Governors, the current Council, and the next two Councils to come.

The Texas Lions Foundation plans to donate our interest in the Texas Lions Museum and office building located at 3301 Legion Drive, Kerrville, Texas 78028 to the Lions of Texas through the newly created Texas Lions Museum and Office Foundation when they have completed and received their 501(c)3 designation from the IRS.

Sincerely
PDG John H. Seale
Chairperson

World Services for the Blind

FEBRUARY 2015 REPORT
TO MD-2 COUNCIL OF GOVERNORS

I would like to report that earlier reports and Little Rock news accounts regarding the pending demise of World Services for the Blind have been proven to be quite premature. I can assure you that WSB is alive and continuing to provide exemplary service to our clients and the community of blind and visually impaired in general.

At present we have 35 clients in training with 4 more in evaluation. Next month we begin a new IRS program with 9 clients expected to take part.

Good news, WSB's application for an LCIF grant has been approved. This grant in the amount of $320,000 will be used to start 3 new programs:

1. *MEDICAL TRANSCRIPTIONIST TRAINING*
2. *CALL CENTER AGENT TRAINING*
3. *NATIONAL REFERRAL NETWORK.*

This referral network is a Pilot program (at the suggestion of LCIF) and will be set up in North Carolina and Texas.

More good news: the downtown Little Rock property has been sold and removes a major drain on our financial resources.

The WSB board and staff are still investigating new and innovative methods to further our mission to "Empower blind or visually impaired adults in the United States and around the world to achieve sustainable independence".

Thank you for the opportunity to serve the Lions of Texas in this capacity.

PDG Jim Coleman
MD2 WSB Chair

Role Models, Leadership in Service and their Common Attributes

There doesn't seem to be an overwhelming geographical quotient to leadership; however, I tend to agree with de Tocqueville that the United States probably produces more grassroots leaders simply because Americans have that unusual knack for stepping in to get things done wherever they see something that needs doing (and nobody else doing it at the moment).

My passport—and recollections—indicate I've met national and governmental leaders in Casablanca, Bangkok, Karachi, Pakistan, Seoul, Helsinki, Kuala Lumpur, Stockholm, Taipei, Vienna, Tokyo, Madrid, Canberra, Australia, Lisbon, Cairo, Wellington, Harare, Zambia, Singapore, Johannesburg, Sri Lanka, Asuncion, New Delhi, Santiago, London, Buenos Aires, Istanbul, West Berlin, Paris, Jerusalem, Mexico City, New York and Washington, D.C., and a lot of other places that don't come to mind at the moment.

The two biggest surprises were usually how different leaders looked, and how much they seemed to think alike.

I don't talk a lot about differences in religion, because I think that is a very personal matter, but I think at least something you might like to call "spirituality" accounts for a lot of leadership. It answered a lifelong suspicion for me when I came across a list of the great spiritual thinkers and their commitment to what we've come to know as "The Golden Rule."

The Christian version, cited in *Matthew 7:12* of the New Testament and dating to about 30 AD, is the most familiar in this country: *"Therefore, all things whatsoever you desire that men should do to you, do you even to them. For this is the Law and the prophets."*

Confucius was quoted some 500 years earlier as saying, *"Surely it is the maxim of loving kindness, do not unto others that which you would not have them do unto you."*

The Judaic code from the Talmud some 1300 years B.C. reads: *"What is hateful to you, do not to your fellow man. That is the entire Law, all the rest is commentary."*

Hindus put it this way in prehistoric times: *"This is the sum of duty. Do not unto others that which would cause you pain if done unto you."*

The Zoroastrian saying, about 600 B.C., was: *"That nature alone is good which refrains from doing unto another whatsoever is not good for itself."*

The Islam rule from the Koran, about 600 B.C., noted: *"No one of you is a believer until he desires for his brother that which he desires for himself."*

The Buddhist belief, dating to about 525 B.C. is: *"Hurt not others in ways that you find hurtful."*

Socrates (470-399 B.C.) was quoted as saying, *"Do not do unto others that which would anger you if others did it to you."*

The teaching of Tao, about 500 B.C., was: *"Regard your neighbor's gain as your gain and your neighbor's loss as your loss."*

And the Sikhs noted, about 1500 A.D.: *"We obtain salvation by loving our fellow man and God."*

Of course, it would be difficult to pick a modern person who better exemplifies the term world leader than Pope John Paul II, whom I met in Rome in 1983. Hardly anybody in the world is busier than the Pope, and Jay and I found ourselves ushered into a confined area at St. Peter's Basilica just before he was due to address a crowd of some 12,000 celebrants in the huge square outside one of the most beautiful and awe-inspiring buildings in the world. Regardless of church membership, one has to be impressed with the Pope, and Jay and I felt like barefoot children before a king as we approached the prelate. It was on Lions club business and the meeting was in the works, so we tried to relax. I had a silver tray to be presented from the Lions, and a little sculpture of a cowboy—which seemed a bit, well, Texan. Jay was carrying a set of rosary beads a friend from Ballinger had asked to be blessed.

His Holiness immediately put us at ease. It seemed as if we were the only two people in the world he wanted to visit with at the moment, and he listened to our report on the Lions anti-drug and diabetes awareness programs that had been chosen as world projects for my administration. We knew he was dedicated to youth and would be interested in the diabetes and anti-drug program. He accepted the silver tray with gratitude and obviously loved the cowboy statue—and carefully and seriously blessed the beads for Jay's friend.

Real leadership is more interested in others than in itself. Pope John Paul II proved this by being one of the most compassionate and caring people I've ever met. His whole personality was radiant with love for others. He then went out on the balcony and showed that love to 12,500 people… in eight different languages. When I recently looked at a photograph of Jay and me with the Pope, I realized that I was wearing a set of presidential cufflinks given to me earlier by Ronald Reagan during a visit to the White House—the U.S. equivalent of the Pope's home.

I'm sorry I didn't get to meet her personally, but I saw that same love and devotion at work in the late Mother Theresa when she was honored with the Lions Clubs International Humanitarian Award for her lifelong mission to the poorest of the poor. And I have often used her saintly statement: *"We cannot all do great things, but we can all do small things with great love."*

And there were other similarities.

President Reagan was surely one of the greatest communicators since Franklin D. Roosevelt. He did with television what FDR had done with the fledgling radio half a century earlier. Roosevelt made it his own, and made millions of Americans feel he was chatting with them in their living rooms. Reagan used television in similar and even more impactful ways.

Jay and I met the Reagans in connection with the Lions anti-drug program in 1983. We had been invited to have lunch in the White House with Dr. Carlton Turner, then administrator of the White House drug abuse program for which Nancy Reagan's "Just Say No" slogan had been the hallmark. There's a different aura about the White House than the Pope's quarters, because we Americans own it and feel a part of proprietorship. Jay and I were made to feel a bit more at home when we ran into a friend from Winters, Texas (a dozen miles up the road from Ballinger). This friend, Love Smith, was the executive director of the Horacio Alger Foundation and a classmate of ours at Baylor. We also ran into two fellow Texans—the late Senator John Tower and billionaire Ross Perot—who were there to share honors for Ross' son with the Freedom Flight Award.

Suddenly, as Jay and I were escorted into the Oval Office—and I was juggling a plaque for Mrs. Reagan and a western sculpture for the President

—I was the barefoot boy in front of the Pope again. I think I handed the gifts off to a Secret Service man, or to Jay, as the President approached with his hand outstretched. Then he said, "Come on, Nancy, they're here," and it was as if we were visiting with friends across the fence at Ballinger. Despite the fact that I must have been the 1,000th person he'd seen that week, the most powerful man in the world was expecting us and seemed excited to see us. Reagan had an incredible ability to be involved with everyone on an individual basis. It was a natural instinct with Reagan, not something he had learned before the Hollywood cameras. He was real, and he was genuinely interested in everyone he met.

Jimmy Carter was just finishing his four-year term as President when I met him during a Lions International Convention in Atlanta in 1982. There was no time to get nervous, because he and Rosalynn entered the coffee room backstage where we were all waiting to be on the program. But talk about the guy next door! Jimmy Carter seemed to have invented the idea of neighborliness. As I was trying to talk about peanuts and world affairs, he kept bubbling up with questions about me and Jay and Ballinger and Lions projects...you could tell he really cared. At one point, I got up to give a seat to Mrs. Carter, but Jimmy pulled my coattail and said, "No, sit down, She can take care of herself. I want to talk to you about Lionism." He had been a Lions District Governor and had attended the International Convention at Dallas in 1968, so he was thoroughly familiar with Lions clubs and Lions club projects. It was no surprise to us when the ex-President and Rosalynn moved right out of the White House and into the Habitat for Humanity program. He not only gave the housing program great publicity—attracting huge membership increases—but he showed up with a hammer and saw at actual conferences around the world. They may have been the best goodwill ambassadors that ever came out of the White House,not to mention some of the best examples of Christianity at work. At this point, Lions Clubs International has joined hands with President Carter in the Habitat for Humanity program.

Of course, I had met fellow Texan President Lyndon B. Johnson, and he was an impressive guy, but in a different way. Lyndon was always on-stage, the consummate politician; but his concern for the poor and the un-educated (and those without electricity, in his early days) was as real as his hearty grin, his Texas charisma, and his abdominal scar. And he no doubt suffered in comparison with the suave, boyish, and Camelot aura of the top half of his presidential ticket in 1960, but Lyndon not only held this country together through some questionable times after the assassination of John F. Kennedy, but went on to change our world with his "Great Society" and "War on Poverty." Of course, his charming and industrious widow, Lady Bird Johnson, is both a Texas treasure and an unprecedented boon to Texas wild flowers and the visual environment. Her National Wildflower Center at Johnson City will be a permanent example for good citizenship.

President George Bush from Texas and President #41, who is the father of George W. Bush (President #43), made an impact on our governmental society for years prior to his becoming President. He served as Vice President and served in China and in many different capacities of governmental service. Many of my friends in Midland knew President Bush, and always touted his expertise and demeanor. We had the opportunity to see him in action in 1981 at a Lions convention in Phoenix, Arizona, as he was in charge of a "Drug Force and/or Program" for the United States and Mexico. He spoke on that subject at the convention, and was probably the impetus needed for us to begin the drug program on an international basis.

We had the opportunity to meet with President Bush at a Lions convention in England. He was the principal speaker and gave a great address. He and Barbara Bush continue to have an impact on the American way of life—having two sons as Governor at the same time, and lastly, to have one who serves as a former President of the United States. They were always involved and always made a difference.

Maybe not quite the same rarefied category with presidents and prelates, but another world-famous VIP, Art Linkletter impressed me with his warmth and outgoing personality when I met him at the airport in Honolulu, Hawaii. And, not unusually, it could have been an embarrassing situation for me. The wonderfully efficient and prescient Lions coordinators out of Chicago had arranged for me to meet Linkletter at the airport. I was returning from my world tour as International Lions President, and having made it through more than 50 countries without major blunders, I was not dissatisfied with myself—particularly since I had enough exposure in media and in Lions events that people recognized me in the waiting area.

I had to acknowledge greetings and give informal reports to a variety of travelers who were arriving for the convention. The main group on this particular flight was a group from South America, and they were very enthusiastic about meeting their President, especially since we had just visited there. It appeared that there was a complete circle around me, and I was trying to shake hands and be the gentleman, while at the same time watching out of one eye for Art Linkletter. I missed the Linkletters in the crowd. By the time I realized it and rushed to the place to check the stewardess, who confirmed that I had missed the television star, I was beginning to feel some of the old panic and embarrassment as I hurried to the baggage claim area...and found the Linkletters retrieving their own luggage like any other travelers. I rushed over and introduced myself and began an elaborate apology when Linkletter turned on that famous thousand-watt smile and said there was no reason to apologize. He knew I had been busy, too, and he had gone on about his business of de-planing. Again, it was leadership in action—thinking of others and working on solutions, not stewing over problems.

It was ironic that a year or so later we were in Kyoto, Japan, for a board meeting and staying in one of the elite suites, which had bulletproof glass. They told us that the suite would be occupied by President Sadat a month or two later. President Sadat was assassinated before he made that trip. I have described meetings with President Sadat at Cairo and Prime Minister Begin in Israel, and although they were among the first big-name world leaders with whom I had brief personal experiences, they remain two shining examples of the epitome of leadership—in both their cases, to the extent of giving their lives for their goals of peace in a troubled region of the world. Sadat's courage has been well-documented in his ultimate sacrifice for peace, but I was impressed with his ability to put me and my associates at ease, despite his own problems at the time.

I'll never forget that Begin took time out to see me on my Lions club mission, despite the fact that he'd just come from a meeting of his cabinet after Iraq had attacked Iran overnight. I later read the biography he gave me with great interest, but I was not surprised to read of his devotion to the democratic way of life, and his struggles to defend his homeland in command of the Irgun. I had seen it in his composure, his steely gaze, and his firm handshake. He was a leader among leaders.

Much more recently, I had occasion to remember Jacques Chirac, who I met years ago when he was the mayor of Paris, one of the world's largest cities. As of this writing, he is the president of France and a leader in European and global affairs.

Those were, admittedly, some of the more spectacular leaders I have had the honor and pleasure to meet personally, but I could go on and on recalling leaders great and small from countries great and small with whose attitudes and abilities I was impressed. For now, it should be useful to try to itemize some of the characteristics I saw in such leaders that may be adapted to leaders of today and tomorrow:

1. They were not afraid - or too busy - to be individually involved.
2. They accepted responsibility.
3. They made a difference.
4. They were ethically tough.
5. They were team-builders, not ego-builders.
6. They were good organizers of time.
7. They practiced the Golden Rule by whatever name they knew it.

Lions Clubs International Foundation

One of the great Lions of our state who does not know the word "Impossible" is one who has been in a leadership position in the U.S. Military for many years before he retired. He became a Lion and his involvement continued. Those of you who are not familiar with the words "Sergeant Major" must be aware of the fact that it holds some significance both in and out of the military. For this PFC who rose to the rank of E2, one becomes quite impressed by a Sergeant Major who has leadership over hundreds of troops in the Armed Services. That leadership was carried forth by Past District Governor and Council Chairman, Dick Robinson when he was Lions Clubs International Foundation Chairman during the time that we were involved in the Sight First Campaign. Dick always stated that if you believe in something and take it to the clubs and the District, the program will sell. That concept and that "challenge" was a part of the finest hours of the Lions Clubs International Foundation and Texas and the SightFirst Program. Dick Robinson believed in it to the extent that he traveled over 56,000 miles during the fruition of this program. He continued his leadership for a four-year period, during which time his belief in the program and resulting service to mankind was passed on from the top tiers of Texas Lionism to grassroots Lions. Goals were set and made from the participation of all the clubs and Lions that were a part of this most successful program. Again, the Sergeant Major believed, and because of that belief, goals were set and achieved.

Women in Lionism

At the Lions Convention in 1917, there was a very controversial vote that decided that women would not be allowed to be members of Lions clubs. However, from the very beginning, women were involved in Lionism through Lioness Clubs, or by different names that were associates of the Lions club. Lionesses became a very strong force in the association, as might be expected, but the "macho"—all but which included a majority of the Lions members—still did not feel that they were part of the Lions club, and that the associates and various names of the organizations that assisted the Lions were appropriate. Through the years—especially through the 70s and 80s—a movement began to make women officially a part of the Lions club, starting in California with Past Pesident Harry Aslan. Finally, at the Convention of 1987, women were made a part of Lions club. There were several from Texas, including Past International Director Mike Butler (and at that time, most of the Past Officers and Past District Governors) were in favor of including women, because it seemed that we had reached our "peak" of Lionism in 1983. We were a little bit on the downhill, and we had depended on women so much in the past to help us that we finally determined that we were very foolish if we did not make them a part of the organization.

It is not difficult to determine that even with the Association's past, that all of the leaders of the Association always had a woman behind them to direct them and be of great benefit to the Association, all we can say is, "THANK GOODNESS!" If it had not been for women being a part of the Association, it would have been very difficult for us to maintain any status in Lionism. Without women in several positions (and now Past District Governors, with one from Texas, Beverly Stebbins, who is a Past International Director along with several others), I think everybody predicts that soon there will be a woman President of our Association.

Some of the first women in Lionism in Texas included Barbara Babcock of Dallas; Camp President and PDG, Pat Carrol; and First International Director from Texas, Beverly Stebbins of District E-2.

Interlude for Men

Why Men Are Never Depressed

Men are just happier people because:
1. The garage is all yours.
2. You never have to drive to another gas station restroom because this one is just too icky.
3. New shoes don't cut, blister, or mangle your feet.
4. Phone conversations are over in 30 seconds flat.
5. A five-day vacation requires only one suitcase.
6. Three pairs of shoes are more than enough.
7. The same hairstyle lasts for years, even decades.
8. You can wear shorts, no matter how your legs look.

BATHROOMS

A man has six items in his bathroom: toothbrush and toothpaste, shaving cream, razor, a bar of soap, and a towel.

The average number of items in the typical woman's bathroom is 337. A man would not be able to identify more than 20 of these items.

ARGUMENTS

A woman has the last word in any argument. Anything a man says after that is the beginning of a new argument.

MD-2 OPPORTUNITIES FOR YOUTH CONTESTS REPORT

COUNCIL OF GOVERNORS MEETING – MAY 22, 2015

All plans for the 2015 Texas Lions MD-2 Opportunities for Youth Contests have been finalized. We have representation from 12 districts with 30 youth participating in 34 contests. Districts are: 2-T2, 2-T3, 2-E1, 2-E2, 2-X1, 2-X3, 2-A2, 2-S1, 2-S2, 2-S3, 2-S4, and 2-S5.

There are 11 participants in the Drug Awareness Speech Contest, 11 in the Diabetes Awareness Essay Contest, and 12 in the Outstanding Youth Contest. Contest coordinators have been working diligently in preparation for each of the contests. Coordinators are as follows: Drug Speech Contest, Lion Mike Wilson from the Seguin Noon Lions Club; Diabetes Essay Contest, Lion Carolyn Stroud from the Graham Evening Lions Club; Outstanding Youth Contest, Lion Debbie King from the Beaumont Founders Lions Club. Judges have been procured for all of the contests. A special thanks to Lion Judy LeUnes of the College Station Noon Lions Club for her help in getting the judges.

A Hawaiian luau around the pool area has been planned for the Friday evening entertainment for all of the contestants. All participants have been assigned their rooms. Curfew time has been set for 11:00 p.m.

There will be a continental breakfast served in the gathering room for all participants, judges, coordinators and other contest helpers.

Plans for the Opportunities for Youth Awards Luncheon have been finalized. I suggest that the incoming Council of Governors continue the Opportunities for Youth contests along with the funding of the scholarships for the next Lions year. This is a wonderful way for young people to see Lionism working in real life. I encourage each incoming District Governor to "Get Connected to Opportunities for Youth" this coming year. Appoint a District Opportunities for Youth chair in your cabinet. I challenge each of you to have participants from your district at next year's state convention contest. *Respectfully submitted, Lion Newton Borlack, MD-2 Opportunities for Youth State Chair*

Past District Governors Association

The Past District Governors Association—composed of those who have been Past District Governors (PDG)—always gathers at each meeting of the Council of Governors and the Camp meeting twice each year. Sometimes, there is not much business to take care of, but PDGs individually have offered their experiences in each district when they're called upon by the District Governor, as they certainly do not want to try to override their authority. However, having served in that capacity, they are able to direct the Governor, Cabinet, and Officers of the District in the proper writings or illustrations of Lions Clubs International, or to the proper past officers of the association for assistance in speaking engagements and with carrying out different facets of the association.

There has been a Lion that, without pay or much recognition, has served in that capacity as Secretary of the association, and the record that we presently have of same would include these Lions that deserve thanks in each and every way for what they do for the association as far as booklets, taking care of dues, and whatever other duties they are called upon to fulfill as far as PDGs are concerned:

Roy Carter: 1961-70, 2-T2 (served as District Governor 1950-51)

Joe B. Redman: 1970-96 (Joe also was known for dancing the last dance at any meeting, and for always wearing red socks so we would know that he was still standing.) Joe was a member of the Beaumont Lions Club, and served as a District Governor of 2-S1 from 1956-57.

C. Lee Smith: of Clyde served from 1996 to present, who among other things other than the duties expounded above would include taking reservations for the banquet on Saturday night at the council meetings, whatever is necessary for the State Convention, and is usually in charge of the Necrology Ceremony for any of the PDGs that have passed during the previous year.

TEXAS
LIONS CAMP

TEXAS LIONS CAMP PAST PRESIDENTS
AND SPOUSES/PARTNERS-IN-SERVICE

1.	PRESIDENT/FOUNDER Jack and Elizabeth Wiech	1949-52
2.	President Frank Robertson	1952-56
3.	President Reagan Smith	1956-60
4.	President Jim Ed Waller	1960-65
5.	President Roland C. Jordan	1965-67
6.	President E. H. Munger	1967-69
7.	President Ebb and Jay Grindstaff	1969-71
8.	President J. P. McCracken	1971-73
9.	President J. L. McPherson	1973-75
10.	President Sam Pakan	1975-76
11.	President James Ward	1976-77
12.	President Herbert F. Barsh	1977-79
13.	President James and Reba Wheeler, Jr.	1979-81
14.	President Fred and Louise Hamilton	1981-83
15.	President R. E. "Bob" Price	1983-84
16.	President N. Davis	1984-85
17.	President Raymond White	1985-86
18.	President J. L. and LaVada Akridge	1986-87
19.	President Marshall and Wanda Cooper	1987-88
20.	President F. Ray McLaughlin	1988-89
21.	President Albert W. and Viola Brown	1989-90
22.	President Gavis D. Gilbert	1990-91
23.	President Charles W. and Bunny Philipp	1991-92
24.	President Fred Stokes	1992-93
25.	President S. R. "Moe" and Henny Cully	1993-94
26.	President John and Jean Kendrick	1994-95
27.	President Carlos E. and Rita Ayub	1995-96
28.	President Charles and Jeane Conner	1996-97
29.	President Kevin Dinnin	1997-98
30.	President George and Theda Conner	1998-99

31.	President David and Elvera Kahlich	1999-00
32.	President Norwood and Carol Brenneke	2000-01
33.	President Ed and Beverly Stebbins	2001-02
34.	President C. A. "Mac" and Mary McCown	2002-03
35.	President Paul and Dale Palmer	2003-04
36.	President Michael and Kim Morgan	2004-05
37.	President Hal and Sandy Griffin	2005-06
38.	President Baron and Karen Cagle	2006-07
39.	President Rick and Lupita Talbert	2007-08
40.	President Ken and Sherry Gleason	2008-09
41.	President Dennis and Jackie Heikamp	2009-10
42.	President Jack King	2010-11
43.	President Pat Carroll	2011-12
44.	President Sam Lindsey	2012-13
45.	President Leon Van Alstine	2013-14
46.	President Jim Wilks	2014-15
47.	President Bill Roe	2015-16
48.	President James Browning	2016-17

Overview of Texas Lions Camp

Our Texas Lions Camp is a noble project of the Lions of Texas. From its beginning in the minds of men of vision, with the courage to make that vision a reality, it has served our fellow man. We cannot measure this service in a material way, because the greatest benefit of the Camp is the hope and inspiration given to those who are our guests. —*Herb Petry, Jr., PIP*

The Texas Lions Camp….
a special place for special people, made possible by special hearts and feelings

gives vivid meaning to these simple words—dedication, desire, determination, beauty, challenge, pride, joy, happiness, giving, sharing, and love.

provides inspiration to all

a positive influence on the world of Lionism

—*Don A. Buckalew, PID*

Through the Years

May 17, 1948 • The idea of a crippled children's camp was presented to Frank Robertson, District Governor of 2-A, by the Kerrville Lions Club committee. After several preliminary meetings, the idea was presented to State Secretary Marlowe C. Fischer on this date.

June 18, 1948 • District Governor Robertson and Texas Lions State Secretary Fischer conferred with the full committee in Kerrville and suggested a plan of procedure.

September 11, 1948 • Three other District Governors heard the story in Kerrville of a crippled children's camp: Jack Wiech of 2-A, Reagan Smith of 2-S and Dave Hudson of 2-E.

March 12, 1949 • Texas Lions League for Crippled Children organized during Council of Governors meeting in Brownsville. Original charter-signers were W. R. Rutherford of Dumas, Schley Riley of Big Spring, Jack

Wiech of Brownsville, Pat Jackson of Nacogdoches, Reagan Smith of Conroe, Virgil Minear of Hallettsville, and J. I. Moore of Kerrville. Named charter officers of the League were Wiech, president Jackson, first vice president Rutherford, second vice president Minear, third vice president, Moore, recording secretary Smith, treasurer and Riley, financial secretary.

April 4, 1949 • Directors of Lions International, Secretary of State approved League Charter and declared the League a tax-exempt organization.

July, 1949 • During International Convention in New York, Directors of Lions International approved camp project and gave permission to use the name of 'Lions'.

September 1, 1949 • First League directors meeting held.

August 1, 1950 • Sales agreement was signed with Federal Security Administration for 504 acres near Kerrville.

September 12, 1950 • Radio broadcast in Austin launched financial drive. Speakers were Governor Allan Shivers, Past International President Herb Petry, Jr. and League President Jack Wiech.

October 14, 1950 • Downtown Dallas Lions Club was the first to see model of camp as President Wiech made his first club speech about the camp.

February 1, 1951 • Lions League completed raising $100,000 for construction to satisfy provision of contract for land.

August 5, 1951 • Lions League directors approved plan of one project per year per club to inject new life in camp idea and voted to build two bunkhouses.

September 28, 1951 • Formal groundbreaking ceremonies were held at camp site, with Secretary of State John Ben Shepperd and Past International President Herb Petry, Jr. as speakers. Contracts for first two bunkhouses were awarded.

September 6, 1952 • Date was set for opening camp. Two bunkhouses, dining room and kitchen, and the arts and crafts building were completed. Pool was near completion.

1952 • Funds for the infirmary were furnished by the Houston Central and Gulf Coast Lions Clubs. Frank Robertson of San Antonio was elected League president, succeeding Jack Wiech.

June 8, 1953 • First Session opened with 40 campers.

July 3, 1953 • Camp was dedicated to the perpetual use and enjoyment of the handicapped children of Texas.

August, 1953 • Camp ended first summer with 236 campers.

1954 • Texas Lions annual dues-paying plan was approved to give Camp financial stability. Two more bunkhouses were completed, along with administration building, Jack B. Wright Memorial Chapel and caretaker's cottage.

1955 • Recreation building was opened, along with the fifth bunkhouse. Wings were added to arts and crafts building.

1956 • The sixth bunkhouse was completed. Camp reached a high of 755 youngsters during the summer.

1957 • Original infirmary was converted to staff housing and program office. A new infirmary and a second staff house were constructed.

1958 • The adult blind program ended its first year with 51 trainees.

1959 • Recreation building enlarged and garage was added.

1960 • Summer sessions provided fun for 720 campers; blind trainees numbered 61.

1961 • The Camp played host to 721 youngsters during the summer; adult blind trainees stepped up to 63.

1963 • The Bill and Gladys Smith Memorial Building was dedicated.

1963 • After providing fun for 6,455 handicapped children in its first decade of service, the Camp started the second decade with 746 youngsters; adult blind trainees numbered 69.

1964 • The William G. Davis Memorial Shelter was dedicated.

1965 • The Pat and Ben Jackson Building was dedicated.

1966 • Summer sessions provided happiness for 750 campers.

1967 • Summer camp equaled a former record of 756.

1968 • The Camp provided a happy summer for 742 campers; 73 blind adults gained new skills in the training program.

1969 • Texas Lions Camp reached a new peak with 762 summer campers and a record number of 84 blind adults in the training program.

1970 • The Camp increased its facilities – additions to the dining hall and bunkhouses one, two and three.

1971 • Lions of Texas added a new dimension of service to handicapped children by opening a pilot program for 111 diabetic campers on leased facilities at Friendswood.

1972 • The Texas Lions Camp for Diabetic Children grew to 150 youngsters. In the past 20 years, 14,358 handicapped children attended the Camp.

1973 • A record number of 1,058 youngsters enjoyed the Camp.

1974 • The Kerrville center served 697 handicapped youngsters. Diabetic campers increased to 311.

1975 • The number of campers served this summer totaled 1,019. At Kerrville, for the first time, an entire session was devoted to diabetics. New facilities include three tennis courts, badminton courts, golf driving range, additional rooms to the infirmary, administration office, garages and a storage shelter at the lake. Frank Robertson retired as Executive Director and J. L. McPherson assumed the position.

1976 • The number of handicapped children at summer Camp increased to 724, while 310 diabetic children were served in two sessions.

1977 • The Camp's 25th year was celebrated by remodeling the dining hall, enlarging the kitchen, erecting a new water storage tank, and replacing all electrical wiring by placing lines underground. Throughout 25 summers, 17.739 handicapped children were served. Seven summers of operation for the diabetic camps helped 1,774 children. In the 20 years of operation, 1,247 blind adults received rehabilitation training.

1978 • J. L. McPherson retired as Executive Director and Glenn Crawford assumed the position. Additional pews and concrete walks were added to the chapel. The Victor Real Estate provided funds for an adult blind residence. Furnishings for the residence were provided by donations from Lions Clubs and friends of the Camp.

1979 • An increased number of camper applications were received—more than could be assigned. A new playground was constructed and the Program Office was renovated.

1980 • A $550,000 goal was set for the Phase I expansion of the Camp. The plans included two new bunkhouses, a second swimming pool, remodeling the kitchen, upgrading utilities and building a pool patio. In September, construction began to increase the Camps capacity to 250 campers per session. A gazebo picnic area was erected and a stonerail fence was built at the Camp's entrance.

1981 • Phase I expansion was completed. The Blind Program was discontinued for the fall.

1982 • The Blind Program began in January. Instruction was received by 42 clients from January to May. The Navy SEABEES from Beeville built the

Campcraft log cabin and prepared a 6/10 mile road and parking lot area for paving.

1983 • Construction of the Herb Petry sports Center began. Alice McCreless gave contribution in memory of Sealy McCreless to provide needed exercise equipment. Started renovating the recreation hall. Horse barn and corral were built.

1984 • The Adult Blind Program was discontinued. The Outdoor Education Center was implemented. The Center will provide year round service to handicapped children. Recreation hall renovation was completed. Corral and horseback riding arenas were expanded.

2014 • 67,000 campers have gone through the camp.

EARLY HISTORY OF TEXAS LIONS LEAGUE FOR CRIPPLED CHILDREN

In 1948, Lionism in Texas was truly on the march. Herb Petry of Carrizo Springs had been elected Vice President of Lions International. District 2-A charted 41 new Lions clubs during that fiscal year to become the largest district in the entire International Association. This growth was reflected in the ambitious programs of individual Lions clubs throughout the State.

The Lions Club of Kerrville—a new club in the heart of the summer camping area of Texas—conceived the notion that the Lions of District 2-A (where Kerrville was located) or the Lions clubs of the whole state should sponsor a summer camp for crippled children, who because of their handicaps, could not participate in the activities of the camps for non-handicapped children.

On September 11, 1948, at the invitation of the Kerrville Lions Club, District Governors from eight Lions Districts of Texas, met in Kerrville to hear the Kerrville story. Jack Wiech, District Governor of District 2-A, expressed the view that his District would undertake the project if it could not be established as a Lions statewide project, but he counseled that every effort should be exerted first to obtain the approval and participation of all Texas Lions Districts. District Governor David Hudson of Weatherford declared that his District would never support such a project located in another District. District Governor Reagan Smith of Conroe was enthusiastic in his approval of the proposed statewide project, and predicted that his district would support it 100%. No decision was reached at that meeting, but the idea was firmly planted. Some had seen a vision and liked what they saw.

There followed many other meetings over the state, all aimed at determining whether or not Lions of Texas could be united behind this great humanitarian undertaking. Studies were made of some 28 programs dealing with crippled children located in various sections of the United States and Canada. From these studies, many ideas were suggested regarding the size of such a project, capital requirements, cost of operation, rehabilitation value of such a project, approximate number of potential enrollees, recommended architecture and layout of such a camp, and other similar suggestions of great value in the final planning stages.

It is an ill wind that blows nobody good, and the widespread incidence of polio in Texas at that time no doubt contributed much to point out the need for such a project in our state. Slowly—and it seemed ever so slowly to those who had caught the vision—the idea began to take hold in the minds of the Lions of Texas.

Finally, on March 12, 1949, at the Council of Governors meeting in Brownsville, the Charter of TEXAS LIONS LEAGUE FOR CRIPPLED CHILDREN, INC. was submitted to the eight Lions District Governors of Texas for their approval and signature. As set out in the Charter, the purpose of the corporation would be to "Support, maintain and conduct, without charge, a crippled children's camp wherein crippled children from all parts of the State may receive supervised rehabilitation training." All but two of the District Governors approved and signed this Charter. Those signing their approval were: W. R. Rutherford of Dumas, Schley Riley of Big Spring, Jack Wiech of Brownsville, Pat Jackson of Nacogdoches, Reagan Smith of Conroe, and Virgil Minear of Hallettsville. and J. I. Moore signed as a representative of the Kerrville Lions Club. The Charter was filed in the office of the Secretary of State and approved by him as a tax-exempt corporation Charter on April 4, 1949.

By-Laws of the League were prepared and adopted, and officers were elected to guide this first Texas Lions statewide project through its first

four very difficult years. They were Jack Wiech, President Pat Jackson, First
Vice-President, W. R. Rutherford, Second Vice-President, Virgil Minear, Third
Vice-President, J. I. Moore, Recording Secretary; Reagan Smith, Treasurer
and Schley Riley, Financial Secretary.

The League's first goal was to obtain a suitable site in Kerr County
for its crippled children's camp. Several tracts of land were examined, but
without any funds, the Board of Directors was unwilling, fortunately, to
commit the League to purchase any property on credit. When it appeared
likely that the League would die in its infancy, the Kerrville Lions Club offered to provide a site, and then put a committee to work to find one. In the
course of its search, the committee learned that 504 acres of the original
grant to the United States government for the establishment of the Legion
Veterans Hospital had been declared surplus federal property. After months
of negotiation and several trips to Washington by Bill Mickelsen of the
Kerrville Club, an Agreement of Sale for the land was consummated with
the Federal Security Administrator on August 1, 1950 at the appraised
value of $15,000—but conditioned that the League have a sum of not less
than $100,000 on-hand within six months earmarked for the construction
of facilities on the site.

Raising $100,000 for a project not even off the planning board proved
to be the greatest hurdle ever to confront the League, and as the six month
campaign came to a close, only $79,000 had been raised. District Governor
Sealy McCreless came to the rescue and "loaned" the League the $21,000
required to make up the deficit, and a deed was delivered to convey the
beautiful 504-acre tract to the League.

What a splendid site for the camp! With a substantial sum of money
in the bank, the League organized a finance campaign in earnest, setting
its initial building and improvements goal at $250,000. Lion Bill Mickelsen
was retained as the camp architect. He constructed a model of the camp,
and it was taken to Lions Clubs throughout the State, where the story of
the Lions' statewide project was told again and again. The campaign was
operated upon the conviction that no Lion who heard and understood
would refuse to help the crippled children of Texas. The only difficulty
was reaching all the Lions of this big state. While six campaigners were
attempting this tremendous undertaking, opposition to the project festered

in several sections, fed by half-truths and misunderstandings.

On October 14, 1950, Jack Wiech, President of the League, displayed the camp model and told the story of Texas' first Lions club, the Downtown Dallas Lions Club. Following the meeting, a member of the club, George R. Jordan, President of International Association, told Wiech that he had been fighting the project, because he had been told that this Lions project was to duplicate the work of the Shriner's Hospital for Crippled Children, of which he was Treasurer. Lion Jordan became a Life Member of the League that day.

September 28, 1951 was an epochal day in the history of the Camp. On that date, a formal groundbreaking ceremony was held with Secretary of State John Ben Shepperd and Past International President Herb Petry as the principal speakers. On the same date, the first phase of the building program got under way with the letting of a contract for the construction of two bunkhouses. While the initial building program was underway during 1951-52, the Board of Directors intensified its efforts to tell every Lion in the state about the Camp. Active and Life Memberships in the League increased in proportion to these efforts.

By the time of the annual meeting of the Board on September 6, 1952, the League had finished construction of the first two bunkhouses, the dining hall and kitchen and the swimming pool. They had acquired sufficient furniture through the vocational school of Texas Southwest College, and had installed its electric, water and sanitary sewer systems. The opening date of the Camp was set for June 1953, with Frank Robertson elected to be President of the League.

Years later, after several seasons of successful operation, Frank Robertson would have a long waiting list of qualified applicants for jobs as counselors at the Camp, but such was not the case in 1953 as he sought camp staff in preparation for the first summer's operation. In fact, within a week of the opening date, the program director and the purchasing agent resigned, creating a very critical situation. President Robertson took personal control, reorganized his staff, and the Camp opened on schedule on June 8, 1953, with 40 crippled children from over the State of Texas in attendance. On Friday, July 3, 1953, at the close of the second camp session of that first year, Texas Lions Camp for Crippled Children was formally dedicated to the perpetual use and enjoyment of the handicapped children of Texas. Its success was assured.

HOW THE TEXAS LIONS LEAGUE IS FINANCED

In the early years, the Texas Lions League was financed with some of the following methods, and were supported by all of the past officers of the Association:

Millions of Texas Lion dollars, hundreds of thousands of gallons of Lion gas has been burned through the years, and billions of sympathetic Lions' heartbeats attest to the merit of this great activity that challenges all Lionism everywhere to match it.
—*Julien C. Hyer, Past President, Lions International*

Working with Texas Lions Camp is one of the greatest contributions a group can make toward helping humanity. It allows the physically handicapped to realize they are not alone in this world, that there is a place in society for them. For some it gives a sense of self-accomplishment, perhaps for the first time in their lives. We know that by working with Texas Lions Camp, we are helping others. It allows us to pay a little rent on the space our Good Lord has allowed us to occupy on this earth.
—*Ed Flood, Past Director, Lions International*

As I have traveled throughout the World for Lionism, what was most rewarding to me was to tell the Lions of the world that I was a Texas Lion, and as such, a part of the Texas Lions Crippled Children's Camp at Kerrville, Texas. This is the most widely-known and most asked-about Lion project anywhere in the world.
—*E. B. "Tex" Mayer, Past Director, Lions International*

There is no question that the Lions of Texas have grown and developed as a result of this project. There is not a person that has visited this Camp that has left not only a better Lion, but also a better person. The image of caring is best shown by the hours and years of dedicated Lions making this camping experience possible for these young people. As a result, one can see that

Lionism has the capacity to change Lions by providing health, sight and hope for those people in need.
—*Ebb Grindstaff, Past President, Lions International*

There are only two past officers of the Lions of Texas who have also served as President of the Camp, that being myself in 1969-71, when we took on the Juvenile Diabetic Program, but also from that stalwart (and one that is involved in everything, and has been involved in every major project in the Lions of Texas, we can never thank him enough for his service) Marshall Cooper. There are some of us that do not have the capacity to understand the Cajun stories, but it is something that no one else can steal, and it is something that he always said that the reason that he came up with the stories was because I was stealing all of his thunder, but I am sure that we both did that in all of our engagements.

Finally, the Camp has been under the able leadership of Stephen Mabry, CAE, CFRE, Chief Executive Director, for the past 25 years, same being the reason for the direction and growth of the camp in so many ways. We are also grateful for Trish Wilson and her enthusiasm as the director of our programs development, who traveled all the way in by jet from Harper, Texas.

Texas Lions Camp: Early Days

Past District Governor Eddie Munger was interviewed at the Camp in February of 2015 at the age of 99, and will soon be 100. Eddie spoke in a very clear tone and was able to get around with just a cane. He has made over 100 trips to the Camp since his first trip in 1953. In 1954, his entire club—the Heights Lions Club—came to the Camp. This was great for the club and the members. Even though they had to ride the bus all night and stayed up all night, they had a good time going and coming. Eddie was President in 1967-1969, at which time Ebb Grindstaff became President from 1969-1971. Prior to the time that Eddie was President, there had been no change in President of the Camp for seven or eight years. Tex Mayer told Eddie that if he would change the committees, he would campaign for him, and he did. Everyone was happy about it, even Jack Wiech said he understood, and he was Chairman of the By-Laws Committee.

In those days, everybody stayed in the hotel downtown—the Bluebonnet—and one key would fit any room. Most of the time, they came up on Friday evening and had dinner, which was usually fried chicken, and everyone enjoyed it, including Ray Elliott who is one of the longtime Lions for District S2.

Eddie was President in 1967, and Frank Robertson was Executive Director and Mildred Newman was his Secretary. Eddie depended on her a lot for many things. The Rehab Program for the Blind was reinstated in the year 1967, and lasted for a couple of years. Eddie and the other officers, including Ebb who was coming in as President, began to think about another project for the Camp, because a lot of the kids with polio in the 1950s were not around, and we felt that we needed to serve more people.

There was a Diabetic Camp at Friendswood, down close to Houston, and Dr. Luther Travis was in charge of that Camp then, as Dr. Ponder is in charge of the Diabetic part of the Camp that we have at the present time. Prior to that time, Roland Jordan, Reagan Smith, Jim McPherson and others were Lions that worked very hard on the programs. Also, Jack Wiech was the one who kept us in line as to the direction that we went. The Board meetings at that time were not held in the daytime, but sometimes began in the daytime, and did not close until 2:00 or 3:00 o'clock in the morning. At least some of the meetings went past midnight, but there were some very difficult times and we had to take care of business as it was. Terrell Lewis, a lawyer from San Antonio, took everything down for Eddie Munger in shorthand, as it was necessary to put together reports for the Board meetings.

Eddie estimated that he made at least 107 consecutive Board meetings for the Camp. At the time of the Rehab Program for the Blind, the Lions gave $50,000 for the Rehab Committee. The Commission for the Blind returned $150,000 to the Camp, and we began to think that too much government was involved. That's when we began the Diabetic Camp. Even though 85-90 trainees for the Rehab Program were involved, a camp up in Arkansas, although out-of-state, seemed to be able to take care of the future of that program. Thereafter, negotiations began between the Camp at Friendswood and our Camp for us to take over the Diabetic Camp, and there was quite a controversy about moving the Camp to Kerrville. Can you imagine a lawyer at Lions Camp and a Doctor at the Camp at Friendswood finally working out the details of this transfer? But it was made and the Diabetic Program was begun. It is absolutely amazing that the Diabetic Program became an International program in 1982-83 when Ebb Grindstaff was International President. It has now moved into so many different facets from just education and research into the many fine programs that have evolved from that particular program—due to the many dedicated and committed Lions. Ebb traveled around the state for the first year trying to convince Lions that this was a program that the Lions needed. At that time, diabetes was something that was not heard of, and even the children were not very pleased to be known as a 'diabetic'. Some of the diabetic kids, when they had a birthday party, would take the cake in the bathroom and flush it down the commode and come out, just as if they had been eating the cake and the sweets that affected their particular metabolism.

What a thrill it was for the Program to become international, and the dedication of Lions' involvement was highlighted during the year 1983-84 when Lions received the Dr. Charles Best Award from the American Diabetes Association—the highest award that could be given. We also received the award from the American Juvenile Diabetes Association at Toronto, also the highest award that could be given.

Texas Lions Camp

by James H. Wheeler Jr., Past President

We need not go into the history of *Texas Lions 1917-1967: a History of 50 years of Lionism* by Julien C. Hyer; *A Few Moments of History District 2E-1 1972-1973* compiled by M.J. Weaver, *Historian; A Few Moments of History,* Revised 1978, compiled by M. J. Weaver, Historian, and updated by Irvin D. Hiler; and finally, *History of Texas Lions Camp* compiled by Herb Petry Jr., but will attempt to list Texas Lions Camp accomplishments since those documents were published.

As the elected director of the Board of Directors in 1965-1971, serving for 6 years, Wheeler was named by President Eddie Munger in 1967 to chair the Camp Improvements Committee. PDG James H. Wheeler, Jr. as an architect has been of great value, and his willingness to serve has been of great value in the building, repair and upkeep of the camp facilities. He served as camp president from 1979-1981, and continues to serve today as Chair of the Camp Improvements Committee.

Under the guidance of four executive directors—Frank Robertson, Jimmie McPherson, Glen Crawford and currently Stephen Mabry—along with the members of the Camp Improvements Committee, the Camp has expanded its original concepts and programs to serve the disadvantaged children of Texas. This has been a team effort.

In 1993, an Ad Hoc Committee named and chaired by Wheeler interviewed architectural firms to assess Camp needs. As a result, Charles Tapley and Associates of Houston was selected and employed to provide a master plan for the future of Texas Lions Camp. Following many interviews with staff and individual committees, a master plan was presented in February 1994 containing projected costs between $5-6 million dollars. Later, Marmon Mok, Architects Engineers of San Antonio was employed to develop and provide construction documents for designs developed by staff, the Camp Improvements Committee following (in general) the Master Plan. This firm had provided services prior to Master Planning. Due to interest of Marmon Mok to aid in benevolent work, this firm has provided

services pro bono for many projects. Many of these projects have been
completed and include:

Bunk House Air Conditioning

Museum

Two new Bunk Houses

ADA Renovations to Bunk Houses

New Dining Hall

Record Storage Building

Infirmary Alterations and Additions

Executive Director Residence Additions

New Swimming Pool

Nature Trail Renovations

Picnic Pavilions

Rec Hall Additions

Fishing Lake Dam Renovations

Fishing Pier

Boat Storage and Docks

Covered Horse Arena

Amphitheater Sun Shades

Pool Change Rooms

Administrative Bldg. A/V System

Endowment Tree

Administrative Donor Wall

Administrative Bldg. Furniture Upgrade

New Maintenance Building

Memorial Bricks Projects

Lion Statue

Amphitheater Concession

Frontier Village, Path and Bridge

Hawkins House Renovations

Smith Bldg. Remodel

Dining Hall Blinds

Street Paving Upgrades

Administrative Office Renovations

As our programs change and 40-year-old buildings need replacement, our ongoing list will require evaluation. All this will be team efforts by the camp committees, staff and the Lions of Texas as we continue to serve the physically handicapped, diabetic and Down Syndrome children of Texas.

James Wheeler and Camp Improvement
by Ebb Grindstaff

Of course James would not say so himself, but he always gives the longest report at the Board meeting that we have every Sunday afternoon at the Camp in February and August, but he always takes it in great spirit, and I believe that is because of a reason. You can see from the above reports that the Camp has made great strides because of the Camp's Improvement Committee, but more importantly because of the direction of the Executive Directors and James Wheeler, who has been involved in each and every one of these projects. He has to come through Ballinger to go to Kerrville. He has been through Ballinger so many times, I have nearly gotten tired of him coming by, but I never have indicated that and would not do so, as James has been one of the outstanding Lions of our Association. During these last 50 years, if it had not been for him, we would have spent many dollars and would not have had the expertise we have had.

TEXAS LIONS CAMP
BUILDINGS AND AREAS DONATED
AND ADOPTED

Bunkhouse #1	Adopted by Dist. 2-S4
Bunkhouse #2	Adopted by Dist. 2-A3
Bunkhouse #3	Adopted by Dist. 2-X1
Bunkhouse #4	Adopted by Dist. 2-S3
Bunkhouse #5	Adopted by Dist. 2-S2
Bunkhouse #6	Adopted by Dist. 2-T1,T2,T3
Infirmary	Donated by Lions Clubs of Lubbock, 1957 Adopted by Dist. 2-E2
Chapel	Donated and maintained by San Antonio Founders
Amphitheater	Adopted by Huffman Lions & Lionesses
Front Gateway	Donated by Dist. 2-S1
Flower Beds Front Gate	Adopted by Kerrville Heart of the Hills Lions
Arts & Crafts	Donated by Lions Clubs of Dallas Adopted by Rowlett Lions Club
Golf Course	Donated and maintained by Texas City Lions
Petry Building Petry Sports Complex	Donated and maintained by Dist. 2-A2
Inspiration Point Shelter	Donated by Houston Tanglewood Lions
Inspiration Point	Adopted by Houston Couples Lions
Rifle Range	Donated/maintained by Houston Westbury Lions
Petting Zoo	Donated/maintained by Navasota Evening Lions

Picnic Area	Donated by Dallas Oak Cliff Lions
Tennis Court	Donated by Conroe Noon Lions
Gazebo between bunkhouse 7 & 8	Donated by San Antonio Founder Lions
Bar-b-que pit by Gazebo	Donated by Del Rio Lions
Flower Bed in front of Old Admin	Donated/maintained by Kerrville Sunrise Lions
New Flag Pole in front of Infirmary	Donated by Kerrville Heart of the Hills Lions
Gazebo by Infirmary	Donated by Dist. 2-T3
James Woolley Plaza by the Pool	Donated by Orange Lions Club
Small Pool	Donated by Lubbock Lions
Program Office	Donated by Lions Clubs of Greater Houston, Gulf Coast Area and KPRC TV-Radio
Playground by water tanks	Plaque is not readable
Smith Building	Donated by Dist. 2-T1
Playground by Bunkhouse #4	Donated by Greater Arlington Lions
Eagle Trail	Donated and maintained by the Fraternal Order of the Eagles
Suddenly Shelter	Donated by Braeburn-Sharpstown Lions Club and Friends, Houston.
Horse Arena	Erected by Santos Lions

Arena Lights	Donated by Kerrville Sunrise Lions
Speaker Stand	Some of the materials were donated and the rest was purchased by Ft. Worth Riveroaks during the work day when they built the stand and installed the sound system that was donated by Corpus Christi Evening Lions
Log Cabin	Labor provided by SeaBees
Gazebo beside Petry Building	Donated by Mrs. Sealie McCreless
New Swimming Pool	Lubbock Lions Club
Remodel Program Office	District 2-X3

TEXAS LIONS CAMP BUILDINGS
AND DATES OF CONSTRUCTION

1952   Arts & Crafts Building: wings added in 1955, renovated in 1993

        Program Office Building: complete renovation in 1979

        Dining Hall & Kitchen: first addition in 1969, second addition in 1977, kitchen addition in 1981, dining area addition in 2000

        Swimming pool and pool house: new swimming pool completed in 1998

        Bunkhouse No. 5: wing added in 1969

        Bunkhouse No. 4: wing added in 1969

        Bunkhouse No. 6: wing added in 1969

1953   Bunkhouse No. 3

        Administration Building: addition in 1975, became Program Office in 1989, renovated in 2000 (in Memory of Herb Barsh)

1954   Jack B. Wright Memorial Chapel: renovation in 2004

        House No. 1: addition 1978 (Den, Utility Room, Bathroom)

1955   Recreation Building: garages added in 1959, renovations 1984/2004
        Bunkhouse No. 2

1956   Bunkhouse No. 1

1957   House No. 2: addition 1978 (Den, enclose carport), addition 1980 (Bedroom, Bathroom, Storage)

        Infirmary: addition (classrooms) added in 1975, renovated 1987 (dedicated to Verne & Babe Carrington), renovated 1998 (dedicated to Albert & Viola Brown)

1959   Garages and maintenance building: addition in 1975

1962	Gladys and Bill Smith Memorial Building
1964	Wm. G. Davis Shelter
1965	Pat & Ben Jackson Building
1969	Shelter at Inspiration Point
1976	Shelter at Camp Suddenly
1978	Real Building
1980	Stone rail fence at front entrance
1981	Gazebo between Bunkhouses #7 & #8
	Bunkhouse #7 & #8
	Lubbock Swimming Pool (small pool)
	Pool Patio
	Upgrading Electrical Utilities
1982	Log Cabin
	Entry road and parking lots added
1983	Herb C. Petry Sports Center (playing fields)
	Horse Barn & corrals
1985	Therapeutic Exercise Trail
	House No. 3
	Eagle Trail: repaved and rededicated in 1998
	Entry Renovation
1986	Amphitheater
	Shooting sports range
	Bunkhouse renovation
	Green house (Green Thumb)
	Large Hay Barn
1987	Riding Arena
1988	Lighting, announcer stand and sound system at riding arena

1989   New Administration Building: renovation in 2000

1990   Petting Zoo
Purchased Spur 100 property

1991   See-Bee Highway and low water crossing
Herb Petry Sports Complex Building
Pole barn and horse sheds

1993   Ropes Course
Sealie McCreless Gazebo

1995   Security gate and entrance
Perimeter fence

1996   Bunkhouses renovation

1997   Equestrian Center Covered Arena

1999   New Golf Course

2000   Picnic Pavilions
Museum and Hall of Honor
Underground utilities
Storage Building at Administration Building
Pool shade and changing rooms

2001   All roads repaved

2002   Fishing lake (dam repaired and stocked with fish)
Fishing pier
Doc Smayda riding trail

2003   Windmill and water well at fishing lake

A Summary History of TLC's Executive Leadership

Stephen S. Mabry, CFRE, CAE
Chief Executive Officer

Disclaimer: There have been many, many instrumental people who have done extraordinary things for children served at Texas Lions Camp. I regret that not every person or contribution can be listed in such limited space, but this in no ways diminishes the impact or importance of their gift. A more expansive chronology is offered at the Camp's website.

If you find and error or omission, or wish to add content, please contact smabry@lionscamp.com.

Executives

The Board of Directors has a number of legal duties and obligations to Texas Lions Camp, Inc.,foremost of which is to ensure that the charitable organization has what it needs to operate. The capacity to identify, employ and support the Chief Executive is paramount not only to achieving this duty, but is vital to safeguarding and maximizing the resources garnered for the organization's charitable purposes.

Since her founding, Texas Lions Camp has had five executive directors and one chief executive officer. The following individuals have been entrusted with championing the mission of Texas Lions Camp:

1. Frank Robertson – Executive Director; 1949-1975
   a. Mildred Newman – Asst. Executive Director; 1953-1979
   b. Jack Roe wrote the first Operational Manual & Model; 1953

2. J.L. McPherson – Executive Director 1975-1978

3. Glenn Crawford – Executive Director; 1978 – 1993
   a. Mike Waldrop – Asst. Executive Director; 1989-1993

4. Dwight Evans – Executive Director 1993-1995

5. Stephen S. Mabry – Executive Director; 1995-2010

6. Stephen S. Mabry – Chief Executive Officer; 2010 – Present

Stephen S. Mabry

Stephen Mabry began his affiliation with Texas Lions Camp in 1989 as the Summer Horsemanship Director. As a student at Texas A&M in College Station, Stephen was hired for the summer by Oscar Lopez, Program Director of TLC during that time period. As an Advanced Western Horsemanship Instructor and Intermediate English Instructor, Stephen led the summer riding program for the Camp that summer.

Following the summer of 1989, Stephen was interviewed by Mike Waldrop and invited to join the full-time staff as Equestrian Director, which he accepted and began on August 1, 1990. While working to finish his degree through Summer-School and graduate in August, Stephen commuted from College Station to Kerrville during the summer of 1990 in order to oversee the riding program.

After marrying his best friend, Shawn Kachtik, in December of 1990, Stephen attended the Cheff Center for Therapeutic Riding in Augusta, Michigan in January of 1991. After graduating, Stephen returned to open and build TLC's first Equestrian Academy, growing the program to include more than 100 students. This aspect of the program made use of the off-season to earn revenue and keep the herd in use by students who learned western pleasure, jumping and therapeutic riding for people with special medical conditions.

In 1993, Stephen was promoted to Asst. Program Director by Dwight Evans, who was Interim Executive Director at the time. Stephen would later be promoted to Program Director in 1994 and in 1995, Stephen was hired by the Board of Directors as TLC's fifth executive director.

By 1995, the Board of Directors was putting the finishing touches on a Master Plan for Capital Improvements. Under the supervision and direction of Camp Improvements Chairman, James Wheeler, Charles Tapley and Associates of Houston, Texas were employed to draft a study to position TLC to meet present and future challenges.

One of Stephen's first assignments, was to further develop and complete the capital campaign known as "CAMPaign 2000." While the campaign had been rough-drafted and begun, nearly no systems existed by which to administer and support the on-going efforts of the campaign. Stephen set about creating the accounting systems and fundraising plans to complete this audacious capital expansion that was estimated at more than $6.5 million dollars. One thing that was done well, was the support from a motivated board and campaign cabinet lead by Past President, Moe Cully of Beaumont, Texas.

"I was amazed and inspired by the Lions of Texas, who turned giving to Texas Lions Camp's campaign into a friendly competition and tried to out-do each other," remembers Stephen Mabry. "Clearly, the beneficiaries of this competition were the children of Texas, some of whom have yet to be born who will need the services offered by Texas Lions Camp" said Stephen.

Armed with a vested Board and campaign success, Stephen set about developing and implementing an approach to include foundation grants of more than $3,000,000. Having garnered a challenge grant from the Mabee Foundation in Oklahoma, Stephen wrote more than 15 grants to garner the remaining funds needed to implement TLC's master plan. By 1997, Stephen was in the construction business in addition to the fundraising business as the Lions of Texas set about the task of fulfilling the Master Plan. By 2002, the Lions could say that most every facility at Texas Lions Camp was either new or recently renovated.

In 2010, Stephen was named as TLC's first Chief Executive Officer, where he continues to serve today.

QUEST FOR ENDOWMENT
TEXAS LIONS CAMP
by PCC John Eads, Endowment Campaign Chair

"Today's Promise…for Tomorrow's Children"

When you sit down to actually think and start writing about history, many stories, people and events come to your mind. (And then again, you may have forgotten some or cannot remember all the facts or names, or you need help in remembering, so bear with me on this, please). My story is from my heart, and one which is my personal dedication and commitment to the Texas Lions Camp and the children we serve—and specifically to the success of endowment. My story will cover the major milestones I remember that contributed toward increasing our endowment funds at our Camp.

Milestone #1   I had been involved occasionally in the Camp prior to the early 80s. My real involvement began when I started attending and serving as a member of the Planned Giving and Endowment Committee of the Camp. I remember quite a number of conversations we had over a few years about how we were going to ensure that the Camp would last beyond our lifetimes. How would it be funded? Who would be involved? We needed to enhance the planned giving and begin earnestly to increase our endowment funds. Being a CPA and dealing with estates, planned giving, and other tax and financial matters, this topic was right down my alley. Endowment! I dedicated myself to do my best to make it happen any way I could.

It was about 1993, and our discussions had taken a new approach in the Planned Giving and Endowment Committee. Instead of talking further about wills, insurance, and gifts to endowment or even the trust fund, we needed to have a fundraiser for endowment. It was that simple. We knew that if we could secure enough funding to endowment, that it would provide enough income to help secure the future of the Camp. I recall that principally, the only funds dedicated to endowment were around $400,000 that had accumulated since 1949 ,and the only real campaign for endowment had come from a wills program that had been established and implemented, and a few gifts from foundations that former Development Directors had secured. Obviously to us, it was not enough to perpetuate the Camp into the future. I remember one meeting when our discussion was centered on auctioning off a Cadillac. It wasn't going to make enough money, but it was a start. Every Lions club was going to be asked to sell tickets. We never completely finalized that discussion to take it further. Finally, I had received a flyer from the University of Texas Ex-Students Association regarding purchasing bricks to be placed around the Alumni Center on the Austin Campus. A bell went off in my head. Ding! This would be a perfect situation we could institute at the Camp to begin raising endowment funds for our Camp.

I presented the idea to the committee as I recall in about 1993. The Executive Committee in October knew of our discussions, and had included memorial bricks in the Master Plan completed in early January 1994. We had originally talked about brick pavers and tiles. We continued our discussions about the bricks over a couple of meetings. We discussed where they would be placed, what size they would be, how much information they could hold, and how we would go about getting approval to begin selling them. We also discussed the price. At first, the discussions boiled down into a price of $1,000 per brick. Before the vote could even be taken on that amount, Jim Nabors from District 2-X3 committed to buy the first brick for $1,000 (you can see the first brick purchased by Lion Jim Nabors hanging in the Administration Building). Discussions continued, and we finally came back to reality that it would be difficult to sell just one brick for that much money. We wanted Lions clubs and as many Lions across the state as we could get to participate. We finally determined that each brick should cost $250. In our February 1994 meeting, we recommended to the Executive Committee that bricks of one color at $250 be used to raise endowment funds and placed in areas visible to our Lions and visitors. I volunteered and was authorized in that meeting to begin setting up promotional materials and sales suggestions for us to review in the August 1994 meeting. I was also authorized to make contact to a number of vendors to see how much it would cost us to have a personalized brick made. I also agreed to draft the plan and documents to sell the bricks to individual Lions and Lions clubs, and provide the information to the committee for approval and ultimately, submission to our Executive Committee and Board for final approval and start of the brick campaign. It took almost seven years to get the brick fundraiser approved and started.

This has been, and still is, a successful endowment fundraiser for us. We had a goal to raise $1 million by selling 4,000 bricks. Currently, since its fundraising inception through August 2015, we have sold 3,050 bricks of the total capacity around our campus of 8,526, and raised $762,500 for our endowment funds. We begin the first installment of 1,127 bricks in the vestibule between the board room in the Administration Building and the History Museum. Bricks were then approved to be placed along the front sidewalk from the parking lot to the Administration Building. The next expansion of bricks was placed in the driveway outside the Administration Building that leads to the vestibule. The Lions statue for the "T Districts" was set up as another location. Currently, placement of the bricks is at the Amphitheater. There are also a few bricks in the area of the Frontier Village dedication. In 2013, the Planned Giving and Endowment Committee obtained approval to add an additional program to the brick sales. Clubs and/or Lions sponsoring our children to Camp were encouraged to purchase an original brick in the name of their camper, and then for a small amount of additional funds, purchase a replica of that camper brick to be presented to them back at the sponsoring Lions club with their family present. This endowment fundraiser has been, and continues to be, very successful. We still seek our $1 million dollar goal and we are getting closer.

Milestone #2 Our Camp continued along a few years concentrating on the brick program, wills and any other foundation or corporate support we could muster. We got a boost in August of 1994, when we began receiving Jack Wiech Fellowship money being designated for endowment by the donor. So now, we were getting $1,000 Jack Wiech Fellowship money for endowment from donors—a great boost in our endowment funds because so many Lions and others wanted to honor one of our founders of the Camp, and the Lion that was instrumental in creating its existence in 1949.

Milestone #3 Our Camp was presented a proposal from Lion Lenny Holzband of District 2-S2 who desired to donate a "tree plaque" in memory of Lion Ernest Pate to help raise endowment funds. It was approved in February 2002 and ultimately, the Endowment Tree was place on the wall in the Administration Building. Lions, Lions clubs and other donors could buy a silver leaf for $500, a gold leaf for $750, a rock for $5,000 and a boulder for $10,000 and have a small space to place their names of honor others. We had to purchase a second tree module later to accommodate the continued success of selling leaves. Eventually, to make way for our Wall of Honor in the Administration Building, the Endowment Tree was approved to be moved to the Recreation Hall, where our Camp Board meetings are held twice a year, and it still resides there today. We were also running out of space for purchases of rocks and boulders, so the move was necessary. This fundraiser has brought the Camp endowment funds in the amount of $768,500 since it was started, consisting of 316 Silver leaves, 194 Gold leaves, 21 rocks and 36 boulders. It continues to raise funds. Thanks, Lenny!

Milestone #4 In 2007, thanks to Lion PDG George Futch and the George & Marie Futch Trust, our Camp Endowment Fund received a $1,113,615 gift. PDG George was always a strong supporter of the Camp. What a boost to our Endowment Funds. Thanks, George!

Milestone #5 "Our Endowment Today...Is Our Children's Tomorrow" In 2001, the Executive Committee and Board of Directors took action to approve a motion to open an Endowment Campaign to raise $1,000,000 in endowment funds by January 1, 2005 in accordance with recommendations of the Strategic Planning Ad Hoc Committee. Our Planned Giving and Endowment Committee was asked to take action. At that time, I believe we had approximately $1 million in endowment funds. In 2002, we began work earnestly in the process with a work session. We formed a Campaign Cabinet composed of myself as Chairman of the Planned Giving and Endowment Committee, and Stephen Mabry, Executive Director for tracking, reporting, consulting and foundation contact. Deb Buehler, Development Director would cover publications and prospect identification. Thus, "Our Endowment Today...Is Our Children's Tomorrow" Campaign was born. It would cover a period from 3-5 years and had six phases to complete. Our first order of business was planning and solicitation to get 100% of the Camp Board of Directors committed to a contribution. We would not begin solicitation of foundations or corporate donors until we had at least accomplished 50% of our goal. I had created a document entitled "Campaign and Marketing Plan" containing the Campaign steps, solicitation , identifying donor prospects, closing the sale and presentation information that was utilized. Board Development to raise $52,500 was co-chaired by Hal Griffin and Norwood Brenneke, with assistance from John Kendrick, Charlie Phillip and Ed Stebbins and Marshall Cooper. We intended to raise an additional $672,000 in giving programs established from honorariums, Jack Wiech Fellows, Tree and even a Wall of Honor. An additional $275,500 was to come from major gifts that would be solicited. Training would be completed in 2002 and we would be underway. John Eads came up with the "Think Endowment" slogan and it was adopted. The Lion's Legacy League was formed and approved by the Executive Committee as an extension of the campaign to raise $1 million during the years 2004-2006. It was an added element to raising endowment funds by adding planned giving elements to our fundraising expanded to include gift annuities, charitable trusts, marketable securities, life insurance and other planned giving tools. This was the beginning for our current Endowment Campaign "Today's Promise… for Tomorrow's Children."

Milestone #6 "Today's Promise… for Tomorrow's Children" This Campaign is the hallmark of our efforts to secure permanent funding for the Camp's future through endowment. President Barron Cagle asked me to become Chairman of the Planned Giving and Endowment Committee again in late 2006. I had indicated to him that I was wholeheartedly committed to establishing long-term endowment benefits for our Camp, and would create a plan with the help of others. He assured me I would have the support of future Presidents Rick Talbert and Ken Gleason. In February 2007, the Planned Giving and Endowment Committee received a new charge from the Executive Committee to study ways and means of securing funds for the League by any means approved by law for charitable donations, and to create and implement any approved fund raising activities or programs for planned giving and endowment in the state. A new brochure on wills that Stephen Mabry and staff had developed had just been mailed out. The planning began. A planning meeting was organized to develop a 3-5 year business plan for meeting the new charge. The basics of the business plan was formation and Board approval in year one, education in year two, and implementation in years three through five. Donors would have the option to designate their donation to endowment or operations.

There were two thrusts: (1) endowment, which would include designated memorials, bricks, endowment tree, and designated Jack Wiech Fellows and the planned giving elements of the Lion's Legacy League as previously described. The business plan included a multiple approach to marketing. In February 2008, the Executive Committee accepted the basic concept as proposed by the Planned Giving and Endowment Committee. The eventual plan has six phases to take place over a five-year period. It basically was the plan I described in Milestone #5.

Before the August 2008 Board meeting, it was determined that we needed to complete a feasibility study to expand the endowment funds much further. At the meeting in August 2008, the Planned Giving and Endowment Committee received three requests for proposal (RFP) and a few others to study and review. Members were asked to submit their questions or issues on each RFP and rate them within two weeks of the meeting. An RFP interview team was developed and was composed of John Eads, Chairman Planned Giving and Endowment Committee, Jack King, 2VP Executive Committee, Steven Mabry, Executive Director, Jim Wilks and Jim Peak. They were asked to finalize the presented information, interview the applicants and recommend the final applicant to the Executive Committee for approval.

Dini Partners was engaged to complete a feasibility study and Fayruz Benyousef held a visioning meeting with members of the Planned Giving and Endowment Committee at their meeting in February 2009. The discussions included campaign planning considerations, review of the 2009 Giving Outlook Survey, vision and objectives, planning study process overview, planning study and interview of donor candidates and outcomes. The Committee was excited and very enthusiastic about moving the Campaign forward. Really felt good to know we were underway with the Campaign. Dini Partners hit the road running. By April 2009, they provided a Mid-Study Report. They completed the feasibility study in June 2009. More than 30 members of the Texas Lions Camp family participated through face-to-face conversations with our campaign consultants, along with 130 Camp board members and 290 camper families that provided feedback through an online survey.

The Planned Giving and Endowment Committee met at the August

2009 Board meeting to discuss details of the Dini Partners proposal for the 12-month Visioning, Infrastructure and Counsel Services at a cost of $120,000, plus outside professional wealth screening services of approximately $10-12,000. It was approved by the Executive Committee and the Board.

The first meeting of the Visioning Task Force was held in Dallas on November 6, 2009, for the purpose of laying out the foundation for the vision/planning work while beginning to shape the plan itself. Members were John Eads, Barron Cagle, Lorraine and Bob Fuller (parents of current campers), Dennis Heitkamp, Ray Hughston, Jack King, Sam Lindsey, Mike Morgan, Dr. Stephen Ponder, Bob Schmerbeck (Kerrville Community Leader), Glen Starr, Sue Steele (former camper counselor), Rick Talbert and Marilyn and Lance Vinson (parents of former camper and staff member), Stephen Mabry, Trish Wilson and Dini Partners. The goal was to begin the process after reviewing the feasibility study information to determine the potential for a comprehensive $25,500,000 campaign that would include endowment and capital components ($20,000,000 for endowment, $3,860,000 capital improvements, and contingency and fundraising expenses of $1,640,000). Another meeting was scheduled for December 4, 2009.

The Campaign Plan draft was ready by January 25, 2010. At the February 2010 Board meeting, the Planned Giving and Endowment Committee pass the following resolution: "Resolved that the members of the Planned Giving and Endowment Committee whole heartedly endorse the endowment campaign for the Texas Lions Camp and recommend the Board of Directors adopt the Plan designed by Dini Partners and recommend the Board of Directors open the Campaign with a Phase I goal of $10,000,000." The Committee also unanimously adopted the name for the Campaign "Today's Promise ...For Tomorrow's Children." The resolution and name passed. The Campaign was underway! (*Author's comment: after a long and difficult process for over 15 years with lots of hard work from myself, Board members, executive committees, Camp staff and many Lions, we finally had a great Campaign for our Camp going forward. Thanks be to God!*) As of August 2015, we have raised $4.2 million toward our Campaign Phase I goal of $10 million.

How does the Campaign operate, you may ask? The Campaign

structure was designed to be relatively simple and functional. Most of the Campaign decisions and direction would be made by the Campaign Steering Committee. Participating Lions in the initial CSC included Campaign Co-Chairs Barron Cagle and John Eads, plus members Margaret Badeaux, Pat Carroll, Hal Griffin, Ray Hughston, Ernest Opella, John Samples, Noah Speer and Nancy Van Alstine. They would manage the Campaign and hold frequent meetings by conference telephone with Stephen Mabry and Trish Wilson to coordinate all Campaign activities. Area Coordinators, District Coordinators and Group Coordinators were invited to participate. Area Coordinators were appointed and responsible for communication and manage the Campaign in a number of assigned Lions Districts geographically. District Coordinators were appointed in each of our 16 Districts to communicate and manage the Lions clubs and other sources of contact and presentations by our Group Coordinators in each of those Districts. Operatively, the Campaign opened Phase I with seeking donations from 100% of our Camp Board of Directors and that would continue throughout the Campaign as new Directors came on to the Board. This was the Board Emphasis part of the Campaign, co-chaired by Dennis Heitkamp and Jack King, and it would always be extremely important to our success in solicitation of donors, especially corporations and foundations. We also made sure that each member of the executive committees was pledged to the Campaign. Not long after we began soliciting the Board, we opened the Club Emphasis part of the Campaign, where we actively started soliciting our clubs. It was principally led by Rick Talbert. We also have opened the Camper Parents and Alumni portion of the Campaign, principally led by Stephen Mabry and Trish Wilson, and are actively soliciting pledges.

One of the main keys to our successes thus far has been our Campaign recognition process, which we are still improving upon, for all gifts made. We researched, presented and obtained approval to move the Endowment Tree to the Recreational Hall and build the "Wall of Honor", dedicated in 2011 in the Administration Building to recognize donations exceeding $10,000 cumulatively from the inception of the Campaign in February 2010 from any source.

Recognitions are on a stairstep approach to various giving levels in color. We also equipped the wall with a kiosk, where you could actually seek donor information.

I thank the Lions and the Camp leadership over the years for having given me the privilege to be involved in the endowment process of our Camp since the early 80s. I am honored to have served as Chairman of the Planned Giving and Endowment Committee of our Camp from 1988-2003, and again from 2006-2012. I have continued to serve on the committee from 1988 until today as liaison from the Executive Committee. I am also privileged and honored to have been involved in the current Endowment Campaign that is underway, serving as Chair of the Campaign "Today's Promise…for Tomorrow's Children." Many milestones have been met along the way and they have been successful thus far. However, without the dedication of our Lions and Lions clubs across this State of Texas, our non-Lion donors, Stephen Mabry, CEO and staff and many Lions involvement as Directors, members of the Executive Committee, members of the Planned Giving and Endowment Committee, our Area, District and Group Coordinators, or Lions and staff serving in any capacity on the Endowment Campaign Team, it would not have happened. As Andrew Carnegie said, "We all teamed up and obtained an uncommon result." As of August 2015, TLC's Endowment Fund is valued at $8,873,040, which includes all of the efforts through the milestones discussed." THINK ENDOWMENT!"

My hat is off to all who have served and are continuing to serve! Thank you for being a part of creating something great… a future for the children "We Serve." Remember, children can at TLC…*because you made it happen! Endowment is the future of our Camp.*

Interlude

As we approach the time that we are closing out the information for the book, it just seemed appropriate to talk about MARSHALL COOPER, one of the UNSUNG HEROES of the Texas Lions. Of course, his involvement was always with youth during the years that he was professionally involved, but since his retirement, it seems that he has been involved in every major activity of the Texas Lions, especially the Texas Lions Camp, Texas Lions Eyeglass Recycling Center, Texas Lions Foundation and all youth activities and organizations.

I am probably one of the few living individuals that had the opportunity to shake the hand of Melvin Jones. It just so happened that when I was in high school, my dad was District Governor of District 2-A that went from Ballinger to Brownsville, and also included San Antonio and the Valley, covering a very large area. On one occasion, Dad had the Council of Governors meeting in Houston, and Melvin Jones was there for that occasion. My dad took me there on purpose (or by accident), but either way, I had the opportunity to meet Melvin Jones. It was a thrill for me, and later on I went to the Melvin Jones Museum in Arizona (where they tried to "hang" me; at least I saw no one smiling, not even Jay) and thought about him being raised on the Calvary Reservation, and then going on to Chicago and becoming a successful businessman—setting forth the idea for our organization.

I have gone from having "senior moments" to easily forgetting moments and names, but you cannot forget the Wilson Club. Roy Lynn Kahlich was a District Governor, as they were in their heyday when they did not have anything but a school in Wilson, but I never saw so many farmers that were involved. They had forty or fifty members in their club, and the Pin Collection of the Wilson Lions Club during our campaign still hangs in my office. There are seven pins in the shadowbox, and each one is made out of the inside contents of a commode. This is mentioned because it is so unusual, as the toilet paper, the plunger, the replica of the outhouse, the other chains that were important to the operation of such hang on my wall.

In the middle of this is "Ebb," which they concocted during the campaign.

It seems that the Texas pins were very popular. There were some great pins that were on saddles, boots, hats and guns. There was one with a boat with "Ride the Ebb Tide" as the theme of the boat; in fact, we gathered all our pins up that we had received throughout the world of Lionism (including a lot of the Texas pins). I'm not sure if I have all of them myself because I've given them to people, or they have been sold. I took all these pins to a pin trader, and told him to go ahead and sell them and get what he could for them. I figured we could make a few hundred dollars. He sold all the pins and we collected $2,500 that we donated to the Camp in a tribute to the many people that were involved.

The State Secretary and Forums

The business of the "Multiple District" was basically handled by three Lions who were known as State Secretaries: Laura Farmer of the Waco Founders Club, who was like a State Secretary, Marlowe Fisher of Austin was one of the first State Secretaries known to me, and from 2-X3 was Tom Kirkham, one of the greatest State Secretaries known to Lions of that era, such as the writer, when I was District Governor. Tom's biography and enthusiasm can be found in the District 2-X3 section in this book.

During the late 70s and early 80s, Ed Skypala from Hereford also did a great job in traveling the State, organizing clubs and working on membership. Ed, along with other Lion leaders, was also responsible for the original Zone Chairman Forum that existed for several years beginning in the early 80s. The Forum became a driving force in Texas for motivation and leadership under the heading of the Texas Lions Forum that started in the 90s, and still exists to the present date. These Forums were patterned after the International Forums that have been in existence for America and Canada, known as USA-Canada Forums.

It was only because of the Leadership of Past District Governor Aubrey Cherry and Past District Governor Frances Cherry that these Forums were a success in Texas. All of these were held in Austin, Texas. Both of these PDGs were very specific in the arrangements of the subjects for the Forums, and obtaining of leaders and speakers from the State of Texas, and also from various Districts of Lions Clubs International. All of these Forums have been held in Austin because it seems to be the most central location. The number has grown each year. This format allows people who were not able to attend USA-Canada Forums to attend a Forum that we would call a "grassroots" Forum for the State of Texas. The success of this Forum and all Forums depends upon the Lions who attend, and the information that they take back to their individual clubs. In addition to having top-notch programs, since the beginning of these Forums it has been of great interest to watch the number of newcomers and those that might come back for a second or third year.

There are always some Past Governors and other leaders of the State that attend these Forums, but the new ones are the ones that are motivated and tend to take back the information to their individual clubs. During a period of time after Ed Skypala was State Secretary, Pat Nations became State Secretary, but more or less in a new role as the Office Secretary, and also the one that would arrange for the meetings of the Council of Governors. These meetings were held mostly in Kerrville, but also in different locations of each District throughout most of Multiple District 2.

After Pat retired, we were very fortunate indeed to have an outstanding State Secretary from Kerrville who has given beyond her calling as Secretary; to be also one that was very efficient in the business of the Governors and then the Vice-Governors, etc. In my opinion, even though their duties have varied depending on the individuals, Sandy Merritt—our present State Secretary—has been one of (or) the best State Secretary we've ever had. Sandy always has a smile on her face and is very anxious to assist any request that a person makes. She has been very cooperative to all the Chairmen-Elects, District Governors and past officers of the Association or any Lion that makes a request. It takes a genius to try to please 50 Governors and Elects and Chairmen and Chairmen-Elects.

Of course, Sandy was very well qualified when she came to our group. She was familiar with service clubs, and was a member of a club that had 150 members. Sandy was raised in San Antonio, and served her tenure with Exxon Oil Company in Houston prior to her move to Kerrville, where she handled a secretarial/employment agency for years. She is involved in a contract for the secretarial work with the Lions of Texas; however, most of the Lions consider her as the State Secretary and as an employee of the Lions of Texas. It seems to make no difference to either party, because the work is always done and Lions are always pleased.

Sandy always takes a personal interest in the people in attendance at each of the meetings, but also in the notification of those Lions that might be ill or have passed away. Indeed, Sandy Merritt has not only been an excellent Administrative Secretary and leader, but one who has fulfilled the needs of the Lions of Texas. She will soon be in charge of the Lions office as it is moved to a different location in Kerrville, and I might note that this is happening while Sandy is also now the President of her Lions club. Thank you, Sandy for all your extra service to a service club.

Texas Lions Forum
and Regional Institute

The Texas Lions Leadership Forum and Regional Lions Leadership Institute is a statewide training event that originated from needed support for a Multiple District dues increase. Part of the increase would be used for leadership training. In 1999, Past International Director Joe Al Picone—at that time a Past Council Chairman—headed a committee that recommended a dues increase from $2 to $7 for Texas Lions. The Committee also recommended that the increase should be annually allocated as $1 for administration, $2 for membership development, and $2 for leadership development. The increase was approved in May 2000. Although the amount budgeted for leadership development has never reached the amount recommended, funding has been adequate to support the Forum and Institute. The event has ascended to become a recognized and certified program.

The originating event was conducted in March 2001. The Pickle Center in Austin was the site. The facility included space for an auditorium of limited seating, one breakout session room and a meal accommodation room. Announced as a Leadership Forum, the program consisted of two general session speakers, two breakout sessions, and three performances by the well-known motivator and entertainer, LaDonna Gatlin. She was accompanied by her brother and a longtime friend as back-up singers. Although this was not particularly a study of Lionism or totally a lesson in motivation, it was some of both, and it was a start for statewide leadership development involving grassroots Lions. Instrumental in preparing and administering the Forum were Council Chairman Michael Rourke and Immediate Past District Governor Aubrey Cherry. Strong support was provided by several Lion Leaders, including Past International President Everett "Ebb" Grindstaff, Past International Directors M. P. "Mike" Butler, Marshall Cooper, and (PID at that time) Jimmy Ross. It was decided that a larger facility with onsite lodging, availability of meals, and more breakout session rooms would be needed for successful future events. As it has worked out, five different Austin locations have been used over the years. They have been The Pickle Center (1 Year), Red Lion Hotel (2 Years), Omni Southpark Hotel (2 Years), Austin Airport Hilton Hotel (9 Years), and the Crowne Plaza Hotel (Formerly the Red Lion, 1 Year).

The process of gaining Regional Lions Leadership Institute approval from Lions Clubs International was initiated with planning for the second event year. This meant submitting the mechanical description of the 2002 training, such as dates, times and site. It also meant providing the curriculum, faculty experience, schedule of events, and appointment of the Coordinator. Regional Institute participants are to be Lions who have not served as Vice District Governor or above. MD-2 leaders wanted to also concurrently include a Forum to accommodate Lions of VDG and higher status. Special effort was made to provide the LCI curriculum for Institute Lions, while offering additional breakout sessions related particularly to MD-2 for those attendees who would not be Institute-eligible. GOOD NEWS! The Institute was approved with a grant of $15,000. The complex approval process is necessary each year, even since LCI reduced grants for any Regional Lions Leadership Institute to $10,000, then to $7,500 for those Multiple Districts who had grants approved two or more times, and more recently changing the rule to provide reimbursement only for first- time participants. Although each of the 16 Texas institutes survived the planning, grant approval process and actually conducting the event, reimbursement from LCI is finalized only after a lengthy and complex report is filed. In other words, if it wasn't done to the LCI Leadership Division's satisfaction, reimbursement is not paid. LCI pays after the work is done. Seems like a pretty good process. Texas has passed the accountability test each year.

One might ask about the value of the Forum and Institute. It is evaluated for curriculum content and for many aspects of the instructors' presentations. These factors, plus the number of participants attending the optional breakout sessions, indicate the quality of the session and the interest of participants. There is also the factor of a large number of Lions returning after their first attendance. Accurately measuring the use of the education back at the club level is much desired for the future. One positive factor is that this is the use of dues money in direct advantage to individual

Lions. Although there is a registration fee, it doesn't cover even the cost of the meals provided. A strong financial draw is that the first 100 Lions, who have not been a Vice District Governor or above, receive one night's free lodging at the event.

The Forum and Institute schedules four meal events with principal speakers, and approximately 40 breakout workshop-type sessions to provide a strong addition to leadership for any Lion dedicating attention to the proceedings. Principal speakers have included a U. S. Army Major General, Past International Presidents, and several Past International Directors. Some of the best instruction has been delivered by teachers called "just Lions." Some of these have been sought out by reputation, and some discovered by observation at other Lion training. A special breakfast at the 10th event was hosted by a "Super Panel"—which consisted of three Past International Presidents and two Past International Directors.

A look at what has occurred with this statewide leadership training event in 15 years indicates the level of success gained. The first event attracted slightly less than 50 attendees. The most recent one registered more than 200 participants. At the first Forum and Institute, no lodging was provided. There is now onsite arrangement for well over 100 rooms. One outside catered meal was provided at the Pickle Center, compared to four sit-down meals currently. More importantly, the program content has moved from entertainment-centered to being very closely aligned with the LCI curriculum aimed at Lions becoming better serving Lions. Rule one: no negativism. The first event was a happy one. The training was minimal, but worthwhile. Everyone had a good time, and it was a happy gathering. The focus has changed to something closer to preparing to accommodate the latest slogan: "Where there's a need, there's a Lion."

Lions frequently consider how to have a better club and how to be a better Lion. Just like the Forum and Institute, those things don't happen overnight. The Forum and Institute has evolved through much work by many. First have been the Councils of Governors. Sixteen of them have said, "We will provide the money to do this." Second has been the MD-2 International Family. Past International Presidents and Past International Directors—every one of them—has supported in some way. Then there are the ones who plan and implement the actual event. The planning physically starts months before the current year's event happens. Who does this? It starts with the Cherry family. PDG Aubrey Cherry is the official coordinator, PDG Frances Cherry is in charge of registration and is the hotel lodging liaison, Lion Melanie Cherry Jones produces all printed material (printed as a donation by her employer, Stewart Title Company of El Paso), and PDG J. P. Kirksey recruits and aligns session introducers and sees that they are in place for each session. PDG Charles and Lion Nancy Handrick do the check-in registration and facility set-up. This may sound easy, but it is a phenomenal piece of work. PDG Michael Smith works with the facility set-up and is ready to take on any need. Then there are the presenters who must study the curriculum and prepare their work. Many, many others have stepped in and helped at any request, sometimes at the last minute. They step forward and simply say, "Let me help." The Texas Lions Leadership Forum and Lions Clubs International Regional Lions Leadership Institute is a real "pain" at times. It is also, from beginning to end, a real "joy."

Lions are providing their own leadership training. Without leadership, there is no membership. Without membership, there is no service.

"We Serve".

Hall of Fame

These are the men and women that have been elected by their respective Districts every so many years as approved by the Constitution and By-Laws, and were designated as some of the most deserving people in their Districts and State.

"Elevation of Lions into the Texas Lions Hall of Fame bestows an honor upon one who has been outstanding in using their time, talents, and resources to further the cause of humanitarian services." (The rules.)

2015

Joe Hargrove, PDG	Crosbyton	2-T2
Dean W. Royalty, PDG	El Paso	2-T3
Charles L. Stout, PDG	Temple	2-X3
Dr. John H. Seale, PDG	Del Rio	2-A2
C. Don Robinson, PDG	Conroe	2-S2
Charles Villaneuve, PDG	Seguin	2-S5

2014

Jack King, PDG	Amarillo	2-T1
Hal Griffin, PDG	Abilene	2-E1
Alvin Z. Owen, PDG	San Angelo	2-A1
Harold Yost, PDG	Lufkin	2-S1
Ernest Opella, PDG	Bay City	2-S4

2013

Rick Stoorza, PDG	Aledo	2-E2
Charles Norwood, PDG	Richardson	2-X1
Lion Jackie Bowling	Mineola	2-X2
Dr. Clayton Roth, PDG	Aransas Pass	2-A3
Dennis Heitkamp, PDG	New Braunfels	2-S3

2012

Chuck Fisher, PDG	Lubbock	2-T2
Frances Cherry, PDG	El Paso	2-T3
Gladys Tramp, PDG	Killeen	2-X3

2012, continued

Ernesto "TJ" Tijerina, PDG	Del Rio	2-A2
Ronald G. Landers, PDG	Houston	2-S2
Clarence Wolfshohl	Giddings	2-S5

2011

Beverly Stebbins, PID	Arlington	2-E2
Wayne Smith *	Dumas	2-T1
H. Allen Lamb, PDG	Abilene	2-E1
Joyce Downie, PDG	San Angelo	2-A1
Paul Mayberry	Lufkin	2-S1
John Carstarphen	Galveston	2-S4

2010

Al Jara, PDG *	Fort Worth	2-E2
Bill Daniels, PDG	San Marcus	2-S3
Brian Whitenack, PDG	Longview	2-X2
John Eads, PCC	DeSoto	2-X1
George Jackson	Corpus Christi	2-A3

2009

Art Cook, PCC	Lubbock	2-T2
Don Peppard, PDG	El Paso Five Points	2-T3
Richard "Dick" Robinson, PCC	Killeen Evening	2-X3
John Kimbrough, PDG	Alamo Heights	2-A2
Dr. Irv Wishnow, PDG	Houston Westbury	2-S2
Ron Heinemeyer, PDG	Seguin Noon	2-S5

2008

Jim Wilson, PDG	Amarillo	2-T1
Bill Terry, PDG	Tuscola/Abilene	2-E1
Jim Wilks, PDG	Sweetwater	2-A1
Bruce Rickert, PDG	Carthage Noon	2-S1
Billy Wheeler, PDG	Victoria	2-S4

2007

Bill R. Graham, PDG	Gainesville	2-E2
Bill Melton, PDG	Dallas Oak Cliff	2-X1
Carol French, PCC	Kilgore	2-X2
Glynn Kaigler, PDG	Portland	2-A3
J. P. Kirksey	Austin Founders Downtown	2-S3

2006

Charles Shannon, PDG	Ropesville	2-T2
Leroy Hufford, PDG *	Ysleta	2-T3
Alvin Coleman, PDG *	Palistine	2-X3
James A. Blocklinger *	Del Rio Host	2-A2
Pat Brennan, PCC	Conroe	2-S2
Uel Stockard. PDG	Bryan	2-S5

2005

Earl Long, PDG	Amarillo	2-T1
C. Lee Smith, PDG	Clyde	2-E1
Ike Fitzgerald, PDG	Midland	2-A1
S. R. "Moe" Cully, PDG	Nederland	2-S1
Jack Grounds, PDG *	Sugar Land	2-S4

2004

William "Bill" Manix, PDG*	Corpus Christi Downtown	2-A3
J.L. Akridge, PDG	Georgetown Evening	2-S3
Alan Howard Snyder, Jr., PDG *	Preston North Dallas	2-X1
C.J. "Smokey" Stevens, Jr., PDG	Texarkana Evening	2-X2
Jack G. Adkison, PDG	River Oaks	2-E2

2003

D.H. "Dick" Alphin	Harlandale	2-A2
Aubrey L. Cherry	El Paso	2-T3
Gerry Chandler Criswell	Bryan	2-S5
James "Bud" McCune *	Huffman	2-S2
Eldon Kenneth "Ken" Schroeder	China Springs	2-X3
Jack F. Strong, Sr.	Lubbock	2-T2

2002

Luren Campbell, PDG	Olney	2-E1
Dr. Bubba Hirsch, PDG	Trinity	2-S1
John P. Richardson, PDG	Beeville	2-S4
Vershel H. Smith, PDG	Sweetwater	2-A1
Dr. Kenneth Waugh, PDG	Canyon	2-T1

2001

David V. "Ike" Boling, PDG	Rockport	2-A3
Connie de la Garza, PID	Harlingen	2-A3
William J. "Bill" Kolozie, PDG	New Braunfels	2-S3
Odis Pharr, PDG*	Pantego	2-X1
Jack Wakin, PDG	Wake Village	2-X2

2000

Ben Baker, PDG *	Waco	2-X3
Vernon Carmichael, PDG *	Missouri City	2-S2
David E. Kalich, PDG	Weimar	2-S5
Francisco "Pancho" Luna, PDG*	Dallas Central	2-X1
Michael Rourke, PDG	San Antonio	2-A2
Tut Tawwater, PDG	Plainview	2-T2

1999

Leon Adickes, PDG *	Hemphill	2-S1
Harland B. Brancel, PDG *	San Angelo	2-A1
Rick Garrett, PDG	Amarillo	2-T1
Stan Sheppard, PDG *	Missouri City	2-S4
Tom Ward, PDG	Breckenridge	2-E1

1998

Roy H. Byars, PDG *	Blanco	2-S3
Herbert "Doc" Daniels, PDG *	Tyler	2-X2
Jack A. Harris, PDG*	Fort Worth	2-E2
Sylvan Mortiz, PDG*	Dallas Oak Cliff	2-X1
Richard "Rick" Talbert, PDG	Weslaco	2-A3

1997

Fred A. Bender, PDG *	Temple	2-X3
George L. Conner, PDG	Houston	2-S2
Francis "Frank" Leroux, PDG *	El Paso	2-T3
Hoyse McMurtry, PDG *	Lubbock	2-T2
Joe Al Picone, PDG	Brenham	2-S3
Mel Smith, PDG *	Universal City	2-A2

1996

Wilbert Boulet, PDG *	Port Arthur	2-S1
Irvin D. Hiler, PDG *	Abilene	2-E1
Paul L. Palmer, PDG *	Early	2-A1
W. R. "Wally" Niemeyer, PDG *	Dickinson	2-S4
James C. Wheeler, PDG	Amarillo	2-T1

1995

Burton E. Diebel *	Alice	2-A3
Marion B. Snider, PDG *	Dallas Park Cities	2-X1
Ed Stebbins, PDG	Arlington	2-E2
R. J. "Jim" Williams, PDG *	Marshall	2-X2
Jack W. Wise, PDG *	New Braunfels	2-S3

1994

Mark Anderson, PDG	Eagle Lake	2-S3
Lytle H. Blankenship, PDG	Uvalde	2-A2
Marshall W. Cooper, PID	Beaumont	2-T2
Crawford H. Drever *	Killeen	2-X3
Joe C. Parish, PDG *	Odessa	2-T3
Charles W. Philipp, PDG	Pearland	2-S2
N. K. Snodgrass, PDG *	Lubbock	2-T2

1993

Dave Donnell *	Brazoria	2-S4
R. Roy Keaton, Past Dir General *	Weatherford	2-E2
John B. Kendrick, PDG *	Mineral Wells	2-E1
William D. "Bill" Mauldin, PDG *	Jacksonville	2-S1
Jimmy M. Ross, PID	Canyon	2-T1

1992

George E. Bushong, PDG *	Dallas Park Cities	2-X1
Garvis Gilbert, PDG *	Cypress Springs	2-X2
Orville Harris *	Corpus Christi	2-A3
J. T. Hinkle, PDG *	River Oaks	2-E2
Willie Kocurek, PDG *	Austin	2-S3

1991

Jack Baggett, PDG *	Corsicana	2-X3
H. M. "Hack" Lasater, PDG *	McLean	2-T2
F. Ray McLaughlin, PDG *	Alpine	2-T3
John J. Tryling, PDG *	Houston	2-S2
Sidney Schwartz, PDG *	San Antonio	2-A2
Freddie A. Wolters, PDG *	College Station	2-S3

1990

Leslie William Collins, PDG *	El Campo	2-S4
Jimmie Pigman, Jr., PDG *	Dalhart	2-T1
Conner S. Scott, PDG	Brownwood	2-A1
Chester E. Stout, PDG *	Carthage	2-S1
James H. Wheeler, Jr., PDG	Abilene	2-E1

1989

Dr. W. R. Cheatham, PDG *	Daingerfield	2-X2
Leroy "Atta-Boy" Cornelius, PDG	Portland	2-A3
W. T. "Dub" Nelson, PDG *	Dallas Oak Cliff	2-X1
Harry E. Rankin, PDG *	Fort Worth	2-E2
Lindall "Lin" Rose, PDG	New Braunfels	2-S3

1988

C. E. Carrruth, PDG *	Andrews	2-T3
J. A. "Abe" Houston, PDG *	Waco	2-X3
C. Howard Leverett, Jr., PID *	Houston	2-S2
J. J. Sharnberg *	Lubbock	2-T2
Melvin R. Smith *	Houston	2-S2
"Zot" Zotarelli, PDG *	San Antonio	2-A2

1987

Carl O. Hyde, PDG *	Midland	2-A1
Glenn C. Portis, PDG	Cuero	2-S4
Joe B. Redman, PDG *	Beaumont	2-S1
Raymond White, PDG *	Hereford	2-T1

1986

Dexter Anderson, PDG *	Eagle Lake	2-S3
M. P. "Mike" Butler, PID	Kerrville	2-A2
F. Hall Brown, Jr., PDG *	Dallas	2-X1
Bill Hudson, PDG *	Denton	2-E2
Ray Hughston, PID	Brownsville	2-A3
Chester E. Penick, PDG *	White Oak	2-X2
T. Loren Maples, PDG *	Graham	2-E1

1985

Doug R. Beauchamp, PDG *	Corsicana	2-X3
Reynold H. "Rey" Costa, PDG *	San Antonio	2-A2
Fred Hamilton, PDG	Hockley	2-S2
W. W. "Bill" Stevic, PDG *	Odessa	2-T3

1984

Larry Fuller. PDG *	Amarillo	2-T1
Dr. D. L. Ligon, PDG *	Wichita Falls	2-E1
John F. Morriss *	Woodsboro	2-S4
Chris C. Roark, PDG *	Groves	2-S1
George M. Thompson, PDG *	Sweetwater	2-A1

1983

Albert W. Brown, PDG *	Denison	2-E2
Don L. Hamilton, PDG *	Tyler	2-X2
James H. Harbin, PDG *	Waxahachie	2-X1
Robert F. Koennecke, PDG *	Seguin	2-S3
Alfred W. Rogers, PDG*	McAllen	2-A3

1982

Herbert F. Bars *	Waco	2-X3
G. S. "Sealie" McCreless, PDG *	San Antonio	2-A2
J. L. "Jimmy" McPherson, PDG *	Houston	2-S2
Allen Reeves	El Paso	2-T3
J. Andrew Smith, PDG *	San Antonio	2-A2

1981

A. G. "Dee" De Martini *	Sugarland	2-S4
George P. Futch, Jr., PDG *	Henderson	2-S1
Roy Minear, PDG *	Midland	2-T2
Dr. Rupert N. Richardson, PDG *	Abilene	2-E1
Edgar O. "Ed" Skypala *	Hereford	2-T1

1980

R. C. Franks, PDG	Bryan	2-S5
Hyman Laufer, PDG *	Kilgore	2-X2
A. B. "Buck" Morgan, PDG *	Grand Prairie	2-X1

1979

Verne L. Carrington, PDG *	Denton	2-E2
Roy N. Davis, PDG*	Weslaco	2-A3
Edwin H. Flood, PID*	Amarillo	2-T1
Raford Hair*	El Paso	2-T3

1978

R. M. "Bob" Arnold, PDG	Gatesville	2-X3
Don A. Buckalew, PID	Conroe	2-S2
Joe E. Childers, PID *	Abilene	2-E1
Joe B. Parr, PDG *	Houston	2-S2

1977

Robert E. Price, PDG *	Port Arthur	2-S1

1975

W. L. Edlemon, PDG *	Friona	2-T1
Dr. Randall D. Watkins, PID *	Abilene	2-E1

1975, continued

D. Schley Riley, PDG *	Big Spring	2-T2
P. E. "Pete" Shotwell, PDG *	Abilene	2-E1

1974

Robert C. "Bob" Coffey, PDG *	Longview	2-X2
Everett J. "Ebb" Grindstaff, PIP	Ballinger	2-A1
Jesse "Guy" Smith, PDG *	Commerce	2-X1

1973

Frank Robertson, PDG *	Kerrville	2-A2
Jack Wiech, PDG *	Brownsville	2-A3
Charles F. Williams, PDG *	Fort Worth	2-E2
J. B. Wooldridge, PDG *	Anahuac	2-S1

1972

Wilbur M. Abbey, PDG *	Port Arthur	2-S1
David A. Evans, PIP *	Texas City	2-S4
Joe Fisher, PID*	Beaumont	2-S1
Fred O. Grimes, PID *	Hillsboro	2-X3
Julien C. Hyer, PIP *	Dallas	2-X1
R. A. Lipscomb, PID *	Lubbock	2-T2
E. B. "Tex" Mayer, PID *	La Grange	2-S3
Wilfred R. McDonald, PDG *	Fort Worth	2-E1
E. H. "Eddie" Munger, PDG	Houston	2-S2
Herb C. Petry, Jr., PIP *	Carrizo Springs	2-A2
Dr. Richard A. Self, PID *	Dallas Oak Cliff	2-X1
W. Bryan Sparks, PDG *	Cooper	2-X2
Don D. Zimmerman, PDG *	Hereford	2-T1

* *Deceased*

LCI Activities

The following are some of the many activities of Lions Clubs International, (LCI) which Texas has contributed to through the Lions Clubs International Foundation (LCIF), and personally through their activities in assisting clubs. There are, of course, other spectacular clubs or organizations that are involved in activities that are just as important, but not as many.

Cape Town South Africa Club (with only 1,250 members and less than 50 clubs) personally feeds 60,000 people each and every day.

2,064,829 people with saved or restored sight through 45 SightFirst grants totaling $12.39 million.

1,141,837 people have a brighter tomorrow through 136 Standard grants totaling $6.17 million.

250,000 youth learning valuable life skills through 38 Lions Quest grants totaling $1.67 million.

More than 75,777 people have clean water and access to health care through 28 International Assistance grants totaling $377,026.

In fiscal year 2010-2011, LCIF received a record $48 million in donations, $13 million or 40 percent increase in donations from previous year!

Restored sight to 7.84 million people through cataract surgeries.

Provided management training for 265 eye care facilities.

Through Opening Eyes, screened more than 325,000 Special Olympics athletes, and gave prescription eyewear to more than 100,000 athletes.

SightFirst restores a person's vision or prevents blindness at an average cost of $6.

Completed more than 17 million vision screenings for children through LCIF's Sight for Kids.

Lions Eye Banks uses 25,436 corneas for transplants and provided 14,280 eyes for research and education (39 of 55 eye banks reporting data in 2011-12).

Campaign SightFirst II is enabling Lions to fund groundbreaking research in eye disease and eye health.

Trained 664,268 eye care specialists.

A gazillion hugs, handshakes and words of comfort and reassurance given to children and adults served by Lions.

Clubs reported 2,077,949 hours of sight-related service last year (actual numbers are higher, because nearly half of clubs do not report their service to LCI).

Strongly supported by many Lions clubs and leaders.

Resolution for Texas Lions 100th Anniversary

The Senate of The State of Texas

WHEREAS, the International Association of Lions Clubs (referred to as Lions Clubs International) was founded in October 1917 at the Adolphus Hotel in Dallas, Texas, by 23 clubs, with 12 being from the great State of Texas. The men from these clubs were inspired by its founder, Melvin Jones, to reach out to individuals in need of service. Today this not-for-profit service organization has grown to 1.4 million members in 209 geographical locations around the world.

WHEREAS, in 1927 at the 10th convention of Lions Clubs International, Helen Keller during her address challenged the Lions to become "Knights of the Blind". The Lions enthusiastically accepted the challenge and therefore hundreds of thousands have been assisted with their vision.

WHEREAS, in the search of service challenges, and meeting the needs of their communities, the Lions of Texas created their crown jewel in 1949, Texas Lions Camp, which has served approximately 70,000 children between the ages of 7-16 with physical disabilities and diabetes. They experience a week of camping activities such as horseback riding, swimming, and overnight camp outs, etc. at no expense to their families.

WHEREAS, In Texas we have the Texas Lions Foundation to support people in times of disaster. Recycling Centers in Texas have been developed to aid in the collection, cataloging, and distribution of approximately 1.5 million pairs of glasses world-wide per year. One Life Program in which Lions have vaccinated 150 million children in 2012 and the One Shot –

One Dollar, Save a Life Measles Project which has joined with the Gates Foundation out of Washington and which has saved millions of lives. Since its inception, $3,995,665.00 has been given to Texas communities in the form of grants and/or disaster relief.

WHEREAS, the Lions Clubs International Foundation (LCIF) was established in 1968 for the purpose of restoring sight and preventing blindness; supporting youth, providing disaster relief and addressing humanitarian needs.

WHEREAS, the Midland Lions Clubs were also the first Regional Recycling Center for the recycling of glasses and sending them overseas. The Lions of Texas have formed five eye-banks throughout the state to assist the medical field in the collection and distributions of cornea for transplantation and for research.

WHEREAS, Lions have worked with Past District Governor Jimmy Carter who was elected as District Governor in Dallas in 1967. We have been proud to work with him through Habitat For Humanity, World Blindness and Former U.S. President Jimmy Carter was the reason for Lions Clubs being nominated for the Nobel Peace Prize in recent years.

WHEREAS, the Lions Clubs International has grown to be the largest and greatest Service Organization in the World, and OUR ORGANIZATION WAS VOTED IN 2012 THE NUMBER ONE NON-GOVERNMENTAL AGENCY IN THE WORLD BY THE UNITED NATIONS.

WHEREAS, a gazillion hugs, handshakes and words of comfort and reassurance are given to children served by Lions.

WHEREAS, three different programs were started in Texas in 1983; one was Journey for Sight to raise funds for another one of the two programs, diabetes which has expanded into such fantastic programs as research to other means and ways to help individuals with diabetes and the result thereof. The idea in Texas in 1983 came from the beginning of the Juvenile Diabetes Program in Texas in 1971-72 has grown to great extents. The drug program also began in Texas the years prior to 1983, through the efforts of many Lions and obtaining the leadership of Lt. General Robbie Riser who spent seven years in confinement in Vietnam and who became the governmental leader and Lions leader of the Drug Program.

WHEREAS, there have been two campaigns in our International Organization; Sight First that has raised approx. half a million dollars for cataract operations or other saved or restored sight programs through grants. Lions are presently involved in several; screening glasses, old glasses beginning in Midland as the first regional project for Lions Clubs International and spreading throughout. There have been nearly twenty million screenings through the Lions LCIF's Sight For Kids. During all this time we have had the opportunity to meet all leaders of the world who have commended the Lions including all the Presidents and the honorary Lion Ronald Reagan and worked with Mrs. Reagan in the "Just Say No to Drugs". Also President Sadat from Egypt, President Begin of Israel, and Pope John Paul II from the Vatican have all praised our programs including many, many other leaders throughout the world.

WHEREAS, the Lions of Texas in 1983 reached 45,000, the highest of Texas Lions and there are still many thousands of Lions involved in these different programs and other programs that are really too typical to mention in such short resolution.

WHEREAS, the Lions adopted in 1970 the motto "We Serve" and has continually used the motto in any manner that might come forth. It's a worldwide organization that can be seen in such places as Cape Town, South Africa where the South African Lions with only 1,250 members in less than 50 clubs personally feeds 60,000 people each and every day. The Lions have had top rating as non-profit organization of all the largest charities including cancer, diabetes, heart, Red Cross, etc. and have now reached over ONE BILLION DOLLARS in donations since 1972.

WHEREAS, as you can tell, we are proud of our organization and proud of all the Lions and the Past Presidents of the Club and the Chairmen of the Council of Governors for each year, and especially the Past Officers of the International Association that have served, beginning with our present Director, Sam Lindsey, Past International Directors Don Buck-alew, Ray Hughston, Mike Butler, Marshall Cooper, Connie De La Garza, Beverly Stebbins and Joe Al Picone; and our two living Past International Presidents—Past President Jimmy Ross from Quitaque, Texas and Past President Everett J. Grindstaff from Ballinger, Texas, from the grass roots to the top.

THEREFORE BE IT RESOLVED that an official copy of this resolution be prepared for the Lions of Texas as an expression of high regard by the Texas Senate.

President of the Senate

I hereby certify that the above Resolution was adopted by the Senate on February 1, 2017.

Secretary of the Senate

Member, Texas Senate

See photo of Resolution-signing ceremony on page 235

"Tankeye"
then and now

Another memorable event was when Jay and I arrived in Karachi, Pakistan on an overnight flight from Rome. It had been one of those flights that was not very pleasant because of storms and other elements that knocked us around. I did not enjoy that flight, and Jay certainly did not; however, we arrived in Karachi at 5:00 a.m. We were combing hair and fixing faces quickly as we walked toward the front door, and we both had mentioned that it was time to put our best face on, even though there might not be many people there.

As the doors of the plane opened, there were some 300 people present, including District Governor Assai Dossani. At least half or more of the people were in attire that indicated that they, too had walked across the desert in order to be present on that occasion. It was not Ebb and Jay Grindstaff, it was the President and First Lady of Lions Clubs International, and they would have given any President the same welcome.

We threw our bags in the car and dropped them off at the hotel, but did not leave the car. This was the day of observation and education of activities of the Pakistanian Lions (little did we know that in 1999, the first female Director of Lions Club International would be from Pakistan, Nilofer Bakhitiar).

At 6:12 p.m., our host told us that Lions Club International had informed them that the guests should have a little time for rest, and they would pick us up for the formal affair at 6:30. I don't know how we did it—it seemed like the activities of the day gave us the adrenaline to keep on going.

During the course of the afternoon, we were taken to a bank. In this room was a blood bank, an eye bank and a crutch bank. Seated at the head table was the President of the project and club, and also the District Governor. There were probably 30 people or so in the room. They were explaining their project and how it worked with great enthusiasm.

I observed a gentleman standing (or leaning) in the corner who appeared to be decrepit, with long unkempt hair, one tooth (that I could see, and it may have been his only tooth) and only one leg. I wondered what part he played in the program or the project.

About that time, they asked me if I would like to participate in the crutch bank program, and I said, "Sure, what can I do?" They said, "We want you to present a crutch to someone." I said "Okay." We got up, I had the crutch, and they brought the man who only had one leg to me in the center of the room. I put the crutch under his arm and he looked up at me and said, *"Tankeye."* He had probably practiced this particular part of the program for months. I will never forget his face, or his eyes of gratitude. And then he walked across the room to the door with the one crutch under his arm, stepped down on the first step and turned around again and said, *"Tankeye."*

How could you express it any better?

"Tankeye" for taking the time to read this book of experiences, leadership, values and life. I hope that it has provoked some thought, and certainly some attitude of humor that we must have in our journey. More importantly, Jay and I would like to take this opportunity to say *"Tankeye"* for all the grassroot Lions who give their time and assets in an unselfish manner in order that they might improve the lives of someone less fortunate.

As we move into a new century, the challenges in front of us abound with even more fantastic miracles if we are to continue as the number one charitable and humanitarian organization in the world. It will continue to grow only if our legacy continues to be a destiny of humble service to all.